SYSTEMS PROGRAMMING
Concepts of Operating and Data Base Systems

SYSTEMS PROGRAMMING
Concepts of
Operating and
Data Base Systems

DAVID K. HSIAO

The Ohio State University

ADDISON-WESLEY PUBLISHING COMPANY

Reading, Massachusetts · Menlo Park, California
London · Amsterdam · Don Mills, Ontario · Sydney

This book is in the
ADDISON-WESLEY SERIES IN
COMPUTER SCIENCE AND INFORMATION PROCESSING

Consulting Editor
Michael A. Harrison

In memory of my grandfather, Hsiao Chio-T'ien 蕭覺天 (1887–1972)

Foreword

The purpose of this book is to discuss general concepts and prevailing notions in systems programming. To this end, we have tried to present the concepts and notions abstractly. Via abstraction, we hope that the basic concepts and notions can be more easily visualized and understood without having detailed expositions of the material involved. Occasionally, we indulge ourselves in closer examination of the systems discussed. In these cases, the aim is to relate our abstract study with real-world problems and to illustrate the feasibility of implementing some of these concepts and notions.

By systems programming we mean the synthesis and analysis of general-purpose operating systems. In this book, the general-purpose operating systems are restricted to assembly systems, input-output control systems, batched processing systems, multiprogramming systems, and data base management systems. There are, of course, many other types of systems worthy of study, e.g., the real-time systems. Due to the lack of time or expertise in developing additional material, we have decided to exclude them from this presentation.

Despite some outstanding theoretical work in systems programming, there is a lack of general theory of systems programming. Thus, we have not strived for a theoretical treatment. Instead, in synthesis and analysis we attempt to separate a whole system into its logical components and to examine the relations among the components. In the process, we identify the components and clarify their roles in the system. Quite frequently we make certain assumptions about the functionality of the system and proceed to substantiate them by demonstrating the logic of the components. We also try to produce a coherent system by logical combination of functionally different components. Whether it is in analysis or synthesis, we always try to select a view or model which tends to provide a better framework for perceiving the complexity of the system. The layered, or structured, approach to input and output control systems and the hierarchical view of off-line batch processing systems are cases in point. These views are, of course, by no means the only views leading toward better system perception for analysis and synthesis.

The advantages of the structural view in synthesis and analysis of a system is that each layer or level of the hierarchy can be dealt with independently, and its relation with other layers or levels of the hierarchy is well-structured. However, there are other views. The finite-state automata and transition-diagrams approach toward the synthesis and analysis of operating systems represents one such view. Here the analysis and synthesis of the system become the identification and clarification of the system in terms of states, transitions of states, physical signals which cause the transitions, and logical signals which hasten the transitions. Logical signals and their generators constitute the heart of systems programming logic. Although the view of an operating system as a finite-state automaton or a transition diagram is not yet in vogue, it may have great potential. We have used this view toward the realization of an input-output control system, and in the discussion of an on-line programming system. We also employ a view from directed graphs to perceive the symbol definition process of assembly systems.

When perceptive views are not available, we rely on generalized models. These models are idealized and are mostly abstract. There are several advantages in developing the generalized models. First, many seemingly diverse and unrelated ideas can be consolidated into a coherent presentation. Second, few working systems have all the needed features for discussion. By incorporating those systems features which underly the principles of these systems, the model can assist in obtaining a better understanding of the systems as a whole. Third, there is less restriction on the nomenclature and conventions used in presenting these systems since the model system need not be the exact image of a working system. This modeling approach has been applied to assembly systems, multiprogramming systems, and data base management systems. Because assembly systems deal with symbols and data base management systems are concerned mainly with logical resources in the form of fields, records, and files, they lend themselves more readily to abstract modeling. On the other hand, multiprogramming systems, which manage physical resources, have somewhat eluded abstraction.

The book is therefore intended as a frame of reference for concepts and notions. We hope that these views and models can provide proper perspective and good insights for those who wish to pursue further study in systems programming. The book is not intended for those who desire to familiarize themselves with the facilities and ramifications of any particular system.

The first chapter is on assembly systems. The study of assembly systems is not aimed at a detailed examination of a present-day assembler. Instead, an abstract assembler is proposed on which the general concepts of the assembly process can be defined and from which the factors, which have complicated the design of assemblers, can be delineated. These factors are directly related to the capability of the assembly language in handling pseudoinstructions of deferred type. Since the flexibility and power of an assembly language are reflected by its capability to handle pseudoinstructions of deferred type, the complexity in assembler design is therefore proportional to the flexibility and power of its assembly language. By studying the abstract assembler, not only can we learn the steps of the assembly process for one of the most powerful and flexible assembly languages, but we can also determine those steps which are directly involved in the resolution of pseudoinstructions of deferred type. The understanding of these steps enables the system designer to determine the degree of flexibility and power of an assembly language which he wishes to propose and to anticipate the amount of design and implementation complexity which has to be incorporated into the assembler. In addition, the function of the linking loader is discussed. Its role in the assembly system and in the input and output system is emphasized.

The second chapter is on input and output control systems (IOCS). In this chapter, we first discuss the prevailing notions in input and output operations such as cycle stealing, memory interference, operational simultaneity, and buffer switching. An idealized model is introduced for the purpose of demonstrating the phenomenon known as concurrent processing with multiple channels. In the model, the concept of system throughput and a measure of concurrence relative to the channel utilization are developed. Although the model is somewhat oversimplified, we hope the essence of concurrent processing and system throughput has been conveyed. The over-simplification is perhaps unavoidable in view of the complexity and amount of detail involved in the real-world situations. We then present two different approaches in designing input and output control systems—a structural approach which concentrates on the design of input and output control systems in terms of layers of subsystems and programs, and a finite-state automata approach which organizes input and output control systems as sequential machines. Because input and output control systems deal mostly with computer hardware elements and operations which can be easily characterized as states and transitions of states, the finite-state automata approach in designing input and output control systems, although seldom used, is promising. By identifying an input and output control system as an abstract se-quential machine with states and transitions of states, the functionality and logic of the input and output control systems can be clearly synthesized, readily understood, and easily programmed.

The third chapter of the book is on batch processing operating systems. Here generalized batch processing operating systems are proposed. The discussion of off-line batch processing concentrates on the characteristics of the system as a hierarchy of processors and subsystems. Efforts to improve the system's ability to accommodate on-line input and output operations and to couple with other systems are also discussed. The characterization of the on-line batch processing operating system in terms of states and transitions of states is straightforward; and the development of the spooling system for on-line job input and output is important.

There are two chapters on multiprogramming systems. In Chapter 4, we identify the factors which have prompted the introduction of multiprogramming systems and classify various multiprogramming systems in terms of the levels of multiprogramming. These levels reflect, to a large extent, the degrees of sophistication of the systems discussed. It is well to note that although the concept of multiprogramming is easy to motivate, approaches to the synthesis and analysis of multiprogramming systems vary widely. These approaches are influenced by the physical resources intended for the systems and by the design experience derived from earlier systems such as the batch processing systems. We then outline mechanisms such as semaphores by which these multi-programming systems can be supported and realized, and point out the problems, such as system deadlock, which are inherent in these systems. Chapter 5 is centered on the multiprogramming systems using virtual space. In our study of virtual space, we attempt to answer the questions: (1) Why do we need virtual space? (2) What are the types of virtual spaces and their capabilities? In answering question (1), we point out that virtual space is designed primarily to resolve problems concerning dynamic storage allocation, repetitive program relocation, program overlay, and run-time growth of programs and data. Because different developers of virtual space have aimed to resolve one or more of the above problems, there are various types of virtual spaces. To this end we try to classify the types of virtual spaces and illustrate them with examples. Thus, we can answer the second question. Finally, we try to describe a generalized multiprogramming operating system which summarizes some of the common characteristics prevailing among the virtual memory operating systems. The role of interrupt analyzer and task initiator in the generalized multi-programming system is outlined. Since physical input and output operations in a multiprogramming system are always performed by the system (instead of by user programs), the expanded function of the input and output control subsystem in the generalized multiprogramming system is discussed. We also contrast the traditional logical input and output operations with the virtual access method which is unique in a virtual space environment. Both dynamic loading and multitasking are also unique to multiprogramming systems. We try to relate these unique system features with material developed in the previous chapters. Solutions to software problems associated with virtual space are also discussed in the context of the generalized multiprogramming operating systems.

The final chapter is devoted to data base management systems. These systems are important because there are indications that future operating systems will be primarily oriented toward data base management. The increasing emphasis in on-line use of computer systems and the improving cost effectiveness of on-line bulk storage have accelerated the development of centralized data bases and multiaccess terminals. Thus the traditional view of an operating system as a computer physical resource manager is too limited. The sheer size of the on-line data bases in a future computer system requires the operating system to become, in addition, a logical resource manager. Logical resource largely consists of on-line data and programs. The management of logical resource is concerned with the organization, security, access, and storage of data and programs in the data base. Because the area of the data base management is still evolving, our discussion will touch upon some problems which need to be resolved. To this end, we have proposed an abstract model of a generalized data base management system by which the concept of storage cell is defined and from which the frequently used structures such as indexed sequential, multilist, and inverted files, and the more recent cellular multilist structure can be derived.

An access algorithm is provided for data structures derivable from the model. The algorithm, due to its unusual characteristics, tends to minimize the movement of the access mechanism for movable-head storage devices, to reduce the number of accesses to secondary storage, and to eliminate imprecise data retrieval.

An algorithm for updating the data structures derivable from the model is provided. Dynamic updating of data structures is needed when an addition, deletion, or replacement of keywords of records occurs.

Mechanisms for access control and privacy protection in data base management systems are also discussed in the model.

Knowledge of computer organization and programming principles is a necessary prerequisite for the book. For a minimal reading of the background material, the reader may refer either to the first six chapters in *Computer Organization and Programming* by C. William Gear (McGraw-Hill) or to Chapters 1, 2, 3, and 8 in *Digital Computer System Principles* by Herbert Hellerman (McGraw-Hill). The latter also contains a very concise, but sufficient, description of the IBM System/360 in Chapter 9. Additional reading on introductory material to systems programming may be found in *Systems Programming* by John J. Donovan (McGraw-Hill). At The Ohio State University, Professor Donovan's book is used in a course which is a prerequisite for the course using the present text.

Preface

The material in the book was originally developed at the Moore School of Electrical Engineering, University of Pennsylvania, for a first course in systems programming in the Fall of 1969. Although the purpose was to present systems programming to the first-year graduate students with a computer science major, the book is presently used at The Ohio State University for a systems programming course in which about half of the students are undergraduate juniors and seniors and the other half beginning graduate students. Knowledge of programming languages (e.g., FORTRAN and assembly language) and programming techniques is required. In addition, basic understanding of conventional, general-purpose digital computer organization and system architecture is assumed.

Some parts of Chapters 2, 3, 4, and 5 were used as an introduction to a summer program on *Multiprogramming System Design Principles* which was held in the Summer of 1970, at the University of Pennsylvania and was supported, in part, by the National Science Foundation. In this program, five specific multiprogramming systems were discussed by their principal designers. We had Professor F. J. Corbató lecturing on Honeywell-GE 645 Multics, Mr. William L. Konigsford on IBM 360/67 TSS, Mr. Norman Weiser on Univac-RCA Spectra 70/46 TSOS, Mr. Bernard I. Witt on IBM 360/MVT and Dr. David N. Freeman on IBM 360 TOS/DOS. We also had recitation leaders who led us into the details of the design of these systems. Professor Michael D. Schroeder was responsible for Multics, Mr. Lee Varian for TSS, Mr. George Bean for MVT, Mr. John Gibson for TSOS and Miss Gwendolyn Gartland for TOS/DOS. Their lectures and recitations have greatly helped the author's understanding of these multiprogramming systems in particular and improved the parts of the book on multiprogramming and virtual memory systems in general. To them the author would like to register his indebtedness.

Considerable material in the chapters on on-line programming and data base systems is derived from the work of the author's colleagues and students and was supported by the Information Systems Program in the Office of Naval Research. Without these persons' diligent work and the support of the Program, these chapters could not have been written. I would like to thank Messrs. Harry A. Freedman and Frank Manola; Drs. Marvin Gelblat, Richard P. Morton, Richard L. Wexelblat and Michael S. Wolfberg; and Professor Noah S. Prywes for their contributions. Mr. Marvin Denicoff, Director of the Information Systems Program, Office of Naval Research, deserves my sincere thanks. His continuing support not only made these contributions possible, but also advanced the state-of-art of systems programming in the areas of on-line programming and data base systems.

The book is organized into six chapters. Each chapter deals with one or more important system concepts. Thus we have assembly languages and assembly systems, input and output operations and input-output control systems, off-line and on-line batch processing systems, multiprogramming, virtual memory systems, and data base systems. Notable omissions are compiler systems and real-time systems. The neglect of the former is deliberate because there is a large number of books on this topic. The omission of the latter is due largely to the author's ignorance of the subject matter. The material in the book is, to a large extent, classical, relying heavily on materials derived from published papers, reports, books, manuals, notes, and private correspondences. To give credit to the original sources of information and to allow further pursuit by the reader, there is a postscript at the end of each chapter which annotates briefly the references made in that chapter.

I would also like to thank Messrs. Joel D. Aron and Charles L. Gold of IBM for their valuable comments and advice which have enhanced the book considerably; my colleague, Professor Douglas S. Kerr, for his careful reading of the manuscript; Professor Andrew Noetzel of the University of Texas for contributing the first draft of Section 3 in Chapter 5; Professor John G. Brainerd who, as the Director of the Moore School, saw the need for a new course in systems programming and was instrumental in getting my course in the curriculum in 1969; and Misses Sally Futrell, Cindy Karr, and Sandy Rich for typing several versions of the manuscript.

Perhaps due to the exposures of the material in the aforementioned summer program and the invited presentation in the 1970 Fall Joint Computer Conference, the earlier drafts of the book have been used either as a text or as a supplement at various institutes by my colleagues, in particular, Professors Stephen W. Ching of Villanova, Richard Eckhous of Massachusetts, Clinton R. Foulk of Ohio State, Lance Hoffman of the University of California at Berkeley, T. Kimura of Delaware, Noah S. Prywes of Pennsylvania, and Richard B. Simmons of Texas A & M. Their enthusiasm about the book is appreciated.

Last but not least, I would like to show my appreciation to my students whose keen interest in systems programming has made the preparation of the book worthwhile, and to the computer industry whose large undertakings in systems programming have provided the field with many fruitful results and challenging problems.

Columbus, Ohio   D.K.H.
June 1975

Acknowledgments

The figures and equations in Section 2.4 (pages 65–72) are derived from "Throughput Analysis of Some Idealized Input, Output and Compute Overlap Configurations" by H. Hellerman and H. J. Smith, Jr., in *Computing Surveys* **2**, 2 (June 1970). Copyright 1970 by the Association for Computing Machinery. Reprinted with permission of the authors and publisher.

The example and figures in Section 2.5.1 (pages 72–77) are reprinted with some revision from *Digital Computer Systems Principles* by H. Hellerman. Copyright 1967 by McGraw-Hill Book Company. Used with permission of the publisher.

The figures in Sections 3.2.4.1 and 3.2.4.2 (page 119) are derived from R. F. Rosin, "Supervisory and Monitor Systems," *Computing Surveys* **1**, 1 (March 1969). Copyright 1969 by the Association for Computing Machinery. Reprinted with permission of the author and publisher.

The stories of the sleeping doctor in Section 4.4.2 (page 165) and the smart banker in Sections 4.5.1.1 and 4.5.1.2 (page 167) are adapted from "Co-operating Sequential Processes" written by E. W. Dijkstra and edited by F. Genuys for *Programming Languages*, London: Academic Press, 1968. Reprinted with permission of the author and publisher.

The list of deadlock conditions and the detection algorithm in Sections 4.5.2 and 4.5.3 (pages 169 and 170) are from "System Deadlocks" by E. G. Coffman, Jr., M. J. Elphick, and A. Shoshani in *Computing Surveys* **3**, 2 (June 1971). Copyright 1971 by the Association for Computing Machinery. Reprinted with permission of the authors and publisher.

Contents

1
Assembly Systems

REMARKS

Before reading this chapter on assembly systems, the reader is assumed to have familiarized himself with the fundamentals of a simple two-pass assembler as, for example, those covered in [3] or [25].*

After going through the material in this chapter, the reader may wish to consult the remaining references for further study. Comments on the references in relation to the material included herewith are provided at the end of the chapter.

1.1 INTRODUCTION

Although the assembler is primarily designed for processing mnemonic machine instructions of an assembly language, as stated in [3] and [25], its complexity is in many ways directly proportional to the flexibility provided in the pseudoinstructions of the assembly language. Unlike the mnemonic machine instructions, the pseudo-instructions do not have corresponding machine instructions. They are provided for the programmer as a means of communicating with the assembler and of facilitating the programming in mnemonic machine instructions. The ease and flexibility provided by the pseudoinstructions greatly increase the complexity in design and the implementation of the assembler.

The traditional view of an assembler as a two-pass processor is oversimplified. We will show this, after discussing pseudoinstructions and the preprocessing of the

---

*   Numbers in brackets refer throughout to the references at the end of the chapter.

input program, by presenting the internal working of an abstract assembler which little resembles a traditional two-pass assembler. The abstraction will allow the reader to concentrate on essentials of the assembler functions instead of on how the essentials were coded.

The remaining sections in this chapter are concerned with the role of the linking loader in assembly systems.

1.2 ASSEMBLY SYSTEMS

As a programming system, the assembly system accepts, as its input, *source programs* written in the assembly language; it translates the programs on the basis of the syntax and semantic rules of the assembly language; and it produces, as its output, *object programs*. Because the assembly language consists of mnemonic instructions which correspond exactly with the computer operations and of pseudoinstructions which directly effect data generation and storage allocation, the assembler can also be used to support compilers in generating data, allocating storage, and employing computer operations. For this reason, the assembler in some systems can accept source programs from either the user or the compiler. In Figs. 1.1(a) and 1.1(b), two-assembly

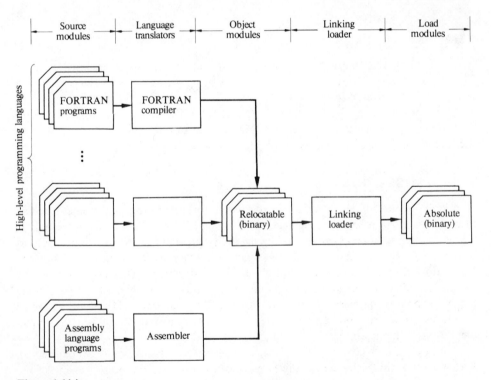

Figure 1.1(a)

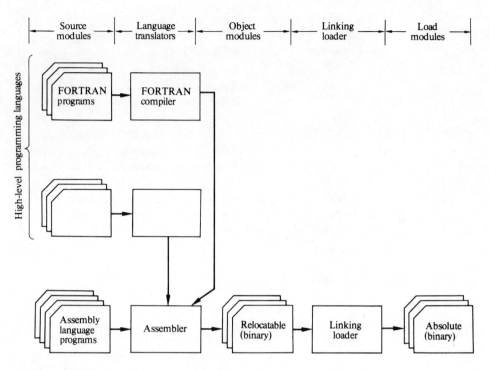

Figure 1.1(b)

system configurations are depicted. For example, the IBM 360/370 assembly system belongs to the former configuration, the IBM 7090/7040 to the latter.

1.3 THE ASSEMBLY LANGUAGE

1.3.1 BASIC FORMAT

The basic format of an assembly language instruction is as follows:

Label	Operation	Operands

Labels are optional symbolic names. The operations are also symbolic and are required. In particular, we refer to those symbolic operations which have counterparts in machine instructions as *mnemonic machine instructions*, and we refer to those symbolic operations which do not have any corresponding machine instructions as *pseudoinstructions*. The operand requirements depend on the syntax rules of the operations. Whether the operands are required or not, they may have symbolic names. For example, we have the following IBM 360/370 program section.

Label	Operation	Operands	Comments
NAME	CSECT		NAME refers to this program segment.
BEGIN	BALR	TWO,∅	Branch and link via register TWO.
	USING	*,TWO	The content of the register TWO is the current value of the location counter.
	⋮		
TWO	EQU	2	TWO has the value 2.
	END	BEGIN	End of this program segment whose first executable instruction is at BEGIN.

The instructions CSECT, USING, EQU, and END are pseudoinstructions whereas BALR is a mnemonic machine instruction. There are three symbolic labels, namely, NAME, BEGIN, and TWO. In addition, the operand of the instruction CSECT and the label of END should be blank, as dictated by the syntax of the IBM 360/370 assembly language [9].

In the following IBM 7090/7040 program segment,

Label	Operation	Operands	Comments
Z	BES	N	Reserve a storage block of N words; label the (N + 1)th word Z.
	⋮		
	USE		Use the main location counter for the subsequent instructions.
X	DEC	1,2	Define two decimal numbers, 1 and 2.
	CLA	X	Clear and add through the accumulator.
W	STO	Z − 1	Store contents of the accumulator into Z − 1.
	⋮		
N	EQU	W − X	The value of N is equal to the value of (W − X).
	END		End of program.

the BES, USE, DEC, EQU, and END are pseudoinstructions; CLA and STO are mnemonic machine instructions. Z, X, W, and N are symbolic labels. For a discussion of this assembly language, the reader may refer to [8].

1.3.2 THE MNEMONIC MACHINE INSTRUCTIONS

Mnemonic machine instructions of an assembly language do not have any important effect on the design complexity of an assembler of the language. In fact, if an assembly language consists of the mnemonic machine instructions alone, the design of an assembler for the language becomes a simple exercise. In this case, the assembler is merely required to perform the following tasks.

1. Maintain and initiate a location counter.

2. Read in an assembly program with one mnemonic instruction at a time.

3. Save the program in a condensed form.

4. Verify the validity of the mnemonics of the instruction.

5. Distinguish for the instruction the types of operands used (i.e., symbolic names, absolute addresses, relative locations, literals).

6. Collect the symbolic names in a table.

7. Collect the symbolic name used to label the instruction in the table, and assign the name with the current value in the location counter.

8. Increase the location counter value by the instruction length.

9. Detect the end of the assembly language program.

10. Replace all mnemonic instruction names with their corresponding codes.

11. Resolve all symbolic names with assigned values in the table.

12. Provide error and diagnostic messages if there are invalid mnemonics or unresolved symbolic names.

13. Provide a machine code program with additional information indicating those addresses which are either relative or absolute, and those values which are designated as literals.

We note that in (1) the location counter is the software counterpart of the hardware program counter. From (1), (2), (3), (4), and (6), we learn that the assembler must have working space for creating a location counter, files for the source program and the consensed program, a list of valid mnemonics, and a table for symbolic names and labels. Such a table is commonly referred to as the *symbol table*.

The verification of the mnemonics of the instructions always takes place at an early stage of the assembly. Furthermore, the list of valid mnemonics is usually incorporated in the symbol table. We may consider these menemonics the built-in symbols of the symbol tables. Once an invalid mnemonic code is detected, the assembly process can be readily aborted. On the other hand, there is considerable flexibility in handling tasks (6) and (7). Some assemblers will not collect symbolic names in the operands until all the symbolic labels are collected and assigned with location counter values. Other assemblers will collect both symbolic names and labels at the same time and attempt to resolve them all, if possible. We note that symbolic names in the operands may appear as labels, which are assigned with location counter values in (7). Thus the symbolic names take the same values of the labels. In this case, we say that the symbolic names are *resolved*. An unresolved symbolic name is one without an assigned value, because it never appears as a label anywhere in the program.

Traditionally, tasks (1) through (9) constitute the first pass and tasks (10) through (13) the second pass of a two-pass assembler, as depicted in Figs. 1.2(a) and 1.2(b).

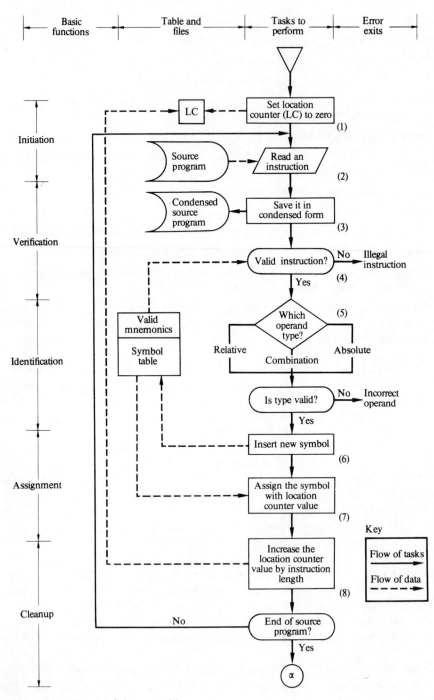

Fig. 1.2(a) Pass 1 of the assembly.

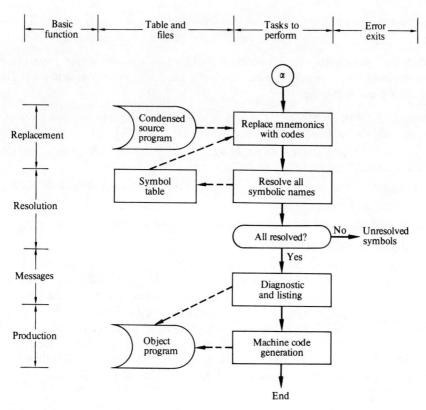

Fig. 1.2(b) Pass 2 of the assembly.

In summary, the assembly process performs the following basic functions:

Pass I

a) Initiation—to set up the symbol table and the location counter, and to open the files for the source program and the condensed program.

b) Verification—to check the validity of the instruction code.

c) Identification—to determine the type and combination of types of the operand.

d) Assignment—to process new symbols and to assign the current location counter value to the symbol.

e) Clean-up—to terminate the work in pass I and to initiate the process in pass II.

Pass II

f) Replacement—to replace mnemonics with their (binary) codes.

g) Resolution—to determine the values of the symbols in the table and to compute the values for the combination of the symbols and constants.

h) Messages—to generate diagnostic messages and listings.

i) Production—to generate the (binary) image of the source program.

Although the design and implementation of a two-pass assembler is simple and straightforward, the assembly language of the assembler is very restrictive. These restrictions prevent the user from

1. writing the instructions of his program in one sequence and executing the same program in a different sequence;

2. incorporating several independently written programs into one so that they can be executed collectively;

3. introducing literals and constants without encoding them in EBCDIC or ASCII;

4. reserving working space; or

5. communicating with the assembler concerning the program listings.

1.3.3 PSEUDOINSTRUCTIONS

Pseudoinstructions are instructions which enable the programmer to communicate with the assembler about the assembly of the mnemonic machine instructions in his program. Thus, via pseudoinstructions, the programmer can affect the process of assembly. For example, every assembly language has an End-of-Program pseudoinstruction which informs the assembler that there are no more instructions in the program. The repertoire of pseudoinstructions varies from system to system. However, we will discuss the pseudoinstructions in terms of their functions. For illustration, we draw sample pseudoinstructions from the IBM 360/370 and the IBM 7090/7040 assembly languages.

1.3.3.1 Location Counter and Location Assignment

As we have learned from the previous section, a location counter is used to keep track of the location of the instruction currently being processed relative to the beginning of the group of instructions. With the availability of several location counters, the programmer can instruct the assembler to assemble various groups of instructions (in the source module) into a prescribed sequence of instructions for execution.

Usually the repositioning of instructions under various location counters is performed by the linking loader at load time (we shall discuss loading and the linking loader in Section 1.5). In other words, location counters provide the user with the facility to write instructions in one sequence to be loaded by the linking loader in another.

Thus each group of instructions, under the control of a location counter, becomes a unit of code for loading. In some assembly systems, such a group of instructions is said to constitute a *control section*. In other words, in these assembly systems each control section is assigned a location counter which keeps track of the locations of the instruction in that control section. However, the programmer is not allowed to introduce any location counter other than the one assigned to the control section. In other assembly systems, a control section may consist of several groups of instructions and each of the groups may be controlled by a unique location counter.

Although these two conventions are different, their effects are the same. To dictate the executing sequence of various units of code in the program, the user either, as in the former case, declares each unit as a control section, or, as in the latter case, assigns a location counter for each unit. The net effect is that units of code are being sequenced either by implicitly assigned or explicitly declared location counters.

In order to use a specific location counter instead of one assigned to the control section (called the *main* location counter), the programmer must specify the location counter in a pseudoinstruction.

To manipulate a location counter and its location assignment, pseudoinstructions with the following capabilities are needed:

1. To name the location counter which is to control the sequence of instructions.
2. To assign an initial value to the location counter.
3. To alter the current value of the location counter.

For example, in IBM 7090/7040 assembly language, the pseudoinstruction

Label	Operation	Operands
	USE	LC1

either establishes a new location counter or switches to an existing location counter named LC1. All instructions following the USE will be under the control of LC1. The pseudoinstruction

Label	Operation	Operands
	BEGIN	LC1, 5

assigns an initial value 5 to the location counter LC1. The same BEGIN can be used to alter the current value of the location counter.

In IBM 360/370 assembly language, the establishment of location counters is implicit. By identifying the beginning of a control section, a location counter is created for that control section. For example, the instruction

Label	Operation	Operands
LC1	CSECT	

establishes a control section (therefore a location counter) whose name is LC1. The instruction

Label	Operation	Operands
LC1	START	5

is used to assign LC1 an initial value 5. START can only be used in the first control section. For altering the location counter value, the ORG is used.

For example, the instruction

Label	Operation	Operands
	ORG	* − 5

decreases the current location counter by 5. Unlike the BEGIN, which can be used anywhere in a program, the ORG of IBM 360/370 assembly language must be used in the control section whose location counter value is to be altered.

1.3.3.2 Control Section and Symbol Dictionary

In writing a large program, the programmer can code the program in pieces, where each piece constitutes a separately assembled control section. The control sections can be executed in any order, allowing them to be debugged as they are completed. Then, the whole program can be loaded for execution when each of its control sections is debugged and tested out.

The advantages in sectioning a program into control sections are many:

1. Coding and debugging of individual control sections can be done in parallel, thereby reducing the time between analysis of the problem and availability of a running program.

2. Modifications to the program, which are usually confined to a few control sections, can be accomplished without the necessity of reassembling the entire program.

3. Duplication of effort can be minimized by incorporating previously checked-out control sections, e.g., library subroutines.

4. Different programming languages can be used for coding various control sections of a large program, thus allowing the programmer to exploit the strong points of these languages.

To handle control sections, pseudoinstructions may be needed in order to

1. identify the beginning of a control section, and

2. indicate the continuation of a control section.

The sample pseudoinstructions given in the previous section have illustrated the handling of control sections.

Communication between programs may involve the transfer of control from one program to another or it may involve reference to common data. The assembler should provide ways and means for such communication. Furthermore, a large program may consist of several control sections—not all of them assembled at the same time. The assembler should therefore provide additional ways and means for communication between independently assembled control sections. Such a program constitutes either one or more control sections. The mechanism by which communication can be established between independently assembled control sections can also be applied to interprogram communications, because programs can be viewed as control sections.

To facilitate this communication, the assembler requires that the programmer, through the use of pseudoinstructions, do the following:

1. identify the symbolic label in the control section that may be referred to by other control sections, and

2. specify the symbolic label in the other (independently assembled) control section to which a reference is made in the control section.

The assembler then creates for the assembled control sections an *external symbol dictionary* which contains the above information.

With the aid of external symbol dictionaries, the linking loader (discussed in Section 1.5) will be able to resolve the cross-references before loading.

In IBM 360/370 assembly language, for example, the pseudoinstruction

Label	Operation	Operands
	ENTRY	LC2, LC3

establishes that symbolic labels LC2 and LC3 in this control section can be used as operands for referencing by other programs or control sections.

The pseudoinstruction

Label	Operation	Operands
	EXTRN	LC3, LC4

establishes two symbolic labels being entries or control section names. Both these labels are, of course, defined in some other control sections.

The use of ENTRY and EXTRN in the IBM 7090/7040 is similar.

1.3.3.3 Data Definition and Generation

To introduce data into storage and reserve storage area in a program, pseudo-instructions of the following categories are usually provided:

1. Define constant: constants of various types and lengths.

2. Define storage: storage of various lengths.

Both IBM 360/370 and IBM 7090/7040 assembly languages have extensive data definition and generation repertoires. For example, in IBM 360/370 the define-constant and define-storage pseudoinstructions can specify various data types—some of which are illustrated on the next page.

Label	Operation	Operands	Comments
	DC	C'AB',	The characters A and B are to be generated.
		X'FE',	The hexadecimal number FE is to be generated.
		B'1Ø1',	The binary number 1Ø1 is to be generated.
		F'12',	The decimal number 12 is to be converted into a full binary word.
		E'46.2',	The decimal number 46.2 is to be generated into a 24-bit mantissa and 7-bit characteristic floating point word.
		A(LC1),	The address value of LC1 is to be generated.
		V(SINE)	The address of an external symbol will be supplied.
AREA	DS	8ØC	80 characters of storage are reserved; the symbolic address of the first character is AREA.

In IBM 7090/7040 assembly language, we single out three examples for illustration.

Label	Operation	Operands	Comments
S	DEC	1,2,3,4,	The decimal numbers, 1,2,3, and 4 are converted to binary numbers and stored in consecutive locations. The symbol S refers to the first of these locations.
AREA	BSS	5	The reservation of 5 locations is accomplished by adding 5 to the current location counter. The symbol AREA refers to the first of these locations.
END	BES	6	The symbol END refers to the first location following the reserved group of 6 locations.

1.3.3.4 Program and Listing Control

There are pseudoinstructions for controlling the program listings, such as space setting, title and subtitle printout, page ejection, etc. Other instructions provide controls over the source program, such as End-of-Program, literal-pool-origin specification, etc.

1.3.3.5 Symbol Definition

Like the data-definition pseudoinstructions, the symbol-definition pseudoinstructions allow a symbol to be introduced and defined in the program. Usually, the mere appearance of a symbol as a label in an instruction results in the symbol being defined. The definition of the symbol is, of course, the current value of the location counter which controls the instruction. In this case, there is no need to use symbol definition pseudoinstructions.

When a symbol is to be assigned a value other than the correct value of the location counter, the use of symbol-definition pseudoinstructions is mandatory.

Both IBM 360/370 and IBM 7090/7040 assembly languages have the EQU pseudo-instruction. The example

Label	Operation	Operand
A	EQU	B

means that the symbol A will be assigned the same value as has already been assigned to B.

1.3.4 DEFERRED SYMBOL DEFINITION

Consider again the use of the pseudoinstruction EQU in the following example.

Label	Operation	Operand
LENGTH	EQU	LISTTOP − LISTEND + 1

It is obvious that LENGTH is defined as the length of a list whose first location is LISTTOP and last location is LISTEND. However, such an instruction is considered invalid in IBM 360/370 assembly language if LISTTOP and LISTEND have not been previously defined.

The rationale is that since the value of LENGTH is based upon the values of LISTTOP and LISTEND, the assembler cannot compute the difference of the values unless they are known prior to the evaluation of this instruction. The fact that both these symbols may be well defined in a later part of the program does not help at all. In other words, this assembler cannot handle symbols whose definitions are deferred. We call these *symbols of deferred type*, and pseudoinstructions whose operands contain symbols of deferred type are called *pseudoinstructions of deferred type*. One way to remove a symbol from being of deferred type is to place (in this example) the EQU instruction at the very end of the program. However, this is not only inconvenient to the programmer, but is also arbitrary. For instance, if the programmer is writing a general list tracing algorithm which requires the length of the list as a parameter, the exact length (i.e., the value of length) does not have to be known.

For the same reason, the pseudoinstruction ORG in IBM 360/370 assembly language cannot be used as follows:

Label	Operation	Operand
	ORG	LENGTH

where LENGTH is *not* previously defined.

The inflexibility of the IBM 360/370 assembly language in handling deferred symbol definition is primarily caused by the construction of the IBM 360/370 assembler as a "two-pass" assembler.

In a two-pass assembler, the following sequence of instructions cannot be resolved.

Label	Operation	Operand
	ORG	A
A	EQU	B
B	EQU	5

We note that in the first pass the pseudoinstruction ORG cannot be processed, because the symbol A is not yet defined. Similarly, the label A cannot be defined in the EQU instruction on account of the symbol B. However, B may be defined in this pass. In the second pass, the processing of ORG is again deferred, since A is still not defined. Nevertheless, when the first EQU instruction is encountered in this pass, the label A can be defined by virtue of B having been defined. It is in the third pass that the pseudoinstruction ORG, with A as an operand, can then be processed. From this observation, we learn that a multiple pass assembler may handle deferred symbol definition. With the ability of an assembler to handle symbols of deferred type, the programmer can now introduce new symbols in place of other symbols which need not be previously defined. The freedom of introducing symbols of deferred type adds considerable flexibility in assembly language programming. However, it also creates more complexity (e.g., more passes) in the assembler. In the following sections we will describe an abstract multiple pass assembler which will resolve symbols of deferred type. Although it is rather complex, the assembler can be used as a general model from which a two-pass assembler can be derived as a special case.

1.4 THE ASSEMBLY

The basic assembly process for a multiple pass assembler consists of the following five functional phases, four of which will be elaborated in subsequent sections.

1. Lexical analysis. The primary function of the assembly process in this phase is to scan and encode the input program string. The encoded form is usually very condensed and easily manipulated by processors in other phases of the assembly process.

2. Syntax analysis. In this phase the assembly process is involved with the verification of the individual encoded statement to determine whether the statement is a valid or invalid assembly statement. Because some of the operands of the statement may consist of arithmetic and other expressions of numerals, literals, and symbolic names, there is the need for parsing.

3. Semantic process. By far the most complex phase of the assembly process is the semantic processing of valid encoded assembly statements. There are two tasks involved. The first is the task of symbol definition. To provide a definition to a symbol is to assign a value to the symbol in a prescribed way. The assignment of values to symbols becomes somewhat complicated if the values of the symbols must be derived from the values of other symbols. Pseudoinstructions are most responsible for these assignments. For this reason, the evaluation of pseudo-instructions is a major task of the semantic process.

4. Production of object program. The generation of object modules for the input program constitutes the task of this process.

5. Program listing and error messages.

1.4.1 LEXICAL ANALYSIS: THE PROCESS OF SCANNING AND ENCODING THE INPUT PROGRAM STRING

The input to the assembler is a program in the assembly language written by a programmer (as depicted in Fig. 1.1a) or produced by a language processor such as a FORTRAN or COBOL compiler (as depicted in Fig. 1.1b). In either case we shall call the input to the assembler the input source program, or, for brevity, the *input program*. In the case of compiler-produced input programs, the compilers serve as preprocessors and usually provide the assembler with input programs which are lexically correct and well encoded. Thus there is no need for the assembler to perform any lexical analysis on compiler-produced input programs. On the other hand, the lexical analysis on a user-submitted input program is extensive. Because it is long and consists of considerable information irrelevant to the process of symbol definition and pseudoinstruction evaluation, the input program is seldom used repeatedly by the assembler. For example, comments and multiple blanks in a statement may be helpful to the programmer, but, except in program listing, they serve no useful purpose in the assembly. In fact, they hinder the assembly process because skipping and detecting characters takes time.

To facilitate the assembly process, the input program is scanned only once. At the end of the scan, an encoded form of the input program is produced which is to be used repeatedly for the rest of the assembly process.

Here we describe a way to encode the input program.

1. As each statement of the input program is scanned, the symbols in the statement are recognized by their type.

2. For each symbol, a search is made over the symbol in the *symbol table* (see Fig. 1.3). An entry in the symbol table consists of two components—a symbol

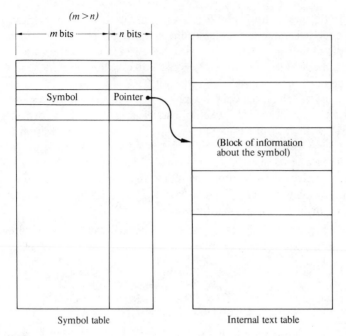

Figure 1.3

and a pointer. The pointer leads to a block of information describing the symbol. Information about symbols is stored in a table known as the *internal text table*. If the search fails, then the new symbol is entered into the symbol table. When a new symbol S_i is entered into the symbol table, the information about the symbol is generated and entered into the internal text table. A pointer P_i to the information is created and stored along with the symbol in the symbol table. Otherwise, the symbol S_i appears in the symbol table. Through its pointer P_i the block of information concerning the symbol in the internal text table is updated. During the update certain conditions, such as multiple defined symbols, can be detected.

3. Now returning to the statement, the symbol S_i in the statement is to be replaced by its pointer P_i. The statement is considered *encoded* if (a) every symbol in the statement is replaced by its pointer, (b) every blank string is replaced by a blank indicator and a blank count, and (c) a pointer to the comment field in the original input program is created if there is comment in the original text.

In this way, all the symbols in an input program are replaced with their corresponding pointers. The advantages are

1. the encoded input program is shorter than the original one, and

2. the use of P_i instead of S_i enables the assembler to fetch from the internal text table the information about S_i directly through P_i in the process of symbol definition (discussed in Section 1.4.3).

This last remark may not be obvious to the reader. We shall elaborate on it. If we were using symbols S_i instead of pointers P_i in the encoded input programs, then each time the assembler encounters a symbol, say, S_5, a search must be made for it in the symbol table. From the table, the assembler can then obtain the pointer P_5 to the information about S_5. But S_5 may be used many times as a symbolic name in different statements, so that the repeated search for S_5 is time consuming.

1.4.2 SYNTAX ANALYSIS: THE PROCESS OF DETERMINING VALID PROGRAM INSTRUCTIONS

Because the assembly statements are simple in syntax, syntax analysis in the assembly process is mainly involved with the parsing of arithmetic expression in the operands. We shall not study parsing algorithms or parsers—both of these have been extensively covered in the literature. What we should be aware of is that syntax rules vary considerably from one assembly language to another. For instance, in IBM 360/370 assembly language, the syntax rules for *valid* expressions are as follows:

1. An elementary expression can only contain either a symbol (one to eight characters of letters and digits with a leading letter), a well-defined value (e.g., B'010' and C'ABC'), a location counter reference (e.g., the use of * to indicate the current location counter value), or a literal (e.g., = F'35', meaning the binary equivalent of a full-word fixed-point decimal number 35).

2. An expression is either an elementary expression or an arithmetic combination of expressions and parenthesized expressions.

3. Arithmetic operators for the combination are restricted to infix operators: addition (+), subtraction (−), multiplication (*), and division (/).

4. No two arithmetic operators can be used in succession.

5. An expression cannot consist of more than 16 elementary expressions.

6. An expression consisting of more than one elementary expression may not contain a literal.

7. An expression cannot have more than five levels of parentheses.
   Thus, the following expressions are *invalid*:

   −A + BCD   Violates Rule 3 because the minus sign is not an infix operator.

   A ** B   Violates Rule 4.

   A = F'0123'   Violates Rules 1, 2, and 6 because the two elementary expressions, A and = F'0123', are not combined with an arithmetic operator.

   A + (B + (C − (D * (E / (F + (2 − G)))))))   Violates Rule 7.

Although the syntax analysis during the assembly process can determine whether an expression of an instruction is valid or invalid, it cannot foresee whether or not the value of the expression exists. To evaluate the expression in terms of symbol definitions, literal definitions, and location counter values, the assembly must enter the semantic processing phase. It is in this phase that definitions of the symbols and literals and values of location counters are determined and the arithmetic combinations of the definitions and values are evaluated. We shall return to the discussion of expression evaluation after we discuss the semantic process in the following section.

1.4.3 SEMANTIC PROCESS: THE PROCESS OF DEFINING SYMBOLS AND EVALUATING PSEUDOINSTRUCTIONS

The processes of defining symbols and evaluating pseudoinstructions are most involved. We will discuss them in some detail. For convenience, the valid encoded input program will simply be called the program. Furthermore, we shall not refer to the encoded form in this discussion because the reader would have difficulty in reading it. Instead, we use the original source form for the study of semantic processing. We note, however, that the assembler does use the encoded form for semantic processing. Thus, whenever we mention a symbol S_i in the discussion, we mean that its pointer P_i is actually being used by the assembler.

Let us first describe the internal tables and the general process. Because the process is rather involved, the reader is forewarned to bear with the presentation. However, we shall illustrate the process by providing a graphical view and a detailed example.

1.4.3.1 The Dictionaries

In processing the symbols in a program, the assembler constructs, in addition to the symbol table and its internal text table, a number of tables for storing information about the symbols. Since a symbol may be defined by other symbols which have not yet been defined, there is the need of going over the symbols several times before they are all defined, as we have illustrated in Section 1.3.4. For this reason, the use of small and compactly coded internal tables, instead of the input program, can result in considerable time-saving in symbol search and processing.

Basically, three additional tables are involved in the process of defining symbols. They are called the

1. instruction dictionary (briefly, I-dictionary),
2. location counter dictionary (L-dictionary), and
3. pseudoinstruction dictionary (P-dictionary).

Although these dictionaries may be considered as logically separate, in a given implementation they may be physically combined. In general, entries in these dictionaries are in the form of tuples generated as the (encoded) input program is read for the first time. To name these tuples, we denote I_i the ith entry of the I-dictionary, L_j the jth entry of the L-dictionary, and P_k the kth entry of the P-dictionary.

The Instruction Dictionary

Conceptually, the process creates an entry for each labeled instruction of the program. That is, each instruction which is referenced in the program will be described in the dictionary. Unlabeled instructions will be skipped by this process. However, the length of the skipped instructions and the location counter by which these instructions are controlled will be reflected in the entry. More specifically, we have for the ith labeled instructions in the program an entry

$$I_i(d, p)$$

where d is the distance (defined as the sum of instruction-lengths) between the ith and the $(i - 1)$th labeled instructions; and p is a pointer to the next entry under the control of the same location counter. In the absence of the next entry, p points to the location counter entry in L-dictionary.

For example, an entry I_0 (6, I_1) would be created for the following IBM 360/370 assembly program, indicating that the first labeled instruction is noted and that the length of previous (unlabeled) instructions is 6 (say, 6 bytes), and that the next labeled instruction under the control of the same location counter is noted by the second entry of the same dictionary. The second entry I_1 is created for the instruction whose label is BADDR.

Location	Label	Operation	Operands	Comments
		CSECT		
000000		STM	14,12,12(13)	Save register contents.
000004		BALR	10,0	Load base.
		USING	*,10,9	
		USING	STORAGE,12,11	
I_0 → 000006	TT	L	9,BADDR	
00000A		B	TT1	
I_1 → 00000E	BADDR	DC	F'12'	
			:	

Consider another example where the I-dictionary contains I_0 (0, I_1) and I_1 (, L_0) for the following IBM 7090/7040 assembly program segment. The second entry would show that the second labeled instruction is noted and that the length of the instructions between this and first labeled instruction is unknown at the time, and that this labeled instruction is the last instruction under the control of the first (or 0th) location counter.

Location	Label	Operation	Operands	Comments
		USE		Use the blank (main) location counter.
I_0 → 000000	ORIGIN	CLA	X	Clear the accumulator and add the content of X to it.
000001		ADD	Y	Add the content of Y to the accumulator.
000002		STO	Z	Store the sum into Z.
000003		TRA	W	Transfer to W.
I_1 → ?	Z	BES	N	
		USE	M	Use location counter M.
		CLA	X	
			:	

The reason that the instruction length is not determined is due to the deferred definition of the symbol N. Unless the value of N is known, the number of reserved locations is not available. Since Z stands for the next location immediately following the reserved block, the value of Z cannot be determined until N is defined. Thus, the label Z, although it causes an entry to be generated in the I-dictionary for the instruction, cannot infer the length of instructions or locations between the previous label ORIGIN and itself. The fact that the pointer entry in I_1 is L_0 means a different location counter is to be used for subsequent instruction control. The USE M pseudo-instruction is very similar to the IBM 360/370 assembly language's M CSECT instruction indicating that the rest of instructions are controlled by a different location counter M.

We note that whether a labeled instruction is a machine instruction or pseudo-instruction, an entry will be created for it in the I-dictionary. The pointers (i.e., the second components) of the entries link together all the labeled instructions under the same location counter; the last pointer of the link always indicates the location counter (entry in the L-dictionary) controlling the instructions in the linked list.

The Pseudoinstruction Dictionary

The P-dictionary will contain entries for pseudoinstruction. These entries are of the form

$$P_k (d, p, 't')$$

where d is defined as above; p is the pointer to an entry in I-dictionary if the entry is under the same location counter, to a location counter entry in L-dictionary if the location counter is initialized by the pseudoinstruction; and t is the text of the pseudoinstruction.

As we have seen in earlier sections, the pseudoinstruction is a directive to the assembler concerning mainly the location counter or data and symbol generation. In the former case, the pointer must mark the location counter concerned. For this reason, we let p be L_j, referring to the jth location counter entry in the L-dictionary. In the latter case, the assembler must know the location where the data and symbols are to be generated. By referring to the labeled instruction immediately preceding the pseudoinstruction, the location from which the data and symbol generation will begin can be determined. Thus, in this case we let p be I_i, referring to the last entry in the I-dictionary. Furthermore, we know that d indicates the distance between the labeled instruction and the pseudoinstruction. If the value of d cannot be determined at the time when the entry for the pseudoinstruction is created, the pseudoinstruction is of deferred type. We shall illustrate it with an example in the sequel.

Special consideration must be given to the cases where the pseudoinstruction itself has a label. For completeness, there is an entry in I-dictionary for the label. The pointer p in the P-dictionary entry for the pseudoinstruction therefore refers to the entry in I-dictionary, and the distance d is of course zero. If the labeled pseudoinstruction is of deferred type, the distance d in the I-dictionary entry (not to be confused with the distance d in the P-dictionary entry) may have to be determined later.

In other words, $P_k(d, p, 't')$ is either in the form of

$$P_k (d, L_j, 't')$$

or

$$P_k(d, I_i, 't').$$

For example, consider the following pseudoinstruction which assigns the value of Z to location counter M.

Label	Operation	Operand
	BEGIN	M, Z

An entry

$$P_1 (, L_2, 'BEGIN M, Z')$$

may be created for the instruction in the P-dictionary. This entry indicates that the distance is unknown (actually, does not apply), that the location counter M has an entry in the L-dictionary which is referred to by the pointer L_2, and that the text of the instruction is saved for later evaluation. The subscript of P_1 reflects that this is the second pseudoinstruction in the program which requires subsequent evaluation. For another instruction,

Label	Operation	Operand
	BSS	5

an entry

$$P_2 (2, I_0, 'BSS 5')$$

may be generated. In this case, the entry indicates that the unlabeled pseudoinstruction has nothing to do with any location counter. Furthermore, its distance from the preceding labeled instruction is 2. Since it is referred to by the pointer I_0, the labeled instruction is the first (or 0th) labeled instruction in the program.

Consider, for example, the following labeled pseudoinstruction

Label	Operation	Operand
Z	BES	N

an entry

$$P_3 (0, I_1, 'BES N')$$

may be created. In this example, the entry indicates again that the pseudoinstruction has nothing to do with any location counter. Because the pseudoinstruction is labeled, there is an entry for the label in the I-dictionary. We know that the entry is pointed by I_1. It is not surprising that the distance is zero since entries at I_1 and P_3 are for the same pseudoinstruction. Nevertheless, the distance d in the entry

$$I_1 (d, I_2)$$

will not be known if the number N has not yet been determined. Such is the case where the pseudoinstruction is of deferred type.

We reiterate that in t there is the directive to the assembler concerning the way in which either the location counter (as designated by L_j) or the instruction (as pointed by I_i) should be handled. The directive must therefore be interpreted by the assembler. The interpretation in the semantic process of the assembly is slow and complex because it is usually performed entirely by software means. For this reason, the so-called "fast" assemblers tend to provide as few pseudoinstructions of deferred type as possible so that the evaluation of the pseudoinstructions can be kept at a minimum. Obviously, this approach has greatly restricted the richness and flexibility of the assembly language.

Few commercial computer systems are designed to provide hardware counterparts of software concepts, such as multiple location counters and data and symbol generations, for more rapid assembly and translation of programming language statements; instead, they attempt to speed up the execution of program (load) modules. And yet, these features merely require the computer systems to incorporate several user-accessible program counters and some data-descriptive machine instructions. High-level language-oriented machines, such as the APL machine, do have some of these features, although such machines are still experimental. For a reading on machines with these features, the reader may refer to [10].

The Location Counter Dictionary

Finally, we come to the make-up of the L-dictionary. Since the L-dictionary consists of entries for location counters, there is a one-to-one correspondence between the entries in the L-dictionary and the location counters used in the input program. For each location counter, four items of information are needed.

1. The initial value of the location counter.
2. The instructions being controlled by the location counter.
3. The location counter which immediately precedes the present one.
4. The location counter which immediately follows the present one.

We note that a location counter may be initiated by a pseudoinstruction, by the last value of the preceding location counter, and by the assembler, if the location counter is the main location counter.* With these considerations in mind, entries in L-dictionary are of the form

$$L_j\,(m, p', p'', p''')$$

where $m = 1$, if the location counter has been initialized by a pseudoinstruction entry in P-dictionary—$m = 0$, if otherwise;

p' is a pointer to an entry either in the I-dictionary or in the P-dictionary under the location counter;

---

* In a sequential machine with a single hardware program counter (PC), there is only one main location counter. All other location counters in the program follow the main one. In a parallel machine utilizing several PC's, there can be several main location counters, each of which may lead to many other location counters. However, main location counters do not precede or follow each other since they simulate parallel processing and control.

p'' is a pointer to the pseudoinstruction entry in the *P*-dictionary that initializes the next location counter; and

p''' is a pointer to the location counter whose initial value is determined by the last value of this counter.

We note from the above definitions that

1. entries (for instructions) under the same location counter—whether they are scattered in the *I*-dictionary, *P*-dictionary, or *L*-dictionary—are chained into a *ring* by their pointers, and

2. location counter entries in the *L*-dictionary are linked with the main location counter entry at the beginning of the *list*.

Furthermore, we observe that each entry in the list leads to a ring. Thus, the pointers in the entries (i.e., p in I_i and P_k entries, and p', p'', and p''' in L_j entries) form a list of location counter entries and rings of instruction entries under the control of the individual location counters. We will illustrate the rings and list in the next section.

An iterative process discussed in a later section can be used for defining all of the symbols in the program by starting at the first entry in the list and tracing through all of the entries in the ring, then taking the next entry in the list and its associated ring, etc.

1.4.3.2 A View From Directed Graph

Let us first illustrate the use of these dictionaries and the flow of the iterative definition algorithm by way of the following example.

Label	Operation	Operand	Comments
	USE	H	Use the location counter H.
	TRA	Y	
Z	BES	N	Reserve a storage block of N words; label the (N + 1)th word Z.
	BEGIN	M,Z	Assign the value of Z to location counter M.
	USE		Use the MAIN or BLANK location counter.
X	DEC	1,2	Define two decimal numbers, 1 and 2.
	CLA	X	
W	STO	Z − 1	
	USE	M	Use the location counter M.
Y	NOP	0	
N	EQU	W − X	The value of N is equal to the value of (W − X).
	END		

We note that there are five labeled instructions whose symbolic locations are Z, X, W, Y, and N and three location counters whose names are H, M, and blank. Further, there are three pseudoinstructions. The first pseudoinstruction

Label	Operation	Operand
Z	BES	N

is of deferred type, where N is not previously defined. Consequently, the label Z cannot be defined. The second one is

Label	Operation	Operand
	BEGIN	M,Z

also of deferred type, where Z is not defined. The third one is

Label	Operation	Operand
N	EQU	W − X

where the N is to be assigned the value of (W − X), instead of the current value of a location counter. The dictionaries for the sample program are as follows.

P-dictionary	*L*-dictionary	*I*-dictionary
P_0 (0, L_0, 'BEGIN, Ø')	L_0 (1, I_1, , L_1) for	I_0 (8, L_1) for Z
P_1 (, I_0, 'BES N')	the blank location	I_1 (0, I_2) for X
P_2 (, L_2, 'BEGIN M, Z')	counter	I_2 (3, L_0) for W
P_3 (0, I_4, 'EQU W − X')	L_1 (0, P_1, P_2,) for H	I_3 (8, L_2) for Y
	L_2 (1, I_3, , 0) for M	I_4 (3, 0) for N

The above dictionaries reflect the final contents of the entries (see also Fig. 1.7). Since there are five labeled instructions, there are five entries in the *I*-dictionary. Again, there are three entries in the *L*-dictionary for the three location counters declared in the input program. The three entries in the *P*-dictionary which correspond to the three pseudoinstructions in the input program are at P_1, P_2, and P_3. From this illustration, we note that:

1. Before any entry is created for the instructions of the input program, the process enters an entry L_0 in the *L*-dictionary. This means that whether or not the user declares any location counter, the process always creates a main (or blank) location counter for his program.

2. To initiate the main location counter, a pseudoinstruction (not part of the input program) which initiates the location counter is also created, as reflected in the entry P_0 in the P-dictionary.

The pointers in the entries are used by the iterative definition algorithm for the definition of symbols and evaluation of pseudoinstructions. The definition algorithm can be viewed as a chaser of a directed graph which follows the directions of the arrowheads (i.e., pointers p, p', p'', p''') and traverses from one ring to another via interconnecting lists. The particular directed graph for this example is depicted below. It provides an understanding of the sequence in which the entries are finally used for symbol definition and pseudoinstruction evaluation. However, it does not reflect the sequence in which the entries are originally made.

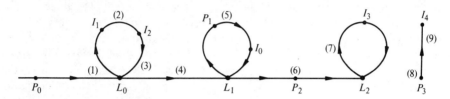

The interpretation of the directed graph is as follows:

1. The definition algorithm begins the process with a standard entry P_0 which leads to a main location counter entry L_0 and sets the counter value to zero.
2. Two labeled instructions are under the control of the main location counter in a prescribed sequence, as reflected in their corresponding entries I_1 and I_2. From the subscripts of the entries, we learn that the instructions appeared in the input program as the second and third labeled instructions.
3. There are no more instructions under the main location counter.
4. A new location counter is called for and designated as L_1. Since there is no pseudoinstruction to set an initial value for the counter, the initial value is determined as the last value of the previous location counter. In this case, it is determined by L_0.
5. The data, or symbol generation, pseudoinstruction P_1 and the labeled instruction I_0 are under control of the location counter L_1.
6. Another new location counter entry, L_2, is initiated by P_2. The initial value of this new location counter is not determined by the last value of the previous location counter. Instead, it is supplied from the same pseudoinstruction P_2.
7. There is only one labeled instruction, namely I_3, under the control of this location counter. Then this list of rings ends.
8. The definition algorithm selects the next entry in the P-dictionary for another list traversing.
9. There is only one instruction whose entry I_4 is led from P_3. The second list ends, and there are no more lists.

From this illustration, we learn that there are two kinds of pseudoinstructions. The ones on the rings are for data or symbol generation; the ones on the lists are for setting location counters and their values.

Unfortunately, the directed graph view obscures the information concerning the number of iterations needed to establish the final version of the directed rings and lists. These iterations result from pseudoinstructions of deferred type. For this reason, we shall return to this example again, apply the semantic process, and take snapshots of the processing at different time instances.

1.4.3.3 Three Stages of the Process

To define the symbols in a program, the assembler performs tasks in three stages. In Stage I, dictionaries are set up and initialized. At the end of Stage II, a sequential pass is made over the instructions of the program. (This is usually known as the first pass of a "two-pass" assembly). During the pass, entries in the dictionary are constructed and updated. For every *labeled* instruction (pseudo or mnemonic) in sequence, an entry is made in the instruction dictionary, *I*-dictionary. Likewise, an entry is made in the pseudoinstruction dictionary, *P*-dictionary, for each pseudoinstruction of deferred type or the type that initializes a location counter. If a pseudoinstruction that names a location counter is present, then an entry is made in the location counter dictionary, *L*-dictionary. The final stage of this process is to resolve all the location assignments to the symbols in the dictionaries.

Stage I

Unless specified in the program with the appropriate pseudoinstructions, the assembler always initializes the dictionaries by creating two entries—one in the *L*-dictionary and one in the *P*-dictionary. The entry in the *L*-dictionary indicates that the program is under the control of the main location counter; and the entry in the *P*-dictionary sets the location counter to zero.

Stage II

In this stage, the process must determine the types of instructions which are being processed. Unlabeled instructions which are not pseudoinstructions of deferred type, and location counter type, will be identified for the purpose of computing the instruction lengths. Thus in the course of processing these instructions, the parameter d in the entries of the *I*- and *P*-dictionaries will have to be initiated and updated. On the other hand, labeled instructions which are not pseudoinstructions of the above types will be handled with additional care, which involves the construction of entries for them in the *I*-dictionary. As we have learned before, the entry must be linked with other entries in the *I*-dictionary under the same location counter in a ring. In other words, care must be given to the construction and updating of pointers to proper entries in the *I*- and *L*-dictionaries. For pseudoinstructions which either name or alter the content of a location counter, the *P*- and *L*-dictionaries will be used for the addition and modification of the entries. Finally, there are the pseudoinstructions of deferred type. These instructions must be saved in the *P*-dictionary as entries for later interpretation. Again, if they are concerned with location counters, then pointers

L_j to entries in the L-dictionary must be created. If they are concerned with symbol and data generation, then pointers I_i to entries in the I-dictionary must be provided. In the former case, the pointers facilitate the lists; in the latter case, the pointers preserve the rings.

Stage III

An iterative algorithm, known as the *definition algorithm*, is given here. The algorithm enables the assembler to systematically trace through the list of location counter entries and rings of instruction entries under the control of the individual location counters.

Step 1. Starting at the initial entry of the P-dictionary, the assembler attempts to evaluate the pseudoinstruction stored in t of the entry. If it can be evaluated, and if the location counter value is known, then either the list (of L_j's) or ring (of I_i's and P_k's) is followed, as indicated by the pointer in the entry. An entry is *defined* by adding the distance to the value of the previous entry. This is terminated if the ring is closed, or if another pseudoinstruction is encountered. In the latter case, the location counter value is recorded.

Step 2. If the entry could not be evaluated (e.g., deferred pseudoinstruction) or if the ring trace has been terminated, the assembler locates the next entry in the P-dictionary and proceeds as described in Step 1.

Step 3. Eventually, the assembler must sweep through all entries in the P-dictionary. There are then two possibilities:

a) All entries have been defined.
b) An entry is not defined. In this case, the assembler returns to reprocess the entry in the P-dictionary, ignoring any previously defined pseudoinstruction entries for which the ring has been followed.

Step 4. The algorithm then terminates in one of two ways—either by Step 3(a), which gives complete definition, or by Step 3(b), which would be without having defined a single pseudoinstruction on the sweep.

In the latter case, an error due to a circular definition must exist in the program.

1.4.3.4 The "Second" Pass. Definition Substitution and Expression Evaluation

Having defined all the entries in the dictionary, the assembler now has the definitions of the symbolic labels, since there is an entry for each labeled instruction in the I-dictionary. With these definitions, the assembler can substitute symbols and evaluate expressions appearing in the operands of the instructions by passing through the entire program again (this pass is known as the second pass of a "two-pass" assembly).

In evaluating expressions, the assembler must determine whether the value of the expression is to be affected by the location of the instruction. If it is affected, the expression is *relative*; otherwise, *absolute*. Obviously, an absolute expression will result in a constant, whereas a relative expression will result in a location relative to the beginning of the program (or control section). The values for determining the arithmetic combination of relative and absolute expressions are as follows:

1. The sum, difference, product, or quotient of two absolute expressions is an absolute expression.
2. The difference of two relative expressions is an absolute expression.
3. The sum or difference of a relative expression and an absolute expression is a relative expression.
4. No other combinations are permissible.

Let us again familiarize ourselves with the following example.

Label	Operation	Operand	Comments
	USE	H	Use the location counter H.
	TRA	Y	
Z	BES	N	Reserve a storage block of N words; label the (N + 1)th word Z.
	BEGIN	M,Z	Assign the value of Z to location counter M.
	USE		Use the MAIN or BLANK location counter.
X	DEC	1,2	Define two decimal numbers, 1 and 2.
	CLA	X	
W	STO	Z − 1	
	USE	M	Use the location counter M.
Y	NOP	0	
N	EQU	W − X	The value of N is equal to the value of (W − X).
	END		

Steps taken in Stages I and II are illustrated as snapshots in Figs. 1.4 through 1.6.

Time	P-dictionary	L-dictionary	I-dictionary
t_0	$P_0\ (0,\ L_0,\ \text{BEGIN},\ \emptyset)$	$L_0\ (1,\ ,\ ,\ )$ for the main location counter	
		At the end of Stage I, a list is constructed.	
t_1	$P_0\ (0,\ L_0,\ \text{BEGIN},\ \emptyset)$	$L_0\ (1,\ ,\ ,\ L_1)$ $L_1\ (0,\ ,\ ,\ )$ for H	
		First statement of the input program has been processed.	

Figure 1.4

Time	P-dictionary	L-dictionary	I-dictionary
t_2	P_0 (0, L_0, BEGIN, Ø) P_1 (, I_0, BES N)	L_0 (1, , , L_1) L_1 (0, P_1, ,) for H	I_0 (, L_1) for Z

First 3 statements have been processed.

Key and explanation

——————————— path of a ring — — — — — — — — path of a list

1. A list that begins at P_0 and ends at L_1 is created.
2. A ring of L_1, P_1, and I_0 is formed.
3. If the components in an entry are unknown at the time, they are left blank in the entry.

Figure 1.4 (*continued*)

Time	P-dictionary	L-dictionary	I-dictionary
t_3	P_0 (0, L_0, BEGIN, Ø) P_1 (, I_0, BES N) P_2 (, , BEGIN M, Z)	L_0 (1, , , L_1) L_1 (0, P_1, ,) for H	I_0 (, L_1) for Z
t_4	P_0 (0, L_0, BEGIN, Ø) P_1 (, I_0, BES N) P_2 (, , BEGIN M, Z)	L_0 (1, I_1, , L_1) L_1 (0, P_1, ,) for H	I_0 (, L_1) for Z I_1 (0, L_0) for X

First 4 statements processed

t_5	P_0 ( ) P_1 ( ) P_2 ( )	L_0 (1, I_1, , L_1) L_1 (0, P_1, ,) for H	I_0 (, L_1) for Z I_1 (0, I_2) for X I_2 (3, L_0) for W
t_6	P_0 (0, L_0, BEGIN, Ø) P_1 (, I_0, BES N) P_2 (, L_2, BEGIN M, Z)	L_0 (1, I_1, , L_1) L_1 (0, P_1, P_2,) for H L_2 (1, , ,) for M	I_0 (, L_1) for Z I_1 (0, I_2) for X I_2 (3, L_0) for W

Key and explanation

——————————— path of a ring — — — — — — — — path of a list

1. Not all the rings and the list are shown.
2. The ring of L_0 and I_1 at time t_4 is enlarged into a ring consisting of the newly processed entry I_2 at time t_5. Note that pointers in I_1 at different times are different, reflecting the enlargement.

Figure 1.5

Time	P-dictionary	L-dictionary	I-dictionary
t_7	P_0 ( ) P_1 ( ) P_2 ( )	L_0 (1, I_1, , L_1) L_1 (0, P_1, P_2,) for H L_2 (1, I_3, ,) for M	I_0 ( ) for Z I_1 ( ) for X I_2 ( ) for W I_3 (0, L_2) for Y
t_8	P_0 (0, L_0, BEGIN, ∅) P_1 (, I_0, BES N) P_2 (, L_2, BEGIN M, Z) P_3 (0, I_4, EQU W − X)	L_0 (1, I_1, , L_1) L_1 (0, P_1, P_2,) for H L_2 (1, I_3, , 0) for M	I_0 (, L_1) for Z I_1 (0, I_2) for X I_2 (3, L_0) for W I_3 (0, L_2) for Y I_4 (, 0) for N

End of Stage II

Explanation

1. By starting at P_0 and utilizing the pointers in the entries followed, we have the list of P_0, L_0, L_1, P_2, and L_2.

2. For each location counter entry, we have a ring. Thus, the ring for L_0 consists of I_1 and I_2. Similarly, by way of the pointers, the ring for L_1 consists of P_1 and I_0. The ring for L_2 consists of I_3 only.

3. Blanks in the entries indicate that the components either are unknown or inconsequential.

Figure 1.6

Steps taken in Stage III are listed here.

1. Process the first entry in P-dictionary starting at P_0. Let d be the distance constant and set $d = 0$.

   $d = 0$ at L_0

   X $= d + 0 = 0$ at I_1

   W $= d + 3 = 3$ at I_2

   $d = d + 1 = 4$ at L_0

   $d = 4$ at L_1

   $d = d + (\ ) = ?$ at P_1

   Because N is not yet defined, the assembler cannot evaluate the pseudoinstruction BES. Thus the process stops at P_1.

2. Process the next entry in P-dictionary starting at P_2.
   Since Z is not yet defined, the process stops right there.

3. Process the next entry in P-dictionary starting at P_3.
   The pseudoinstruction EQU is evaluated in terms of W and X. Since W and X are defined in earlier processes, we have

   $$N = W - X = 3 - 0 = 3 \quad \text{at } I_4$$

4. Since entry at I_4 does not lead to any other entry, and since there is no new entry in the P-dictionary to process, the assembler starts at the first entry in P-dictionary that is not yet completely processed.

5. Process the entry at P_1.
   The pseudoinstruction BES N can now be evaluated, for N has been defined. The evaluation of the instruction results in the following change of d.

   $$d = d + N + 1 = 4 + 3 + 1 = 8$$

   Thus

   $$Z = d + 0 = 8 \quad \text{at } I_0.$$

   This process terminates at L_1.

6. Process the entry at P_2.
   The pseudoinstruction BEGIN M, Z causes the value of d to be set to the value of Z, i.e.,

   $$d = Z = 8.$$

   Thus

   $$Y = d + 0 = 8 \quad \text{at } I_3,$$
   $$d = 8 + 1 = 9 \quad \text{at } L_2.$$

7. The symbol definition is completed without error and the dictionaries have all their entries updated. The final version of the dictionaries is depicted in Fig. 1.7.

Time	P-dictionary	L-dictionary	I-dictionary
t_9	P_0 (0, L_0, BEGIN, ∅) P_1 (, I_0, BES N) P_2 (, L_2, BEGIN M, Z) P_3 (0, I_4, EQU W − X)	L_0 (1, I_1, , L_1) L_1 (0, P_1, P_2,) L_2 (1, I_3, , 0)	I_0 (8, L_1) for Z I_1 (0, I_2) for X I_2 (3, L_0) for W I_3 (8, L_2) for Y I_4 (3, 0) for N

Fig. 1.7 End of stage III.

1.4.4 THE PROCESS OF PRODUCING OBJECT PROGRAMS

If the semantic process is successful, this process will produce for the input program the object module, or program.

As we have discussed earlier, there are symbolic labels (e.g., entry points) and symbolic names (e.g., external names) in the other control section to which a reference is made in the control section. These entry points and external names cannot be defined by the assembler because these other control sections were simply not available at the time of assembling that control section. Information concerning the entry points, external references, and names of the control sections is kept in the object module known as the external symbol dictionary (which is discussed earlier in Section 1.3.3.2).

The internal symbols in a program are defined by the definition algorithm incorporated in the assembler. As discussed earlier, the definition of a symbol is the current value of the location counter under control. Since the location counter keeps track of the location of the instruction currently being processed *relative* to the beginning of the group of instructions, the definition of a symbol is commonly referred to as the *relative address*. Thus, the relative (or absolute) expression of symbols appearing as operands in an instruction will be assembled into a relative address (or constant). The rules used for determining whether an expression of symbols is a relative or absolute one have been discussed in Section 1.4.3.3. Simply, a relative expression will result in a relative address and an absolute expression will end up with a constant. Furthermore, the definitions of symbols can be introduced as data for address manipulation. This is accomplished by specifying the symbol in a pseudoinstruction of the data definition type. For example, the following instruction

Label	Operation	Operand
ADDR	DC	A (LC1)

allows the programmer to manipulate the content of ADDR which refers to a symbolic location LC1 (see Section 1.3.3.3 on data-definition pseudoinstruction). In evaluating the pseudoinstruction, the assembler recognizes the symbol and generates a relative address. In order to distinguish those definitions which are relative addresses from those definitions which are constants, a dictionary is constructed by the assembler as part of the object module. The dictionary known as *internal relocation symbol dictionary* has for each relative address an entry that indicates its location in the module.

In general, an object module is composed of two parts:

1. The symbol dictionaries—

    a) The external symbol dictionary.
    b) The internal relocation symbol dictionary.

2. The program proper—

    a) The assembled instructions and data.

1.4.5 CONCLUSIONS

Interestingly it is possible to write an IBM 360/370-like assembly program which is equivalent to the example given in the previous section. As an exercise, the reader may verify for himself that the same semantic process and its definition algorithm developed in the previous sections can be used to define the symbols and evaluate the pseudoinstructions of the new program. The only difference between this exercise and previous illustrations is that the definitions of the symbols, and the values of the expressions, of these programs do not have the same numeric values. This is due to the byte-oriented addressing scheme in the IBM 360/370 system. Nevertheless, the new program can be correctly assembled by the algorithm used above.

An equivalent IBM 360/370-like program			Example given in Section 1.4.4		
Label	Operation	Operand	Label	Operation	Operand
	START				
	USING	*,15			
H	CSECT			USE	H
	B	Y		TRA	Y
	DS	(N)F	Z	BES	N
Z	EQU	*			
M	CSECT				
	ORG	Z		BEGIN	M,Z
	CSECT			USE	
X	DC	2F'1,2'	X	DEC	1,2
	L	1,X		CLA	X
W	ST	1,Z − 4	W	STO	Z − 1
M	CSECT			USE	M
Y	NOP	0	Y	NOP	0
N	EQU	W − X	N	EQU	W − X
	END				

However, the IBM 360/370 assembler will not assemble this program successfully. There are five errors given:

1. An error in the branch instruction

   B   Y

   indicates that the symbolic address Y refers to a location outside the present control section.

2. An error in the define-storage instruction

   DS   (N)F

   occurs because the number N of reserved full-word storage is not previously defined.

3. Another error in the same define-storage instruction is the use of duplication number N. The use of the parenthesized expression is illegal.

4. An error in the set-location-counter instruction

ORG   Z

occurs because Z cannot be symbolic.

5. An error in the store instruction

ST   1,Z − 4

indicates that the expression (Z − 4) cannot be evaluated because Z is a symbolic label in another control section.

Except for the error in (3), all errors result directly from the use of symbols whose definitions are deferred. In the case of the error in (3), the valid duplication number must be a constant instead of a symbol. This constraint, of course, precludes the use of parentheses. Since a constant must be given, the use of the symbol of deferred definition type is unwarranted.

The IBM 360/370 assembler restricts the use of set-location-counter instructions, limits duplication factors, and prohibits referencing symbols in other control sections. These constraints eliminate the need for the assembler to handle deferred symbol definition. Consequently, the number of passes that the assembler takes to sweep the input program is reduced to two. More specifically, the iterative definition algorithm does not have to reprocess the entry in the P-dictionary after the first sweep (as was indicated in Step 3(b) of the algorithm in Section 1.4.3.3). With the first sweep and the "second" pass, the IBM 360/370 assembler is truly a two-pass assembler.

The lessons we have learned in this study are:

1. The flexibility of an assembler in handling deferred symbol definition is related to the iteration of the definition algorithm of the assembler.

2. The two-pass assembler makes no iterative use of the definition algorithm.

3. Without the use of an iterative definition algorithm, the assembler cannot handle deferred symbol definition. Consequently, the assembly language programmer is restricted in his freedom in symbolic referencing and is prevented from employing pseudoinstructions of deferred type.

4. On the other hand, the advantage of a two-pass assembler over a multiple pass assembler lies in a reduction of the size of the P-dictionary and a simple one-sweep definition algorithm. A small P-dictionary implies less interpretation, and a single sweep dictates no reprocessing, both of which save time.

In this abstract assembler, we hope that the dichotomy between the speed of an assembler and the richness of its assembly language has been characterized. Such characterization is intended to enable the system programmer to evaluate the trade-offs in designing the assembly language and the assembly system.

1.5 THE LINKING LOADER

In the absence of pseudoinstructions in the assembly language, the object module resulting from a single control section can be used as input to the loader. The loader then produces as its output the *load module*, which can be entered into the main storage for execution. With some minor additions, the loader can be extended to accept as its input several independently assembled modules and to produce as its output a combined load module.

Although this type of loader can be rather useful, it does not facilitate inter-module communication in terms of direct references.

Some of the pseudoinstructions, such as EXTRN and ENTRY, are specifically designed to facilitate intercontrol section communication, enabling a control section to make symbolic reference to another control section. In order to resolve such cross-references, we must again extend the capability of the loader to accept several independently assembled and cross-referenced object modules and to resolve the symbolic names for loading.

For our discussion, we call such an extended loader the *linking loader*. The major tasks of the linking loader are, therefore,

1. to determine the operational locations of the program proper of each object module;
2. to process and to remove the external symbol dictionaries;
3. to translate all relative address of data and instructions to their absolute forms and to remove the internal relocation symbol dictionaries;
4. to make certain determinations relative to channel, input, and output unit assignment;
5. to make certain determinations relative to the number, location, and assignment of buffers; and
6. to make the initial placement of data and instructions in the main memory so that the program may be properly executed.

Functionally, tasks (1), (2), and (3) are concerned with program relocation and memory utilization; tasks (4) and (5) are concerned with input and output device utilization; and task (6) is loading. The function of the linking loader in relocation and memory utilization will be elaborated in Section 1.5.1. Since the discussion of the function of the linking loader in device utilization requires the knowledge of input and output operations, it is included in the chapter on input and output operations. We shall not discuss the straightforward loading function of the linking loader.

In addition to these basic functions, a linking loader may have some new capabilities. One of these capabilities is called *chaining*, which enables a large collection of programs to be overlayed in a small memory space; the other capability is called *dynamic loading*, which enables the loading of a subroutine by call during the execution of the calling program. Both these additional functions of the linking loader will be discussed in the following sections.

1.5.1 RELOCATION AND MEMORY UTILIZATION

In referring to tasks (1), (2), and (3) in the previous section, we note that the linking loader performs the process of translating all the program references (e.g., relative addresses, external symbols, internal relocation symbols, and entries) into their absolute forms. By an absolute form we mean the form which the CPU can decode. Such a process is known as *relocation*. Obviously, the linking loader, not the assembler, does the relocation.

If the absolute forms are the main memory addresses, then the process is called *relocation-at-load-time*. If the absolute forms are the addresses of some address space other than the main memory, then the process is called *relocation-at-execution-time*. In this case, the absolute forms are often called the *virtual addresses*, and their address space the *virtual space*. The discussion of virtual addresses and space will be included in the chapter on virtual memory systems. Here we concentrate on the case of relocation-at-load-time.

Because the main memory is relatively expensive, much attention has been given to its better utilization. The relocation capability of the linking loader greatly enhances the effective use of the main memory.

Through the proper organization of a program and the use of the linking loader, the program, especially one larger than the available main memory, can efficiently utilize the main memory.

Here we include some of the methods which can enhance the memory utilization.

1.5.1.1 Chaining and Overlay

This is perhaps the most classic method for utilizing the main memory. The method requires that the programmer divide his program into sections (usually, routines or control sections) of which one must be designated as the *main section*. The remaining sections are called the *dependent sections*. A feature of the linking loader, known as *chaining*, enables the main section at run time to call in the dependent sections for execution. By placing the main section in the available main memory and sharing the rest of the available memory for the dependent sections, the main section can replace a dependent section when it is no longer needed with another dependent section. The technique of using the same area for different dependent sections of a program is known as *overlay*.

Although overlay technique enables the user to utilize small main memory for a large program, it has many shortcomings:

1. The user is responsible for the organization of his program into main and dependent sections.

2. Careful job preparation must be performed so that the operating system is informed of the relationship between the main sections and its dependents, e.g., the order in which the decks of the sections are inputted.

3. References between sections are restricted, e.g., a previous dependent section may not refer to an entry that is defined in a subsequent dependent section.

4. Once the main memory is allocated to the main section and its dependents, it remains so during the entire execution. Although sections may reduce their size during execution, the extra memory space resulting from the reduction will not be available to the other sections of the program. On the other hand, if a dependent section increases its size, part of it may be overlayed when another dependent section is brought in by the main section.

5. All of the sections of a program must be presented at the job preparation time, enabling the operating system to set up the proper linkages for using the chaining feature of the linking loader at load-time.

6. Only the main section can call on the dependent sections. The dependent section is not allowed to call on the other sections. If this should happen, then the return address to the main section saved in the chaining mechanism would be wiped out.

1.5.1.2 Dynamic Loading

The *dynamic loading technique* differs from chaining in that the sections of a program are defined dynamically instead of at the job preparation-time. In other words, the number of sections which constitute a program can vary, depending on the need of the main section. Furthermore, sections can be assembled separately and call on each other. To accomplish the dynamic loading technique, the linking loader requires that at a location known to the linking loader, there is a *symbolic reference table*. In relocating the main section, the loader creates for each entry to the main section two pieces of information: the symbolic name of the entry and the absolute location of the entry.

Whenever the main section calls on the linking loader for a dependent section, the loader processes the external symbols of the dependent section by searching through the symbolic reference table. If the symbol is found, then its corresponding location value is used for relocation. Otherwise, the external symbol is undefined, and the loading of the dependent section is aborted. To communicate with the linking loader for bringing in the dependent section, a macro call is usually provided. The macro call requires as its parameters the name of the dependent section and the absolute location at which the section is to be loaded. On issuing the macro call, the section's request will be sent to the operating system's request handling routine, either through interrupt, trap, or program transfer. This routine will, in turn, activate the linking loader for relocating the section. The return of the call indicates either the completion of the relocation or the abortion of the loading. If the relocation is successful, the calling section can then branch and link to the dependent section in the usual way.

If the dependent section requests the loading of another dependent section, it can issue a similar macro call. The only restriction is that the dependent section to be loaded will have all its external symbols defined in the symbol table. (What would be the price for removing the restriction?)

Because memory allocation of various dependent sections is not done at job preparation time, as in the case of chaining the overlay, there arises a problem of dynamic memory management. Whenever a dependent section is to be loaded, the calling section should consider the following:

1. Is there enough main memory for the dependent section?
2. If not enough, can the main memory occupied by a previous dependent section be reclaimed?

In other words, either the operating system or the main section must provide the management capabilities for

1. keeping track of the available main memory,
2. reclaiming the main memory occupied by the previous dependent sections (this process is known as garbage collection), and
3. combining the reclaimed areas for larger available areas.

In summary, solutions to dynamic linking and loading of control sections are very much complicated by the problem of dynamic memory management. Because virtual space plays an important role in dynamic memory management, the study of dynamic linking and loading will be examined again in the chapter on virtual memory systems.

1.6 POSTSCRIPT

The generalized assembly system is an abstraction of the work in [15] and [24]. The discussion of particular assembly languages is derived from [8], [9], and [22]. The study of the function of the linking loader is based on the material in [6], [13], [18], and [20]. Hashing algorithms used in the exercises are collected from [2], [12], and [17]. For a discussion on table search, collision, and other uses of hashing algorithms, the reader may refer to [7], [16], and [19]. The detailed layout of the load and object modules is not relevant in this study. However, they can be found in [18] and [21]. The study of macroassembly instructions is not covered in this chapter. The author believes that macroassembly instructions can be considered as pseudoinstructions. The process of macroexpansion can be facilitated by the employment of location counters. Furthermore, the process of code generation for macroinstructions is analogous to the evaluation of pseudoinstructions of data and symbol-generation type. For this reason, the macroprocessor can be designed with the kind of definition algorithm employed in the assembler. Macroprocessors used as macroassemblers and macrogenerators for high-level languages are discussed in [1], [4], [5], and [23].

REFERENCES

1. P. J. Brown. "The ML/I Macro Processor." *Comm. of the ACM* **10,** 10 (October 1967): 618–623.
2. W. Buchholz. "File Organization and Addressing." *IBM Systems Journal* **2** (January 1963).

3. J. J. Donovan. *Systems Programming.* New York: McGraw-Hill, 1972, Chapters 1–3.

4. I. D. Greenwald. "A Technique for Handling Macro Instructions." *Comm. of the ACM* **2**, 11 (November 1959): 21–22.

5. M. I. Halpern. "Toward a General Processor for Programming Languages." *Comm. of the ACM* **3**, 4 (April 1960): 214–220.

6. R. Hedberg. "Design of an Integrated Programming and Operating System—Part III: The expanded function of the loader." *IBM Systems Journal* **2** (September, December 1963): 298–310.

7. F. A. Hopgood. "A Solution to the Table Overflow Problem for Hash Tables." *The Computer Bulletin* **11** (March 1968): 297.

8. "IBM 7040/7044 Operating System (16/32k)—Macro Assembly Program (MAP) Language," File No. 7040-21, Form C28-6335-2, Minor Revision, 1965.

9. "IBM System/360 Operation System—Assembler Language," File No. S360-21, Form GC28-6514-8m Eighth Edition 1971.

10. J. K. Iliffe. *Basic Machine Principles.* London and New York: MacDonald/American Elsevier, 1968.

11. W. Kent. "Assembler-Language Macroprogramming: A Tutorial Oriented Toward the IBM 360." *Computing Surveys* **1**, 4 (December 1969): 183–196.

12. W. D. Maurer. "An Improved Hash Code for Scatter Storage." *Comm. of the ACM* **11**, 1 (January 1968): 35–38.

13. J. McCarthy, F. Corbató, and M. M. Daggett. "The Linking Segment Subprogram Language and Linking Loader." *Comm. of the ACM* **6**, 7 (July 1963): 391–395.

14. M. D. McIlroy. "Macro Instruction Extensions of Compiler Languages." *Comm. of the ACM* **3**, 4 (April 1960): 214–220.

15. G. H. Mealy. "A Generalized Assembly System," Rand Memorandum RM-3646-PR, The Rand Corp., Santa Monica, California, August 1963, AD 411 835. (Excerpts were included in the book entitled *Programming Systems and Languages*, Edited by Saul Rosen, New York: McGraw-Hill, 1967, pp. 535–559.

16. R. Morris. "Scatter Storage Techniques." *Comm. of the ACM* **11**, 1 (January 1968): 38–44.

17. W. W. Peterson. "Addressing for Random Access Storage." *IBM Journal of Research and Development* **1** (1957): 130–146.

18. L. Presser and J. R. White. "Linkers and Loaders." *Computing Surveys* **4**, 3 (September 1972): 150–167.

19. C. E. Price. "Table Lookup Techniques." *Computing Surveys* **3**, 2 (June 1971): 1–65.

20. "SPECTRA 70—70/35-45-55 Operating System (TOS) Utility Routines," 70/35-302, May 1968, pp. 6-43 through 6-62 on Linkage Editor.

21. "SPECTRA 70 All Systems—System Standards Reference Manual," 70-00-610, June 1967, pp. C-1 through C-7.

22. "SPECTRA 70 Time Sharing Operating System (TSOS)—Assembler Reference Manual." 70-00-625, June 1969.

23. C. Strachey. "A General Purpose Macrogenerator." *Computer Journal* **8**, 3 (October 1965): 225–241.

24. R. R. Talmadge. "Design of an Integrated Programming and Operating System—Part II: The Assembly Program and Its Language." *IBM Systems Journal* **2** (June 1963): 162–179.

25. P. Wegner. *Programming Languages, Information Structures, and Machine Organization.* New York: McGraw-Hill, 1968, Chapter 2, pp. 107–144.

EXERCISES

1. Consider the following subset of IBM 360/370 mnemonic and pseudoinstructions:

   L, ST, A, C, D, M, S, CL, MVI, N, O, X, BAL, BC, LA;
   and USING, START, END, DC, DS, and EQU.

   The operands of these instructions are restricted to constants and symbolic labels; no arithmetic expressions are allowed. For DC and DS instructions, only full-word specification of hexadecimal numbers and memory space is permitted. The use of asterisk to indicate the current address in a USING instruction is included. Symbolic labels may be, at most, four characters long.

   For each of the following two assignments, you are required to provide five simple test programs written in the aforementioned assembly language. In writing these programs, you must manage to use each aforementioned assembly instruction at least once. Each program should be assembled twice—first by the standard IBM 360/370 assembler and then again by the assembler of yours. Although the binary object modules produced by the IBM assembler and your own assembler may be different in format, these modules should be similar in content. Furthermore, the ability of these two assemblers to detect errors with respect to these test programs should be close.

   a) Design and implement a two-pass assembler which can process the programs written in the aforementioned assembly language.

   b) Design and implement a single-pass assembler for the proposed assembly language.

2. Expand one of the assemblers in (1) to include two new pseudoinstructions: EXTERN and ENTRY.

3. Design and implement a linking loader which will

   a) accept the object modules produced by the expanded assembler in (2),

   b) resolve the cross-references among the modules in terms of their external symbols and internal entries,

   c) produce the load modules if the cross-references are properly resolved, and

   d) generate error messages if loading must be aborted.

   There is no need to place the load modules in core for execution. However, a listing of the load modules and their corresponding object modules should be submitted. In the listing, at least two object modules with the EXTERN and ENTRY instructions should be used to illustrate the cross-reference. The corresponding load modules should be organized, with some simplification, similar to the ones produced by the IBM 360/370 assembler.

4. The symbolic labels of the following sample program are to be defined. In other words, show the values of Z, X, W, Y, and N, and explain the way that the values are derived

if these symbolic labels can indeed be defined. Otherwise, indicate the reason that some of the symbolic labels cannot be defined.

```
        USE      H
        TRA      Y
Z       BES      N
        BEGIN    M,Z
        USE
X       DEC      1,2
        CLA      X
W       STO      Z - 1
        USE      M
Y       NOP      0
N       EQU      W - Y
        END
```

5. Design and implement the part of the assembly system which performs the lexical analysis as outlined in Section 1.4.1.

6. Design and implement the part of the assembly system which handles the syntax analysis as outlined in Section 1.4.2.

7. Design and implement the part of the assembly system which performs semantic process as outlined in Section 1.4.3. Mechanisms for producing snapshots of dictionaries and tables should be built into the process.

8. Propose a standard format for object modules, then design and implement a linking loader with the first three and last capabilities outlined in Section 1.5.

9. Combine the above four designs and implementations to produce an integrated assembly system.

10. On the basis of the definition algorithm developed for the pseudoinstructions, design and implement an algorithm for macroexpansion and instruction generation.

11. Incorporate the algorithm for macroexpansion and instruction generation into the integrated assembly system to form a macroassembly system.

12. Write a program in an assembly language other than the IBM 360/370 and 7090/7040 assembly languages which is equivalent to the sample assembly program included in Section 1.4.3.2. Should the program fail to be assembled, indicate the causes of the failure.

13. Hashing Algorithms. Write programs to compare the following hashing algorithms in terms of their capability in generating uniformly distributed addresses over the symbol table.

As the input to the programs, a collection of 500 distinct symbols should be selected from some randomly chosen assembly program listings. Each symbol may have 1 to 8 characters. The size of the symbol table is 132.

The output from the programs should include for each algorithm a histogram with 130-some columns. Each column presents the number of collisions occurred. A computation of standard deviation is also required.

The discussions of the results should include a discussion of the factors which attribute to one algorithm over another in generating more uniformly distributed addresses.

Listing of the symbols used should also be included. (Don't let blank characters dominate the symbols.)

Algorithm One [17]

splits the 8-character symbol into four 2-character parts;
adds the four parts together;
divides the sum by the table size; and
uses the remainder as the relative address.

Algorithm Two [17]

adds the first four characters of the symbol to the remaining four characters of the same symbol;
squares the sum;
uses the center four characters;
divides them by the table size; and
uses the remainder as the relative address.

Algorithm Three [2], [12]

performs "exclusive or" between the first four characters and the last four characters of the symbol;
divides the characters by the prime number which is nearest to but less than the table size; and
uses the remainder as the relative address.

Algorithm Four [H. F. Guckes]

converts each of the 4-character parts of the symbol to a packed decimal equivalent;
concatenates these two packed decimal numbers;
divides the concatenated number by the prime number (in packed decimal) nearest to, but less than, the table size;
converts the remainder to a binary number; and
uses the binary number as the relative address.

14. Sequential and Binary Search [C. W. Gear]

   a) Sequential search. Consider an assembly program with N different symbolic names and suppose that each is used $(M + 1)$ times. If the definitions and uses are distributed evenly, and no name is used before it is defined, then, at the stage where K names have been defined, we can expect a search to take about $K/2$ comparisons. This will be done M times before the next name is defined, or a total of $M(K/2)$ comparisons will be made.

   Show that the total expected number of comparisons is about $[MN(N + 1)]/4$.

   b) Binary search. The prerequisite for the use of the binary search technique is that the symbol table be sorted into order. Keeping the table in order as it is generated is a slow process, since it is necessary to move existing information. What can be done is to pass the assembly program once and gather together all symbol names and leave the symbol table unordered. No check is made on multiple defined and undefined symbols.

   Before passing through the assembly program once more, the table is sorted, using binary search technique. At this stage, checks can be made on multiple defined and undefined symbols. The symbol names in the address fields can then be looked up by the binary search technique during the next pass.

If the number of different symbols is N and each is used M times, then the sort at the end of first pass will be in the order of $N \log_2 N$ operations.

Show that the total expected number of comparisons is at least $(M + 1)N \log_2 N$.

c) Compare the sequential and binary search techniques for large N's and draw some conclusive remarks.

15. Design and implement a compacting routine which can compact items in the main memory in order to consolidate all blocks of available space into a large block. The organization of the main memory which has been allocated to the user is depicted in Figs. 1.8, 1.9, and 1.10. The following definitions are used.

AVLIS   Contains a pointer to the
           first block of available space.
ARTOP   Contains a pointer to the
           beginning of the main memory.
L_i Length of the ith block.
C_i Address of the ith block.
item   Contains only address-inde-
           pendent data and programs.

$C_i < C_j$ for $i < j$

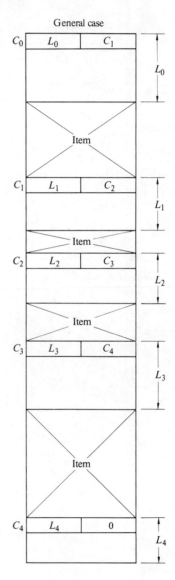

Figure 1.8

Special case

Result

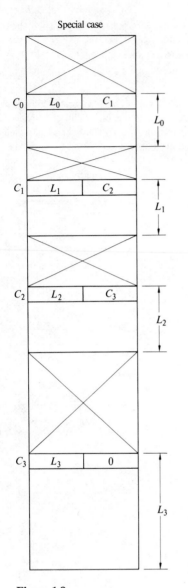

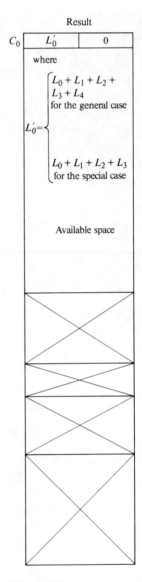

Figure 1.9

Figure 1.10

16. In referring to Section 1.4.3.1, we recall that the distance d in entries $I_i(d, p)$ and $P_i(d, p, 't')$ is meant to be the sum of instruction-lengths between the ith and the $(i - 1)$th labeled instructions. Now consider the following special situations.

a) What if there is no $(i - 1)$th labeled instruction. In other words, the ith labeled instruction is the very first labeled instruction under the control of a location counter. How is the distance calculated in this case? (See the first example on page 19 for suggestions.)

b) Will the calculation be complicated if the location counter is initiated either with a constant or with the last value of a previous location counter?

c) When a pseudoinstruction of deferred type is labeled, two entries will be created for the pseudoinstruction: One in the I-dictionary for the label and the other in the P-dictionary for the text of the pseudoinstruction. Since there are two entries, there are two distances. How are these distances calculated? (See the second example on page 19 for a labeled pseudoinstruction.)

d) In view of the aforementioned situations, expand the definition of the distance d so that the calculation of instruction-lengths can take care of these special cases.

2
Input/Output Operations and Input/Output Control Systems

REMARKS

It is assumed that the reader of this chapter has familiarized himself with the following terminology and notions as described in [2], [4], and [11] regarding hardware characteristics of I/O operations, devices, and configurations.

I/O operations, I/O operation completion flag or signal, I/O device, and I/O control unit.
Data channel.
Sequential access device: tape.
Direct access device: disk, disk access mechanism, track, cylinder, track address and number, cylinder address and number; drum, drum access mechanism, sector and sector address and number.
CPU, main memory, memory cycle, instruction execution time.

The following terminology and notions are frequently used in the chapter. We shall provide a brief discussion here.

Record, logical record, and physical record.
File and file label.
Block, block size, and blocking factor.
Buffer, buffer size, buffer switching, and buffer pool.

Information stored on a storage medium is usually organized into units of data, called *physical records*. The choice of the physical record size depends on the medium on which the records reside. It is designed to make the optimal use of, and to reduce the total access time to, the storage space of the medium. Of the disk-like (drum-like) devices, the minimal size is the size of a track (sector) since it takes the same amount of time to access either the track (sector) or a portion of the track (sector). Large record sizes are a multiple number of track (sector) sizes. Among them the cylinder (consecutive sectors) size is a popular one. Of the tape-like devices, the choice of record size can be more flexible. To distinguish one record from another, physical records on the tapes are separated by some fixed space known as *record gap*. By sensing the record gaps, the tape device can initiate its I/O operation correctly on the variable-length records. However, if the record size is too small, say smaller than the record gap, then the tape contains less useful information than it should. Furthermore, variable length and small records require more process considerations than fixed length and large records. Thus, whether it is direct access or sequential access devices, the common practice for general-purpose systems is that

1. there is one-to-one correspondence between the physical records and the storage units of a device; and

2. physical records on the device are of equal length.

Because physical records must be copied onto storage devices from the main memory (and received from the devices to the main memory), there is the need of main memory space for accommodating them. The main memory space for copying (receiving) physical records is called the *output (input) buffer*. Obviously, the buffer must be able to accommodate at least one physical record at a time. The size of the buffer is therefore related to the length of physical records. We have the dichotomy that the physical record should be large to off-set the relatively slow access time and comparatively inexpensive storage space of devices, on the one hand, but should be small to conserve the relatively fast and more expensive buffer space, on the other hand. One way to conserve the buffer space is to form a *buffer pool* so that a buffer in the pool can be used for either input or output operation as long as it is available. Thus, the dedication of the buffer for specific operation is unwarranted. To determine the availability and the intended use of the buffer, *buffer switching* is used. The following discussion illustrates a buffer switching technique.

In a simple case of using two fixed-length buffers—one for input and one for output—the problem is how to write onto a device a collection of physical records in an input buffer which has just been read in and computed upon. An obvious, but uneconomical, solution is to transfer the data in the input buffer to the output buffer and then initiate the write-onto-the-device operation. The uneconomical aspect of the solution lies in the necessity of performing a memory-to-memory transfer operation which ties up the CPU for the entire duration of the transfer. Now consider a different solution as follows. For each buffer, there is an entry which consists of

1. the status, S, of the buffer (say, "0" means idle; "1" means busy);

2. the length, L, of the buffer, and

3. the main memory address, A, of the buffer.

The intended use of the buffer is determined by the position of the entries. In this example, the first entry always points at an input buffer, and the second points at an output buffer. In referring to Fig. 2.1, we note that the buffer at address A_j is the input buffer, because the first entry contains the address A_j. Likewise, the buffer at address A_i is the output buffer, because the second entry contains the address A_i. When data in the input buffer is ready to be written onto a device (i.e., the input data

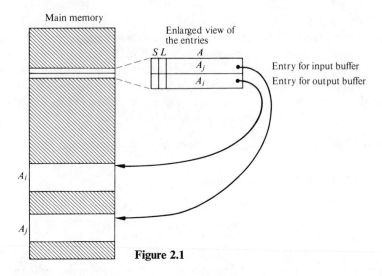

Figure 2.1

entered has been computed upon), and the status of the output buffer is idle, we merely interchange A_i and A_j in the entries, as depicted in Fig. 2.2. After the interchange, the write-onto-the-device operation is initiated. Furthermore, the input operation can be started if a new input operation is required. Using this technique, not only does the memory-to-memory transfer operation become unnecessary but also the new input and output operations can be started readily. The interchange of buffer addresses amounts to a logical, not physical, transfer of data from one address to another and enables an input buffer to be used as an output buffer, and vice versa. Such is a technique for buffer switching.

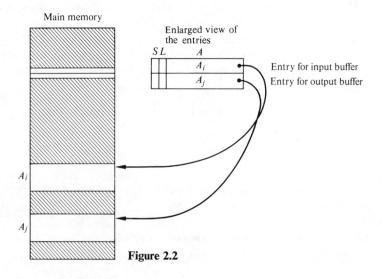

Figure 2.2

Let us call the smallest unit of user's information for storage and retrieval the *logical record*. It is obvious that the size of the logical record does not imply the size of the physical record. In order to maintain the optimal use of and minimal access to the storage space on a medium, the user's logical records must be transformed into physical records for storage. Furthermore, when physical records are retrieved from the medium, they have to be returned to the user as logical records. The process of organizing logical records into a physical record by placing the logical records one at a time into a buffer of the size of the physical record (plus a few for control words, i.e., delineators) is called *blocking*. When the buffer can no longer hold any more logical records, the content of the buffer is written onto the medium as a physical record. For this reason, the physical record is also called the *block*. The process of separating a retrieved physical record into logical records, and presenting them one at a time to the user, is called *deblocking*.

A collection of logical records with common characteristics, such as format and use, can be designated as a *file*. In the system, the file is stored as blocks. To distinguish blocks of one file from another file, unique *file labels* are assigned to files.

The *blocking factor* of a file is the ratio of the number of logical records in the file to the number of blocks for the file. Thus, the blocking factor represents the average number of (fractions of) logical records needed in blocking.

2.1 AN EXAMPLE OF I/O OPERATIONS

The logic of a simple write-onto-disk routine is flowcharted in Fig. 2.3. This routine can write data in a buffer onto consecutive tracks of a disk provided that the beginning track number of the disk, the buffer address, and the buffer size are given. The routine employs two input/output operations. The first is the seek-the-track instruction. Obviously, if the proper track is not found based on the given track number, the instruction will result in an error signal or flag. The second is the write-the-track instruction which causes the data in the buffer to be written onto the consecutive tracks. We learn that (1) although the CPU execution time* of the seek-the-track instruction is comparable to the execution time of other computer instructions, such as addition and store, the time needed by the disk to seek the proper track (i.e., the access time) is, as a factor of thousands, greater than the execution time; and that (2) in the case of the write-the-track instruction, the execution time of the instruction is also small. However, the transfer time required to move data from the main memory buffer to the consecutive tracks is the product of the buffer size and the transfer rate, which is, of course, large.

We note in (1) that during the access time, no new input/output operations should be issued which may prevent the right track from being found. Thus, there is a waiting period before the write-the-track instruction can be issued. On the other hand, there is no reason why this period cannot be taken up by the execution of instructions other than I/O instructions. If this should be the case, the CPU can be busily executing

---

* The execution time is a time that the CPU is not free for other operations.

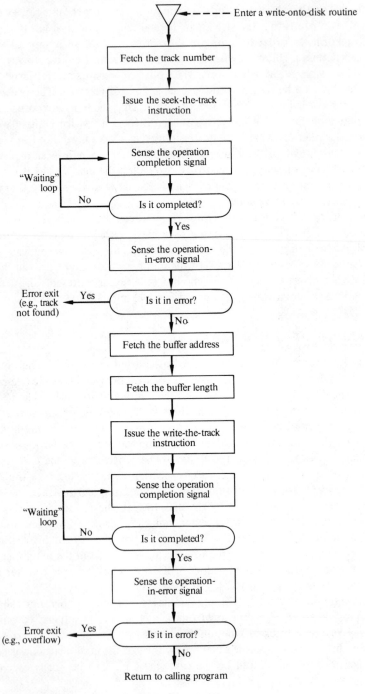

Figure 2.3

instructions and the input/output device can continue its seek operation. Ideally, when the seek operation is completed (i.e., the track is found), the CPU has just reached a logical conclusion of a series of instruction executions which may include the work in filling up the buffer. Thus, the write-the-track operation can now be executed right away because the tracks are ready and the buffer is full. The attempt to fully utilize both the CPU and the I/O operations is a goal that the system programmer wants to achieve. In achieving the goal, the access time should overlap with the execution time. Such overlap of CPU and I/O operations requires careful programming of I/O routines.

We observe in (2) that during data transfer to disk the program, we must refrain from issuing new I/O instructions to the same device. Otherwise, the write-the-track operation cannot be properly completed. Due to the long transfer time, there is again a waiting period before the issuance of another I/O instruction. Unlike the waiting period mentioned previously, this period involves the following kind. Each time a physical record is fetched for transfer, there is the access to the main memory buffer. The general rule is that whenever a memory access is needed by an I/O device for data transfer, the CPU must yield the memory access to the I/O device even at the expense of the suspension of an ongoing execution. However, the memory access time is short, compared to the transfer time. There is again the reason to utilize the CPU to execute non-I/O instructions during the waiting period since the memory access by I/O device is short and the suspension and continuation of instruction execution by CPU is automatic. From these observations, we may conclude that whether it is during the access time or transfer time, the overlap of the CPU and I/O operations is desired. Furthermore, we term a program with full overlap of CPU and I/O operations a *balanced program*.

2.2 BUFFER SIZE AND BUFFER ALLOCATION

2.2.1 CAN WE ACHIEVE A BALANCED PROGRAM?

From the discussion in the previous section, it seems that balanced programs can be readily achieved. To aid our understanding, we have provided a more thorough treatment of the notions of balanced programs and overlap of CPU and I/O operations in the sequel. The treatment is developed around a detailed example.* The reader is urged to bear with the details. As we have done previously, our aim is to perceive the notion, rather than to belabor the point with the example.

The first one is the main program which calls on the second program DSCWT—a subroutine for writing a block of words onto disk. Not included in the illustration is the part of the main program which constructs the words to be placed in the buffer

---

* The programs written in PDP-8 assembly language are included here for illustration. However, no knowledge of the PDP-8 assembly language is required. The PDP-8 I/O instruction execution time is 3.75 μsec. Other instructions have execution time ranging from 1.5 μsec to 4.5 μsec. The minidisk has a transfer rate of 66 μsec/word and an average access time of 16.67 msec. These are summarized in the tables on the following pages.

and fills up the buffer whenever the content of the buffer has been written onto disk. However, we will assume here that the construction of such a word requires the execution of approximately 35 instructions, with an average of 3 μsec per instruction. Furthermore, these words are stored in a buffer of size 200 words at location 1000. The buffer is not shown in the illustration either.

The subroutine DSCWT can write a block of words onto disk provided the following information is properly supplied:

1. the main memory address of the first word to be written onto disk,

2. the number of words to be written consecutively,

3. the track address and track number, and

4. the error and normal return addresses.

The number of words to be transferred onto disk is in the order of thousands. We note that the routine DSCWT in Fig. 2.4 resembles the program logic outlined in Section 2.1.

Label	Operation or constant	Operand	Comments
MAIN	JMS	DSCWT	Jump to the write-disk routine.
	1000		Core address of the first word is to be written onto disk.
	700		Disk track number.
	−200		Negative value of the word count.
	0		Disk track address.
	HLT		Error return from the routine.
	HLT		Normal return.
			Disk transfer rate 66 μsec/word. Average access time 16.67 msec.

Let us denote

n the number of words in the buffer, i.e., the buffer size;

r_{io} the I/O unit transfer time per word; and

t_a the I/O unit access time.

Then the total I/O processing time of n words:

$$t_{io} = t_a + nr_{io}. \tag{1}$$

In this example, we have

$$t_{io} = 16{,}670 + (200) \cdot (66)$$
$$= 16{,}670 + 13{,}200 = 29{,}870 \ \mu\text{sec}. \tag{2}$$

Label	Operation, operands, and constant	Comments	Required execution time in μsec
DSCWT	Ø	Entry to the write-disk routine.	
	CLL CLA CMA		1.5 + 1.5 + 1.5
	TAD I DSCWT		4.5
	DCA I CA	Store at CA the main memory address of the first word to be written onto disk.	4.5
	ISZ DSCWT		3.0
	TAD I DSCWT	Place the track number in the accumulator.	4.5
	DEAL	*Seek the track.*	3.75
	ISZ DSCWT		3.0
	CLA CLL		1.5 + 1.5
	TAD I DSCWT		4.5
	DCA I WC	Store the word count at WC.	4.5
	ISZ DSCWT		3.0
	TAD I DSCWT	Place the track address in the accumulator.	4.5
	ISZ DSCWT		3.0
	DMAW	*Write words from main memory to disk.*	3.75
	DFSC	Set the completion flag and skip the next instruction, if completed.	3.75
	JMP.−1		1.5
	DFSE	Set the error flag if there is an error. Otherwise, skip the next instruction.	
	JMP ERR		1.5
	CLA		1.5
	ISZ DSCWT		3.0
	DCMA	Clear the completion flag.	3.75
	JMP I DSCWT	Return to the calling program.	3.0
ERR	DEAC		
	JMP I DSCWT		
			$\overline{72.0}$
WC	775Ø	Fixed main memory location for storing word count.	
CA	7751	Fixed main memory location for storing address.	

Figure 2.4

Similarly, we denote

r_p the amount of CPU processing time required for each word in the buffer, and
t_p the amount of CPU processing time required for executing the I/O routine.

We have the total CPU processing time

$$t_{CPU} = t_p + nr_p. \tag{3}$$

Because, as mentioned in the example, it takes the execution of 35 instructions to produce a word to be placed in the buffer,

$$r_p = 35 \times 3 = 105 \ \mu sec.$$

We have

$$t_{CPU} = 72 + (200) \cdot (105)$$

$$= 21,072 \ \mu sec. \tag{4}$$

Comparing (2) and (4), we note that when the seek is issued at the same time that the CPU starts to fill the buffer, then

$$t_{io} > t_{CPU}.$$

This means that the program is I/O-*bound*. In other words, the CPU is idle part of the time.

One might conclude that a "balanced" program where $t_{io} = t_{CPU}$ would leave neither I/O unit nor CPU idle. This is accomplished by adjusting the buffer size so that we can achieve the equality

$$t_{io} = t_{CPU} \qquad \text{or} \qquad t_a + nr_{io} = t_p + nr_p.$$

Thus,

$$n = \frac{t_a - t_p}{r_p - r_{io}} = \frac{16,670 - 72}{105 - 66} \cong 426 \ \text{words}.$$

However, a "balanced" program does not assure the full utilization of CPU and I/O unit. The reason for this is that we cannot write on the disk until (a) the seek is complete and the read/write head is positioned over the correct track, and (b) the output buffer is completely filled.

If we were using a buffer size of 426 words, we could initialize the disk seek operation DEAL before constructing the first 426 words to be placed in the buffer. Since the disk seek time requires

$$16,670 \ \mu sec,$$

and the time required to construct 426 words consumes

$$nr_p = 426 \times 105$$

$$= 44,730 \ \mu sec,$$

the overlap of the CPU and I/O processing time is 16,670 μsec. The remainder

$$(44,730 - 16,670) = 28,060 \ \mu sec$$

results in I/O idling. In other words, the I/O unit must wait to start the data transfer until the CPU has filled up the buffer.

From the above discussion, we note that the "balanced" program is, in fact, *computation-bound.*

Another reasonable approach is, perhaps, to choose a buffer size which can result in a full overlap of the CPU time with the I/O unit's access time. In this case, we choose the buffer size

$$n' = \frac{t_a}{r_p} = \frac{16,670}{105} = 159 \text{ words.}$$

Thus,

$$
\begin{aligned}
t'_{io} &= t_a + n' r_{io} \\
&= 16,670 + (159) \cdot (66) \\
&= 16,670 + 10,494 = 27,164 \ \mu\text{sec}
\end{aligned}
\tag{5}
$$

$$
\begin{aligned}
t'_{CPU} &= t_p + n' r_p \\
&= 72 + (159) \cdot (105) \\
&= 72 + 16,695 = 16,767 \ \mu\text{sec.}
\end{aligned}
\tag{6}
$$

Comparing the pairs of equations (2), (4) and (5), (6), we note that from (2) and (4),

$$
\begin{aligned}
t_{io} - t_{CPU} &= 29,870 - 21,072 \\
&= 8,798 \ \mu\text{sec}
\end{aligned}
$$

and from (5) and (6),

$$
\begin{aligned}
t'_{io} - t'_{CPU} &= 27,164 - 16,767 \\
&= 10,397 \ \mu\text{sec.}
\end{aligned}
$$

From the above, we learn that the choice of the buffer size 159 does not provide an improvement over the original size 200. Although disk access time has been completely overlapped with the computation time, the CPU is partially idle during the time of data transfer from main memory to disk.

In general, the access (i.e., the seek) time of most movable-head disk devices varies. It is proportional to the amount of movement that the read/write head must have in order to reach the desired track. Thus, by choosing a fixed-size buffer the best one can achieve is to overlap the *average* access time. In reality, the program may be I/O-bound in one run and computation-bound in another run.

The equations used in aforementioned discussion can be generalized to reflect the I/O operations of records and blocks. Obviously, a record can be a word. However, we will have

$$t_{io} = t_a + n r_{io} \tag{7}$$

where

n denotes the number of records in the buffer,

r_{io} denotes the I/O unit transfer time per record, and

t_a denotes the I/O access time.

And

$$t_{CPU} = t_p + nr_p$$

where

r_p denotes the amount of CPU time required for each record processing in the buffer, and

t_p denotes the amount of CPU processing time required for executing the I/O routine.

Because t_p is a fixed overhead and is comparatively small for large n, the above equation can be simplified as follows:

$$t_{CPU} = nr_p. \tag{8}$$

Equations (7) and (8) will be used in later sections.

In summary, we note that the disparity in the I/O access time, I/O transfer rate, process time, and program logic, make it difficult, if not impossible, for the program to achieve full utilization of the I/O units and CPU. This is especially evident in an environment where one program is processed until completion without another program being processed concurrently.

In such an environment, the overwhelming concern is to utilize the CPU as much as possible, even at the expense of inactivity of the I/O units. In other words, unless full computation and I/O overlap is possible, every effort is directed to make the user's program computation-bound.

As we have seen from the above illustration, a way to make a program computation-bound is to assign a large buffer. This observation motivates many operating systems (e.g., the assembly system in Chapter 1) to allocate as much available main memory as possible to the user's program buffer, either through the system's input and output control system (IOCS) or the linking loader. We can thus discuss the role of the linking loader in handling I/O unit and buffer assignments, which was deferred in the section on linking loader in the previous chapter.

On the other hand, in a less restricted environment, where several programs may be processed without requiring any one of them to complete first, we can achieve considerable overlap between CPU operations of one program and I/O operations of another program. Furthermore, with additional I/O devices, channels, and buffers, we can even overlap between I/O operations of one program and I/O operations of another. Such overlaps among programs are known as *concurrent processing*, which will be discussed in Section 2.4.

2.2.2 BUFFER ALLOCATION ALGORITHMS

Since large buffer size can improve the utilization of CPU, the aim of the buffer allocation algorithm is to assign as much main memory (i.e., the amount of main memory left after all the computation parts of a program have been loaded) as possible to the I/O operations which require buffers.

The minimum buffer size for an I/O operation is usually specified in the user's program for the I/O operation. If not specified, it is determined by the system, based on the characteristics of the I/O unit or the physical layout of the information on the unit.

The following is a simple buffer allocation algorithm which assigns additional buffers to an I/O operation based on the following:

1. The frequency of the I/O operation relative to the frequency of all the other I/O operations—since high frequency implies high I/O activity, the program may become I/O-bound. Thus, for improving the utilization of CPU, additional buffers, if available, should be assigned first to the I/O operation with high frequency.

2. The number of I/O operations which may share the additional buffer—by pooling buffers of the same size, the I/O operations associated with these buffers can share the buffers in the pool. This has the effect of enlarging the buffer size.

In general, the number of I/O operations associated with a pool varies from one pool to another. By assigning it to the pool associated with more I/O operations than the pool with fewer I/O operations, the new buffer can be more effectively shared. This will result in better CPU utilization.

Let us consider a program with nine I/O operations $IO_1, IO_2, \ldots, IO_9$. The minimum buffer size and relative frequency of each I/O operation is listed below. The available main memory for assignment is, in this example, 1600 words.

I/O operation	Minimum buffer size (words)	Relative frequency of usage
IO_1	200	2
IO_2	200	1
IO_3	100	0
IO_4	100	0
IO_5	100	1
IO_6	50	0
IO_7	50	3
IO_8	50	1
IO_9	100	2

To combine buffers of the same size in a pool, we have grouped the I/O operations as follows:

Pool	Buffer size	Number of I/O operations	Number of buffers required	Sum of frequencies	Minimum size requirement
1	200	$2(IO_1, IO_2)$	2	3	400
2	100	$4(IO_3, IO_4, IO_5, IO_9)$	4	3	400
3	50	$3(IO_6, IO_7, IO_8)$	3	4	150

From the above chart, we note that the minimum storage requirement is 950 words. To double every buffer would require $(2 \times 950) = 1900$ words. If the available main memory is greater than 1900, we can proceed to triple the original storage requirement. However, in this example, the available storage is less than 1900. Thus, we first assign 950 words to satisfy the minimum requirements. We then proceed to distribute the remaining 650 words among the pools.

Let A_i be the additional buffer desired for pool i, and S_i be the frequency of I/O operations.

We form the weight

$$W_i = A_i \times S_i \quad \text{for } i = 1, 2, 3.$$

Step 1. The remaining main memory is distributed to the pools whose weight is a maximum.

Step 2. When a pool has been assigned an additional buffer, its A_i is immediately reduced by one. In this way, the weight of the pool will drop by a factor of S_i.

These steps will be repeated until there is not enough main memory for the assignment.

Since we had intended to double every buffer, the additional buffers desired, A_i, would be

$$A_1 = 2$$

$$A_2 = 4$$

$$A_3 = 3.$$

Available main memory	Pool 1 Buffer size = 200			Pool 2 Buffer size = 100			Pool 3 Buffer size = 50			Pool selected by weight
	A_1	S_1	W_1	A_2	S_2	W_2	A_3	S_3	W_3	
650	2	3	6	4	3	⑫	3	4	12	Pool 2
550	2	3	6	3	3	9	3	4	⑫	Pool 3
500	2	3	6	3	3	⑨	2	4	8	Pool 2
400	2	3	6	2	3	6	2	4	⑧	Pool 3
350	2	3	⑥	2	3	6	1	4	4	Pool 1
150	1	3	3	2	3	⑥	1	4	4	Pool 2
50	1	3	3	1	3	3	1	4	④	Pool 3
0	1	3	3	1	3	3	0	4	0	

In summary, we have

Pool	Buffer size	Number of I/O operations	Sum of frequencies	Number of buffers required	Additional buffers assigned	Total number of buffers
1	200	2	3	2	1	3
2	100	4	3	4	3	7
3	50	3	4	3	3	6

In this algorithm, the pool that has the combined maximum in terms of the number of I/O operations and the sum of frequency of usage receives the maximal additional buffers.

In general, buffer allocation algorithms may depend on a number of other factors, such as type of buffer (e.g., the input type and the output type) and mode of I/O operations (e.g., supervisory mode and user mode).

2.3 I/O INTERFERENCE AND I/O FACILITY UTILIZATION

2.3.1 THE PHENOMENON OF MEMORY CYCLE STEALING

In referring to the example given earlier in this chapter, we learn that each time a word is to be transferred from the main memory to the disk, three memory cycles—i.e., 4.5 μsec—are needed to initiate the transfer. One such cycle is used to fetch the word from the main memory; the other cycles are used to fetch, update, and restore the control words WC (word count) and CA (core address of the word to be fetched). These three cycles are not available to the CPU, should the computation performed by the CPU require access to the main memory at the same time. In the IBM 360/370 system, the repertoire of channel commands and device orders is rather elaborate, because this system can support various types of channels and devices (see the discussion in Section 2.3.2). These commands and orders are usually stored in the main memory as data, known as *channel command words*. When an I/O operation is requested, the system fetches the appropriate channel command words from the known location of the main memory and sends to the designated channel and device. Again, memory fetches require cycles which are not available to the CPU for other use. This phenomenon is commonly called *cycle stealing* for data transfer.

The reason that the access to the main memory is given to the I/O transfer operation over the CPU is based on the belief that cycle stealing for data transfer is infrequent. In the example, since it takes 66 μsec to transfer a word to the disk, the stolen cycle time will not exceed one-fifteenth (4.5/66 = 1/15) of the total transfer time.

The cycle stealing phenomenon can be minimized with additional hardware in the data channel and I/O unit. For instance, in the example, if the disk unit and its data channel were provided with two hardware registers—one for storing the control word WC and the other for CA—then there would be no need of stealing two of the three memory cycles, as mentioned earlier, because these two control words no longer have to be fetched from the main memory for every data transfer, except for the very first data transfer. Similarly, the channel command words of the IBM 360/370 system can also be stored in local memories of the channels. Secondary storage devices such as disks, drums, and tapes are designed for storing large amounts of data. Data transfer between main memory and the secondary storage devices usually involves hundreds and thousands of words, or bytes. The addition of some hardware facility, such as the two registers in this example, and local memories as proposed for the IBM 360/370, can avail hundreds and thousands of memory cycles to the CPU for memory-reference computation. However, any minimization of cycle stealing must be weighted against the additional cost for hardware registers and local memory of channels.

2.3.2 USING THE CPU FOR PART OF THE I/O OPERATION

In the example, we note that two memory cycles are used to fetch the control words and no memory cycles are needed to update and store them, because update and store is performed by the hardware facility built in the data channel. Without the hardware facility, the programmer will have to provide at least six instructions for

1. sensing the completion flag of the word transmitted,
2. decrementing the word count by one if it is not already zero,
3. terminating the I/O operation if the word count is zero,
4. incrementing the core address by one,
5. placing the current word to be transferred in a specified register,
6. executing the I/O instruction, and
7. resetting the completion flag.

In other words, each time a word is to be transferred, the CPU will be tied up by these six instructions for at least $(6) \times (1.5) = 9$ μsec.

Since the updating of control words is performed by the CPU through programming, there is no need of the additional hardware facility in the data channel. However, by using the CPU's logical and arithmetic facility for updating control words, an I/O operation can prevent the CPU from performing computations which are independent of the I/O operation.

In summary, the cycle-stealing phenomenon prevents the CPU from executing memory-reference instructions, because access to memory is given preference to I/O operation. The use of the CPU for part of the I/O operation ties up the CPU for that part of the operation. Collectively, these delays due to I/O operations are called I/O *interference*.

2.3.3 DATA CHANNELS

Logically, the data channel can be considered a satellite computer placed between I/O devices and main storage under the control of the CPU.

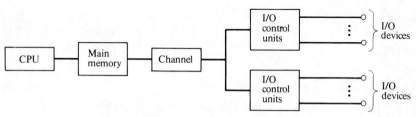

Figure 2.5

Depending on its capacity, a channel may have either its own memory registers, arithmetic, and control units, or share part of the CPU's main storage and logic. The data channel with its own memory and logic is more costly, and in some configurations it is more expensive than the CPU. Therefore, it may not be economical to employ dedicated memory and logic for data channels.

On the other hand, in sharing the CPU's main memory and logic, there arises the problem of I/O interference. In summary, unless it is justified by the system configuration and economy, the use of a data channel with its own memory and logic is preferred. In this case, efforts can be made to minimize the tying-up and idling of the CPU. Thus the objective in employing a data channel is to enable the CPU to

1. initiate an I/O operation with minimum memory access and process time, and
2. proceed with its computation concurrently with I/O data transfer with minimal interference.

Instructions executed by the channel are often called *channel commands*. The channel command program resides either in the channel memory or in the main memory. In the latter case, the CPU will have to transfer the channel command program to the proper channel for execution by the channel. Basic command types are:

1. read—causing data to be transferred from an I/O device to main memory,
2. write,
3. sense—requesting I/O device for device-dependent status information, and
4. control—causing a string of bits, the *device orders*, to be sent to an I/O device control unit. The I/O control unit decodes them and causes the device to function accordingly.

The execution of a channel command results in sending one or more device orders to the I/O control unit. Most of the device-dependent orders are sent to the I/O control unit by the control command of the channel. For example, there are orders for:

tape rewind and tape backspace,
to load tape cartridge, and
to position the access mechanism.

Since the data channel is an autonomous entity, a CPU attached to several data channels can sustain multiple I/O operations. The number of channels that a CPU can have is determined by the memory cycle of the CPU and the data transfer rates of the data channels. Let

m be the memory cycle of the CPU, and

d_i be the data transfer rate of the ith data channel.

Then, the number n of data channels is determined by

$$\frac{1}{m} \geq \sum_{i=1}^{n} d_i.$$

For example, a CPU with the memory cycle of 1.5 μsec/byte can have two data channels each of which has a data transfer rate of 275 kilobytes/second (kb/sec). Because

$$\frac{1}{m} = \frac{1}{1.5} = .666 \text{ bytes}/\mu\text{sec}$$

$$= 666 \text{ kb/sec} \tag{9}$$

$$d_1 = 275 \text{ kb/sec}$$

$$d_2 = 275 \text{ kb/sec}$$

$$\sum_{i=1}^{2} d_i = 550 \text{ kb/sec.} \tag{10}$$

Comparing (9) and (10), we have

$$\frac{1}{m} > \sum_{i=1}^{2} d_i.$$

Intuitively, the above figures indicate that the CPU is capable of keeping both data channels busy to sustain multiple concurrent I/O operations by providing the channels with as many cycles as they can "steal." Thus, the objective of having several data channels is to enable the CPU to sustain multiple I/O operations.

2.3.4 BALANCED CHANNEL AND DEVICE UTILIZATION

The I/O devices of an operating system can be grouped by their types and their attached data channels. To each type a symbolic name may be assigned. When the user's program requests the service of an I/O device by referring to the symbolic name, the operating system—either the IOCS or the linking loader—can select a physical device for the assignment. A selection algorithm may be based on the following criteria:

1. The device is attached to the data channel with more available devices.

2. The device is in ready-to-go condition, i.e., requires no initialization.

3. The device has been requested by fewer I/O operations than others.

The above selection criteria tend to minimize the number of machine halts, such as required to mount tapes and disk packs and balance the channel usage for efficient overlapped I/O operations among channels. The use of symbolic device assignment requires the characterization of the system's I/O facilities into manipulatable information, which is included in the later sections. The execution of the assignment algorithm and the establishment of the information "path" between the source and the device assigned requires the presence of system programs known as the *Input and Output Control System* (IOCS). In an effort to better utilize the available I/O facility for a program, the language translator—say, the assembler—usually delays the physical device assignment until the load time. Thus the linking loader, with the aid of the IOCS, performs the actual assignment.

2.4 THE INFLUENCE OF THE BUFFER ALLOCATION AND CHANNEL MULTIPLICITY IN OVERLAPPING INPUT, OUTPUT, AND COMPUTE OPERATIONS

From the discussions on buffer allocation and channel utilization, we note that if the memory cycle of a computer system is reasonably short and the size of the memory is considerably large, the computer system not only can sustain multiple concurrent input and output operations by providing a large number of channels, but also can have some control over the behaviors of the programs by adjusting their buffer sizes in order to make the programs either computation-bound or I/O-bound.

An ideal situation for a computer system with a large number of channels would be that for any mix of programs, the system could determine the sizes of the buffers for the programs so that both the CPU and some, if not all, channels would be utilized simultaneously. In other words, the computations resulting from these programs would be carried out concurrently with the input and output activities of the channels. In this way, the CPU and all the needed channels and devices would be utilized at all times. Since the CPU and some of the channels would be utilized simultaneously to the maximal capacities, we may infer that the time required by the system to process these programs would be minimal. A computer system which processes a given set of programs with minimal time is said to have achieved the maximal *throughput* for that set of programs.

The goal of achieving maximal throughput is, of course, a goal that every computer systems programmer would like to reach. The issues involved lie in the following:

1. With fixed main memory, the buffer allocation algorithm is limited by the available space of the main memory. Furthermore, a larger size implies a higher cost.

2. A prior knowledge of the input and output behaviors of a given set of programs is difficult to obtain, while without this knowledge, the buffer allocation algorithm cannot assign the available space to the program intelligently.

3. The high cost of sustaining a number of channels, not all needed to achieve maximal throughput, may not be justified.

Thus we have the impression that the memory size, the buffer allocation algorithm, and the number of channels have a definitive effect on the cost/throughput of the computer system.

The study of the buffer allocation algorithm, and memory size, has been illustrated in previous sections. Here we shall study the influence of the memory size and the channel multiplicity. To this end, we again introduce some abstract models. It is hoped that these abstract models, although simple and idealized, can lead to better understanding of the cost/throughput issues in computer systems.

2.4.1 TWO MODELS AND FOUR CASES

Let us repeat here the computer system with a single channel, as depicted in Fig. 2.5. Let us also consider a computer system with two channels.

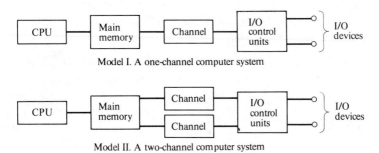

Model I. A one-channel computer system

Model II. A two-channel computer system

Figure 2.6

In this discussion, a program P consists of exactly three operations, namely, an input operation I, a set of computations C, and an output operation O. Since they are in the same program P, these three operations must be carried out sequentially. In other words, the initiation of C cannot take place without I being completed. Likewise, O can only be invoked when C has indicated its completion. Let m be the number of independent programs $P_1, P_2, \ldots, P_m$ to be processed one after the other by the computer systems. By an independent program P_i, with corresponding input operation I_i, computation C_i, and output operation O_i we mean that the starting of some of the operations in P_i does not have to wait for the completion of all the operations in P_{i-1}. More specifically, I_i can be started as soon as I_{i-1} has completed. This also applies to C_i and C_{i-1}, and O_i and O_{i-1}, respectively. An interesting phenomenon may occur, for example, I_i may start, due to the completion of I_{i-1}, while C_{i-1} is still ongoing. In this case, C_{i-1} is obviously independent of I_i. We call this phenomenon an I_i-C_{i-1} *overlap*. For short, we refer to it as *I-C overlap*. In general, we are interested in the occurrences of *I-C*, *I-O*, *O-C*, and *I-O-C* overlaps.

For each program P_i, there are three associated areas—an input buffer, a working area for computations, and an output buffer. To facilitate our discussion, we shall consolidate into one the following areas:

1. All m working areas.

2. All m input buffers.

3. All m output buffers.

4. The available space in the main memory which has not been taken up by the programs, working areas, and buffers.

The consolidated area is denoted by M.

We note that the buffer allocation algorithm of the computer system can assign the available space—as indicated in (4)—to a program either as additional working area for computations, or as additional buffers. In other words, we shall consider in the following cases that the program is either computation-bound or I/O-bound. When the program is being considered I/O-bound, we shall assign a larger time unit to I_i and O_i. Likewise, if the program is computation-bound, we shall assign a larger time unit to C_i.

2.4.1.1 Case I: Serial Processing

Serial processing is the simplest way to utilize the computer system. Since the entire area M is dedicated to an operation until its completion, there is no need of an additional channel.

The total time required to process the program P_i is

$$I_i + C_i + O_i$$

as depicted in the following time sequence figures where the solid lines represent active time, the dotted lines represent idle time, and a pair of arrowheads indicates the time frame under consideration. Furthermore, the time frame also characterizes the elapsed time.

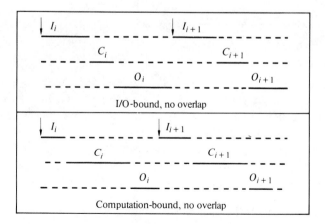

Fig. 2.7 Serial processing with one channel.

In this case, there is no overlap of operations. Since buffer switching allows an area to be used for input, output, and computation operations, we know that the entire M is used for this purpose. Obviously, the single channel configuration in Fig. 2.6 will suffice. However, even in this configuration, there is the possibility of some overlap.

2.4.1.2 Case II: Concurrent Processing By Employing One Channel

Since there is only one channel, there can be no I-O overlap. On the other hand, there may be either I-C or O-C overlap. To achieve such an overlap, we must divide the area M into two parts where one part can be used for the input (or output) operation and the other part for the computations during the I-C (or O-C) overlap.

Again via buffer switching, either one of the two areas can be used for input, computation, and output operations. Due to the lack of channel multiplicity, it is not possible to have one area with an ongoing input operation and the other area with an ongoing output operation. Thus, by employing a single channel, we can only achieve either I-C or O-C overlap.

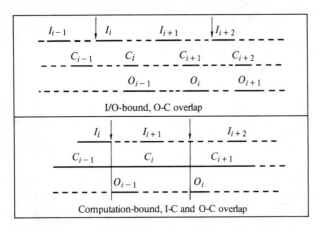

Fig. 2.8 Concurrent processing with one channel.

Now let us examine the time sequence for the I/O bound case. We note that although computations C_{i-1} in program P_{i-1} have been completed, the output operation O_{i-1} in the same program cannot be started right away because the only channel is being used for a new input operation I_i. As soon as I_i is completed, the output operation O_{i-1} can be started. Meanwhile, the computations C_i in the program can also be carried out since they require no use of the busy channel. Thus, C_i overlaps with O_{i-1}. By the same token, C_{i+1} overlaps with O_i as depicted in the time sequence diagram.

The total time required to process the program P_i, in this case, is still

$$I_i + C_i + O_i.$$

However, in the same time frame not only P_i has been processed, but also some of the operations in other programs have been accomplished. These are the output operation, O_{i-1}, in the previous program and the input operation, I_{i+1}, and computations, C_{i+1}, of the next program. If the output operations in the previous program and the next program take approximately the same amount of time, i.e., $O_{i-1} = O_{i+1}$, then both P_i and P_{i+1} have been processed in the same time frame.

The elapsed time for processing these *two* programs, P_i and P_{i+1}, is

$$I_i + O_{i-1} + I_{i+1} + O_i.$$

The reason that C_i and C_{i+1} do not show in the above expression is that they have been overlapped by O_{i-1} and O_i, respectively. Furthermore, the elapsed time for processing a simple program, say P_i, is approximately half of the above expression.

Let t_i be the approximate elapsed time to process the program P_i. Thus, we have

$$t_i = \begin{cases} \frac{1}{2}(I_i + O_{i-1} + I_{i+1} + O_i) \cong I_i + O_i & \text{if } P_i \text{ is I/O-bound,} \\ C_i & \text{if } P_i \text{ is computation-bound.} \end{cases}$$

2.4.1.3   Case III: Concurrent Processing By Employing Two Channels

If we are given another channel, then we can have *I-O* overlap in addition to either *I-C* or *O-C* overlap. In this case, we can still use the two parts of M for input, output, and compute operations.

The approximate elapsed time required to process the program P_i is

$$t_i = \begin{cases} \frac{1}{4}(I_i + C_i + I_{i+1} + C_{i-1} + O_{i-1} + O_i) \\ \qquad\qquad\qquad \cong \frac{1}{2}(I_i + C_i + O_i) & \text{if } P_i \text{ is I/O-bound,} \\ C_i & \text{if } P_i \text{ is computation-bound.} \end{cases}$$

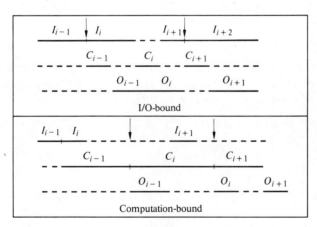

Fig. 2.9 Concurrent processing with two channels.

2.4.1.4   Case IV: Highly Concurrent Processing By Employing Two Channels

Finally, we will see how to achieve an *I-C-O* overlap with two channels. Taking the same I/O-bound situation as in Case III, the extra area allows us to accommodate three operations simultaneously. Thus, M is to be divided into three parts. We will not illustrate the computation-bound situation.

The approximate elapsed time required to process the program P_i is

$$t_i = \begin{cases} \frac{1}{4}(I_i + I_{i+1} + x \cdot O_{i-2} + O_{i-1} + y \cdot O_i) \\ \qquad\qquad\qquad \cong \frac{1}{2}(I_i + O_i) \quad \text{if } P_i \text{ is I/O-bound,} \\ C_i \qquad\qquad\qquad\qquad\qquad\quad \text{if } P_i \text{ is computation-bound.} \end{cases}$$

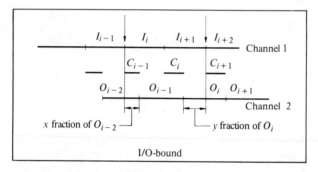

Fig. 2.10 Highly concurrent processing with two channels.

2.4.2 THROUGHPUT FORMULAS

In order to arrive at some formulations of the throughput studies in the preceding section, we shall make some more simplifications and assume that each program has the same average input, computation, and output times, i.e., that

$$I = I_i, \quad C = C_i, \quad O = O_i \qquad \text{for each } i.$$

In the fourth case, we shall also assume that the sum of the time fractions is one, i.e., $(x + y) = 1$. Furthermore, in cases where the area M must be divided into parts, we assume that the parts are of equal length. Finally, we adapt the notation

$$[a, b]$$

to mean the greater of a and b. For example,

$$t = [5, 2] = 5.$$

The elapsed time for processing the program P is therefore in the serial processing case,

$$T_1 = I + C + O \qquad\qquad \text{(no overlap);}$$

in the case of concurrent processing with one channel,

$$T_2 = [C, (I + O)] \qquad\qquad \text{(I-C or O-C overlap);}$$

in the case of concurrent processing with two channels,

$$T_3 = \tfrac{1}{2}(C + [C, (I + O)]) \quad \text{(I-C, O-C, I-O overlap);}$$

in the case of highly concurrent processing with two channels,

$$T_4 = [C, \tfrac{1}{2}(I + O)] \qquad (I\text{-}C\text{-}O \text{ overlap}).$$

Recalling Eqs. (7) and (8) in Section 2.2.1, we have

$$t_{io} = t_a + nr_{io}$$

$$t_{CPU} = nr_p$$

To apply the above equations, we assume that (1) the buffer area can accommodate just these n records, (2) all n records are of identical size, and (3) every one of the m programs has n records for processing. With these assumptions, we note that

$$I = O = t_a + nr_{io}$$

$$C = nr_p.$$

The formula T_1 therefore becomes $(t_a + nr_{io}) + nr_p + (t_a + nr_{io})$, i.e.,

$$T_1 = nr_p + 2t_a + 2nr_{io}.$$

Since the program P has n records for processing and T_1 is the elapsed time for processing n records of P, the elapsed time, T'_1, required for processing *one* record of P can be derived by dividing T_1 with n. Thus,

$$T'_1 = \frac{T_1}{n} = r_p + \frac{2t_a}{n} + 2r_{io}.$$

In accordance with the assumption that the buffer for P can accommodate n records, the entire consolidated area M is, therefore, in this case used to accommodate just these n records. In other words, we have

$$T'_1 = \frac{T_1}{n} = \frac{T_1}{M} = r_p + \frac{2t_a}{M} + 2r_{io}.$$

Now consider T_2. With substitution, we derive

$$T_2 = [nr_p, ((t_a + nr_{io}) + (t_a + nr_{io}))] = [nr_p, (2t_a + 2nr_{io})].$$

$$T'_2 = \frac{T_2}{n} = \left[r_p, \left(\frac{2t_a}{n} + 2r_{io}\right)\right].$$

In this case, we note that the consolidated area M must be divided into two buffers to accommodate concurrent processing. On the basis of the assumption that each one of the buffers must be able to handle n records, we have $n = (M/2)$. Thus

$$T'_2 = \frac{T_2}{n} = \frac{T_2}{M/2} = \left[r_p, \left(\frac{2t_a}{M/2} + 2r_{io}\right)\right] = \left[r_p, \left(\frac{4t_a}{M} + 2r_{io}\right)\right].$$

Formulas for T'_3 and T'_4 can also be derived with similar considerations. In summary, the elapsed time required to process one record of the program P is, for the four cases, as follows:

$$T'_1 = \frac{T_1}{M} = r_p + \frac{2t_a}{M} + 2r_{io},$$

$$T'_2 = \frac{T_2}{M/2} = \left[r_p, \left(\frac{4t_a}{M} + 2r_{io} \right) \right],$$

$$T'_3 = \frac{T_3}{M/2} = \frac{1}{2} \left(r_p + \left[r_p, \frac{4t_a}{M} + 2r_{io} \right] \right),$$

$$T'_4 = \frac{T_4}{M/3} = \left[r_p, \left(\frac{3t_a}{M} + r_{io} \right) \right],$$

where M is the consolidated area for buffering, as defined in Section 2.4.1. It is divided into either two parts or three parts for the purpose of supporting either two concurrent operations, or three concurrent operations, as the case may be.

The notion of the computer system *throughput* is characterized by the amount of time (i.e., elapsed time) that the system must devote to the processing of its programs. Obviously, the less time that is required to process the same collection of programs, the higher will be the throughput of the system. In other words, a system with greater throughput can get the processing done sooner. The above formulas give the elapsed time required to process a record of the program P. We can perceive the relative throughput of the systems considered by comparing their elapsed times.

2.4.2.1 Effects on Computation-Bound Programs

Let us now examine the cases where the processing is computation-bound. The above equations become

$$T'_1 = r_p + \frac{2t_a}{M} + 2r_{io}$$

$$T'_2 = r_p \quad \text{for } r_p > \frac{4t_a}{M} + 2r_{io},$$

$$T'_3 = r_p \quad \text{for } r_p > \frac{4t_a}{M} + 2r_{io},$$

$$T'_4 = r_p \quad \text{for } r_p > \frac{3t_a}{M} + r_{io}.$$

We can infer from these equations the following comments.

1. In the serial processing case, a large M may offset the long access time t_a of the I/O unit and improve the system throughput (with a large M the term $2t_a/M$ drops out, leaving a small T'_1).

2. In order to make a user program computation-bound, the user program and the system buffer allocation algorithm must be intelligent enough to assign an M so large that it can offset more than four, or three times the access time (without a large M, the terms $4t_a/M$ and $3t_a/M$ will be dominated by I/O units' access time t_a).

3. The throughput of a computer system cannot be improved substantially by employing a multiple number of channels for concurrent operations if the programs are mostly computation-bound (because their throughputs all have the same value r_p).

2.4.2.2 Effects on I/O-Bound Programs

For I/O-bound programs, the four cases lead to the following, where

$$T'_1 = r_p + \frac{2t_a}{M} + 2r_{io},$$

$$T'_2 = \frac{4t_a}{M} + 2r_{io},$$

$$T'_3 = \frac{1}{2}\left(r_p + \frac{4t_a}{M} + 2r_{io}\right),$$

$$T'_4 = \left(\frac{3t_a}{M} + r_{io}\right).$$

Again, we can make some generalizations based on these equations.

1. A large memory implies a large M, so that we have

$$T'_1 \cong r_p + 2r_{io},$$

$$T'_2 \cong 2r_{io},$$

$$T'_3 \cong \frac{r_p}{2} + r_{io},$$

$$T'_4 \cong r_{io}.$$

In other words, a two-channel computer system can transfer records twice as fast as a single-channel one. With a large main memory, the two-channel computer system definitely has a lead over the single-channel one.

2. If the computation rate and transfer rate are close, i.e., $r_p = r_{io}$, we have

$$T'_1 \cong 3r_p,$$

$$T'_2 \cong 2r_p,$$

$$T'_3 \cong \tfrac{3}{2}r_p,$$

$$T'_4 \cong r_p.$$

In other words, with a large memory and close rate of computation and I/O transfer, the two-channel system with *I-O-C* overlap can improve the throughput, at best, three times over the serial processing one.

3. Despite a good transfer rate, none of the more sophisticated configurations and processings can fare much better than the serial processing one if the main memory is small and the access time is slow.

2.5 INPUT/OUTPUT CONTROL SYSTEMS

Due to the complexity in handling I/O operations, program computations, buffers, channels, and devices, the Input/Output Control System (IOCS) is designed to aid the user, as well as the operating system itself, in performing I/O operations. As we shall see in the following sections, the I/O routines require considerable coding effort, which may be disproportional relative to the user's program. By undertaking this major coding effort, the system programmer removes the user not only from this source of errors which are not detectable during the assembly time, but also from many debugging runs.

In this section, we shall emphasize the conceptual design of the IOCS instead of the coding efforts needed.

2.5.1 THE DESIGN OF THE IOCS AS A FINITE STATE AUTOMATON

The design must, obviously, be directed toward a prescribed computer system con- figuration. In this section, an approach to the design of an IOCS using the two- channel configuration, as depicted in Fig. 2.6, will be described. We know that with two channels the system throughput can be improved considerably via concurrent processing of programs. For this reason, *we shall design the* IOCS *to achieve I-C-O overlap and other overlaps whenever possible.*

The design of the IOCS as a finite state automaton is revealing. This technique has, perhaps, the best potential as a systematic approach to software design.

In a finite state automaton, there are the states, the transitions between states, and the signals which trigger the transitions. In this design, each of the three areas (i.e., input buffer, working area for computation, and output buffer) will be in one, and only one, of three possible states at any one time:

Idle—available for the next block of data,
Busy—in the midst of handling a block of data,
Ready—completed handling of a block of data and readiness to transmit it to the
    next area.

By "transmitting to the next area" we do not mean that the block of data must be physically moved from one buffer area to the next area. Instead, the interchange of pointers to the buffer areas may be used as a buffer switching technique.

The transition between states for each of the three areas is shown below:

$$\text{Input buffer} \quad \hookrightarrow \text{Idle} \rightarrow \text{Busy} \rightarrow \text{Ready} \supset$$
$$\text{Working area for computation} \quad \hookrightarrow \text{Idle} \rightarrow \text{Busy} \rightarrow \text{Ready} \supset$$
$$\text{Output buffer} \quad \hookrightarrow \text{Idle} \rightarrow \text{Busy} \supset$$

(The output buffer does not have a Ready state since it has no next area.) The first step is to construct a state-transition table listing the state transitions, using the abbreviations B for busy, R for ready, and I for idle, as shown in Figs. 2.11(a) and 2.11(b). Also listed with each state transition is the source of the signal which triggers the transition. The following signals are presumed available to trigger state transitions:

   i input operation complete
   o output operation complete
   c computation complete

For the moment, consider state transitions due to these signals only. Thus, the first row in Fig. 2.11(a) says that, if the input buffer is currently busy (B) while the working area and output buffer are idle (I), the completion of an input operation (i) will trigger a transition to a new state in which the input buffer will then be ready (R) for another operation. Although all possible combinations of signals and states can be listed, it is easy to see that some will never occur and need not be shown. For example, since an i signal denotes completion of an input operation, it must accompany an input-buffer state of B, and hence rows whose arguments are of the form $iIXX$ or $iRXX$ need not be listed. Similarly, rows whose arguments are of the form $cXRX$, $cXIX$, or $oXXI$ are excluded. In each row of the table the signal gives the successor state which corresponds to the current state. This is obtained by changing only the state of the area signaling completion to R (ready). In constructing the table, all rows are considered independently of all other rows, and rows can be listed in any order, although a systematic enumeration is included here.

Signal triggers the transition	Current state			Successor-state		
	Input buffer	Working area	Output buffer	Input buffer	Working area	Output buffer
i	*B*	*I*	*I*	*R*	*I*	*I*
i	*B*	*I*	*B*	*R*	*I*	*B*
i	*B*	*B*	*I*	*R*	*B*	*I*
i	*B*	*B*	*B*	*R*	*B*	*B*
i	*B*	*R*	*I*	*R*	*R*	*I*
i	*B*	*R*	*B*	*R*	*R*	*B*
c	*I*	*B*	*I*	*I*	*R*	*I*
c	*I*	*B*	*B*	*I*	*R*	*B*
c	*B*	*B*	*I*	*B*	*R*	*I*
c	*B*	*B*	*B*	*B*	*R*	*B*
c	*R*	*B*	*I*	*R*	*R*	*I*
c	*R*	*B*	*B*	*R*	*R*	*B*
o	*I*	*I*	*B*	*I*	*I*	*I*
o	*I*	*B*	*B*	*I*	*B*	*I*
o	*I*	*R*	*B*	*I*	*R*	*I*
o	*B*	*I*	*B*	*B*	*I*	*I*
o	*B*	*B*	*B*	*B*	*B*	*I*
o	*B*	*R*	*B*	*B*	*R*	*I*
o	*R*	*I*	*B*	*R*	*I*	*I*
o	*R*	*B*	*B*	*R*	*B*	*I*
o	*R*	*R*	*B*	*R*	*R*	*I*

Fig. 2.11(a) State transitions caused by input, computation, and output completion signals.

The next task in table construction is the *s* (signal issued by the IOCS) section of the table. The major purpose of the *s* is to start new operations whenever possible. Using this principle, the successor-state entries are determined and listed in Fig. 2.11(b).

In addition to the *i*, *o*, *c*, and *s* signals, the IOCS is also assumed to receive two less-frequent signals: START and LAST, denoting the start of the program and a notification that the last block has entered the input area. Although these could be shown in separate rows, compaction of space in the table is gained by showing each with a slash separating a LAST entry from one due to some other signal.

The tables constitute the heart of the IOCS program logic. They may be referenced by a simple scan program whose function will now be described. Consider that the system is in one of its states with an ongoing execution. Eventually, an *i*, *o*, or *c* signal will be generated. As indicated previously, this causes a machine interrupt that includes identification of the signal. The scan program then does the following:

1. Uses the signal to identify the first table (as depicted in Fig. 2.11c) to be searched.

2. Searches this table, using the current state as an argument. When a match is found, the successor-state becomes the new current state.

3. The new current state is used as an argument to the *s* table. If a match is found, then the following takes place: the successor-state replaces the current state; the associated action is taken; and execution returns to the preinterrupt activity, or continues with a new activity. If no match is found, this indicates an error in the design.

We note that this IOCS can improve the system throughput by taking some intelligent actions. These actions are involved with buffer switching, starting new input and output operations and computations, and taking no action when no new operation can possibly be initiated. In starting new operations, the IOCS attempts to achieve as much concurrent processing as possible via overlapping of these operations. Thus the original goal, as stated at the beginning of this design, is met.

Signal triggers the transition	Current state			Successor-state		
	Input buffer	Working area	Output buffer	Input buffer	Working area	Output buffer
START	*I*	*I*	*I*	*B*	*I*	*I*
s/*LAST*	*I*	*I*	*B*	*B*/*I*	*I*	*B*
s/*LAST*	*I*	*B*	*I*	*B*/*I*	*B*	*I*
s/*LAST*	*I*	*B*	*B*	*B*/*I*	*B*	*B*
s/*LAST*	*I*	*R*	*I*	*B*/*I*	*I*	*B*
s/*LAST*	*I*	*R*	*B*	*B*/*I*	*R*	*B*
s	*B*	*I*	*I*	*B*	*I*	*I*
s	*B*	*I*	*B*	*B*	*I*	*B*
s	*B*	*B*	*I*	*B*	*B*	*I*
s	*B*	*B*	*B*	*B*	*B*	*B*
s	*B*	*R*	*I*	*B*	*I*	*B*
s	*B*	*R*	*B*	*B*	*R*	*B*
s/*LAST*	*R*	*I*	*I*	*B*/*I*	*B*	*I*
s/*LAST*	*R*	*I*	*B*	*B*/*I*	*B*	*B*
s/*LAST*	*R*	*B*	*I*	*R*	*B*	*I*
s/*LAST*	*R*	*B*	*B*	*R*	*B*	*B*
s/*LAST*	*R*	*R*	*I*	*B*/*I*	*B*	*B*
s	*R*	*R*	*B*	*R*	*R*	*B*

Fig. 2.11(b) State transitions caused by signals resulting from the IOCS intervention, starting of a program, and inputting the last block.

After the state transitions tables are constructed, they are partitioned into four smaller tables, each for a single triggering signal (see Fig. 2.11(c) for the first three and Fig. 2.11(d) for the last one). Also, any row whose current state cannot be found somewhere as a successor-state (except for *START*) may be deleted.* In the *s* table, each state transition is caused by a signal from the IOCS. The signal is intended to improve the system throughput by either initiating a new program or overlapping as many operations as possible. Since the signal *LAST* can also cause the IOCS to take actions, the *s/LAST* table shows that the IOCS does, indeed, act intelligently. By act intelligently, we mean the ability to switch buffers, start operations, achieve overlaps, and, therefore, skip intermediate states.

i table

States	
Current	Successor
BII	*RII*
BIB	*RIB*
BBI	*RBI*
BBB	*RBB*
BRI	*RRI*
BRB	*RRB*

c table

States	
Current	Successor
IBI	*IRI*
IBB	*IRB*
BBI	*BRI*
BBB	*BRB*
RBI	*RRI*
RBB	*RRB*

o table

States	
Current	Successor
IIB	*III* → A USER
IBB	*IBI* PROGRAM
IRB	*IRI* ENDS
BIB	*BII*
BBB	*BBI*
BRB	*BRI*
RIB	*RII*
RBB	*RBI*
RRB	*RRI*

Fig. 2.11(c) Transitions requiring *no* intervention from the IOCS.

---

* The designer of the IOCS may have to list exhaustively all possible states for examination. There are exactly 324 (= $(3 \times 3 \times 2)^2$) state transitions that must be examined for each type of triggering signals. Fortunately, large numbers of transitions do not take place and can thus be eliminated from the tables.

s and *s/LAST* table

Signal	States		Action taken followed by return to prior activity	Overlap achieved
	Current	Successor		
s/START	*III*	*BII*	Start input (and start program)	
s/LAST	*IIB*	*B/I, IB*	Start input; *LAST* (no action)	*I-O/*
s/LAST	*IBI*	*B/I, BI*	Start input; *LAST* (no action)	*I-C/*
s/LAST	*IBB*	*B/I, BB*	Start input; *LAST* (no action)	*I-C-O/C-O*
s/LAST	*IRI*	*B/I, IB*	Move *c* to *o* (i.e., buffer switching), start output; start input	*I-O/*
s/LAST	*IRB*	*B/I, RB*	Start input; *LAST* (no action)	*I-O/*
s	*BII*	*BII*		
s	*BIB*	*BIB*		
s	*BBI*	*BBI*		
s	*BBB*	*BBB*		
s	*BRI*	*BIB*	Move *c* to *o* (i.e., buffer switching), start output	*I-O*
s	*BRB*	*BRB*		
s/LAST	*RII*	*B/I, BI*	Move *i* to *c* (i.e., buffer switching), start computation, start input if not *LAST*	*I-C/*
s/LAST	*RIB*	*B/I, BB*	Move *i* to *c* (i.e., buffer switching), start computation, start input if not *LAST*	*I-C-O/C-O*
s	*RBI*	*RBI*		
s	*RBB*	*RBB*		
s/LAST	*RRI*	*B/I, BB*	Move *c* to *o*, *i* to *c* (i.e., buffer switching), start output, start computation, start input if not *LAST*	*I-C-O/C-O*
s	*RRB*	*RRB*		

Fig. 2.11(d)

Let us elaborate, for example, the action in (3) that the IOCS will take in a case where an input completion signal *i* occurs which changes the state of the computer from *BIB* to *RIB* (see the *i* table in Fig. 2.11c). Knowing that system throughput can be improved if concurrent processing is utilized, the IOCS takes the action by

a) switching the input buffer and working area (Because data in the input buffer are ready (*R* in *RIB*) to be computed upon, and the working area is idle (*I* in *RIB*), the buffer switching effectively, not physically, moves the data from input buffer to the working area.);

b) starting computation in the working area (By now the state of computer is in *IBB*. Although it has improved system throughput considerably with new computation, the IOCS can still do more. We note that the input buffer, nevertheless, is idle.); and

c) starting a new input operation for the input buffer, since the buffer has been idle (*I* in *IBB*). The state of the computer is finally in *BBB*, indicating that there is an *I-C-O* overlap for highly concurrent processing. The only special situation which may limit the extent of processing concurrence is when no new input operation is available, i.e., when the very last record has been read by the previous input operation. In this case, the state will be in *IBB*, allowing only *C-O* overlap. This example is also summarized in Fig. 2.11(d) as an entry.

2.5.2 THE DESIGN OF THE IOCS AS LEVELS OF PROCESSORS AND SUBSYSTEMS

The design approach of the IOCS as a finite state automaton, although revealing, tends to provide the reader with a simplistic view toward IOCS design. To understand the scope of the design, let us identify some of the factors which may complicate the design.

A. User requirements

From the user point of view, the issuance of I/O instructions should not differ greatly from the issuance of other instructions. In other words, the user expects that

1. the I/O instructions are simple and symbolic;

2. the reference to secondary storage areas is made by symbolic names, and relative addresses;

3. the data to be stored into and retrieved from the secondary storage devices must be in the source format that the user desires, without undue consideration of the physical characteristics of the devices; and

4. the system performs I/O operations efficiently.

B. System design criteria

In order to meet the user requirements, the IOCS must be able to

1. relieve the user from concern about the exact formation of the I/O instruction, and its related channel commands and associated device orders;

2. provide symbolic names for the secondary storage areas;

3. safeguard the devices on which the user's data are stored;

4. perform blocking, deblocking, and buffer allocation; and

5. improve system throughput.

The above criteria require the IOCS to have information concerning the characteristics and utilization of the devices, the size and usages of the symbolically named storage units, and the relations between devices and units. With this information, the IOCS can then perform the following four functions:

1. interpreting user I/O requests,

2. executing required I/O operations,

3. verifying data and devices, and

4. buffering user data.

2.5.2.1 Organization of the Information Concerning I/O Operations, Channels, and Devices

Since the IOCS provides I/O routines and carries out I/O operations for the user, it must have knowledge of the available I/O facilities in the system. To this end, the information about these facilities must be organized into tables which are first initialized at system generation time and then maintained by the IOCS throughout the entire operating period of the system. We shall provide a way, by no means the only way, to organize the information and structure the IOCS.

2.5.2.1.1 PHYSICAL DEVICES

Each I/O device is associated with a table known as the *device control block*. The device control block contains all the information about the I/O device's current status and the entries of the routines which can initiate and maintain the device. Included is information such as the following:

(D1) the flags which tell whether or not the device is busy, whether or not the channel to which the device is attached is busy, and whether or not the device has been requested for use;

(D2) the number of physical records read or written on this device;

(D3) the address of the routine which can construct the proper sequence of instructions, channel commands, and device orders for I/O operations of the device;

(D4) the address of the routine which can keep track of the progress of the operation;

(D5) the address of the routine which can process and recover errors;

(D6) the statistics concerning the permanent and recovered read/write errors incurred during the I/O operation;

(D7) the pointer to the next control block whose device is also attached to the same channel; and

(D8) the pointer to the symbolic unit name table where a symbolic unit name is assigned to the device (explained in the sequel).

We note from the above that the user no longer needs to write the exact sequence of instructions and channel commands and device orders for an I/O operation, since these actions are done for him by the routine addressed in the device control block. Furthermore, checking progress and recovering errors of an I/O operation become the functions of the system, since routines and statistics are maintained by the IOCS in the device control block.

From (D7) we learn that all the device control blocks whose devices are attached to the same data channel are linked by their pointers. Thus, the IOCS can keep track of the number of devices and their activities for the channel by tracing through the pointers from one device control block to another. In addition, the priority in terms of, say, device usage for a channel can be established by simply arranging the device control blocks of the devices of that channel in such a way that the device control block of the device with the highest priority (marked with some indicator) points to the one with next highest priority, and so on.

2.5.2.1.2 SYMBOLIC UNITS

In general, the user refers to an I/O device by referring to its symbolic name. The advantages of using symbolic names are many.

1. Symbolic names are easier to use and can be made meaningful to reflect the type of device for which they stand.

2. By referring to the device as a symbolic unit, and allowing the system to establish the correspondence between the symbolic unit and a physical I/O device, the user enables the system to balance the use of devices and channels on the one hand, and relieve the user from such considerations on the other hand.

3. As long as the symbolic unit names are still the same, the actual assignment of the symbolic units to the physical I/O devices can be changed from time to time. Thus the user's program written and compiled (or assembled) at one time can be run at another time, even if the configuration of the physical device has been changed.

A symbolic unit does not always correspond to a physical I/O device. Devices such as disks and drums are usually partitioned into many sections, each of which is assigned to a symbolic unit because these devices can be accessed *directly*, i.e., the partitioned sections can be located by moving the access mechanism directly to that section. Thus, in general, there is a many-to-one correspondence between the symbolic units and the directly accessible devices. To reach a certain part of a tape, buffers must be created. Records on the tape must be read sequentially until the specified information is found, a time- and space-consuming process. For this reason, there is a one-to-one correspondence between the symbolic units and the sequentially accessible I/O devices.

For each symbolic unit, a *unit control block* is created. Like the device control blocks which provide information and routines to control the physical devices, the unit control blocks contain information about the symbolic units. Since several symbolic units may share a physical device (because of the many-to-one correspondence), there may be more than one I/O operation outstanding on the same device. The information concerning the individual I/O operations resides in the unit control blocks. Therefore, the unit control block provides information to keep track of the progress of the individual I/O operation.

Basic information included in a unit control block is:

(U1) the device type and the channel used;

(U2) the I/O operation currently requested for the unit;

(U3) the address of the routine which can construct the proper sequence of instructions, channel commands, and device orders for the I/O operations of the device;

(U4) the address of the routine which can keep track of the progress of the operation;

(U5) the address of the routine which can process and recover errors;

(U6) the beginning and last addresses of the partitioned section of the directly accessible device assigned to the unit;

(U7) the statistics concerning the current address of the directly accessible device, number of records per address, and current record number; and

(U8) the pointer to the symbolic unit name table where a symbolic unit name is assigned to it (explained in the next section).

By placing the addresses, as in (U3), (U4), and (U5), instead of the actual routines in the unit control block, the IOCS provides the user with an option to supply his own routines. If the option is exercised, the IOCS merely substitutes the address of the user's routine in the unit control block in place of the standard address supplied by the IOCS.

2.5.2.1.3 SYMBOLIC UNIT NAME

To establish the correspondence between the symbolic names and the I/O devices, a table known as the *symbolic unit name table* is constructed. Each entry in the table consists of three parts:

(S1) the symbolic name,

(S2) the pointer to the unit control block of the symbolic unit for which the symbolic name stands, and

(S3) the pointer to the device control block of the I/O device to which the symbolic unit is assigned.

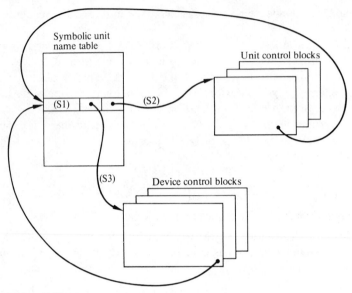

Figure 2.12

2.5.2.2 Four Basic Functions of the IOCS

The Input/Output Control System consists of four basic subsystems for interpreting and executing the I/O operations, and for verifying and buffering the data to be processed by these I/O operations. They are known as the I/O operation interpreter, the I/O operation executer, the I/O verification subsystem, and the I/O buffering subsystem.

2.5.2.2.1 INTERPRETATION OF I/O OPERATIONS

The I/O instructions, channel commands, and device orders for an I/O operation require careful and tedious preparation, because they are device-dependent. To relieve the user and the system programmer from the preparation, the I/O *operation interpreter* is provided for analyzing and generating the proper sequence of I/O instructions, channel commands, and device orders for the I/O operation. The I/O operation is generally composed of

1. the name of an I/O operation;
2. the name of the symbolic unit involved;
3. the list of parameters needed for the operation; and
4. the entries to the normal and error returns.

Examples of the I/O operations are read/write operations associated with various devices.

Information concerning the I/O operations is recorded in the unit control block of the symbolic unit specified in (S2).

2.5.2.2.2 EXECUTION OF I/O OPERATIONS

When the proper sequence of instructions, commands, and orders are ready to be executed, the sequence is passed to the I/O *operation executer* which carries out the execution.

The I/O operation executer schedules the use of data channels, monitors the channel activities, performs the error-recovery, provides code conversions, and handles normal or error returns. Information concerning the channel activities, location of the error-recovery routine, and return addresses are kept in the device control block and maintained by the I/O operation executer. It is at this level that the overlap of operations to improve system throughput is performed.

In Fig. 2.13, we illustrate the role of the I/O operation interpreter and executer with a scenario.

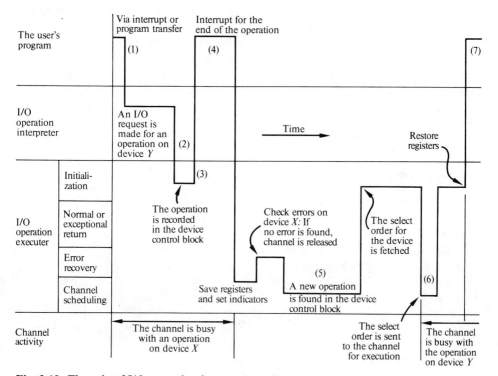

Fig. 2.13 The role of I/O operation interpreter and executer.

The I/O request of a user's program is usually in the form of a system macro (see Exercise 7). Obviously, the macro is transformed by the assembler with macro-processing capability into a series of machine instructions and a list of parameters. One of the machine instructions is likely a supervisor call (SVC), which causes control of the user program to be interrupted and transferred to the IOCS during execution.

Such transfer is known as *interrupt*. On the other hand, for computers which do not have supervisor calls, the transfer is accomplished by a standard program transfer instruction. Whether via interrupt or program transfer, the instruction will direct the user's I/O request to the I/O operation interpreter. This is depicted as Step (1) in Fig. 2.13. The interpreter then determines the device on which the I/O request is made. As we recall, the assignment of a device for a unit may change from time to time. This information may not be available at the assembly time of the macro. However, the latest assignment of a particular device for a known unit is established and maintained by the IOCS in the unit and device control blocks and the symbolic unit name table. By consulting the list of parameters in the macro and the control blocks, the device can be determined (2).

The executer schedules the use of the channel to which the device, i.e., Y, is attached. If the channel is busy, as in this case, the use of the channel must be deferred (3). One of the options is to return control to the user's program with the hope that the time for channel waiting can be utilized for running other parts of the program (4). As soon as the channel is free, the executer schedules the channel for device Y (5). As we recall, the device control blocks of the devices attached to the same channel are linked by pointers. Thus, via the device control block of the device X, it is possible to determine the next device control block which is queued for the channel. In this case, it is the device control block of device Y. The device is then activated (6). By now both the channel and device are ready for subsequent input/output operations such as read and write; control is therefore returned to the user's program for the operations (7).

2.5.2.2.3 VERIFICATION OF DATA AND DATA STORAGE

The I/O operation executer does not know whether the data being processed by the I/O operations is correct or not because it simply carries out the prescribed I/O operations. To prevent starting I/O operations on the wrong data, data are organized into blocks of files. A label can be created and assigned to the file. By verifying its label each time a file is used, the system can be assured that the file is the correct one on the right device. The I/O *verification subsystem* performs all of the label verification and creation functions. The user supplies the name of the label to the subsystem which places the label and records onto the medium in a standard form. For example, if tapes are used as the storage medium and if the file is to occupy the length of two tapes, then the subsystem will create at the end of the first reel an end-of-reel trailer label, switch the reels, "close" the first tape, "open" the second one, write a header label on the second one, and then close the second tape with an end-of-file trailer label. Record gaps are also created and sensed by the I/O verification subsystem. These gaps are used to separate records and labels on the tapes.

2.5.2.2.4 BUFFERING DATA

In order to maintain the optimal use of, and minimal access to, the storage space on an external device, the IOCS performs the function of organizing the user's logical records into physical records for storage. Furthermore, when physical records are retrieved from the device, the IOCS performs the function of returning them to the user's program as logical records. As there are as many physical record sizes as there are types of physical devices, the task of the IOCS in performing such functions is considerable. However, the user is not aware of the correspondence between his logical records and the system's physical records.

The process of organizing the logical records into a physical record is, as we have mentioned earlier, called *blocking*. The IOCS accomplishes the blocking by placing the logical records one at a time into a buffer slightly larger than the physical record. (The buffer also has space for a few control words.) When the buffer is full, its contents are written onto the device as a physical record, or block. The process of separating a retrieved physical record into logical records and presenting them one at a time to the user's program is called *deblocking*. In addition to blocking and deblocking, there is the need of buffer switching which is indispensable if the overlap of I/O operations and computations performed by the I/O operation executer is to be effective. The part of IOCS which performs above functions is known as the I/O *buffering subsystem* (*IOBS*).

We recall that the buffer allocation algorithm of the linking loader may assign an I/O operation with several buffers. The function of IOBS is to utilize these buffers so that the continuous flow of information, being read or written out, can be maintained. When a buffer is full (empty), the IOBS immediately directs the data flow to (from) another buffer. While data is flowing into (from) the other buffer, the IOBS performs the deblocking (blocking) of the buffer. In this way, the overlap of computation and I/O operation is achieved.

2.5.2.3 Physical versus Logical Input/Output Control System

We note that at the lowest level of the IOCS is the I/O operation executer. It assumes that the I/O instructions, channel program, and/or device orders for an I/O operation are in proper sequence and forms, so that the instructions can be processed by the CPU, channel commands can be sent to the data channel, and device orders can be sent to the device for appropriate responses. At a higher level lies the I/O operation interpreter which identifies the I/O operation and constructs the proper sequence of I/O instructions, channel commands, and device orders for the operation. In some operating systems, such as the IBM OS 360, the sequences of instructions, commands, and orders for individual operations have already been composed and stored in the main memory. The I/O interpreter merely identifies the operation, fetches its corresponding sequence, and sends the sequence to the data channel if necessary. At a level still higher resides the I/O verification subsystem which employs I/O operations for reading and writing labels. In this case the interpreter and executer are used for carrying out these operations. At the highest level, there is the I/O buffering subsystem. Unless the label of a file is positively verified or created, there is no need to perform the rest of the I/O operations on the file. When the label is correctly matched or created, the I/O buffering subsystem then carries out the rest of the I/O operations. The collection of these four levels of I/O subsystems and processors is known as the I/O *control system*.

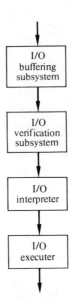

In organizing the I/O programming facilities into levels, the IOCS can provide the user and system programmer with as few and as many subsystems as they desire. For example, if the user desires to write a nonstandard label for his file, he can bypass the I/O label verification subsystem, using only the interpreter and executer for this purpose. A more elaborate buffering scheme can be employed should the user decide that the facility provided by the I/O buffering subsystem is inadequate. He can then bypass the I/O buffering subsystem and introduce his own buffering system.

On the other hand, the IOCS can provide the user with easy means and conventions:

1. to specify the I/O operations in the form of requests (say, macros) and relieve him from concern about the exact formation of I/O instruction, channel commands, and device orders;

2. to create and verify the labels of the files; and

3. to read/write logical records.

At the same time and without being apparent to the user, the IOCS tries to utilize the physical facilities more efficiently by

1. storing and retrieving data as physical records;

2. providing the capabilities to detect the end of a device or channel operation and to start at another;

3. maintaining continuous data flow through buffer switching; and

4. allowing computation and I/O operation to overlap.

The IOCS discussed here is considerably more sophisticated than the one presented in Section 2.5.1. Although both of them can store and retrieve physical records, detect the completion of the device and channel operations, maintain data flow via buffer switching, and achieve I/O and computation overlaps, there are subtle differences. The IOCS presented in Section 2.5.1 does not handle logical records, cannot verify labels, and performs no deblocking and blocking operations. Because it is restricted to the handling of physical records and physical I/O operations, that IOCS is termed the *Physical* IOCS (PIOCS). By the same token, the IOCS discussed in this section is often referred to as the *Logical* IOCS (LIOCS).

2.6 POSTSCRIPT

The first design of an operating system as a finite state automaton is attempted in [6]. To illustrate this approach to the design of an IOCS, we have borrowed a well-developed example from [4]. The discussion on the throughput formulas is derived from [5] with some simplifications. The buffer allocation algorithm is due to [3]; and the generalized model of the IOCS at the end of the chapter is based on the material from [7], [8], and [9].

   Although the concept of organizing the operating system in terms of "layers" of operating subfunctions and functions is credited to [1], the notion of levels of processors and subsystems for the IOCS, as outlined in [7], may have been the forerunner of the concept.

REFERENCES

1. E. W. Dijkstra. "The Structure of the THE System." *Comm. of the ACM* **11,** 5 (May 1968): 341–346.

2. J. J. Donovan. *Systems Programming.* New York: McGraw-Hill, 1972, pp. 350–366 and 401–424.

3. R. Hedberg. "Design of An Integrated Programming and Operating System—Part III: The Expanded Function of the Loader." *IBM Systems Journal* 2 (September-December 1963): 298–310.

4. H. Hellerman. *Digital Computer System Principles.* New York: McGraw-Hill, 1967, pp. 115–135.

5. H. Hellerman and H. J. Smith, Jr. "Throughput Analysis of Some Idealized Input, Output, and Compute Overlap Configurations." *Computing Surveys* **2,** 2 (June 1970): 111–118.

6. R. E. Heistand. "An Execution System Implemented as a Finite State Automaton." *Comm. of the ACM* **7,** 11 (November 1964).

7. "IBM 7040/7044 Operating System (16/32K) Input/Output Control System." File No. 7040-30, Form C28-6309-5, IBM Corp., (September 1966).

8. G. H. Mealy. "Operating Systems." Rand Report No. P-2584, The Rand Corp., Santa Monica, California, May 1962, AD 603146.

9. A. Padegs. "The Structures of System/360—Part IV: Channel Design Considerations." *IBM Systems Journal* **3,** 2 (1964): 165–180.

10. C. P. Wang and W. Anacker. "Performance Analysis of Multiprocessor Systems with Hierarchical Memories." *IEEE Trans.* **EC-16** (December 1967): 764–773.

11. P. Wegner. *Programming Languages, Information Structures, and Machine Organization.* New York: McGraw-Hill, 1968, pp. 66–72.

12. P. White. "Relative Effects of Central Processor Input-Output Speeds Upon Throughput on the Large Computer." *Comm. of the ACM* **7**, 12 (December 1964): 711–714.

EXERCISES

1. Propose a buffer allocation algorithm which gives biased considerations to input/output operations using small buffers. Illustrate the algorithm with example.

2. Propose a buffer allocation algorithm which gives biased considerations to certain types of input/output operations regardless of their sizes of buffers. Demonstrate the algorithm with example.

3. (Hellerman and Smith) Examine the graph where numerals inside the parentheses designate the following configurations:

    1 — Sequential, i.e., no overlap.

    2 — Either input and computation, or output and computation may take place at the same time.

    3 — Two of the three combinations of input, computation, and output operations may take place at the same time.

    4 — Input, output, and computation operations may take place at the same time.

    For example, by $(2 < 4 < 1 < 3)$ we mean that the relative performance in terms of throughput of configuration 2 is worse than 4, which in turn is worse than 1, which is worse than 3.

    After the examination, provide an interpretation of the graph. For your reference, the elapsed time required to process one record of the program P, for the four configurations, are repeated here.

    $1 — r_p + (2t_a/M) + 2r_{io}$
    $2 — [r_p, (4t_a/M + 2r_{io})]$
    $3 — 1/2(r_p + [r_p, 4t_a/M + 2r_{io}])$
    $4 — [r_p, (3t_a/M + r_{io})]$

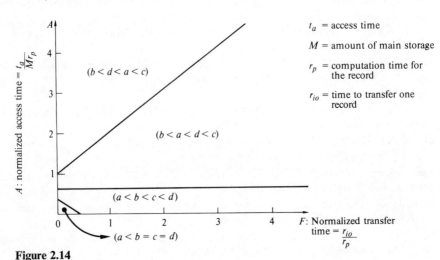

t_a = access time

M = amount of main storage

r_p = computation time for the record

r_{io} = time to transfer one record

Figure 2.14

4. Develop a set of throughput formulas for the cases where a three-channel computer system is given.

5. (F. K. Ng) The PIOCS in Section 2.5.1 can also be characterized by a state-transition diagram. The diagram can generate the sequence of transitions on the basis of the status of the computation area and I/O buffers. In addition to states I, C, O, and S, we introduce two look-ahead states, LO and LC. When in LO, the status of the state C will be examined. If it is ready, R, the computation area and output buffer, will be switched. Furthermore, the status of C will be changed to idle, I, the status of O will be busy, B, and the next state to enter will be C. A similar course of action will take place when the state is LC. The diagram is depicted herewith.

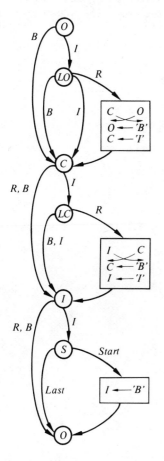

Figure 2.15

Propose an equivalent transition diagram without the two look-ahead states.

6. Implement the PIOCS as characterized by the transition table in Fig. 2.11(d). In order to illustrate the working of the PIOCS, a system environment must be designed and implemented so that the occurrences and transitions of the states as depicted in Fig. 2.11(a) and Fig. 2.11(b) can be used by the PIOCS as input.

7. Design and flowchart a set of input/output macros for the use of the LIOCS, as outlined in Section 2.5.2. These macros must include the following logical operations:

opening of a file,
closing of a file,
retrieval of a logical record,
storage of a logical record.

To facilitate the above operations, the user must provide some information about his files and records. Furthermore, the LIOCS must extract from the unit and device control blocks, and the symbolic name table, certain information concerning the blocks, buffers, and device-dependent parameters about the files and records. The collection of this information is called the *file control block*.

Based on the aforementioned macros, outline the necessary information in the file control block.

8. Implement the LIOCS in the aforementioned problem.

3
The
Batch Processing
Operating
Systems

REMARKS

It is difficult to characterize a typical batch processing operating system. The problem lies not in the lack of batch processing operating systems, but in the finding of a typical one. In fact, there are many types of batch processing systems. In this discussion, we shall concentrate on two important types of batch processing systems, namely, the off-line and the on-line types.

By *on-line programming* we mean that the user can input his job control commands, program statements and data into, and receive output from, the system directly, without going through an intermediate storage medium such as punched cards or tapes. However, in order to enter jobs and receive results directly, the user must utilize terminals to access the system via communication lines. On the other hand, in an *off-line* environment, jobs are submitted as decks of cards (or card images on tapes or disk packs) which are handled by operators and read by card readers (or tape and disk units). The output is listed on paper by printers (on tapes and disk packs by tape and disk units) and dispatched to the user by operators. Although the readers/printers for job input/output may be physically remote from the system via communication lines, the user is still required to handle his jobs as decks and his results as listings. In this case, we simply have an off-line batch system with remote stations.

Among the off-line batch processing systems, the system of programming language subsystems is widely used and easily constructed. We shall attempt to characterize this type of system with some general guidelines and detailed notions.

The sheer size and great complexity of on-line batch processing systems tend to prevent us from gaining a good abstraction of their architectural and functional makeup, without which we cannot perceive and understand them well. Nevertheless, we shall try, as we have done before, to concentrate on their functionality and architecture via abstractions.

The terminology used in this chapter is by no means standard. In fact, there are no standard vocabulary terms particular to batch processing systems. On the other hand, the notions and organizations to be discussed here can commonly be found in batch processing systems.

3.1 INTRODUCTION

Batch processing systems were developed with the aim of *job automation*. By job automation we mean an automatic procedure to prepare, introduce, execute, and terminate jobs consisting of programs and data for better system throughput.

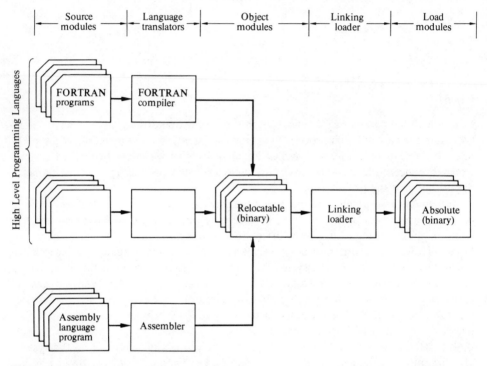

Figure 3.1

For example, in referring to the programming languages system depicted in Fig. 1.1(a), and again reproduced above, we note that the following steps constitute a reasonable procedure for processing a user job.

1. Determine the programming language used in the source modules of the job.

2. Select the proper language translator for the compilation or assembly of the modules.

3. Handle any abnormal termination due to conditions such as compilation or assembly errors.

4. Manage the normal completion of the compilation or assembly by saving the object modules.

5. Oversee the transition from the language translator to the linking loader.

6. Prepare the object modules for inputting to the linking loader.

7. Handle any abnormal termination due to conditions such as missing external symbols and modules.

8. Manage the normal completion of the linking by saving the load modules.

9. Load the modules and their associated data into main memory for execution.

10. Dispatch the output generated by the executing modules.

11. Handle any abnormal termination due to conditions such as program check or prolonged execution.

12. Manage the normal completion by updating, for example, the job accounting information.

13. Return to step (1) for the next user job.

Before the advent of batch processing systems, the operator (or the user) was the one who performed the steps of the procedure. The determination of the language used in the deck of source modules, as dictated in step (1), was done by a personal examination of the modules included for the job. The operator selected the proper translator by fetching a deck of cards which constituted the load modules of the translator. He also loaded both the decks into the main memory. The execution of the translator then followed, as outlined in step (2). If the object modules produced by the translator were punched on the cards, the operator must fetch them from the hopper. The newly punched object modules would be transported to the input hopper and be read into main memory along with the deck of load modules for the linking loader. The execution of the linking loader would then have to follow. These are required by steps (3), (4), (5), and (6). Again, the punched deck which constitutes the load modules of the user program would have to be retrieved from the hopper, transported to the input hopper, appended with user data cards, and read into the main memory for the execution. These are, of course, steps (8) and (9). Finally, when the execution of the user programs was completed, the operator would have to prepare the next set of programs and data to be run.

Such a procedure by the operator can hardly improve the system throughput. While decks are being examined, fetched, transported, and handled, the computer system is idling. The use of punched cards as an intermediate medium for storing object and load modules is not only unnecessary if the computer system has either magnetic tape or disk storage, but also is cumbersome. Unit-record devices such as card reader/punch are slow, and punched cards are sensitive to manual handling. The aim of batch processing systems is, therefore, to replace the operator in carrying out the aforementioned procedure so that job automation can be accomplished with better system throughput.

We have also learned in the previous chapters that better system throughput involves more effective utilization of CPU, channels, and I/O devices. One way to achieve an effective utilization is to keep the CPU busy at all times, even at the expense of some I/O idling if concurrent utilization of both CPU and I/O is not possible. With fast CPU and large memory, the manual preparation, loading, and supervision of job processing by operators, although routine, cannot always keep up the pace of the hardware. Further, manual operations on repetitious job routines are accident prone. There are also certain system throughput improvements, such as concurrent processing and interrupt handling, that can best be dealt with by carefully developed system programs, such as the IOCS and interrupt handler, because the complexity of the problems involved precludes the operator from making on-the-spot decisions. It is therefore not surprising that the automatic procedure for preparing, introducing, executing, and terminating jobs is taken over by the "built-in" programs of a computer system. Batch processing systems are those "built-in" programs which can provide job automation with improved system throughput. However, the degree of job automation of a processing system is mostly limited by the available main and secondary memories for the system and the speed of hardware components such as CPU, channels, and devices.

In this chapter we shall illustrate both a simple system which can run in a computer system with limited memory (8K bytes of main memory and one disk of secondary memory), as well as a more sophisticated system which requires large main memory (32K words of main memory and a family of disks and tapes). We will also discuss ways to improve job automation and system throughput by way of coupling.

3.2 A HIERARCHY OF PROCESSORS AND SUBPROCESSORS: A VIEW OF OFF-LINE BATCH PROCESSING OPERATING SYSTEMS

A simple way to view the off-line batch processing operating system is to look at it as a hierarchy of processors and subprocessors (see Fig. 3.2). At any level of the hierarchy, the processors at that level are in control and perform some tasks. An interesting phenomenon inherent in the batch processing operating system hierarchy is that the processors at the same level cannot be performing their respective tasks at the same time. Furthermore, for a subprocessor to communicate with another subprocessor at the same level, the communication must be done via the processor which is the immediate predecessor of the subprocessors in the hierarchy. We can conclude from this discussion that any processor in the hierarchy must be able

1. to select some of its subprocessors for a given task;
2. to oversee the transition from one of its subprocessors to another one of its subprocessors;
3. to provide communication for its active subprocessors;
4. to handle exceptional conditions due to the abnormal termination of an active subprocessor; and
5. to return to the processor of which it is, in turn, a subprocessor.

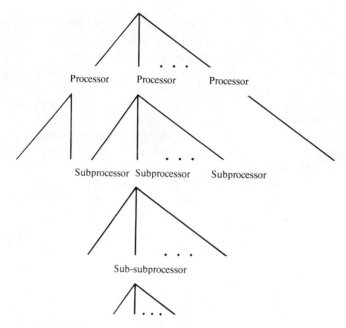

Fig. 3.2 The hierarchy of processors and subprocessors.

The aforementioned performance of a processor, of course, applies to its subprocessors, its subsubprocessors, and so on. The important observations are that, for a processor,

1. the proper selection of subprocessors is determined by the information communicated to the processor from other processors at the same level of the hierarchy;

2. the overseeing of the transition from one subprocessor to another involves the loading, initiating, controlling, and terminating of the selected subprocessors;

3. communication among the subprocessors—since they are being executed at different times—may be accomplished via a dedicated area which is known to all subprocessors at all times;

4. an exceptional condition may require the processor to alter its detailed execution sequence of the subprocessors; and

5. a normal or abnormal return to the superior processor may require the processor to deposit some information about its return in an area known to all processors at that level.

What are these processors which play the roles of selectors, overseers, communicators, and alterers in a system hierarchy? If we have a clear definition and delineation of various software and hardware components in terms of hierarchical processors, then the overall system architecture will be straightforward. However, a definition and delineation of components of an existing system in terms of hierarchical processors is laborious. Not only is the definition and delineation of any existing system voluminous, and not appropriate for this presentation, but few designs of existing systems are based on the concept of hierarchy. Nevertheless, the hierarchy approach to off-line batch systems is perceptive. At the lowest level of the hierarchy, the processors include hardware components such as arithmetic units, interval timer, channels, and CPU. A common processor of the aforementioned hardware (sub-) processors is the interrupt handler. The interrupt handler receives information from arithmetic units, in terms of overflow and underflow signals, from the interval timer in the form of the timer overflow signal, from the I/O operation executor in the form of the channels' signals on I/O, and from the CPU in the form of the program checks (say, incorrect addressing) and supervisor calls (say, halting an I/O operation). As a selector and overseer, the interrupt handler upon receiving an interrupt (i.e., a signal check, or call) determines the next subprocessor to be activated. For example, if the interrupt is a timer overflow signal, the interrupt handler will ignore the signal if there is no timer-overflow-processing routine (a subprocessor) available, and will process the signal by loading (if not already in the main memory), initiating, and executing the routine if available. When the processing of the timer overflow is completed or aborted, the routine (subprocessor) returns to the interrupt handler (processor) for a termination. In this case, the interrupt handler is a software processor whose subprocessors consist of both hardware units, such as the timer, and software modules, such as the timer-overflow-processing routine. We shall provide the reader with an outline of an off-line batch system in terms of a hierarchy of processors. In order to avoid voluminous details and refined delineation at the lower levels, we proceed to describe the system from the root of the hierarchy.

3.2.1 AN OFF-LINE BATCH PROCESSING OPERATING SYSTEM OF PROGRAMMING LANGUAGE PROCESSORS

The off-line batch processing of user programs written in various programming languages has been traditionally considered to be the main function of a typical batch processing operating system. In this case, we shall view the system as a rooted and labeled hierarchy of many programming language subsystems (e.g., one of the subsystems is the assembly system), as depicted in Fig. 3.3.

The root of the hierarchy is where the system processing begins. In referring to Fig. 3.3, we note that the root of the hierarchy is the resident control programs. To batch process a collection of programs, a lower level of processors is called, which, in turn, determine what subprocessors are needed. The labels of the nodes are intended to reflect the functions of the processors. We shall elaborate on these labeled processors in terms of their functions.

3.2.1.1 The Root of the Hierarchy

The development of the Input/Output Control System (IOCS), which enables the various subsystems and programs to use a set of standard and basic I/O facilities, leads to the practice of the resident control programs. For example, the I/O operation executor of the IOCS is kept in the main memory at all times, because the activities

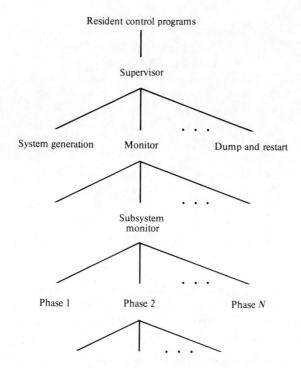

Fig. 3.3 The hierarchical organization of an off-line operating system.

of the data channels have to be constantly monitored in order to keep them busy. We recall that by monitoring the data channel and I/O activities, the I/O operation executor can readily schedule the use of the data channel, perform error-recovery, provide code conversions, and handle normal or exceptional returns. Furthermore, control blocks needed by the I/O operation executor, such as the unit control blocks, the device control blocks, and the symbolic unit name table, must also be in the main memory. They contain, among other things, the status information concerning the progress of the I/O operations and the usage of channels and devices. This information must be constantly maintained and available. For these reasons, a part of the memory, usually at the lower end, is permanently allocated to the I/O operation executor and its associated control blocks.

3.2.1.1.1 THE RESIDENT CONTROL PROGRAMS

The supervisory programs permanently kept in the main memory are called the *resident control programs,* and their associated data, working spaces, and communication areas are called the *nucleus* (see Fig. 3.4 for the memory layout). Because the resident control programs and the nucleus are vital to all the subsystems and user programs, their memory area is always protected from access by the user's program. (Many early computers and present minicomputers with limited main memory have neither resident control programs nor memory protection features.)

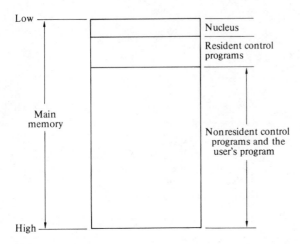

Fig. 3.4 Memory layout.

The resident control programs must be small in size and few in number, since they remain in the main memory at all times; otherwise, the remaining memory available to the susbystems and the user's program will be very limited. Thus, system functions made resident are those necessary

1. to respond to unscheduled requests, interrupts, or traps; and

2. to initiate, maintain, and terminate a subsystem (e.g., a programming language monitor system).

In order to respond to unscheduled requests, interrupts, or traps, the resident routines must be able to handle

a) the operator's requests;

b) the running program's requests for service, e.g., the I/O operations; and

c) machine interrupts or traps due to arithmetic overflow or underflow, channel signal, illegal instruction, address error, interval timer overflow, machine check, etc.

In some cases, the handling routines do not themselves service the request, interrupt, or trap. They simply analyze the conditions which caused it, and determine whether such conditions warrant further processing. If a request requires additional processing, the handling routine will cause the loading of the proper routine from the secondary storage into a working area either in the nucleus, or elsewhere, for servicing the request.

In the case of the I/O operations, the processing routine (e.g., the I/O operation executor) already resides in the memory. Thus, the I/O requests and channel interrupts can be processed readily.

For initiating, maintaining, and terminating a system, the resident control programs must provide routines which can cause the loading of the system functions.

One of the most important functions of the operating system is to determine the type of processing requirements which have been requested by the user. Based on these requirements, the function can then initiate subsequent subfunctions for the intended processing. The *supervisor*, which supervises the transition from one user job (e.g., all the work for a user's collection of consecutive programs and data) to another job, is such a function. The subfunctions, which are under the control of the supervisor, include the following:

a) *the monitor*—to monitor the transition from one subsystem (e.g., the FORTRAN programming system) to another subsystem (e.g., the assembly system);

b) *the system dump and restart*—to save the main memory information in a system utility unit (e.g., disk or tape) for later listing or execution; and

c) *the system generation*—to produce new, and edit current, copy of the system.

In referring to (a), we note that each subsystem can have its own monitor, called *subsystem monitor*, which monitors the transition from one phase of a subsystem (e.g., the input program scanning phase of the FORTRAN system) to another phase of the same subsystem (e.g., the storage allocation phase of the FORTRAN system).

The actual loading of the above system functions is performed by the *system loader*. For this reason, the system loader is also made resident. In other words, the system loader is the part of the residence control programs which performs the second function of the resident control program mentioned earlier in the section. The function of the system loader is

1. to position the I/O device to the beginning of the physical records which contain the system function involved;

2. to read and verify the records;

3. to initiate the positioning of the device to the beginning of the records involved in the next part of the system function; and

4. to transfer control to records which have just been loaded.

We note that the system loader performs none of the six functions attributed to the linking loader as described in the chapter on the assembly system, and it loads the program in load modules only. Because its function is simple, the loading of the system functions is rapid and involves minimal overhead.

3.2.1.1.2 THE NUCLEUS

In addition to the control blocks and working areas, the nucleus may contain

1. regions for intersubsystem communications, such as the name of the subsystem in control, phase name of the subsystem in control, time allocated for the run, and main storage limits available to the load modules;

2. system data such as the current date and time;

3. fixed locations assigned to machine functions, such as interrupt or trap entries (e.g., channel interrupt), and transfer points (e.g., to the I/O operation executor); and

4. pointers to various tables and control blocks, such as
   a) the pointer to the unit control blocks by channel,
   b) the pointer to the device control blocks by channel,
   c) the pointer to the system's utility units, and
   d) the pointer to the system library's table of contents.

We note that (a) and (b) are used by the I/O operation executor for scheduling the channel activities; (c) is used by the subsystems for assembly and compilation and system functions for memory dump and restart; and (d) is used by the system loader for loading the system functions and subsystem phases.

3.2.1.2 The Remaining Hierarchy: The Nonresident Control Programs

The sheer size of the supervisor, the monitor, the subsystem monitor, the dump, and the restart makes it impractical to keep them permanently in the main memory; instead, they reside in a secondary storage device, such as disk or tape. To facilitate the loading of these system functions, each and every system function is assembled and relocated into its absolute form. Furthermore, in the case of the subsystem consisting of several phases, each phase is separately assembled and relocated. Collectively, they are stored in a standard format on a system utility known as the *system library unit*.

A two-level table, known as the *system library's table of contents*, of the following form may be constructed and maintained by the *system library update subsystem* during the assembly and relocation of the system functions and subsystems, where

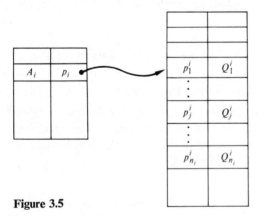

Figure 3.5

A_i is the name of the subsystem (e.g., FORTRAN) or system functions (e.g., DUMP);

p_i is the pointer to the block of information concerning the subsystem or system function A_i;

p_j^i is the name of the jth phase of A_i;

Q_j^i contains information concerning the main memory address at which the phase p_j^i is to be loaded, and the beginning secondary memory address of the physical records which contain the phase p_j^i.

Furthermore, the order in which p_j^i appears in the table determines the loading sequence of the phases. In other words, for the subsystem A_i (say, the FORTRAN), the loading of the phase p_1^i (the scanning of the input program phase which classifies the FORTRAN source statements, produces diagnostic messages, forms symbol dictionaries, and translates statements into internal text) precedes

the phase p_2^i (the storage allocation phase which generates constants, reserves storage, generates equivalences, and translates FORMAT statements), which precedes

the phase p_3^i (the arithmetic and logical translation phase which reorders arithmetic and logical statements into computation order), which precedes

the phase p_4^i (the indexing analysis phase which optimizes the use of subscripts and allocates index registers), which precedes

the phase p_5^i (the instruction generation phase which generates the executable machine instructions).

3.2.1.3 The Command Language

A language, known as the *command language*, or *job control language*, is used to communicate with the operating system. Unlike programming languages, such as FORTRAN, COBOL, and Assembly, which require compilation, assembly, and relocation, the command language is essentially an interpretive language. Basically a statement in the command language consists of the name of a command and a set of parameters for the command. The process of interpreting the statement involves the following steps:

1. Read and save the statement.
2. Verify the command name by matching it with the entries of the table consisting of the valid command names.
3. Transfer to the error processing routine if the command name is invalid, i.e., not in the table.
4. Transfer to the system routines which carry out the command so named. Since the needed system routine may not be resident, the interpreter must call on the system loader for loading the routine. The system loader will search the system library's table of contents for the routine name and then load the routine from the system library for execution.
5. Pass the parameters to the routine.
6. Return to (1) when the routine completes its process.

Because of the hierarchical organization of the operating system, the first command of a job should be the command which can cause the loading of the supervisor. When the supervisor is in control, the commands followed should be recognizable by the interpreter of the supervisor. Should there be an invalid command, the supervisor will either skip this command or terminate the job, depending upon the nature of the job. To bring in the monitor, an appropriate command recognizable by the supervisor would have to be issued. When the monitor is in control, the subsystems can be brought in through the use of the appropriate commands. Usually, the name of the command contains the name of the subsystem. If an unrecognizable command is encountered by the monitor, the command is either skipped, or causes the control to return to the supervisor. When a subsystem is in control, the subsystem monitor interprets its own commands. Invalid commands can cause the control to return to the monitor.

In summary, the hierarchical organization of the operating system requires the control system at each level of the hierarchy to have its own interpreter and table of valid command names. Control is returned to the system immediately superior in the hierarchy. Although physically there may be one interpreter shared among the control programs, and a combined table of valid command names is stored in the system library for ready access, a valid command for the supervisor may cause the termination of a subsystem if the command is being interpreted by the subsystem monitor. In other words, commands in the table of valid commands must be used in the right level of the hierarchy for proper interpretation.

Since commands are related to the functions that the various system components and subsystem can provide, we can anticipate the repertoire of commands by studying their functions. Thus we will discuss the roles of the supervisor, the monitor, and the subsystem monitor, instead of compiling a list of possible commands. Nevertheless, we will show some sample commands and their roles in activating the supervisor, monitor, and submonitors in Section 3.2.3.2.

3.2.2 THE COMPONENTS OF THE OFF-LINE OPERATING SYSTEM
3.2.2.1 The Supervisor

Usually, a job begins with the command (say, the JOB command) which can cause the loading of the supervisor if it is not already in the main memory. The supervisor is thus the first "component" of the operating system to be brought into the main memory from the system library for initiating a user's job. Once the supervisor is in the main memory, the process of the job initiation begins, and includes the following:

1. The verification and update of the user's job account. In recognition of the JOB command, the supervisor passes the control immediately to an installation accounting routine. The accounting routine checks the user's identification, his available funds, the job type and class, and performs the log-in procedure.

2. The time allocation. The time allocated to the job is recorded in the interval timer as a part of control information in the nucleus. The timer will cause an interval-time-overflow-interrupt should the time allocated to the job be exceeded.

3. The establishment of I/O configuration. As we recall, the I/O configuration is defined in the unit and device control blocks and symbolic unit name table. The supervisor is responsible for maintaining the control blocks and table because it is the first, as well as the last, component to be brought into main memory for a job. On the one hand, the supervisor enables the user to alter the configuration

through the commands to facilitate the flexible use of I/O units, and on the other hand, the supervisor maintains a standard configuration to relieve the user from considering the I/O configuration.

The subroutines provided by the supervisor can carry out the commands for

a) reserving certain units for the user;
b) making certain units unavailable to the user;
c) interchanging two units;
d) performing certain end-of-file functions, such as rewind and unload a tape;
e) reestablishing the standard I/O configuration; and typing out the current I/O configuration for the operator.

4. The initiation and termination of system functions. These include the dump and restart and monitor for specific job processing requirements.

5. The return to the resident control programs. Upon the termination of a job, the supervisor is either brought in by an end-of-job command or by the operating system itself. In either case, the supervisor will release all the units reserved for the job, log-out the job, and initiate the next job. In some cases, the supervisor also reestablishes the standard I/O configuration for the next job.

3.2.2.2 The Monitor

While the supervisor is concerned with the initiation and termination of a job, the monitor is mainly concerned with the initiation and termination of a subsystem, or a system function of the operating system. Although the number of subsystems and system functions of a given operating system varies from installation to installation, the basic types can be identified as follows:

1. language processors—FORTRAN, COBOL, assembly, linking loader, etc.;

2. system library update;

3. language library update;

4. sort/merge;

5. utilities; and

6. user program execution phases.

Before initiating a subsystem, the main function of the monitor is to determine whether the subsystem requires the use of certain basic system functions for its entire run. For example, the system library update subsystem handles system library programs in physical record format; it does not need the aid of the input/output buffering subsystem (IOBS) for blocking and deblocking records. On the other hand, language processor subsystems with compiler and assembler may use input/output operations which require the presence of the IOBS. Thus, the monitor must prohibit the loading of IOBS in the first case and initiate the inclusion of IOBS in the latter.

When a subsystem is terminated, the monitor must clear the main memory area and initiate the next subsystem.

3.2.2.3 The Subsystems

3.2.2.3.1 THE SYSTEM LIBRARY UPDATE SUBSYSTEM

As we recall, the system library consists of system programs and subsystems in absolute forms. The system library update subsystem is provided for adding, modifying, and deleting any load modules of the system programs or subsystems in the system library.

Since input to the subsystem may be in various languages and forms (e.g., FORTRAN source language form, relocatable binary, absolute column binary, and system library's physical record form), and may involve the use of a number of units for compiling, assembling, and editing the input and library, a subsystem monitor is needed as follows for keeping track of the activities.

The system library update subsystem monitor does the following:

1. Processes the commands which control the addition, deletion, and modification of the system library.
2. Determines which I/O units will be used and initializes them.
3. Checks the label of the old system library unit containing the system library and the new system library unit on which the new system library is to be created.
4. Retrieves relocatable programs from language libraries if the input is previously stored in these libraries as relocatable subroutines.
5. Calls on the language processor subsystems and linking loader to produce programs in absolute form if the input program was not already in absolute form.
6. Directs the execution of the phases involved in the update run.

The system library update program involves the following phases:

1. The blocking and sorting of input records to confirm the sequence in which the input records will appear as phases in the system library.
2. The creation of the new entries or modification of the old entries in the system library's table of contents for the above phases.
3. The writing of the new table of contents on a utility unit.
4. The merging of the phases in the old system library and the newly created phases.
5. The writing of the new system library on the utility unit.

3.2.2.3.2 THE LANGUAGE LIBRARY UPDATE SUBSYSTEM

The function of this subsystem is similar to the one discussed in the previous section. The major difference is that the programs in the language library are stored as subroutines (more precisely, control sections) in their relocatable forms, instead of absolute forms. For this reason, the language library is often called the *subroutine library*. In general, each language processor subsystem has its own subroutine library. Thus, for example, the FORTRAN compiler subsystem has its FORTRAN subroutine library and the assembly subsystem has its macro definition library. However, in practice, these libraries may be physically combined, and collectively called the language library or the relocative library. Conceptually, the same technique used to construct the two-level system library's table of contents can be extended here to construct the *language library's table of contents*.

Because a subroutine may consist of several control sections, and different subroutines may share the same control sections, the language library's table of contents requires considerable refinement. (See Fig. 3.6.)

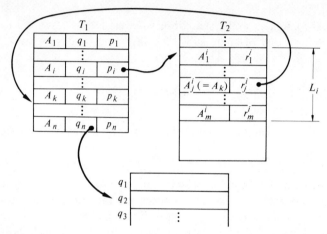

Figure 3.6

To locate all of the control sections needed for a subroutine, the search is first made with the subroutine name. The subroutine is, of course, a control section name A_i in the part of the table of contents T_1. Associated with A_i are two addresses p_i and q_i. If p_i is null, then the indication is that the subroutine consists of one and only one control section whose whereabouts is at q_i. If p_i is not null, then there is a list L_i of m control sections $A_1^i, A_2^i, \ldots, A_m^i$ which constitute the subroutine. In this case, the search continues on the part of the table of contents T_2.* With the aid of p_i, an entry in the list L_i is found. The entry consists of a control section name A_j^i and an address r_j^i which indicates the whereabouts of the A_j^i in T_1. Along with A_j^i in T_1 are, again, two addresses p_j^i and q_j^i, as mentioned earlier. Assuming all of the p_j^i are null, then the control sections needed for the subroutine are:

$$A_i \quad \text{at} \quad q_i,$$
$$A_1^i \quad \text{at} \quad q_1^i,$$
$$\ldots,$$
$$A_m^i \quad \text{at} \quad q_m^i.$$

---

*   The number m (of control sections) is not needed for the search since the control sections are linked by way of the pointers r_j^i to form a list with the beginning of the list at p_i. We introduce m here solely to facilitate the discussion.

However, in general some of the p_j^i may be pointers to the lists L_j^i. In this case, iterative use of the above searching scheme is applied until the application terminates with the null pointers. Although the iterative searching scheme requires some effort in avoiding any circular search and in tracing through the multiple number of entries, it enables the programmer to add additional subroutines (therefore, control sections) which may make external references to the existing subroutines (or control sections), without ever having the need of reprocessing the existing subroutines and their tables of contents.

In implementation, the language and system library update subsystems are usually combined, because the functions of their subsystem monitors and programs are similar.

3.2.2.3.3 THE LANGUAGE PROCESSOR SUBSYSTEMS

A. The Assembler

The discussion on the assembler can be found in the chapter on the assembly system.

B. The Linking Loader

The linking loader accepts as its input a program in one form—the relocatable form—and produces as its output the program in another form—the absolute form. For this reason, it can be considered as a language translator. Unlike most translators (e.g., ALGOL and FORTRAN compilers), which do not concern themselves with the effective use of the computer resources, such as the allocation of buffers and utilization of devices and channels, the linking loader is the only translator which directs itself to this problem. Since all of the compilers and the assembler produce relocatable programs which are then loaded by the linking loader, the effective use of the main memory, devices, and channels can be beneficial to all the compilers and the assembler.

In cases where the size of the main memory is limited and the size of the re-locatable programs is large, the linking loader is divided into several execution phases. Each phase is brought in by the linking loader subsystem monitor which monitors the transition from one phase to another.

Phase 1. The input reduction phase

The input to the loader on a medium such as tape and disk is called the *load file*. In general, the load file consists of a set of relocatable programs, along with commands about the modification to be made on the programs. Phase 1 of the loader identifies the program proper and the following control information of the relocatable programs:

1. the symbol dictionaries including, for each control section, the external symbol dictionary and the internal relocation symbol dictionary;

2. the file control blocks; and

3. the commands to the loader.

It stores the above control information in a condensed form in the main memory. The remaining memory is used to store the relocatable program proper. Since the program proper may be larger than the available space, Phase 1 organizes the program proper into physical records which can be written onto and read from a system utility unit through the use of the IOCS. In this way, the size of the program does not impose a limitation in using the loader. The only restriction is that the control information must be small enough to be condensed and stored in the main memory. At the end of Phase 1, the file control blocks and the tables for the symbol dictionaries are constructed (see Fig. 3.7). If the control blocks and tables require more space than they were allocated, then the formatted program proper is spilled to a system utility tape or disk to make room for the control blocks and tables.

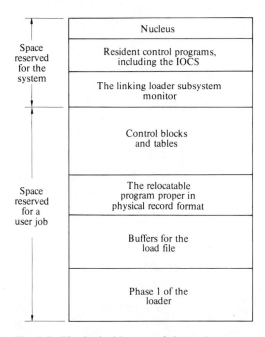

Fig. 3.7 The logical layout of the main memory at the end of Phase 1.

Phase 2. The cross reference and subroutine analysis phase

The main function of Phase 2 of the loader is to determine which set of subroutines will be needed from the subroutine library. Since a subroutine may consist of several control sections and different subroutines may share the same control sections, Phase 2 must consult the table of contents of the subroutine library to determine the control sections which comprise the set of needed subroutines. Once the control sections are determined, Phase 2 calls on Phase 1 (which is still in the main memory) to process the control sections, condense the control information, and insert them in the control blocks and tables. Commands to the loader are then processed and the control blocks and tables are updated (see Fig. 3.8).

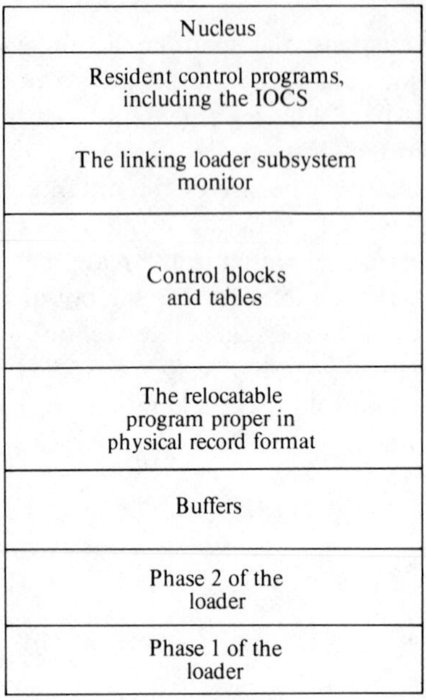

Nucleus
Resident control programs, including the IOCS
The linking loader subsystem monitor
Control blocks and tables
The relocatable program proper in physical record format
Buffers
Phase 2 of the loader
Phase 1 of the loader

Fig. 3.8 The logical layout of the main memory at the end of Phase 2.

Phase 3. The absolute location assignment

The main functions of Phase 3 of the loader (Fig. 3.9) include the following:

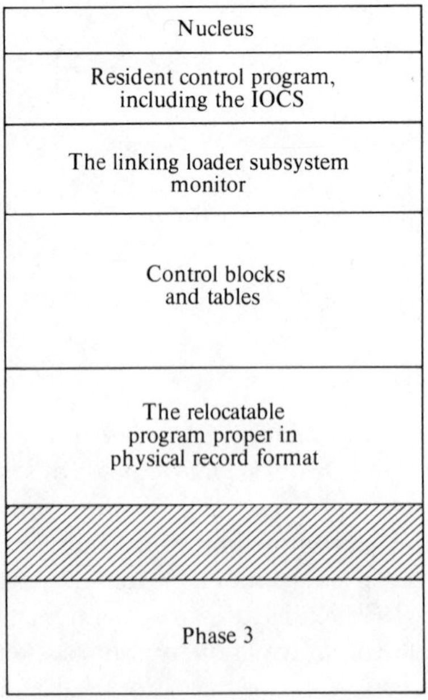

Nucleus
Resident control program, including the IOCS
The linking loader subsystem monitor
Control blocks and tables
The relocatable program proper in physical record format
/////////
Phase 3

Fig. 3.9 The logical layout of the main memory at the end of Phase 3.

1. The assignment of absolute locations to the names of the control sections (not the program proper) as they are indicated in the control blocks and tables.
2. The assignment of physical devices to the symbolic units requested by the relocatable program. The assignments are made to try to achieve a balanced channel and device utilization as discussed in the chapter on the I/O operations and the IOCS.
3. The allocation of buffers. As we recall, the buffer allocation algorithm has been included in the chapter on the I/O operations and the IOCS.

Phase 4. The program proper relocation phase

Because the symbolic names and references in the control blocks and tables have been assigned the absolute locations, they can now be used for the relocation of the program proper. In other words, based on the above information, it is possible to generate the absolute program proper from its relocatable form. However, until the entire program proper has been converted into its absolute form, the control blocks and tables must remain in the main memory. Since the control blocks and tables are kept in the lower end of the main memory (see Fig. 3.9), the upper portion, excluding Phase 4, is available for storing the absolute program proper. If this area is not enough, the absolute program proper is spilled to a system utility unit. By processing all physical records of the relocatable program proper, Phase 4 can relocate the program proper into its absolute form. The absolute program proper is stored mainly in the main memory. Unless it is large, it will not be spilled to the utility unit.

It should be clear from the discussion so far that the time required to complete linkage loading varies according to the number of control sections used, the size of the program proper, and, of course, the space reserved in memory for other user programs. This helps to explain why simple figures for system performance do not exist.

Phase 5. The absolute program proper load and execution phase

Phase 5 is brought in for the final movement of the absolute program proper to its position of execution. Since the segments (usually the control sections) of the absolute program proper may not be in contiguous loading order, some machines require that they be reordered into the proper order for execution. In this case, the reordering is performed by scatter-writing the segments into their proper order. When the program proper is reordered, the execution of the program may begin (see Fig. 3.10).

C. The Compilers

To incorporate a compiler into the operating system as a language subsystem, the compiler writer needs to know the organization of the compiler in terms of subsystem monitors and execution phases. Since numerous books have dealt with the subjects of compiler writing and compiler systems development, we shall forgo the discussion here.

3.2.2.3.4 THE PROGRAM PHASES EXECUTION SUBSYSTEM

Absolute programs can be saved permanently in private files or public libraries of the system. In either case, the preparation of user or system programs for inclusion in the files and libraries must first be handled by the linking loader. It is the linking loader

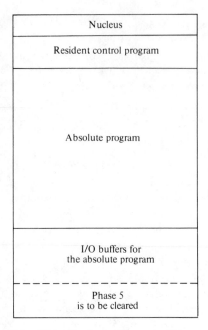

Fig. 3.10 The logical layout of the main memory at the end of Phase 5.

which generates absolute programs, i.e., load modules, as depicted in the previous section. However, when a job requires the execution of absolute programs, the program phases execution subsystem must be brought in. This system can retrieve the absolute programs from the libraries and files, if they are in permanent residence, or read the absolute programs from input devices. Like compilers, large user and system programs may require the linking loader to organize them into execution phases for orderly execution in a memory squeezed environment. The subsystem monitor must therefore be able to identify the phase names, monitor the transition from one phase to another phase, and terminate the phase execution.

3.2.2.3.5 OTHER SUBSYSTEMS AND SYSTEM PROGRAMS

Other important subsystems and system programs, such as the sort/merge subsystem and the debugging system programs, will not be covered in this text. They should be investigated by the students as possible topics for further study.

3.2.3 SUMMARY OF THE OFF-LINE BATCH PROCESSING OPERATING SYSTEM

The batch processing system described in the previous sections is a general one (see Fig. 3.11). The unique features of the system are:

1. the presence of a centralized input/output control system which handles the input/output operations for all of the subsystems and programs;

2. the capability to create and verify labels for all of the subsystems and programs residing in the system library, language library, and private files;

3. the availability of system and language library update subsystems for maintaining all of the subsystems and the subroutines of every language processor; and

4. the use of the hierarchical structure of the nucleus, supervisor, and monitor for intersubsystem communication and job automation.

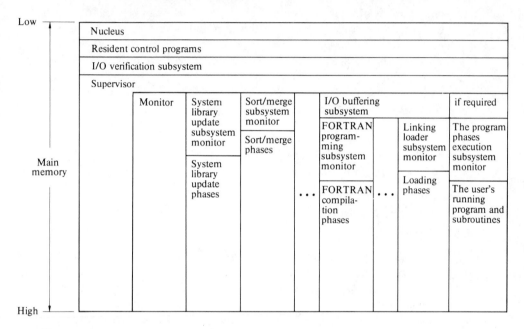

Fig. 3.11 Logical main memory layout of the subsystems involved in the off-line batch processing operating system.

This system basically serves as a host system for various programming language processors and subsystems.

As a host system, it imposes a hierarchical organization to the various programming subsystems. Very often the user will find that his programs and data are terminated prematurely by the operating system, due to improper use of the job control language. Further chaos may be created should the organization of the operating system become more complex.

In order to use the job control language properly, programmers are required to understand the architecture of the operating system. Thus, they must be taught not only the problem-oriented language, but also the system architecture and job control language. Some improvements have been made to facilitate the use of the job control language; for example (1) all of the system commands start with a symbol which is different from the symbol preceding subsystem commands; and (2) the use of the macro command for replacing the more frequently used set of commands. Nevertheless, in most cases, the command language is still designed as an afterthought for a given operating system architecture. It may be useful for future designers of operating systems to begin with the design of the command language which then influences or dictates the design of the operating system.

3.2.3.1 An Example

With some simplification, the generalized system hierarchy can be used to characterize a conventional batch processing system, the IBM 360 Basic Operating System (BOS), as a hierarchy of processors and subprocessors.

The root of the hierarchy is composed of resident control programs and nucleus. A common input and output control system, the Physical IOCS (PIOCS), is permanently in the main memory. More specifically, the resident control programs known as the *Supervisor* consist of the following routines:

1. PIOCS,
2. supervisor-call-interrupt-processing routine,
3. external-interrupt-processing routine,
4. program-and-machine-check-processing routine,
5. operator-communications-processing routine, and
6. fetch routine.

Because the routines in (2) through (4) process interrupts, they are collectively called the *Interrupt Handler*. Furthermore, the fetch routine which loads programs and data in absolute form from a dedicated disk is an absolute loader. It is also called the *System Loader*. Thus the four major functions of the Supervisor are those which monitor the input/output requests and executions, handle the interrupts, load nonresident system subfunctions, and communicate with the operator. The nucleus is made up of four basic areas:

1. A table of physical unit blocks (PUB Table). There is an entry in the table for each symbolic I/O unit used. Normally, a symbolic unit is assigned a physical device. However, two or more symbolic units may be assigned to a single device if it is a direct-access device, such as a disk.

   The position of an entry in the table implies the intended symbolic name of the entry. For example, the second entry always represents the card reader for job control cards. Each entry consists of four pieces of information which characterize the assigned device—the channel to which the device is attached, the unique device identification number, the device type, and recording density and specification.

2. A communication region. In this region, system data such as date and configuration are recorded. There are areas for intersystem communications such as the name of the program in control and the name of the phase of a program in execution.

3. Fixed locations assigned to machine functions such as the timer and the return entry for the user timer-processing routine.

4. A transient area for loading and executing logical input/output packages (such as OPEN and CLOSE), system dump, restart, and checkpoint routines.

We note that the nucleus of the IBM 360/BOS consists of the types of information which are similar to the ones in the nucleus of the generalized system discussed in the previous sections (See Fig. 3.12). The only difference is in the handling of the control blocks. In the IBM 360/BOS, control information about the physical devices and symbolic units is included in the nucleus as the table of the physical unit blocks. On the other hand, the generalized system which can support more elaborate logical input/output activities, such as buffering and label verification, requires more sophisticated control blocks. These control blocks are considerably larger. Like the logical I/O packages such as OPEN, CLOSE, GET, and PUT, they are stored in the system's transient and the user's area. (See also Section 2.5.2.3 in Chapter 2 on the physical IOCS versus logical IOCS).

The PIOCS is another name for the I/O operator executer which handles the physical I/O requests and executions. In monitoring the requests and executions, the

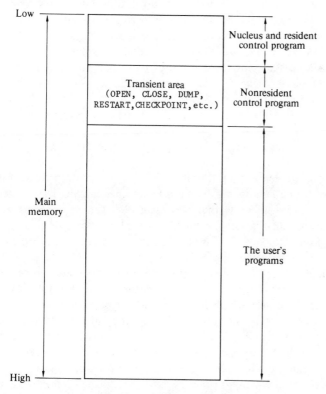

Fig. 3.12 Memory layout of the IBM 360/BOS.

PIOCS can schedule the use of the channels. Thus, another name for the PIOCS is the *Channel Scheduler*.

The system program which supervises the transition from one user job to another job is called the *Job Control*. The Job Control also monitors the transition from one subsystem to another subsystem. In the IBM 360/BOS, the subsystems include the assembly, report generating, sort/merge, program execution phases, and debugging systems. Because each use of a subsystem must be handled as a job, the supervision of job transition and the monitoring of subsystem transition are one and the same task. Furthermore, the function of monitoring the subsystem is taken over by the Job Control. For example, in monitoring the assembly, the Job Control determines (based on user's job control card specification) whether the object modules are to be included in the system's relocatable library, or whether the load modules are to be placed in the core-image library. If the user has requested an assemble-and-execute option in his job control card, the Job Control will load and execute the assembler, direct the assembler to insert the object modules into the relocatable library, call and execute the linking loader (called *linkage editor*), direct the linking loader to place the load modules in the core-image library, and finally cause the load modules to be executed in the main memory. Unless there is a specific user request, the load and object modules in the libraries will not be saved for future use. On the other hand, catalogs will be created for these modules and will be permanently kept by the Job Control if such requests are made. Because both the assembler and the linking loader are rather large and the IBM 360/BOS is configured for a small main memory of 8K bytes with a standby disk, the load modules of these two processors are also organized into execution phases. The names of the phases are, of course, in the catalog, and the phases are in the core-image library. Both the catalog and library are stored on the disk. Similarly, the load modules of the user program are also organized into phases. It is, therefore, the Job Control's function to call the System Loader for loading the execution phases of the (language) processors and of the user program (Fig. 3.13).

From this discussion, we learn that the Job Control does not provide fully automated transition from one language subsystem to another language subsystem. Since user programs written in different languages must be organized into different jobs, and intermediate results must be either manually passed from one job to another or specifically included in a cataloged file for subsequent use, the user and operator are responsible for the job preparation (Fig. 3.14).

On the other hand, the Job Control does provide good automatic procedures for language processing and user program execution. In the former, the Job Control serves as a language system monitor which brings in the language processor for the translation of user programs, enters the translated programs into the (relocatable) library, and calls in the linking loader for program-phase organization and core-image-library insertion. In the latter case, the Job Control supervises the execution of the user programs by calling the linking loader to prepare program phases for the library, loading and executing the program phases, and monitoring their executions. Thus, in these cases the Job Control functions as the monitor outlined for the gen-

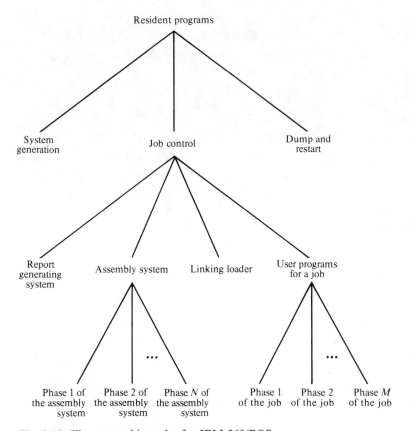

Fig. 3.13 The system hierarchy for IBM 360/BOS.

eralized batch processing system. For a detailed exposition of the IBM 360/BOS, the reader may refer to [10] and [11].

3.2.3.2 The Use of Job Control Languages

The command language or job control language of a batch processing system is used by the operator and the user to activate and select the processors and subprocessors of the system for intended services. Although the syntax of these commands varies from one system to another, the correct use of these commands lies not only in detailed attention to the syntactical peculiarities of the individual commands, but also in careful preparation of the sequence of commands. The sequence has a great deal to do with the way that the hierarchy of processors and subprocessors is structured and can be activated.

For example, because in the IBM 360/BOS the command //EXEC will cause the Job Control to prepare programs for execution, it must be placed properly in the job deck. In order to prepare the programs, the Job Control must decide whether or not the linking loader is to be used for the job. Since the programs can be either

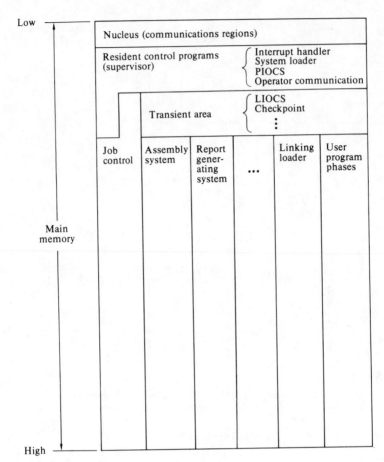

Fig. 3.14 Logical main memory layout of the subsystems involved in IBM 360/BOS.

fetched from the libraries (the permanently cataloged core-image library or the temporarily entered relocatable library), or read from the system's input device, there are three possibilities. We shall discuss them in sequel.

Case 1. The user program is already in the core-image library.

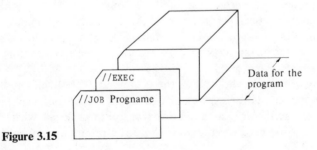

Figure 3.15

When the command //EXEC is encountered, the Job Control will *not* activate the linking loader. Instead, the Job Control will direct the system loader to fetch the first program phase of the program named in the //JOB card from the core-image library, and will supervise the execution of all program phases of the program fetched from the library.

To include program phases in the core-image library for subsequent executions, the command //JOB SYSCMAINT must be used in a prior job for the program phases.

Case 2. The user program is in the system's input device.

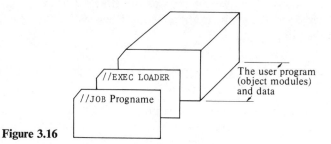

Figure 3.16

In this case, the Job Control will activate the linking loader when the job control card //EXEC is encountered. The linking loader will read from the system's input device the program named in the //JOB card, prepare the program into execution phases, and return to the Job Control for program phase execution.

Case 3. The user program is in the relocatable library.

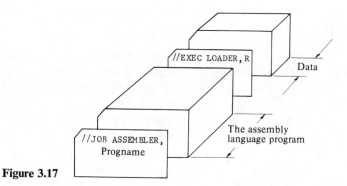

Figure 3.17

In this case, an assembly language program is to be assembled; the object module of the program is to be stored temporarily in the relocatable library; the linking loader is to be brought in for program phase preparation; the linking loader is to be informed of the temporary residence of the object modules (by the letter R in the //EXEC card); and the program phases are to be executed.

In view of the system hierarchy, it is reasonable to expect that the execution of the user program phases constitutes the last transition from job preparation and translation to job processing by the Job Control. Thus, the use of //EXEC at the end of a job is not inconvenient. However, the necessity for the user to inform the Job Control about the whereabouts of his program modules in specifying the //EXEC command is not convenient. Sophisticated systems can determine the whereabouts of the program modules by systematically searching the libraries, system's input devices, and user's input files. Although these sophistications can alleviate the cumbersome task in using the job control commands, they contribute to the size and complexity of the systems. For systems such as the IBM 360/BOS, which are restricted to meager memories, the control programs must be small. Thus, the user is still burdened with the job preparation.

3.2.4 SOME IMPROVEMENTS OF THE OFF-LINE BATCH PROCESSING OPERATING SYSTEMS

In batch processing systems, as developed to this point, full I/O and computation overlap is difficult to achieve. This problem is largely due to the fact that the instructions of a program are seldom (and sometimes cannot be) organized for the purpose of the overlap. Since there is only one program to be executed in the main memory until its completion, the CPU usually idles while the I/O operation is ongoing. An acute case is the simple case of *on-line job I/O* where the input of jobs into the operating system is through a card reader. As each job control command is usually punched on a card, the reading of the job control cards, program decks, and data leaves the CPU idling most of the time. A similar situation exists when a large quantity of output information has to be punched and printed on the card punch and printer.

3.2.4.1 Off-line Job I/O

To circumvent the aforementioned situations, magnetic tapes are used for batching the jobs. A computer is usually used to read the batch of jobs from its card reader, and write them onto a tapé while the main computer is processing the previous batch of jobs. The tape is then mounted onto the tape unit of the main computer when the main computer is about to process the batch. Since the tape unit is a faster I/O device than the card reader and punch, its use for inputting and outputting jobs can reduce the CPU idling time.

As we learned from our earlier discussion, the units for the card reader and the input job tape can be switched through the use of appropriate commands recognizable by the Supervisor. Thus, the I/O instructions in the user's program which refer to the card reader are now effectively referring to the tape. By switching the printer and card punch with a tape, the output from the job batch can be saved on the tape as backlog. The tape is later processed by the computer, which will then produce the listing on its printer and punched cards on its card punch unit.

Such handling of a job batch is called *off-line job I/O*.

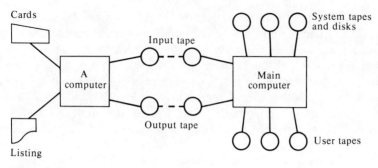

Figure 3.18

3.2.4.2 Directly Coupled Systems

One particular system with off-line job I/O capability has been implemented at Yale [18] (see Fig. 3.19). In this system the following modification of machines and operating systems are included.

1. The small and slow computer handles all of the I/O operations and serves as the master; the big and fast computer performs computation only and serves as the slave.

2. To give the master computer the capability of loading, starting, and monitoring the processing function of the slave computer, several features are added to the system:

   a) the capability of each computer to interrupt the other, and
   b) the modification of a TRANSMIT instruction of the master computer which can cause the movement of a block of data between the two main memories.

3. The capability of the operating system of the master computer to schedule computation for the slave computer.

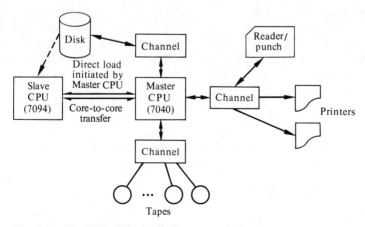

Fig. 3.19 The Yale 7094–7040 direct coupled system.

Item (b) requires the two main memories of the system to be directly coupled. For this reason, such systems are called *directly coupled systems.* In these systems high volumes of large batched jobs can be processed with considerable ease.

Recent experience with directly coupled systems shows that a heavily loaded master computer can get bogged down in I/O operations while the bigger slave computer is idle. Thus installations of this type, such as OS/360-ASP and VS/370-JES2, tend to make the master computer the bigger of the two. Furthermore, by modifying the master-slave concept slightly, the slave can have selected I/O of its own (as long as its average performance remains computation-bound) and the master can do some local processing (as long as its local work does not interfere with I/O processing) [12].

3.3 THE ON-LINE BATCH PROCESSING SYSTEMS

Whether employing an off-line job I/O, or an on-line job I/O technique, the off-line batch processing system requires the user to enter his jobs on punched cards. The use of the teletypewriters, for example, is not permitted. The preparation of jobs in the format of card decks is arbitrary; the exclusion of terminals such as teletypewriters is inconvenient.

Attempts have been made to provide on-line programming with batch processing systems. By *on-line programming* we mean that the user can input his job control commands, program statements and data, and receive output from the operating system directly, without going through an intermediate' storage medium, such as punched cards or tapes. Batch processing systems with on-line programming capability are referred to as *on-line batch processing systems.*

On-line terminals such as teletypewriters and keyboard/display units are usually used for such purposes. However, since their I/O capabilities are much slower than card reader and punch, the same problem of CPU idling exists and becomes worse. The problem is further multiplied by the fact that on-line programming is intended to facilitate the use of a number of terminals.

The use of terminals such as teletypewriters and keyboard/display units to enter jobs can eliminate the need of preparing jobs on punched cards. It effectively replaces keypunching of jobs. However, each time the same job is to be entered for processing, it would be absurd if we had to type the entire job again on the teletypewriter. Naturally, the on-line system must have a file system which can save the user's programs, data, and commands for later processing.

From the above discussion, we conclude that for an off-line batch processing system to become an on-line system, it must have

1. on-line terminals such as teletypewriters and keyboard/display units;
2. satellite computers to process low-speed inputs from the on-line terminals;
3. a central computer for general computation; and
4. a centralized file system.

A simple on-line batch processing system may be composed of two computers: a small one, and a big one coupled through a data channel or communication line.

The small computer is equipped with terminals such as teletypewriters and keyboard/ display units. Its operating system forwards the jobs as messages to the big computer. In addition, the operating system provides control functions which can cause the big computer to begin, alter, and terminate the process of a job. The extended batch processing operating system of the fast and big computer can perform complex computation and process files for the on-line jobs as well as the background jobs (e.g., jobs entered through the off-line job I/O). Through interrupts, the small computer can communicate with the big computer in real time.

A more sophisticated on-line batch processing system may consist of one big computer and several satellite computers. For example, the IBM 3791 communication controllers are such satellite computers, which are coupled with a big computer, the IBM 360/370, via communication lines. As a satellite computer, the IBM 3791 communication controller has its own secondary storage, such as the disk and diskette for backup and filing, main storage for data buffering and processing, and control logic for instruction decoding and program execution. It supports a number of keyboard/printer, keyboard/display, and communications terminals [1].

3.3.1 A SIMPLE ON-LINE BATCH PROCESSING SYSTEM

We shall discuss the simple on-line batch processing system in terms of its functional and architectural elements (see Fig. 3.20).

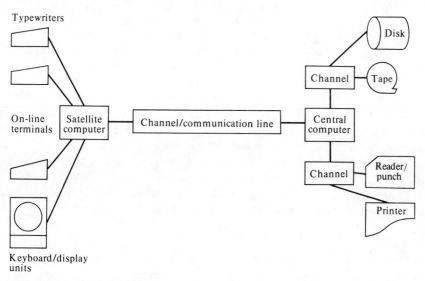

Fig. 3.20 A simple on-line batch processing system.

3.3.1.1 The Table, Buffers, and Commands

A. Buffers and New Commands

Since job input and output via on-line terminals are performed in terms of characters, the system must provide buffers for collecting these characters. In fact, there are three types of buffers.

1. Buffers in the satellite computer. These buffers are usually very small—64 characters for example. The size of the buffers is determined by the number of characters to be transmitted to the central computer, the I/O rate of the terminals, and the available main memory in the satellite computer.

2. Buffers in the central computer. These buffers are somewhat larger than the ones in the satellite computers. However, they are still rather small relative to the size of the main memory of the central computer—500 words for example. The size of these buffers is determined by the number of characters to be transmitted to the satellite computer, the I/O rate of the secondary devices such as disks, and the available main memory of the central computer.

3. On-line buffers. These buffers are even larger. They are created by the system on the secondary devices such as disks. The size of these buffers may be several thousand words. Again, the size of these buffers is determined by the number of words to be transmitted to the central computer, the "average" user job size, and the available secondary memory.

Input buffers in the satellite computer are created for the purpose of collecting every character (if it is from a teletypewriter) or line (if it is from a display console) as soon as the character or line is entered by the user, converting the character code from one (say, ASCII) to another (say, EBCDIC) if required, compacting the characters for the transmission. Output buffers in the satellite computer are intended for the purpose of receiving messages from the central computer, decoding the control bits about the messages, converting the character code if necessary, sending as many characters as the terminal can output, and keeping the terminal busy.

We shall not elaborate on the buffers in the central computer. Both the satellite and central computer buffers are transparent to the user. Their role in handling job I/O is intended to bridge the disparity in speed, capacity, and function of the terminal, satellite computer, central computer, and secondary storage device. However, the on-line buffers are highly visible to the user. The user can accumulate his program statements, data, and commands for batch processing and amass his output in these buffers. For this reason, there is a one-to-one correspondence between the on-line terminals and the pair of on-line input and output buffers. Furthermore, the on-line batch processing system provides a set of new commands for the user:

1. to clear the input or output buffer;

2. to append lines (program statements, data, or systems commands) to the input buffer;

3. to delete lines;

4. to insert lines;

5. to edit lines;

6. to print the lines in the input or output buffer; and

7. to start processing the job in the input buffer.

When the terminals are on-line display consoles, the addition, deletion, insertion, edition, and printing of lines can be extended to characters.

For our convenience, we shall simply refer to the on-line buffers as buffers. We shall also refer to the statements, data, and commands in the buffers as lines, and by their line numbers.

B. The Table and Some More Commands

For the on-line batch processing system to keep track of the users, the jobs, and the terminals, there is a *system operation table*. This table contains information concerning the following:

1. Terminal identifications. There is a unique identification number for every terminal whether it is an on-line or an off-line device.

2. User identifications.

3. Buffer assignments. For each terminal there is associated a pair of buffers, namely, the input buffer and the output buffer. The entries in the table are originally the symbolic unit names. (For a discussion on the symbolic unit names, the reader should consult Section 2.5.2.1 in the chapter on IOCS.) Subsequently, the entries become the pointers to the unit control blocks of the units to which the buffers are assigned at system generation time.

4. Operating status. This is information regarding the current status of the central computer system. The system is either running a job for this terminal, or waiting for the completion of a job being run for some other terminal. In either case, the line number of the line with which the job begins is always saved in the table entry. When it is not running a user job, the system is performing clearing, addition, deletion, edition, or printing of lines. Such performance is noted in the table entry. Since the lines are involved, the line numbers are needed there too.

After the signing-in command is issued at a terminal, the terminal identification and user identification will be verified and entered. Similarly, after the signing-out command is issued, the user identification will be removed from the table.

3.3.1.2 The Satellite Computer Operating System: A Finite State Automaton with Few States

The organization of the operating system of the satellite computer system is influenced by the following factors.

1. Communication with teletypewriters is asynchronous, character-by-character. These characters may be entered at a maximal rate of ten per second, for example. For outputting characters, it is desirable to keep the teletypewriter at the full rate.

2. Communication with display consoles is synchronous, character-by-character, via certain register.

3. Communication with the central computer system is in a form called a handshake. A message initiated by the satellite operating system must be acknowledged by a reply from the operating system of the central computer system.

On-line job preparation functions, such as clearing of the buffers and editing of lines and characters, are all performed by the central computer operating system. The logic of the satellite computer operating system generally includes the following states:

Dormant state. No characters are to be inputted from, or outputted to, the teletypewriters or display consoles.

Read state. One character is to be read into the (64 character) buffer.

Write state. A line of characters is to be outputted to a device. The line of characters will be printed or displayed unless it is interrupted by a special stop-printing-and-outputting signal. In this case, the emergency state is entered.

Emergency state. The special signal indicates that a character must be read immediately. Otherwise, the character may be lost or written over by another character. Thus, in this state, the system immediately sends a temporary "time-out" signal to the device and records the number of remaining characters to be outputted in a table for subsequent resumption of the output operation. When this is accomplished, the next state is the read state.

Handshake state. A line of characters is to be outputted to the central computer operating system. The line of characters will be sent over if the handshake is accepted. Otherwise, this state is reentered at a later time for outputting the line of characters. An interruption can occur if the stop-printing-and-outputting signal appears.

Processing state. Code conversion and character packing are the basic processing tasks in this state. (However, for more advanced satellite computer, such as the IBM 3791 communication controller, the processing tasks may include message editing, display formatting, etc.) By performing these tasks, the satellite computers can relieve the central computer from such tasks.

The design of the satellite computer operating system as a finite state automaton is not a difficult task. We shall leave it to the reader as an exercise.

3.3.1.3 The Central Computer Operating System

The inclusion of the system operation table and interrupt handling routines requires the enlargement of the nucleus and the resident control programs. Furthermore, the number and size of the nonresident control programs must be greatly expanded. One of the major expansions must be the file system, which allows both the system and the user to store, retrieve, and update his programs, data, and command procedures (see Fig. 3.21).

3.3.1.3.1 THE CHANGING ROLE OF THE RESIDENT CONTROL PROGRAMS: A STUDY OF THE INTERRUPT HANDLER

In order to communicate with the central computer operating system, the satellite computer operating system issues a request via the data channel which will trigger an interrupt in the central computer system. This interrupt will be processed by the

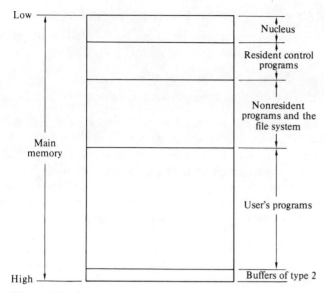

Figure 3.21

Interrupt Handler, one of the resident control programs. At the occurrence of the interrupt, the system is in one of the following three states.

Ready state. The system is running a program which has nothing to do with any on-line programming service, such as appending, deleting, editing, inserting, starting the processing of a certain line in the input buffer, or clearing the buffers. In this case, the interrupt handler saves the request from the satellite computer operating system, the current contents of all the registers used by the interrupted program, and the contents of the program counter for later continuation of the interrupted program. Furthermore, the interrupt handler checks the parity of the request, delays until all necessary I/O operations are completed, and decodes and services the request. When the requested service is completed (e.g., deletion of a line from a certain input buffer), the interrupt handler restores the contents of all the registers, and resumes the interrupted program.

Busy state. In this state, the interrupt handler is in the middle of servicing a request. Since a new request cannot be honored until the present request is completely serviced, the interrupt handler returns a message to the satellite computer operating system, causing it to reissue the request at a later time. Meanwhile, the interrupted program resumes its run.

Wait state. In this state, the interrupt handler is expecting more data from the satellite computer operating system in order to continue the service routine.

When the service cannot be disturbed, the busy state is entered. When data are needed for the service, the system will wait for them by remaining in the wait state. Thus, the interrupt handler always gives priority to the on-line programming services.

3.3.1.3.2 THE EXTENDED NONRESIDENT CONTROL PROGRAMS

The major extension to the nonresident control programs is the addition of the file system. We observe that there are two kinds of on-line use of the file system:

1. the use of the file system during job preparation, and
2. the use of the file system for run-time access to data and programs.

The second kind of on-line use of the file system will not be discussed in this chapter. For the first kind of on-line use of the file system, we are concerned with the commands needed for job preparation. As we have mentioned before, we have commands to clear, append, delete, edit, insert, and print lines of the job in the input buffer. However, we have not provided commands for specifying the data, programs, and command procedures stored in the file system, which must be included as a part of the job. For this reason, new commands must be provided for such purpose.

Thus these additional nonresident control programs (excluding the file system), which provide the interface between the satellite and central computer system, have the following three major functions:

1. preprocessing the job input held in the input buffer for the central computer operating system,
2. postprocessing the job output from the central computer operating system, and
3. interpreting the on-line commands.

A. Input Preprocessing

There are three reasons to require preprocessing of jobs held in the input buffer.

1. The job statements must be scanned for interpretation of the on-line commands.
2. The job statements in the input buffer may not be in proper format to be handled by the central computer operating system.
3. Some additional commands, besides the ones supplied by the user, must be inserted by the control programs to allow postprocessing of system output for the job.

By preprocessing the job statements, the system enables the user to have a freer command language syntax. For example, conversion of the line of freer syntax to the card image is performed by the preprocessor.

When a collection of programs and data must be transferred from the buffer into the main memory for processing, the user does not know that this collection must constitute a batched job, since the system is a batch processing system. For this reason, the end-of-a-job command and other necessary commands must be provided by the preprocessor. Furthermore, standard practices of using system input/output units for the running job must be avoided. Unless specifically requested by the user, the units on which the input and output buffers reside must be used. Commands for unit switching are inserted during the preprocessing phase.

B. Output Postprocessing

There are two conditions requiring postprocessing of the job output.

1. Binary output, which is normally punched, is instead stored in the file for use at a later time.

2. Alphanumeric output, which is normally printed, is diverted to the user's output buffer. As with the input, there is a format difference requiring an additional conversion step.

C. On-line Command Language Interpretation

Allowing the user to include source or binary information previously stored in the file as a part of his job, the system does not require that all the necessary job information is actually in the user's input buffer. For example, there is no way to get binary decks in the buffer from the terminals. Thus, binary decks must have been stored in the file and should be retrieved into the buffer by the file system. For retrieving the stored information, the system produces appropriate job control cards which are inserted in the user's job in the buffer.

D. The Biased and Perpetual Supervisor

D.1 The Job Scheduler. The job scheduler is the part of the supervisor which actually determines the next job to be run. In the off-line batch processing system, the job scheduler always initiates the next job in the batch (see Section 3.2.2.1)

1. by reading a card (or card image),
2. by determining whether the card indicates the beginning of a job, and
3. by activating the accounting routine if it does.

In the on-line batch processing system, the job scheduler, which always gives the preference to the terminals, does the following steps:

1. reads a card (or card image);
2. determines whether the card indicates the beginning of a job;
3. continues to step (5) if the card is the beginning of a job;
4. resumes the interrupted job and skips the remaining steps;
5. determines whether it is an on-line job if it is a job;
6. looks for an on-line job if it is not an on-line job;
7. activates the accounting routine for the on-line job, if there is one, or for the background job, if there is none; and
8. continues with the new job.

D.2 The On-line Job Priority Controller. Not only do on-line jobs have priority over background jobs, but there can be preferential considerations among the on-line jobs. The assignment of priority can be arbitrary. However, we can incorporate a priority controller which always schedules the next job to be processed on the basis of the order of the entries in the system operation table as mentioned in Section 3.3.1.1.

D.3 The Perpetual Supervisor.　　Unknown to the terminal user, the concepts of the job in the off-line and on-line batch processing systems are entirely different. In an off-line environment, the user submits a job by placing all his programs and data between a beginning-of-the-job card and an end-of-the-job card. However, in the on-line environment, the user expects to sign in and sign out only once, enter many programming tasks in-between, and wait for various results at different times. Thus, as far as the user is concerned, his concept of the job is an interactive session of programming tasks between a signing-in and signing-out. However, the system, in fact, handles each of his tasks (initiated by a start-at-the-line command) as a job, in the sense of the off-line batch processing system. As we discussed in Section 3.2.1 the transition between jobs is handled by the supervisor. To reduce the overhead and to facilitate job transition, the supervisor (automatically) sets the interval timer and maintains the same I/O configuration for the terminal user. For this reason, a part of the supervisor is perpetually kept in the main memory.

3.3.1.4　The File System

The file system is not only essential to an on-line batch processing system, but is also an integral part of the systems discussed in later chapters. For this reason, we shall defer the discussion of the file system to latter parts of the book.

3.3.2　A SUMMARY AND SOME IMPROVEMENTS OF THE ON-LINE BATCH PROCESSING OPERATING SYSTEM

The on-line batch processing system can be useful for small on-line programming jobs with a limited number of terminals. Graphic displays, which require considerable computation of their coordinates, can be sent to the central computer for faster results. The on-line programming information—programs, data, and job control commands—can now be saved in the files for later retrieval and updating. Although neither the satellite nor the central computer alone provides multiprocessing capability, (i.e., parallel computation by the CPU's, not including the I/O and computation overlap), the combined system is in fact a multiprocessing system with two CPU's.

As each user signs in the system, the operating system of the central computer creates for the user two buffers on disk—the input buffer and the output buffer. The input buffer is used to stack the user's commands, programs, and data, which can be edited and examined through the use of the input and edit functions provided by the system. When the input is ready to be processed by the central computer, an on-line command is issued by the user. The command causes the central computer to schedule the processing of the job in the user's input buffer. The processing of the job may involve

1. the storage of commands, programs, and data as records into the user's files;
2. the retrieval of commands, programs, and data from the public and user's private files,
3. the assembly, compilation, interpretation, and execution of programs and procedures; and
4. the creation, updating, and deletion of files and records.

The output of the job is accumulated in the user's output buffer. On demand of the user, the output buffer can be examined and listed through the use of the on-line output command of the system.

3.3.2.1 Indirectly Coupled Systems

The basic system concept of the on-line system is to interconnect the input-output computer with the large scale computational computer, by means of commonly shared disk buffers and files. We note that there is no direct connection between the main memory units of the two computers, and each computer schedules its own work. For this reason, this type of coupled system is referred to as an *indirectly coupled system* or a *shared file system*.

An indirectly coupled system with an advanced file system capability has been implemented at the University of Pennsylvania (see Fig. 3.22). A more elaborate system configuration for an indirectly coupled system has been proposed in [2].

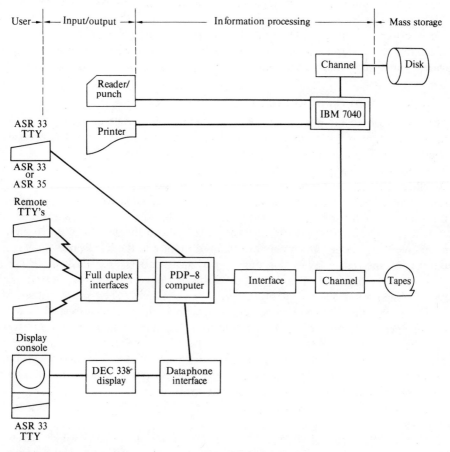

Fig. 3.22 The University of Pennsylvania's Moore School coupled system/PDP8-IBM 7040.

Results of simulation studies indicated considerable improvement in terms of job turnaround time (i.e., the elapsed time between the submission and return of a job) and job throughput (i.e., the amount of work that can be performed by a given set of resources) of the coupled system over the stand-alone batch processing system.

3.3.2.2 Remote Job Entry

For indirectly coupled systems, the use of high-speed reader/printer terminals, for example, to enter job decks at remotely placed stations via communication lines is in vogue. These terminals are called *remote job entry* terminals. Unlike off-line job I/O (Section 3.2.4.1) where the job decks are copied on tapes or disk packs and then transported to the central computer for processing, the job decks at remote job entry terminals are entered directly into the central computer via communication lines. Thus, the remote job entry is a more advanced form of on-line job I/O and is characterized by its high speed, great volume, and long distance. The indirectly coupled systems with remote job entry capability are also referred to as on-line systems. By referring to our earlier discussion, we note, however, that there are important differences between on-line job I/O and on-line programming. The reader should be aware of the differences. Here, an on-line processing system is always meant to be a system with on-line programming capability, whether it utilizes on-line or off-line job I/O.

3.3.2.3 System Configurations

The discussion so far has indicated that for an on-line system there is a need for satellite computers for terminal I/O, and a central computer for batch processing. Such a configuration is of course a functional one. In physically organizing computer hardware and software, the same functional need may be obtained in various ways. Whether to implement some of the functional components with hardware and other functional components with software is a complex decision from which a spectrum of computer hardware and software organizations has resulted. The CDC 6600 system [21] perhaps represents one end of the spectrum in which the functional components of the on-line system are realized mainly in the hardware. This system consists of one central processor and ten peripheral processors. Each processor has its own main memory. The memories of the peripheral processors are connected with the memory of the central processor via ten channels. The control of the system is always in one of these peripheral processors. In addition, the peripheral processors can independently pursue the task of monitoring its channel activity and transferring data between its peripheral memories and the central memory, without respect to other processors. The central processor is designed to process computation-bound programs requiring floating point arithmetic. The peripheral processors are intended for small tasks involving heavy input/output operations. Thus, tasks such as program preparation and file editing are mostly performed on the peripheral processors (see Fig. 3.23).

On the other end of the spectrum, there are on-line systems whose functional components are mainly implemented in software. Physically, both the peripheral and central processing is supported by the same CPU. An example of these systems

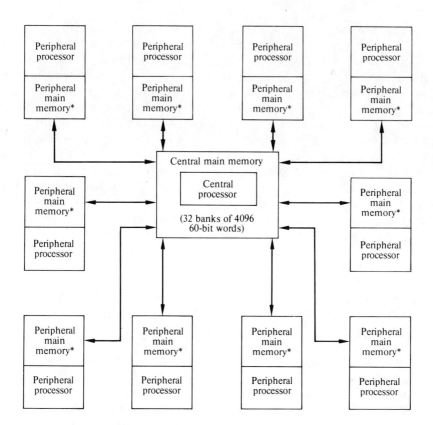

*Each peripheral main memory is composed
of 4096 12-bit words.

Fig. 3.23 The Control Data 6600 processors configuration.

is the IBM OS 360/370 with HASP [19]. Even in these systems there is a clear distinction between the role of the central processing system, such as OS 360/370, and the role of the peripheral processing system, such as HASP.

We shall concentrate our attention in the following section on the functional role of the peripheral processing system and the relation of the peripheral system to the central one.

3.3.2.3.1 JOB SPOOLING SYSTEMS

In Section 3.2.4.1 we discussed an improved method of handling job batches for off-line batch processing systems, known as off-line job I/O. In the discussion, the intermediate devices which facilitate the off-line job I/O are tapes. For on-line batch processing systems, there is also a need for improved job handling. As in the case of off-line job I/O, the need for an improved job handling is prompted by the following:

1. The desire to reduce device and channel interrupts and to increase device and channel throughput.

We learned in the chapter on I/O operations that each I/O operation is composed of a sequence of channel commands and device orders. The execution of an I/O operation by the I/O executor (a part of the IOCS) amounts to fetching the appropriate sequence of channel commands and device orders from the main memory and forwarding the commands to the channel and the orders to the device controller. The I/O instructions for these devices (terminals), such as read-a-card (print-a-line) can only cause the input (output) of one job card (line). To handle job batches, there must be frequent execution of these instructions. However, frequent executions of the I/O instructions create interrupts, such as read-completion signals. One way to reduce the number of interrupts is to "chain" the I/O instructions into longer sequences of channel commands and devices orders. Instead of reading one card (line) between interrupts, a series of cards (lines) can be read before an interrupt or pause occurs. Consequently, the card readers/punches and terminals can function at their top speed.

2. The desire to provide specialized blocking, deblocking, and buffer allocation facilities.

   Although the IOBS (a part of the IOCS) has general buffering facility, the need of specialized buffering capability for job I/O is warranted. Both terminals and unit-record devices are involved with fixed-length card and line images, so that buffer sizes can be fixed. Thus, there can be more efficient buffer management for job I/O. Furthermore, the number of terminals and devices is also known. Consequently, the number of needed buffers can be determined on the basis of the available main memory. Buffer switching and pooling can be readily accomplished since buffers are of the same size. Thus with specialized buffering management, the flow of job batches to and from unit-record devices and terminals can be maintained with fewer interrupts and pauses.

3. The desire to manage job priority and multiple entries of jobs.

   Although constituting a logical collection of user programs and data for processing, a job usually consists of many parts. It will be beneficial to the user if different portions of the job can be submitted to the on-line batch processing system at different terminals and devices. As long as appropriate job control cards and commands are included in the job concerning the mix of the job portions, the collection and preparation of the portions into a single job for processing should be possible. In the process of collection and preparation, the job priority externally assigned by the operator or the user can be accommodated by arranging the job processing queues.

4. The desire to preprocess and postprocess jobs.

   Since jobs have to be read in from terminals and devices before they are processed, preprocessing of jobs (or job cards) can be done easily. In preprocessing, certain jobs can be skipped or eliminated for subsequent processing due, for example, to over-size or high-time estimation. Output generated by the jobs can be suppressed via postprocessing for similar reasons. In preprocessing, data and programs stored in the file system and libraries can be fetched for the requesting job. In postprocessing, permanent output from the job can be stored in the file system and libraries directly without having to submit the output as another job.

In summary, the improved job handling is aimed to reduce interruptions to the central processing system, to increase the throughput of devices and channels dedicated to the peripheral processing system, to keep constant the flow of job batches from various dedicated devices and terminals to the peripheral processing system, and to perform preprocessing and postprocessing of job batches.

Let us now examine some of the algorithms and designs of a peripheral processing system utilizing disks as an intermediate storage, the Houston Automatic Spooling Priority system (HASP) [19].

Basically, HASP performs the following tasks:

1. Reads all user jobs (i.e., job cards or job statements) from all of the system's input terminals and unit-record devices.

2. Stores temporarily all the incoming jobs on intermediate high-volume disks.

3. Preprocesses jobs.

4. Communicates with the central processing system which will then process the preprocessed and stored jobs.

5. Accumulates all the output generated by the running jobs.

6. Postprocesses jobs.

HASP accomplishes the first task effectively by reducing channel and device interrupts and improving channel and device throughput by means of chaining I/O instructions, by providing specialized buffering facility, by managing job priority, and by allowing multiple entries of job batches.

To perform tasks (2) and (5) effectively, HASP must be able to manage efficiently the intermediate storage which consists of modules of disks. In order to take advantage of the parallelism in the disks' movable access arms (mechanisms), and to keep track of the disk space, HASP employs several tables and algorithms.

I. The Tables

A. Master cylinder map

There is only master cylinder map in HASP (see Fig. 3.24). Because the access time to any track within a cylinder remains the same, and access time to another cylinder from the present cylinder requires considerably more time, the smallest unit of disk storage to be considered for access efficiency is the cylinder.

The master cylinder map is a binary bit map with a one-to-one correspondence between the bits in the map and the cylinders in the disk modules. Initially, all bits are 1, indicating that all cylinders are available for allocation. As soon as a cylinder is allocated, the bit is set to 0.

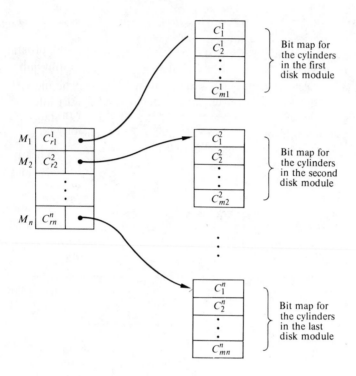

M_i For the ith disk module.

C_j^i The jth cylinder on the ith module.

C_{ri}^i The most recently referenced cylinder (i.e., the $r$ith
          cylinder) on the ith module.

1. If all disk modules are of the same type, then they all have the same number
   of cylinders. In this case, we have $m1 = m2 = \cdots = mn$. However, HASP can
   support different disk types.
2. The C_{ri}^i for each i is dynamically updated.

Fig. 3.24 The master cylinder map.

B. Job cylinder maps

For each job, HASP creates a pair of job cylinder maps—one for the job and its
input data, and the other for the job's output data. Essentially, the job cylinder maps
for a job are copies of the master cylinder map in which the allocated cylinders are
those cylinders for the job and its input and output data. Furthermore, the track
address of the last track used in a cylinder, which was noted in the job cylinder map,
is also recorded. With this track address, one can determine the next track to be
allocated for the job input or output. Since there are two cylinder maps, there are
two last track addresses.

C. Job control table

For each job, there is a job control table. The table contains accounting information about the job, data appearing on the job cards, pointers to the cylinder maps with their associated last track addresses, and some extra space. In other words, the job control table serves as a directory to the cylinder maps.

D. Job queue element

Each job is associated with a job queue element which includes the internal job identification, the external priority assignment of the job, the location of the control table, and the location of the address of the next element in the queue.

II. Storage (i.e., cylinder and track) Allocation Procedure

A. The storage allocation procedure is designed to efficiently utilize the dedicated disk modules. The efficiency is achieved by the following strategy.

1. Cylinders are allocated on the basis of the dynamic positions of the access arms (mechanisms). Thus, repositioning of access arms can be kept at a minimum.
2. Because access arms of the disk modules move independently of one another, simultaneous use of several modules for storage is possible. It is therefore possible to spread a single file over a number of cylinders on different modules.
3. Although the cylinder is the smallest unit for access consideration, tracks within a cylinder are carefully assigned. First, each track is organized as a multiple number of card images. Because card images are fixed in length and small in size, and all jobs are handled as job cards, there is very low fragmentation of track storage. Furthermore, all job cards of a job lie in consecutive tracks of a cylinder.

Two maps are consulted for storage allocation. If the allocation is for a storing input (output) job, then the master cylinder map and the input (output) job cylinder map are employed. An elaborate search algorithm is used to determine the available cylinder as reflected in the master cylinder map. We shall examine the algorithm more closely. Meanwhile, we depict the storage allocation in the following flow chart (Fig. 3.25).

III. Cylinder Searching Algorithm

A. The only table used by the cylinder-searching algorithm is the master cylinder map, as depicted in Fig. 3.24. There are three stages of search. The first, an *immediate search*, determines whether there is a more recently referenced cylinder on any module that is available. This determination is accomplished by examining the C_{ri}^i entries in the master cylinder map for every i. If there is an available cylinder, then, for some j, C_{rj}^j is associated with a 1 bit, indicating that the most recently referenced cylinder on the jth module is available for allocation. Since there are n modules, there are n most recently referenced cylinders. Thus, the immediate search requires a check of, at most, n entries of C_{ri}^i in the master cylinder map. This check is swift.

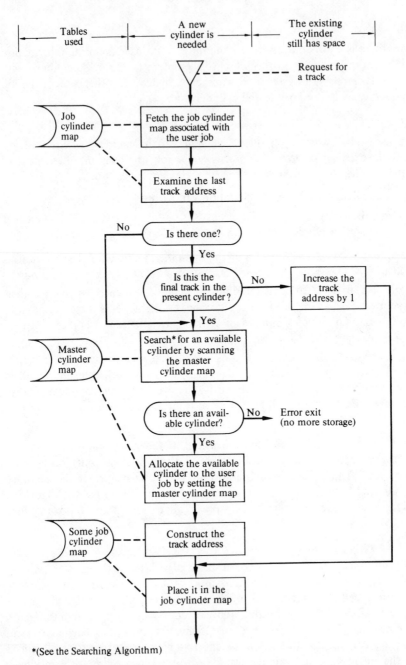

Tables used   A new cylinder is needed   The existing cylinder still has space

Request for a track

Job cylinder map

Fetch the job cylinder map associated with the user job

Examine the last track address

Is there one?   No

Yes

Is this the final track in the present cylinder?   No   Increase the track address by 1

Yes

Master cylinder map

Search* for an available cylinder by scanning the master cylinder map

Is there an available cylinder?   No   Error exit (no more storage)

Yes

Allocate the available cylinder to the user job by setting the master cylinder map

Some job cylinder map

Construct the track address

Place it in the job cylinder map

*(See the Searching Algorithm)

Fig. 3.25 The storage allocation procedure.

Furthermore, by using the most recently referenced cylinder for allocation, there is no need to reposition the disk's access arm. If there is no most recently referenced cylinder available for allocation, then the second stage, a *neighborhood search*, is entered. In the neighborhood search, the adjacent cylinders (eight on either side) of a most recently referenced cylinder are searched. Unless there is an available cylinder for allocation, the adjacent cylinders of every most recently referenced cylinder will be searched. In other words, for C_{ri}^i on module M_i, where $ri = k$, the search algorithm will check to see whether either

$$C_{k-1}^i \quad \text{or} \quad C_{k+1}^i$$

is available. If not,

$$C_{k-2}^i \quad \text{and} \quad C_{k+2}^i$$

will be checked, and so on. Unless either

$$C_{k-8}^i \quad \text{or} \quad C_{k+8}^i$$

is available, the search algorithm will repeat the checking on the $(i+1)$th module M_{i+1}.

The neighborhood search is based on the theory that the access time for a disk access arm to reach an adjacent cylinder is less than the access time of an arbitrary cylinder. When the neighborhood search fails, the third stage of the search begins. In this stage, an *exhaustive search* is conducted. The exhaustive search begins its examination of C_1^1, C_2^1, ..., and C_{m1}^1 for the first disk module M_1, then repeats the examination for the next disk module until an available cylinder, say C_j^i, is found. Otherwise, there is no cylinder available at all.

In general, the design of the algorithm enables the immediate search to be used frequently, the neighborhood search occasionally, and the exhaustive search rarely. The cylinder search algorithm is depicted in Fig. 3.26.

To perform tasks (3) and (6) (i.e., pre- and post-processing of jobs), HASP makes use of the job control tables and job queue elements. The job priority determines the queue formation. Obviously, jobs of the same priority have their queue elements linked together, and in high priority jobs their linked elements are queued ahead of low priority elements. The allowable processing time and output volumes are determined by the information in the user's account which can be referred to by means of the job control table. Thus preprocessing and postprocessing of jobs can be facilitated by HASP.

To perform task (4) (i.e., communicating with the central processing system), HASP replaces the IOCS of the central processing system to handle all I/O operations related to terminals and unit-record devices. Requests for these types of I/O from the running (user) program will be accepted by the IOCS. However, in this case the IOCS will not process the requests, but will relegate the requests to HASP. When the result of the requested I/O becomes available, HASP passes it to the IOCS for returning to the requesting program. The basic relation of HASP and OS 360/370 is depicted in Fig. 3.27.

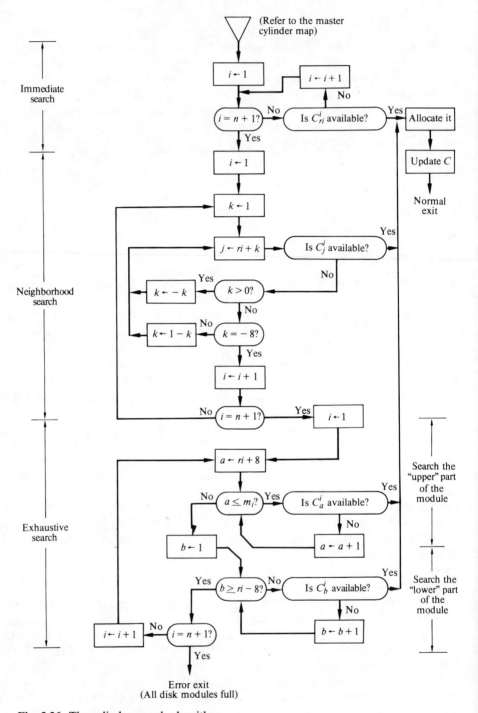

Fig. 3.26 The cylinder search algorithm.

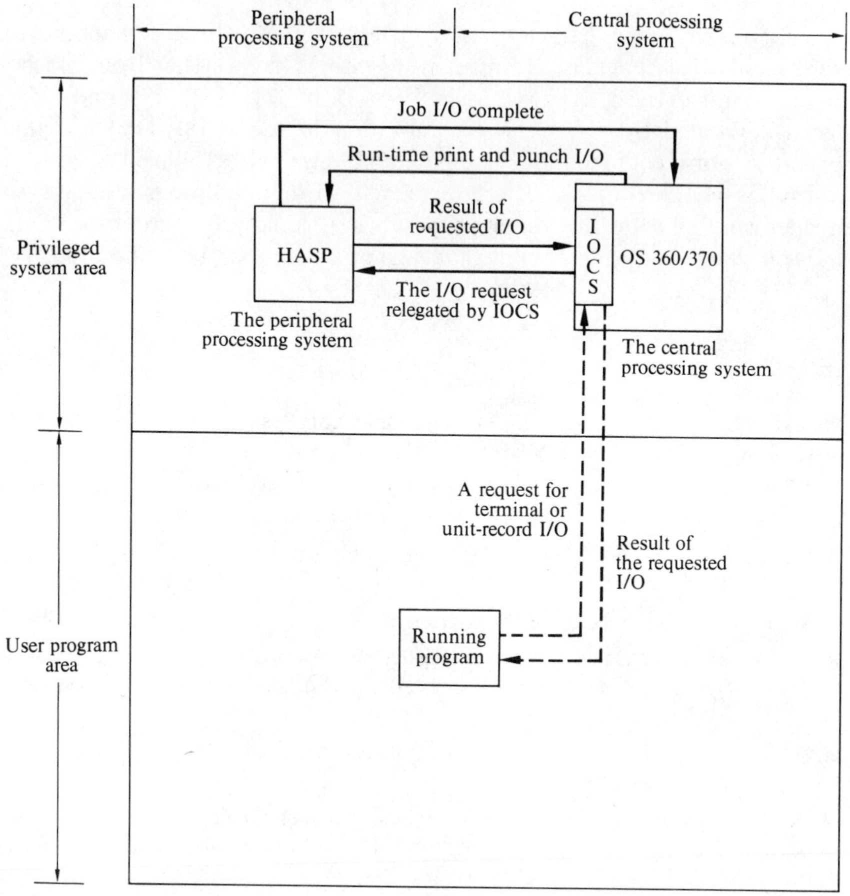

Fig. 3.27 Memory layout of the roles of the central and peripheral processing systems for HASP and OS 360/370.

In summary, we have discussed a peripheral processing system for job I/O in some detail. The specialized and sophisticated job I/O systems is prompted by the advent of on-line processing systems. Because they collect jobs and utilize intermediate storage, the job I/O systems are also termed *job spooling systems*.

3.4 POSTSCRIPT

For a survey of batch processing systems, the reader may refer to [17], and [18]. The off-line batch processing system is based on the general guidelines in [14] and the detailed notions in [5], [8], [9], [10], [11], [13], [16], and [24]. The view of the off-line batch processing system as a hierarchy of processors and subprocessors is mine. However, it is eloquently argued in [4]. On-line batch processing systems do not lend themselves easily for characterization and abstraction. This is perhaps inevitable, due to the author's intimate involvement in the on-line batch system from which most of the material is derived. The system is the work of [7], [15], [23], and [25], and has been advocated by [3]. The generalization of the HASP [19] for multiple peripheral systems configuration can be found in [12]. Coupled systems have generated considerable interest before the advent of the multiprogramming systems. The reader can find some interesting proposals in [2] and [20]. Problems related to the implementation of programming language processors can be found in [22].

REFERENCES

1. "An Introduction to the IBM 3790 Communication System," File No. 370-01, Form GA27-2767-0, First Edition, November 1973.

2. F. R. Baldwin, W. B. Gibson, and C. B. Poland. "A Multiprocessing Approach to a Large Computer System." *IBM Systems Journal* 1 (September 1962): 64.

3. J. W. Carr and N. S. Prywes. "Satellite Computers as Interpreters." *Electronics*, November 1965, pp. 87–89.

4. E. W. Dijkstra. "The Humble Programmer." *Comm. ACM* **15**, 10 (1972): 859–866.

5. R. T. Dorrance. "Design of an Integrated Programming and Operating System— Part IV: The System's COBOL Compiler." *IBM Systems Journal* 2 (September– December 1963): 322–327.

6. H. H. Goldstine. *The Computer from Pascal to von Neumann.* Princeton, N.J.: Princeton University Press, 1970.

7. D. K. Hsiao. "A File System for a Problem Solving Facility." The Moore School Report No. 68-33 (May 1968), The Moore School of Electrical Engineering, University of Pennsylvania. Also NTIS AD 671 826.

8. "IBM 7040/7044 Operating System (16/32K)—Programmer's Guide." File No. 7040-36, Form C28-6318-7, Eighth Edition, 1966.

9. "IBM 7040-7044 Operating System (16-32K)—Systems Programmer's Guide." File No. 7040-36, Form C28-6339-4, Major Revision, October 1965.

10. "IBM System/360 Basic Operating System—Programmer's Guide." File No. S360-20, Form C24-3372-6, Seventh Edition, September 1967.

11. "IBM System/360 Basic Operating System—System Control Program Logic Manual." Form Y24-5002-0, First Edition, December 1965.

12. "IBM System/360/370 Attached Support Processor System (ASP)." Version 2, System Programmer's Manual, Form GH20-0323-8, Ninth Edition, March 1971.

13. R. Larner. "Design of an Integrated Programming and Operating System—Part IV: The System's FORTRAN Compiler." *IBM Systems Journal* 2 (September–December 1963): 311–321.

14. G. H. Mealy. "Operating Systems." Rand Report No. P-2584, The Rand Corp., Santa Monica, California, May 1962, NTIS AD 603146. Excerpts appeared in *Programming Systems and Languages*, S. Rosen (Editor), New York: McGraw-Hill, 1967.

15. R. P. Morton. "On-Line Computing with a Hierarchy of Processors." Moore School Report No. 69-13, The Moore School of Electrical Engineering, University of Pennsylvania, December 1968.

16. A. S. Noble. "Design of an Integrated Programming and Operating System—Part I: System Considerations and the Monitor." *IBM Systems Journal* 2 (June 1963): 153–161.

17. Saul Rosen. *Programming Systems and Languages.* New York: McGraw-Hill, 1967, pp. 4–23.

18. Robert F. Rosin. "Supervisory and Monitor Systems." *Computer Surveys* 1, 1 (March 1969).

19. T. H. Simpson, R. P. Crabtree, and R. Ray. *HASP-II/Houston Automatic Spooling Priority System With Remote Job Entry.* Program Order No. 360D-05.1.014, IBM, September 1968.

20. E. C. Smith, Jr. "A Directly Coupled Multiprocessing System." *IBM Systems Journal* 2 (September–December 1963).

21. J. E. Thornton. "Parallel Operation in the Control Data 6600." *AFIPS Proc. FJCC* 2, 26 (1964): 33–40.

22. Peter Wegner (Editor). *Introduction to System Programming.* London and New York: Academic Press, 1964.

23. R. L. Wexelblat and H. A. Freedman. "The MULTILANG On-line Programming System." *Proc. AFIPS 1967 SJCC* 30: 559–569.

24. B. White and J. Trimble. "Design of an Integrated Programming and Operating System —Part VI: Implementation on the 7040/44 Data Processing System." *IBM Systems Journal* 3, 1 (1964): 79–94.

25. M. S. Wolfberg. "Control, I/O, and Editing Functions in the Problem Solving Facility." The Moore School Report No. 65-31, The Moore School of Electrical Engineering, University of Pennsylvania (June 1965).

EXERCISES

1. In view of the hierarchical structure proposed in Section 3.2, design an off-line batch processing system generator which can produce tailor-made off-line batch processing systems on the basis of the specific processing need at an installation. We may assume that the generator is provided with a large collection of well-defined processing functions such as language translator subsystems. We must show nevertheless how various functions are being put together by the generator.

2. Elaborate on the differences between on-line programming capability and on-line job I/O capability in terms of software functional requirements and hardware component and device support. Show that it is possible to have systems with one capability and without the other. Give examples.

3. Describe a real-world system both with on-line programming and on-line job I/O capabilities.

4. Assume the main memory of an on-line system is divided into three partitions. The first partition is dedicated for high-priority (I/O bound) jobs, called *foreground jobs*, involving

on-line programming. The second partition is reserved for medium-priority (I/O bound) jobs, *background-one jobs*, which are entered via remote entry terminals and may require overlay. The last partition is kept for low-priority jobs, *background-two jobs*, which are mostly computation-bound.

Represent the running and scheduling of jobs in the on-line system by state-transition diagrams. As an aid, the states, the factors which trigger the transitions and the outline of a diagram, are included herewith.

A job can be considered in one of the three following states:

Running
Blocked
Ready

a) Draw a state transition diagram for each type of job (i.e., foreground, background-one, and background-two jobs) in terms of the aforementioned three states, and indicate by way of examples the factors which cause the transitions.

b) Complete the transition diagram depicted in Fig. 3.28 with the states (s_i) and factors (f_j) listed below.

s_1 Ready list of high-priority (I/O bound) jobs
s_2 Ready list of medium-priority (I/O bound) jobs
s_3 Ready list of low-priority (CPU-bound) jobs
s_4 Blocked jobs for terminal I/O
s_5 Blocked jobs for overlaying I/O and remote job entry I/O
s_6 Blocked jobs for disk or tape I/O
s_7 Running
f_1 Request a dependent section (for overlaying)
f_2 Request terminal I/O
f_3 Request disk or tape I/O
f_4 Overlaying I/O completed
f_5 Terminal I/O completed
f_6 Disk or tape I/O completed
f_7 Exceeded time limit (as indicated in user's job control card or determined by the system)
f_8 Run for specific time period

5. List the factors which trigger the transitions, develop a state-transition diagram for the satellite computer operating system proposed in Section 3.3.1.2, develop also a state-transition diagram for the interrupt handler of the central computer operating system as outlined in Section 3.3.1.3.1, and then combine these two state-transition diagrams to reflect the interface between the satellite and central systems.

6. Read and comment on some of the historical papers on operating systems included in Part 5 of Rosen's book [17].

7. Read and comment on Goldstine's book on the computer [6].

8. Explain the following design decisions made for the cylinder search algorithm in HASP.

a) In the neighborhood search, only eight adjacent cylinders (on either side) of a most recently referenced cylinder are searched. Why eight?

b) Instead of searching all of the nearest neighboring cylinders (on either side) of most recently referenced cylinders of all the modules involved and then the next nearest

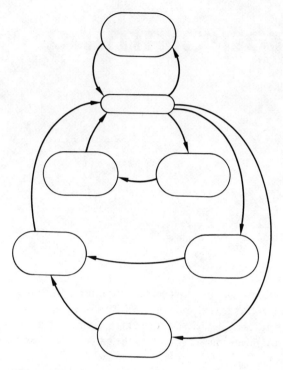

Figure 3.28

ones, the neighborhood search algorithm, before checking any cylinders of the next module, checks all of the eight cylinders (on either side) of a most recently referenced cylinder of the current module. Why is the search designed to work on one module at a time instead of all modules as a whole?

4
Multiprogramming

4.1 REMARKS

In studying multiprogramming systems, we first concentrate our efforts on examining those systems which employ conventional real memory. Not only do their system architectures resemble the architectures of the batch processing systems, but also their program organization and linkage convention are similar to the batch processing ones. We shall point out the similarities.

On the other hand, the more powerful multiprogramming systems are structured on the basis of the notion of tasks. The necessity of synchronization of running tasks and interlocking of tasks on common resources leads to the study of semaphores and p and v operations. The semaphores can be associated with resources which are to be shared among tasks; the operations can post, defer, and invoke the progress of the tasks.

A new phenomenon, known as system deadlock, may occur when resources are scarce and tasks are unyielding. To this end, we attempt to derive the conditions which define the system deadlock. Furthermore, we propose algorithms which can prevent and detect the system deadlocks, and provide system recovery from deadlocks.

4.2 WHY MULTIPROGRAMMING?

As we recall, the use of off-line job I/O and coupled systems is aimed to increase the utilization of the CPU's of the batch processing systems and to reduce the job turnaround time (i.e., the elapsed time between the submission and return of a job) for the users. Because of the slowness of the system and the predominance of off-line computation-bound programs of small and medium size, it is possible to achieve some success in using the above techniques for utilizing the CPU's computation capability and speeding up the job turnaround time.

With the recent advances in hardware and changes in user's programming demands, the above techniques become quite inadequate. The internal processing speed* of the CPU has been improved greatly; and the user's demands for direct access to the computer system and fast job turnaround time have prompted the development of on-line programming and the consideration of job scheduling.

In order to access the computer system directly, terminals are needed. Furthermore, storage devices such as disks are required for storing resident data and programs which are subject to on-line storage and retrieval by the users.

For accommodating fast turnaround of off-line jobs in various sizes and better response time to the users of on-line jobs, each job is given a unit of processing time, i.e., the *time slice*; the job processing is based on a turn-taking procedure (see Fig. 4.1). When a job exhausts its time slice or must wait for the completion of an I/O operation, the job is deactivated (i.e., placed in a wait state) and another job, either new or already partially processed, is activated for processing. In this way no single job can dominate the system, and the CPU's waiting time for the I/O completion in one job can be used to compute another job. Furthermore, by keeping several jobs ready in the system, better CPU performance can be obtained, thus improving job turnaround and response. However, to be constantly ready to serve a job and to reduce the job turnaround time, input to the job and output from the job require additional management. A stack of the job's input for the card reader and a backlog of the job's output for the card punch and printer should be created on a faster I/O device, say the disk, so that the running of the current job will not be held up excessively by the slowness of the job I/O (see Section 3.3.2.3.1 on Job Spooling Systems in Chapter 3).

Furthermore, to make the main memory storage occupied by the deactivated job available to the active ones, the job may have to be transferred to a secondary storage device for later activation.

---

*   The internal processing speed of a CPU is determined by the speed with which the CPU can interpret and execute the machine instructions. To interpret a machine instruction, the instruction must be fetched from the main memory since conventional computers are mainly of von Neumann stored program type. In order to fetch the right instruction, the main memory address of the instruction must be maintained (in the program counter, PC) and be given to the memory controller (via memory address register, MAR). When it is fetched (via the memory buffer register, MBR), the instruction in the original main memory address must remain intact and the copy of the instruction must be saved in a temporary working register. The time required to fetch an instruction from the main memory and to place it in a working register is termed a *memory cycle*. The identification of the operation type and verification of the operands of the instruction then follow. Because operands may refer to information in the main memory, additional fetches may be necessary. Thus, the interpretation of an instruction by the CPU may result in more than one memory cycle. In this case, several working registers will be used.

When the operation type is properly identified and its operands are successively verified, the execution phase of the instruction takes place. During the execution, the working registers involved will be used. Furthermore, the result of the operation may have to be stored in the main memory, causing another memory access. Thus, the time required to carry out the execution is determined by the performance of the hardware circuit for the operation, the access time of the registers, and additional memory cycles.

From the preceding discussion, we learn that the internal processing speed of a CPU is effected by the frequency of main memory access, the main memory cycle time, the performance of hardware circuits for the operations, and the access time of the registers. To

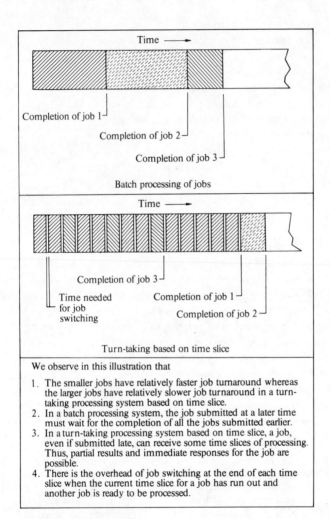

Fig. 4.1 Job processing.

improve the internal processing speed of the CPU, one must therefore reduce the frequency of main memory access, shorten the memory cycle, upgrade the circuit performance, and speed up the register access. There are several technology advances which facilitate the improvement.

1. Main memory technology. The present technology can reduce the cycle time of magnetic core to 0.5 μsec at a cost of 0.5¢/bit. Although slightly shorter cycle time at a higher cost can be achieved, the majority of the core memory has a cycle time ranging from 0.75 to 2.0 μsec at a cost under 0.5¢/bit.

The core memories may be gradually replaced by all semiconductor or semiconductor/ bipolar hybrid main memory at a cost approaching 0.25¢/bit.

The number of bits that can be fetched in a cycle is determined by the width of *data path* (i.e., the number of bits that can be transmitted in parallel) and the multiplicity of *memory interleaving* (i.e., the number of simultaneous access to different modules of the main memory without interference). Obviously, wide data path requires more data buses and high multi-

We note that all these requirements result in heavy I/O activities. The situation is made more acute by the fact that the improvement of I/O devices has not been on a par with the improvement of the CPU. In disks, for example, improvements in transfer rate, access time, and rotational delay have been only in the order of 1.5 to 2 (as noted in the following table), whereas the improvement of the internal processing speed of the CPU has been in the order of 5 to 10 as reviewed in the footnote.

The disparity of the hardware improvement in terms of the CPU's internal processing speed and the I/O device's transfer and access time, and the user's demand for faster job turnaround and direct access, prompt the introduction of multiprogramming. By *multiprogramming* we mean the technique by which more than one program

---

plicity of interleaving demands modular memory organization, both of which will result in additional cost. Nevertheless, these are effective means to cut the memory cycle time and reduce the frequency of memory access. For example, if the width of the data path is 64 bits and the cycle time is 0.75 μsec, then in one memory cycle sixty-four bits can be fetched. Because of the wide data path, more information can be fetched for interpretation and execution. Consequently, there is less frequency access to memory. In addition, if the multiplicity of memory interleaving is 2, an effective cycle of 0.40 μsec is possible.

2. High-speed memory technology. The traditional use of high-speed registers has given way to either addressable scratch-pad memory, such as the one used in UNIVAC 1108, or nonaddressable cache memory, such as the one used in IBM 370/165. These memories, largely of bipolar configuration, are characterized by memory cycles ranging from 54 to 115 nanoseconds, capacities from 8K to 32K bytes, and cost from 3¢ to 6¢ per bit. For a higher cost, a memory cycle of 15 nanoseconds is attainable. Because nonaddressable high-speed memory is transparent to a program, the program does not have to keep track of the addresses of the information presently being moved into the high-speed memory for faster interpretation and execution. Consequently, the use of cache memory is gradually replacing the use of addressable scratch-pad memory. Information is moved in "chunks" from the main memory to the high-speed memory for interpretation and execution by the CPU; thus the cycle time of the high-speed memory plays an important role. Furthermore, if the program references are localized (i.e., confined in the same chunk), and program instructions involve few store-into-main-memory operations, then the performance obtained will be dominated by the high speed, nanosecond, memory, rather than by the slower speed, microsecond, memory. For example, with a 16K-byte cache memory of 80 nanosecond cycle time and over-half-a-million byte main memory of one microsecond cycle time, experimental study shows that a performance approximately equivalent to 80% of that obtainable with a single memory of 80 nanosecond cycle. Thus, the use of cache memory yields an effect that the large main memory appears to be operating in the cycle time of the small cache memory.

3. Circuit technology. Circuit technology has been advanced noticeably from discrete devices to integrated circuits (IC). The propagation delays of the popular IC's, such as emitter-coupled logic (ECL) and transistor-transistor logic (TTL), have been improved from 20 nanoseconds a few years ago to subnanoseconds. Meanwhile, with the aid of computerized design and testing, the packaged logic (LSI) can have 50 to 1000 gates per chip. For example, the IBM 370/145 utilizes packaged logic chips with the following characteristics on each chip: 174 complete circuits consisting of 128 storage cells and 46 supporting circuits including decoding, drive and sense functions, and output signal amplification.

4. Microcode technology. Machine instructions have been realized internally as compositions of series of microcodes. The execution speed of the machine instruction can be improved if there is a high parallelism among the operations of its microcodes. Furthermore, the functional ability of the machine instruction can be increased if the repertoire of microcode is rich.

Year	Disk	Transfer rate (character or byte per second)	Access time (msec) min/average/max	Average rotational delay (msec)
50's	IBM 1301	90K	50/120/180	17
	IBM 1302	180K	50/120/180	17
60's	IBM 2311	156K	25/75/135	12.5
	IBM 2314	312K	25/60/135	12.5
70's	IBM 3330	806K	10/30/50	8.3

resides in the main memory and one program can be activated or resumed for execution before the execution of the currently running program is completed. In this way, several programs can be run concurrently in the computer system to utilize more fully the computing resources. Such resources are, for example, the CPU, main memory, and peripheral devices. By running several programs in the system, it is hoped that the following will result:

1. In processing a program's I/O requests, the CPU's waiting time for the completion of the I/O operations can be significantly reduced by executing another program. Thus, the CPU can be utilized more effectively when several jobs are multiprogrammed by the system. In addition, the job spooling system, for example, can be run as a "perpetual" job of the system.

2. The turn-taking procedure based on certain time slice (see Fig. 4.1) can be employed (a) to ensure better turnaround time. This is especially useful in an on-line programming environment where the turnaround time—more specifically, the *response time* (i.e., the elapsed time between the demand of output and the arrival of the output)—becomes critical, and (b) to create a more balanced utilization of the system resources, e.g., keeping both the CPU and peripheral devices busy.

4.3 LOAD-TIME RELOCATIVE MULTIPROGRAMMING SYSTEMS

Although the definition of multiprogramming is a simple one, the implementation of a multiprogramming system includes many variations. There seem to be two schools of thought concerning the implementation of multiprogramming systems— those who believe that multiprogramming systems may be implemented in computer systems where program relocation is done at load time, and those who believe that multiprogramming systems may be implemented in computer systems where program relocation is done at execution time. The former has the advantage of using more conventional computer systems and employing some experience and approaches which have proven useful in designing batch processing systems. The latter requires unusual hardware known as *memory translation*, and special memory organization, management, and program linkages.

In this chapter, we shall concentrate on load-time relocative multiprogramming systems. The discussion of run-time relocative multiprogramming systems using virtual memory will be dealt with in the next chapter.

4.3.1 MULTIPROGRAMMING JOBS ONLY

The simplest multiprogramming operating system is the one in which more than one job can be run concurrently while programs within a job must be processed sequentially one at a time. In other words, programs within a job cannot be multiprogrammed. When a program of one job is deactivated due to running out of its time-slice or due to waiting for the completion of an I/O operation, a program of another job is activated for processing. Meanwhile the deactivated program may be left in the main memory or transferred to a secondary device for later activation.

These systems are relatively simple in design and in operation because they involve no multiprogramming among programs of a given job. Many of their design considerations are derived from those of batch processing systems with some modifications and extensions. An example is the IBM 360 Tape/Disk Operating System (TOS/DOS).

4.3.1.1 The Organization of Input/Output Control Blocks and IOCS

The organization of IOCS and its control blocks within the IBM 360 TOS/DOS resembles very much the one described in the chapter on Input/Output Operations and IOCS. We will try to show their similarities and differences. However, the reader should be aware that although the organization of these two systems in terms of I/O may be similar, their terminologies are not.

To allow symbolic reference to input/output devices, unit control blocks were created for the devices as we have learned from earlier discussion. A unit control block contains information which keeps track of the progress of the individual I/O operation on a symbolic unit. Furthermore, for each I/O device there is associated a device control block which contains all the information about the I/O devices' characteristics and current status. Because the IBM 360 TOS/DOS is designed for a computer configuration with small memory (6-24K) allocated to the resident supervisor, the control blocks are simplified to conserve storage, thereby eliminating some of the flexibility in unit and device assignment. By placing the information concerning the device type and the channel used by a symbolic unit (referred to as item U1 in Chapter 2) in the unit control block, the operating system can dynamically assign an available physical device of like type on the same channel to the unit. In IBM 360 TOS/DOS, unit-device assignment is done by the operator or by explicit specification of user's job control statement, but not by the operating system. It is assumed that the operator knows the nature of the symbolic units and available devices so that they will be assigned to each other properly. Thus this information (i.e., item U1) is now absent from the unit control blocks. Information (known as item U2 in Chapter 2) concerning the I/O operation currently requested for the unit in the IBM 360 TOS/DOS is facilitated by a pointer to a queue, known as the *I/O Request Queue* or *Channel Queue*. The use of the queue is prompted by the fact that in a multiprogramming environment there may be several requests for the same unit. Information (known as items U3 and U4) concerning the format and execution of channel commands and device orders is now placed alongside the request entry in the I/O request queue. This is logical since different requests for the same unit may involve different I/O operations which result in different channel commands and device orders. For recovery due to I/O errors, the addresses (item U5) of the error recovery routines must be kept. Because IBM 360 TOS/DOS provides a standard tape I/O recovery routine and does not provide the user with the option to use his own recovery routines, there is no need to keep track of the addresses of various recovery routines. Thus, there is simply a pointer to an entry of a table, known as *Tape Error Block* (TEB) containing the statistics of the recovery operation in the unit control block.

Information (items U6 and U7) concerning the partition of a directly accessible device is kept in a separate table, known as *Job Information Block* (JIB). To relate a unit control block to the symbolic name assigned to the unit, a pointer to the symbolic unit name table is needed. This pointer (item U8) is placed alongside the entries in the I/O request queue. In IBM 360 TOS/DOS, the symbolic unit name table is called *Logical Unit Block* (LUB).

In summary, the unit control information for a unit which has not otherwise been included in JIB, TEB and I/O Request Queue is collected in a block for the unit known as *Physical Unit Block* (PUB). Much of the information in the device control block, as listed in Chapter 2, is incorporated into the PUB and TEB. More specifically, the flags (known as D1 in Chapter 2) which tell whether or not the device is busy, whether or not the channel to which the device is attached is busy, and whether or not the device has been requested for use are included in PUB. (Items D2, D3, D4, D5, and D8 have the same meaning as U2, U3, U4, U5, and U8, respectively. They have been incorporated into TEB along with D6.) For scheduling devices, the devices attached to the same channel are grouped together by means of pointers (D7). This is done in IBM 360 TOS/DOS by arranging the entires of PUB in the order of their channel numbers. Since each entry of PUB corresponds to a device, devices attached to the same channel are thus grouped together by the same channel number.

From the above discussion, we learn that in IBM 360 TOS/DOS the only unit control information which has not been combined with the device control information is included in the JIB. Basically, therefore, the JIB represents the simplified unit control block and PUB represents the device control block.

The Logical Unit Block (LUB) is in essence the symbolic unit name table as defined in Chapter 2. By definition, each entry of the block can associate a symbolic unit name with its unit and device control blocks. Since unit and device control blocks are now incorporated in JIB and PUB, there are pointers to these blocks in an entry of the LUB. The symbolic name of the unit is implicitly defined by the position of the entry in the LUB. For example, the first entry corresponds to SYSRES, second SYSRDR, etc. (See Fig. 4.2.)

The organization of the Input/Output control system in IBM 360 TOS/DOS is similar to the one described in Chapter 2. However, there is no buffer allocation algorithm employed in the linking loader. Consequently, the capability of allocating

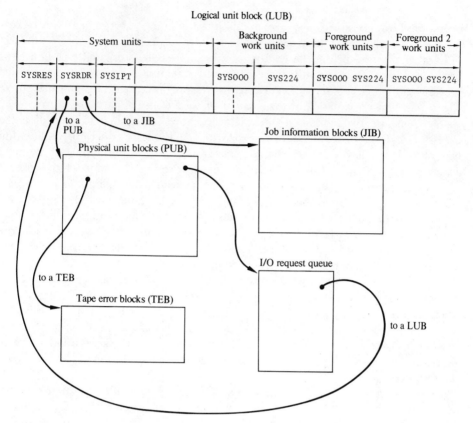

Fig. 4.2 The I/O control blocks.

the extra main memory (after the loading of a user program) as additional buffers to I/O operations is not there.

Because input/output requests are queued, the channel scheduler of the I/O operation executor will schedule the I/O operations in the queue for execution.

Entries in the queue are linked by channel so that it is possible to utilize a given channel by performing I/O operations on that channel in close succession. In a round robin procedure, the entry at the beginning of the queue receives execution first, unless the device is busy. If a channel is busy, then all entries associated with the channel are skipped and the first entry associated with another channel is scheduled.

4.3.1.2 Considerations of File Integrity and I/O Deadlock

We recall that in Chapter 2 it was stated that direct access devices, such as disks, may be partitioned into several units, each of which may have a symbolic unit name. By referring to the symbolic unit name, the user's I/O request can cause the access mechanism of the device to be positioned at the partition assigned to the unit. Subsequent read/write operations on the partition can then be performed by the I/O operation executor. However, in a multiprogramming environment, the access mechanism of the device may be moved to a different position upon the I/O request of another user job before the read/write operations on the original partition have been carried out. Consequently, there is the need of reinitiating the I/O request for the previous job; otherwise, the subsequent read/write operations will be performed on the wrong partition—a violation of the *integrity of the files* in the partition.

To reinitiate the request, additional access time is required to reposition the access mechanism for the subsequent read/write operations. Furthermore, a situation may occur that a new I/O request could cause an immediate positioning of the same access mechanism to a different partition just before the execution of the present read/write operations. In order to carry out the read/write operations, the access mechanism must be repositioned again. In other words, these two I/O requests have prevented both of the requested read/write operations from being carried out. A hopeless situation may result in a perpetual access contention without any read/write operation being performed. Such a situation is said to have created an *I/O deadlock*. The problem of file integrity and I/O deadlock will be reexamined in the context of resource sharing and system deadlock in Section 4.5. Here, we begin to note the appearance of the problem. Furthermore, we note that the problem of integrity and deadlock is due mainly to the advent of the multiprogramming. It is in the multiprogramming environment that several I/O requests may appear simultaneously. Because I/O devices and channels are shared, contention for access and usage of shared resources may result in a violation of integrity and creation of deadlock over the resources.

To protect the integrity of the user's information, the I/O operation executor *always* executes a CYLINDER SEEK operation (consisting of channel commands and device orders) upon *first* receiving a user's I/O request. The CYLINDER SEEK operation enables the access mechanism to be positioned at the proper cylinder for the unit requested by the user's program. Furthermore, no user is allowed to issue physical I/O instructions involving the CYLINDER SEEK operation. In other words, the I/O operation executor will examine the channel command program (words) and invalidate all the commands which may cause a CYLINDER SEEK operation.

To minimize the repositioning of the access mechanism and avoid deadlock due to multiple I/O requests, one approach is to "lock" the access mechanism to its position. The I/O operation executor accomplishes it by chaining all the channel commands and device orders for a given I/O request so that the read or write operations after the seek operation cannot be interrupted before their completion. In this way the access mechanism cannot be repositioned until the current I/O request is completely honored.

4.3.1.3 The Hierarchical Structure of the Operating System

Referring to Fig. 3.3, we note that the batch processing operating system's hierarchical organization may be generalized and applied to the design of multiprogramming systems with the capability of multiprogramming jobs only. In general, there may be several supervisors, each of which supervises a collection of jobs and oversees the transition from one job to another job of the collection. Consequently, in the generalized organization the number of jobs that can be multiprogrammed is equal to the number of job supervisors incorporated in the operating system. Furthermore, jobs under the supervision of the same supervisor cannot be multiprogrammed, because the organization under the supervisor is basically a batch processing one. (See Fig. 4.3.)

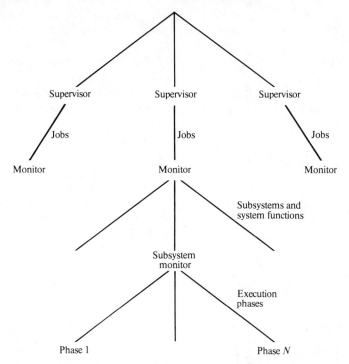

Fig. 4.3 The hierarchical organization of a multiprogramming operating system.

The organization of the IBM 360 TOS/DOS resembles the one outlined above. Due to the meager computer configuration, there is considerable simplification. At the system generation time, an IBM 360 TOS/DOS can partition the main memory into four areas. As in the batch processing system, the system area consists of resident control programs and nucleus. The other three areas are for users' programs. They are named *Background Program Area*, *Foreground-One Program Area* and *Foreground-Two Program Area*. The nonresident control programs are loaded dynamically either in the system area or users' program areas, depending on the nature of control. Because there are three program areas, the IBM 360 DOS/TOS creates three job supervisors—one for each area. As each job supervisor can bring in its jobs for processing, the operating system has the capability of multiprogramming three jobs. The scheduling of jobs for multiprogramming is of course performed by the job scheduler of the resident control programs. When the program of a job is waiting for the completion of an I/O operation, or runs out of its allocated time, the job scheduler selects the program of another job, based on the following priority criteria, and passes control to that program. The priority of a job is determined by the area in which the job resides. The Background Program Area has the lowest priority and the Foreground-One has the highest priority. With this fixed priority, it is possible for a job in Foreground-One Program Area to dominate the use of the CPU. For this reason, the operator must carefully select jobs for running in the Foreground-One and Two Program Areas. In general, these jobs are heavily I/O-bound and are constrained by real-time considerations.

The supervisor in each program area is basically a batch job-processing supervisor, as described earlier in Chapter 3. The main differences are that (1) the control programs which constitute the supervisor are largely nonresident and are loaded in respective program areas of execution; and (2) the region for intersubsystem and inter-execution-phase communications (as described in Chapter 3) is also located in the program area. There is one communication region for each supervisor.

In addition, there are differences between the supervisor for the Background Program Area and supervisors for the Foreground Program Areas. The latter cannot host any programming language subsystem. To have their programs compiled or assembled, the users are compelled to run these programs as background jobs. The reasons for sacrificing foreground compilation and assembly capabilities in designing

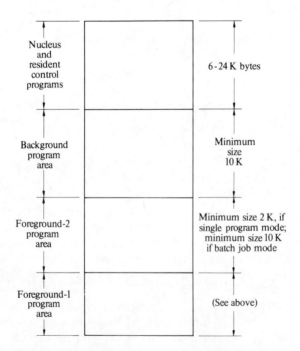

Fig. 4.4 IBM 360 TOS/DOS main memory layout.

the supervisors are the following:

1. Device limitation. Because compilers and assemblers in their compilation or assembly process use tape or disk units as working space for intermediate steps, there may not be enough peripherals for such undertakings simultaneously in more than one partition. (Keeping in mind that in IBM 360 Model 30 to 50 series, the cost or peripherals in terms of disk and tape units may overshadow the cost of the CPU.)

2. Main memory limitation. The main memory allocated to the resident control program is about 6 to 16K bytes. With this much storage, it is not possible to develop a sophisticated I/O control system (IOCS) so that I/O device allocation can be done dynamically by the IOCS instead of by the operator or through the explicit specification of the user. A more advanced multiprogramming operating system of similar organization with automated I/O device allocation capability would require a main memory storage of at least 32K bytes. An example is the IBM 360 multiprogramming with fixed number of tasks (MFT) operating system. (See references.)

4.3.1.4 Summary

We note that design considerations of the IBM 360 TOS/DOS are mostly derived from advanced batch processing systems. Thus it is not surprising that its multiprogramming capability is limited to jobs only. Job selection and I/O request scheduling which are required in a multiprogramming environment are incorporated in the system. Automatic I/O device allocation by the operating system, as found in many batch processing systems, is not available here. Thus, the bulk of the IOCS is reduced to a minimum. Because it is expected to run in a device-limited environment, the operating system does not provide capabilities for compiling and assembling foreground programs.

4.3.2 MULTIPROGRAMMING BOTH JOBS AND PROGRAMS WITHIN A JOB

There is a subtle difference between multiprogramming jobs only, and multiprogramming programs within a job as well as jobs. The more elaborate system capability of the latter allows not only the jobs to compete for system resources, but also the programs within a job to compete with each other for the same resources.

With the program as the smallest unit for multiprogramming instead of the job, there is greater and more acute competition for system resources. This is especially useful in a system environment where the system resources are not very restricted.

Since a job is defined by its job control language statements, the operating system can easily identify the job for multiprogramming. However, to identify a program for multiprogramming, there is the need of additional information for the operating system. Whenever a subroutine is called dynamically by a program, the program must inform the operating system whether or not the subroutine is to be multiprogrammed with the calling program. Although this information may be provided in the job control statements in the preparation of the program, it is difficult to provide the information about the routines which may, in turn, be called by the subroutine.

For this reason, additional means are provided for the user's program to communicate with the operating system about the running of these routines, either in a multiprogramming mode or batch mode with the calling programs.

This enables the user's program (1) to call a subroutine dynamically from secondary storage for loading and execution; (2) to inform the operating system whether or not the subroutine being called is to be multiprogrammed with the calling program; and (3) to synchronize the running of the rest of the program and the subroutine if the subroutine is to be multiprogrammed with the calling program.

To accommodate the dynamically called subroutines and data, the operating system must provide means for the main storage allocation—a necessary condition which is forever imposed on the systems utilizing conventional (real) main memory. With this feature, the user's program can request additional main storage for its subroutines and data. When the main storage becomes scarce, the operating system can return the user's request for main storage with the following:

1. An indication of no-space-available is given, causing the abortion of the loading and execution of the user's subroutine.

2. An effort is made by the operating system to transfer (i.e., swap out) another multiprogrammed program whose program priority is lower to a secondary device for later execution. The space thus emptied is given to the one which requested the space.

A system with (2) is one with *swapping* capability. A working multiprogramming system with swapping capability as an option is the IBM 360 MVT system—multiprogramming with variable tasks system.

4.3.2.1 The Organization of the Operating System in Terms of Tasks and Subtasks

To distinguish those programs running in the batch mode from those running in the multiprogramming mode, the concept of a *task* is introduced. Tasks are meant to be multiprogrammed. On the other hand, programs requiring batched processing are always meant to be processed serially. To accommodate serial processing of programs in systems with multiprogramming capability, the notion of a *job step* is included. Job steps of a job are therefore meant to be serially (i.e., batched) processed. In general, a job is composed of one or more job steps and each job step consists of one or more tasks. Although tasks within a job step can compete for system resource concurrently, the job steps for a given job must utilize system resource in a serial manner. Nevertheless, job steps of different jobs can compete for the same system resource concurrently. Consequently, the tasks of different jobs (but not of different job steps of the same jobs) can compete for the same system resource concurrently.

The macroinstruction which enables a program to be called and multiprogrammed with the calling program is called the *attach macro*. The calling program is said to be a *(main) task* and the called program its *subtask*. In other words, a subtask is attached to a (main) task upon the issuance of an attach macro by the (main) task.

With the availability of the attach macro, subtasks can be created very easily. In fact, the entire MVT operating system can be viewed as an organization of subtasks. At the top of the organization, there is the built-in *main system task*, which is not a subtask of any task. Logically, the main system task is composed of the console operator, the console commands, and the programs which can process the commands, issue the attach macro, and create proper subtasks as directed by the operator through his commands. Among the various types of subtasks created by the main system task are the *reading subtasks* which read user's input job stream from input devices, the *initiating subtasks* each of which supervises the processing of a job, and the *writing subtasks* which write job output to output devices. A user's job may consist of at least one task which is, of course, the subtask of the initiating subtask, which, in turn, is a subtask of the main system task. The number of reading, initiating, and writing subtasks to be attached to the main system task is a matter to be decided by the operator. In other words, the MVT operating system cannot make an educated guess of the number of needed reading, initiating, and writing subtasks based on the system resources and job load. Furthermore, these subtasks are multiprogrammed in an asynchronous fashion, although different priorities can be assigned to different subtasks.

It is important to utilize certain system resources which require careful synchronization of several tasks. For example, if there are several reading subtasks in the MVT, it is important to synchronize these subtasks so that input devices (say, card readers), from which input jobs are read and job streams are formed, can be kept running at top speed with minimum stopping. On the other hand, the ease in creating subtasks enables the operator to vary the mix of the reading, initiating, and writing subtasks which may enhance overall system resource utilization.

The organizations of the MVT and the TOS/DOS are very different. The former is task-oriented, and the latter job-oriented. Furthermore, the MVT is built with a dynamic organization of tasks. The number of subtasks to be created in a given environment depends on the needs of the operator and users. In particular, there can be as many memory partitions as there is memory available.* Thus the number of system functions, such as reading, initiating, and writing subtasks, can vary. In the TOS/DOS the hierarchy of subsystem and system functions is fixed. It is not possible for the system to accommodate more than three partitions, should additional resources become available.

4.3.2.2 The Synchronization of Running Tasks

Because they are intended for multiprogramming, the tasks are essentially independent of each other during execution. In many situations where the resources such as memory, device, and data are shared among the tasks, a part of a task may be dependent upon the results of other tasks even though the major part of the task has been run

---

* The maximal number of memory partitions for MVT is 16. This limitation is due to the IBM 360's hardware memory protection feature which can only protect 16 mutually exclusive areas because there are only 16 protection "keys." On the other hand, the MVT operating system architecture does not have such design limitation.

in a multiprogramming environment with other tasks. Without explicit synchronization, the task may not receive the correct results in order to pursue its remaining work properly. For this reason, two macroinstructions have been provided to allow the synchronization of interdependent tasks.

The *wait macro* in a task permits the task to be delayed until one or more results from (or resources assigned to) other tasks become available. The *post macro* enables a task to signal to other tasks that the results (or resources) are indeed available. By employing the macroinstructions, the tasks can

1. communicate with each other,
2. coordinate their work progress, and
3. interlock themselves on system resources.

System resources, of course, include storage media such as main memory, physical devices such as disks, and logical items such as files and library subroutines.

Consider the example in Fig. 4.5 where tasks T_1 and T_2 are interlocked on the system resources R_a and R_b. Since T_1 and T_2 are being multiprogrammed, the use of

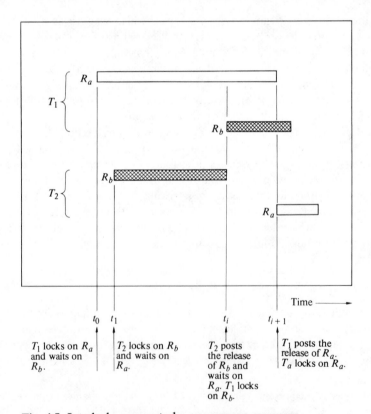

Fig. 4.5 Interlocks among tasks on common resources.

these resources can be represented concurrently by horizontal bars. We note that in this example, the task T_2 has issued a post macro at the time t_i, indicating that the use of resource R_b has been completed. Since the task T_1 has been waiting for the resource via a wait macro, the resource R_b is immediately assigned to T_1. However, T_2 must wait for R_a since T_1 has not yet relinquished the use of R_a. Until the time t_{i+1}, the wait macro in T_2 delays the work progress of T_2. As soon as a post macro is issued by T_1 at t_{i+1} on R_a, the progress of T_2 is resumed. In this example, we note that these two tasks are interlocked on common resources. Without the synchronization mechanisms, the tasks will not be able to proceed properly.

In addition to explicit interlocks among tasks via post and wait macros, the requests issued by the tasks for resources under the operating system control can also create interlock. In other words, the operating system may defer the progress of a task until the requested resources become available to the task. In this case, the synchronization is handled by the operating system without the explicit use of post and wait macros.

4.3.2.3 Controlled Access to Common Resources

Consider as common resources the data which are not under the control of the operating system. In a batch processing environment, access control over common data is entirely the responsibility of the user. That is, the user must arrange his programs for execution (either batch them or overlay them) so that each program can access the common data in a prescribed serial manner. In this manner, the access to the common data by a program is made possible only when the running of all the preceding batched or overlayed programs has been completed. The most the operating system can do is to pass some error condition codes from one batch phase of a job to another batch phase of the same job. These error condition codes may be considered as common data of the job maintained by the operating system.

In a multiprogramming environment, it is desirable to have the operating system controlling the tasks' access to common data in an orderly way. For example, while data are being changed as a result of an update, there should be no access to data. In this case, the data are being used exclusively by the task and are not accessible to any other task. On the other hand, read-only data can be accessed by authorized tasks at all times.

For this reason, provisions are included in the system to allow the user to define and name the common resources. Furthermore, two macroinstructions, *enq* and *deq*, are provided for the user's task to control access to named resource. The enq macro causes a request to be put on the queue for a named resource; the deq macro requests removal from the queue because the use of the resource is completed. The named resource can be defined for exclusive or concurrent use.

4.3.2.4 Resource Allocation Strategy

The allocation of system resource to user jobs is a function of the operating system. More specifically, the system's initiating subtasks allocate the system resources since these subtasks supervise the jobs and process job requests for system resources.

The need of a strategy in allocating system resources to incoming jobs is for the purpose of

(S_1) maximizing the utilization of system resources,

(S_2) minimizing the access contention over system resources,

(S_3) safeguarding the integrity of the system resources, and

(S_4) avoiding deadlock among the initiating subtasks and their jobs.

The item S_4 is overwhelmingly important. Deadlock not only can prevent a system resource which has been allocated to a job from being made available to other jobs, but also can render the system completely useless. For example, in Fig. 4.6(a), there are three initiating subtasks, I_1, I_2, I_3, and three system resources R_a, R_b, R_c. Assume that R_a has been allocated to job 1, R_b to job 2, and R_c to job 3 by their respective initiating subtasks. At time t_i, job 1 requests system resource R_b. Since R_b has not been released from job 2, job 1 must wait. Similarly, job 3 halts at t_{i+1} and job 2 at t_{i+2}. By the time t_{i+2} there is clearly a deadlock—all three jobs have been halted due to the deadlock over system resources. The entire system is, therefore, doing no useful work.

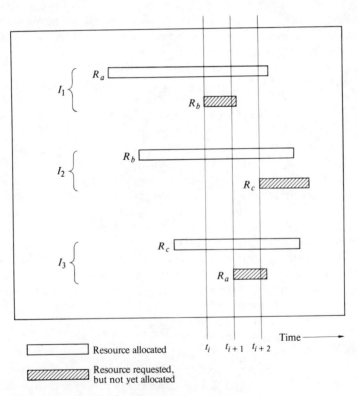

Resource allocated

Resource requested, but not yet allocated

Fig. 4.6(a) Deadlock on resources.

Because the initiating subtasks are responsible for the allocation of system resources and are familiar with the nature of the system resources, it is desirable for the initiating subtasks to develop a strategy to avoid system deadlock.

Although avoidance of deadlock is of primary importance in developing the strategy, considerations of S_1, S_2, and S_3 must also be emphasized. For example, if we were to adopt a strategy that a job must be given all its requested resources at the beginning and the job will not be initiated until all its requested resources have become available, then there would be no system deadlock. However, such a strategy is costly, since some of the system resources allocated to the job may remain unused for long periods, and other jobs which have requested the same resources must wait for even longer periods. Obviously, this strategy does not satisfy S_1. On the other hand, if we were to adopt a strategy that (1) a job must release a formerly obtained resource before obtaining an additional resource, when holding the original resource may prevent the acquisition of the additional resource, and (2) the job must rerequest the original resource along with the additional resource should they be needed collectively, then there would be a greater utilization of system resources. However, this strategy is unsound in the case where system resources are mainly data files. Releasing formerly acquired data files and rerequesting the data files along with new data files cannot prevent the data files from being contaminated (i.e., a violation of file integrity) by other jobs to which the same data files have been allocated. Therefore, in this case, there is a violation of S_3. The allocation of system resources in the MVT system does not take place at individual task level; instead, it is at the job step level.

The strategy incorporated in the initiating subtasks is as follows:

1. Determination of the type of system resources requested for the jobs is performed by the system.

2. Allocation of each type of system resource is based on special considerations in accordance with the nature of the resources.

3. When several types of system resources are requested, a prescribed sequence of allocation steps is taken.

In the MVT system, system resources are of three types: files (called data sets), devices, and main memory regions.

The allocation of data sets for a job is based on the belief that the integrity of the data sets can best be maintained if the data sets are allocated to the job for the entire life span of the job. Thus, no task of the job can proceed until all required data sets have been obtained—an approach satisfying S_3.

The allocation of devices for a job is based on the consideration that devices such as tape drives can be used for one set of information at a time when the previous set of information is no longer required. Unlike data sets, devices do not have integrity problems. There is no need of allocating all the requested devices for the job for the entire job span. Furthermore, to allocate all requested devices for the entire life span of a job tends to create access contentions among jobs. For this reason, device allocation is performed by the initiating subtask at the job step level. At the end of a step, all devices allocated to the step are released—an approach tending to satisfy S_2.

Considerations of main memory region allocation are similar to the ones on devices. By not allocating a memory partition (called region) at the job level, the system does not have to reserve for the job a region which must be as big as the largest region required by any one of its job steps.

In other words, main memory region allocation at the job step level enables the initiating subtask to reserve just enough main memory for the job step or the initiating subtask itself (if the size of the initiating subtask is bigger than the size of the job step). As in the case of devices, at the end of a step the region allocated to the step is released and a new region for the next job step is allocated. Thus, conditions S_1 and S_2 are fulfilled.

When all three types of resources are requested by the job, the strategy involves the following:

1. data sets for the job are to be allocated first,
2. main memory region for the job step is allocated next, and
3. devices for the job step are allocated finally.

The above order of allocation is important. Without the proper data sets, there is no need to proceed. Thus, allocations for the job step do not have to take place. Region allocation comes before device allocation because the system's device allocation routine must be executed in the region of the new job step. By allocating a region to a job step, the device allocation requirements for the job step can then be carried out by the routine.

A schematic diagram of the system resource allocation mechanisms is depicted in Fig. 4.6(b).

4.3.2.5 Restrained Competition

As we noted earlier, the MVT system can create many identical subtasks to perform system functions and to serve as subsystem monitors. These subtasks are, of course, programs residing on the secondary storage. To conserve main memory and to allow a copy of the program to be used by several identical subtasks on different input, most of these system programs are coded *reentrantly*. The discussion of reentrant programs is included in Section 4.6. Although we shall not dwell on it here, it is important to note that (1) logically we may be referring to several subtasks, but physically there are fewer programs in the main memory carrying out the functions of these subtasks, and (2) a mechanism is available in MVT so that the operating system can be informed whether a reentrant program is to be shared by several subtasks. With this information the system can keep track of those reentrant programs which have already been loaded in the main memory and those which have not. An analogy between reentrant programs and read-only data sets is noted in that they both can be accessed by authorized tasks at all times.

One of the goals of designing the multiprogramming system is, as we stated at the beginning, to maximize the use of system resources. In order to accomplish this goal, the notion of task is introduced. It is hoped that more refined delineation of job units can result in more effective resource utilization. Instead of few large jobs contending

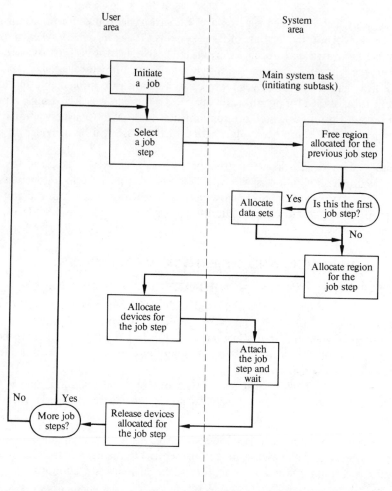

Fig. 4.6(b) A resource allocation mechanism.

for system resources infrequently, there are more job units (tasks) available to make proper request and prompt use of the same resources. However, there are other design goals such as the one emphasizing resource sharing. Furthermore, in reality, system resources are seldom abundant. In fact, multiple requests and exclusive use of limited and shared resource may result in system deadlock. When a deadlock occurs, no utilization of system resources can take place. In this situation tasks must be deferred and resources must be reallocated to avoid system deadlock.

4.3.3 CONCLUSIONS
The study of multiprogramming systems in previous sections concludes that the systems must provide effective synchronization mechanisms to enhance interlocking of tasks on common system resources on the one hand, and prevent possible system deadlock which may render the system useless on the other hand.

The post, wait, enq, and deq macros are software synchronization mechanisms which have been incorporated in some of these systems. However, many synchronization mechanisms have recently been incorporated into hardware. Furthermore, it has also been recognized that more primitive synchronization mechanisms can be developed which may lend themselves more easily to hardware implementation and software realization of the aforementioned macros. To this end, we shall discuss a pair of synchronization primitives which are fundamental and have been incorporated in the "fourth generation" computers. Illustration of their use will be provided in the examples.

To avoid system deadlock, we must identify the necessary conditions for its occurrence. With these conditions, we can then study strategies and algorithms to prevent and detect system deadlock. However, sufficient conditions are difficult to derive. Without knowing the sufficient conditions, any prediction of system deadlock is not possible.

4.4 SYNCHRONIZATION AND INTERLOCK MECHANISMS

4.4.1 SEMAPHORES AND SYNCHRONIZATION PRIMITIVES

Synchronization among tasks can be achieved with (1) a semaphore, and (2) a pair of instructions called *v*-operation and *p*-operation in each task. *Semaphores* are hardware registers or special memory locations which contain integers. Because there are several synchronizing tasks using the same semaphore, the system forms a queue of all the tasks on that semaphore.

The *v-operation* is a machine instruction with one operand. The operand is the name of the semaphore. Whenever it is executed, the *v*-operation performs the following work:

1. If the value of the semaphore is nonnegative, the value is incremented by one. The instruction is now complete, and control returns to the next instruction of the task which was running when the execution of the current instruction was started.

2. If the value of the semaphore is negative, the first task in the queue (other than the running task) is placed in the ready state. The value of the semaphore is incremented by one.

The *p-operation* is also a machine instruction with the name of the semaphore as its operand. Whenever it is executed, the *p*-operation performs the following work:

1. If the value of the semaphore is greater than zero, the value is decremented by one. The instruction is now complete, and control returns to the next instruction of the task which was running when execution of the current instruction was started.

2. If the value of the semaphore is nonpositive, the task which was running when execution was started is put in the queue. The value is decremented by one.

For interlocking tasks on a common resource, the value of the semaphore and performance of the *v*-operation and *p*-operation can be interpreted as follows.

The supplier of the resource will employ the *v*-operation to post the availability of the resource; the consumer of the resource will employ the *p*-operation to wait for the resource if the resource is not yet available. When the value of the semaphore is greater than zero, it indicates that the resource is available. Each *v*-operation will result in more plentiful supply. Thus, the value of the semaphore increases with the additional executions of *v*-operations. As long as there are available resources, the *p*-operation can be executed without having the task deferred. When the resource is consumed, the value of the semaphore decreases. By the time the value of the semaphore becomes zero, indicating no resource available, the execution of a *p*-operation in a task will cause the task to be suspended, since there is no resource for the task to consume. Negative values in the semaphore indicate resource is urgently needed. In this case, even if a *v*-operation is being executed, the increase of the resource will not offset the shortage, since the *v*-operation will only increase the value by one. For this reason, new tasks should be activated. If these are suppliers, then the resource will be replenished and the value of the semaphore will be positive. Otherwise, there is either an acute shortage of the resource or more consumption than supply. In such a situation, the task whose *p*-operation is being executed will be put to wait.

4.4.2 THE SLEEPING DOCTOR: AN EXAMPLE

The story of the sleeping doctor is centered around the clinic as depicted below.

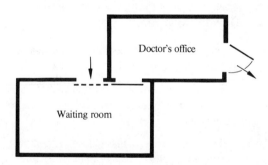

The clinic is composed of a waiting room and an office. The waiting room has an entrance. Next to the entrance there is an opening to the doctor's office. Both the entrance and the opening share the same sliding door, which always closes one and opens the other. Furthermore, the entrance is so small that only one patient at a time can go through.

When the doctor has treated a patient, he slides open the door to the waiting room and asks the next patient to come in, if there is a patient. He goes to sleep in the waiting room if there is no patient.

The patients behave as follows: When they find some patients in the waiting room, they just wait their turn. However, when they find the sleeping doctor, they wake him up.

In this example, there are two tasks. The patient task and the doctor task. The semaphore can reflect the number of patients in the waiting room. If the value is greater than zero, the doctor task can proceed without interruption. Each time he asks a patient to come to his office, it amounts to the execution of the *p*-operation in the doctor task. If the value is zero, the execution of the *p*-operation renders the doctor task inactive, i.e., puts him to sleep. The patient task is thus activated.

On the other hand, the patient task may have been active long before the doctor task arrives at the scene. In this case, the semaphore can easily accumulate a large positive integer. Otherwise, the doctor task will be activated each time the semaphore has the value 1. In other words, the doctor will be wakened each time a new patient enters the empty waiting room.

4.4.3 SUMMARY

Although many synchronization and interlock mechanisms have been proposed in the literature, the ones included in the previous sections have actually been built in the computer hardware. Theoretically, it is possible to propose more primitive mechanisms than the ones included here. For example, the semaphore can restrict the integers to binary 0 and 1. The *p*-operation and *v*-operation can be simplified to exclude the use of the task queue. These primitive mechanisms can produce the same effect as the more elaborate ones. Nevertheless, for practical reasons and ease of use, hardware and software mechanisms tend to be more elaborate.

What we have to recognize here is that these synchronization and interlock mechanisms are characterized by the following:

1. semaphores which enable the tasks to associate the names of the semaphores with interlocked resources and on-going events;

2. *p*-operations which allow the tasks to make known that some resource has been taken and that a certain event has occurred and which delay the task when the resource and events are not there; and

3. *v*-operations which allow the tasks to make known that the resource has been replenished and that the event has indeed occurred, and which wake up the supplier of resource and producer of events when the resource and events are low.

4.5 SYSTEM DEADLOCK

4.5.1 THE PROBLEM OF SYSTEM DEADLOCK

The problem of system deadlock has been studied in the cases of IBM 360 TOS/DOS and MVT systems. However, it is universal in all multiprogramming systems. The problem arises only when resources are shared and are not plentiful. The solution to the problem should avoid deadlocks, without being unnecessarily restrictive in resource sharing and without being unusually demanding in resource supply. To illustrate the problem and a solution, we include the following example.

4.5.1.1 The Bank's Problem

A bank has limited capital. To maximize the utilization of its capital, the bank would like to make loans to its customers in such a way that each and every individual customer's loan ceiling is below the bank's capital, whereas the total loan ceilings may exceed this capital.

A deadlock certainly exists if the following situation occurs where the capital is 100 thousand dollars.

Customer	Loan ceiling (in 1000 dollars)	Present loan	Available credit
c_1	80	41	39
c_2	60	21	39

Thus, in this situation, the bank is left with a cash of 38 thousand dollars [$100 - (41 + 21) = 38$]. If either of the customers wants to claim his full remaining credit before returning a single dollar to the bank, there is not enough money in the bank to honor the claim. In other words, the bank must either cancel the other loan or refuse the new claim. In either case, the bank's reputation is at stake.

4.5.1.2 The Bank's Solution

To safeguard its reputation, the bank adopts the following conditions for granting loans so as to avoid a deadlock situation.

1. A customer must first establish with the bank a loan ceiling for the intended business transactions. He can secure as many loans as he desires, provided the sum of loans is below the ceiling.

2. For every loan secured by the customer for a business transaction, there is an assurance that the business transaction will be completed in (fixed) time and the loan will be repaid when the transaction is completed.

3. The first loan request from the customer will be considered if the requested loan does not exceed the ceiling established for the customer. The remainder is a loan credit which can be requested by the same customer as additional loans for his subsequent business transactions.

4. When a customer asks for a loan below his loan ceiling and within his credit, he should expect the approval of the loan. However, he should not be offended if the bank cannot execute the loan immediately. Nevertheless, the bank will process the loan request, and in due course the customer will get the loan money.

5. The bank is rather certain that the approved loan for the customer can be honored since other customers whose transactions are due for completion will soon return the borrowed money with interest.

6. The bank will accept any customer whose desired loan ceiling does not exceed the bank's capital.

Before advancing a loan to a requesting customer, the bank will go through the following procedure.

The bank has a fixed CAPITAL; each new customer i establishes with the bank a loan CEILING (i). For each customer (i.e., for all i), the following must hold:

CEILING (i) $\leq$ CAPITAL.

Whenever customer i (i.e., for all i) applies for a LOAN (i, j), the bank must see to it that at the time of application the following must hold:

$$0 \leq \sum_j \text{LOAN}(i, j) \leq \text{CEILING}(i).$$

In other words, the sum of all the outstanding loans (there are $j - 1$ of them) and the present loan request of the customer must be below the customer's loan ceiling.

Thus, the loan CREDIT (i) for the customer i can be derived from

$$\text{CREDIT}(i) = \text{CEILING}(i) - \sum_j \text{LOAN}(i, j).$$

Furthermore, the bank knows how much CASH is on hand. Since

$$\text{CASH} = \text{CAPITAL} - \sum_i \sum_j \text{LOAN}(i, j),$$

obviously,

$$0 \leq \text{CASH} \leq \text{CAPITAL}$$

has to hold.

In order to decide whether an approved loan is to be executed or not, the bank essentially inspects the situation that would arise if the loan had been executed. If this situation is "safe," then the bank advances the loan. Otherwise, the bank will stall.

Determination of whether a situation is safe amounts to inspecting whether all customer transactions can be guaranteed to finish. The procedure starts by determining whether at least one customer has a loan credit which does not exceed the cash. If so, this customer can complete all his transactions. The procedure then investigates the remaining customers as if the first one had finished all his transactions and had returned all his loans. Safety of the situation means that all transactions can be finished. In other words, the bank can get all its money back. In this situation, no transaction can be delayed indefinitely due to the lack of cash for advancing a loan credit.

If for the bank's capital we substitute system resources, for the customers we substitute jobs, for the customer credit ceilings we substitute total resources requested by jobs, and for the loans we substitute resources allocated to jobs, the bank's problem has a direct analogy to the multiprogramming deadlock problem. It shows that we should be able to test how "safe" our resource allocations are at every job step initiation, i.e., each time a customer applies for a new loan.

4.5.2 CHARACTERIZATION AND PREVENTION OF SYSTEM DEADLOCK

System deadlock can be characterized in terms of the following conditions:

1. Mutual exclusion condition—tasks claim exclusive use of the resources they require.

2. Wait-for condition—tasks hold resources already allocated to them while waiting for additional resources.

3. No preemption condition—resources cannot be forcibly removed from the tasks holding them until the resources are used to completion.

4. Circular wait condition—a circular chain of tasks exists such that each task holds one or more resources that are being requested by the next task in the chain.

In fact, these are necessary conditions whose existence defines a state of system deadlock.

In Section 4.3.2.4, we noted that the resource allocation strategy of the IBM MVT system has successfully avoided the deadlock situation.* The strategy's approach to the allocation of data sets, such that no task can proceed until all required data sets have been obtained, clearly removes the wait-for condition. Its strategy on main memory region and device allocation—where the task must release its original region and device and request them again with additional resources—eliminates the no preemption condition. Finally, the strategy that the allocation of resources in a serial order (i.e., first, data sets at job level; second, main memory region at job-step level; and third, device at job-step level) effectively prevents the circular wait condition.

However, the mutual exclusion condition is difficult to deny. For example, in Section 4.3.2.3 the use of enq and deq macros for exclusive use of named resource will create a mutual exclusion condition.

Nevertheless, the prevention of system deadlock can be accomplished by denying at least one of the four aforementioned conditions.

4.5.3 SYSTEM DEADLOCK DETECTION AND RECOVERY

Let $r_1, r_2, \ldots, r_n$ represent resource types and $w_1, w_2, \ldots, w_n$ represent the number of resources of each type. At an arbitrary time instant t, let p_{ij} denote the number of resources of type r_j allocated to task T_i, and let q_{ij} denote the number of resources of type r_j requested by task T_i in excess of those already allocated to task T_i. Define the *allocation* and *request* matrices $P = ((p_{ij}))$ and $Q = ((q_{ij}))$, and let P_i and Q_i denote the row vectors giving the resources allocated to T_i and requested by T_i, respectively. Furthermore, by summing the columns of the allocation matrice P, we have the total number of allocated resources of type r_j. In other words, $\sum_{i=1}^{m} p_{ij}$ is the total number of allocated resources of type r_j for m tasks. Let $V = (v_1, v_2, \ldots, v_n)$ be an *available*

---

* Of course, it is conceivable that some job may never get started due to a deadlock situation outside the computer system.

resources vector whose jth element $(v_j \leq w_j)$ indicates the number of resources of type r_j that are currently available. Note that

$$v_j = w_j - \sum_{i=1}^{m} p_{ij}.$$

That is, the sum of the resources allocated and those available of type r_j must be equal to the total number of that type in the system. In the following, 0 will indicate a (row) vector each of whose n elements is 0. Also, $x \leq y$, where x and y are vectors, is defined to hold if and only if it holds for each pair of corresponding elements from x and y.

The algorithm below is designed to reveal a deadlock by simply accounting for all possibilities of sequencing the tasks that remain to be completed. Suppose at time t the state of the system is available in the matrices P and Q, and suppose V is also given. Furthermore, we denote the rows of allocated and requested resources for task i at time t with $P_i(t)$ and $Q_i(t)$, respectively, and the available resources vector at time t with $V(t)$.

1. Initialize $W \leftarrow V(t)$. In other words, the number of resources of each type at time t is determined by the available ones as indicated in V. All rows in P are assumed to be "unmarked" at the outset.

2. Search for an unmarked row in P, say the ith, such that $Q_i(t) \leq W$. In other words, the algorithm tries to identify a task whose requested resources are available. If one such task is found, go to step (3). Otherwise, the algorithm terminates here.

3. Set $W \leftarrow W + P_i(t)$, mark the ith row, and return to step (2).

If all the rows in P are marked, then there exists a sequence $\{T_i\}$ of tasks such that the execution of the tasks based on the sequence (i.e., the order in which the rows are marked) will not result in a deadlock on the resources. On the other hand, if there are unmarked rows at the termination of the algorithm, there is a deadlock. From step (3) we learn that even if all previously scheduled tasks (i.e., whose rows are marked) release their allocated resources to the system, there is still not enough resource for requesting task whose row in P is unmarked. More specifically, the unmarked rows correspond exactly to the deadlocked tasks. Thus, the algorithm can be used for deadlock detection.

Since deadlock is detectable, one can then consider ways to recover from a deadlock. One way to recover from a deadlock is to abort all the deadlocked tasks (whose rows are unmarked).

This algorithm is very similar to the procedure used in the solution to the bank's problem. The only differences are that in the bank's problem there is but one type of resource (namely, the money), whereas in a computer system there are n types; in the bank's problem the bank would not risk dropping a customer, whereas in a computer system a task may often be aborted. The cancellation of tasks can be avoided if for each task one agrees to establish, a priori, a quota of allowable resources and to take into account that the processing of the task may be deferred considerably due to limited resources.

4.5.4 CONCLUSIONS

We have motivated the phenomenon known as deadlock with examples. Necessary conditions which constitute a deadlock situation are included. An algorithm for deadlock detection by ordering the resource requests by size and associating with each task a count of the number of resource types being requested is outlined. This algorithm can lead to a solution to deadlock recovery by task abortion.

4.6 PROGRAM ORGANIZATION IN A MULTIPROGRAMMING ENVIRONMENT

In a multiprogramming environment, a common subroutine may be called upon by several programs. In order to conserve main storage and minimize the I/O and CPU activities in reading and loading additional copies of the subroutine, the same copy in main storage should be shared by all of the calling programs. In sharing the subroutine, there arises the following problem.

The subroutine may be called by another program before the execution of the entire subroutine for the previous call is completed. If the subroutine is entered before its completion, then there may be a loss or alteration of the information concerning

a) the return address to the calling program,

b) the list of parameters,

c) the working areas,

d) the program logic, and

e) the operating environment, such as machine register contents.

An expedient way to resolve the above problem is to incorporate program conventions in the subroutine for checking its completion before permitting the entry of another call, on the one hand, and in the calling programs for testing the successiveness of the calls, on the other hand. In this way, the subroutine cannot be entered and no other calling program can get a successive call until the execution of the subroutine for the current calling program is completed. The question is then raised whether the calling programs should be kept waiting for the completion of the subroutine or whether additional copies of the subroutine should be brought into main memory. In the former case, there is a decrease of program performance due to its waiting for the subroutine. In the latter case, there is a loss of processing time and main memory storage. A solution is therefore needed to allow concurrent entry to a subroutine by calling programs and to save the variant information listed above from (a) through (e).

Solution requires that a common subroutine is to be organized in the following ways in order to be shared in a multiprogramming environment:

1. The subroutine is delineated into a procedure part and one or more data parts.

2. The procedure part is composed of the instructions and, perhaps, some constants of the subroutine. However, neither the instruction nor the constants in this part is to be modified during execution.

3. The data part consists of the return address to the calling program, list of parameters, working areas, and contents of the general registers. Furthermore, there is a data part for each call for the subroutine.

4. Between the calling program and the subroutine, a convention is agreed upon, so that the storage can be acquired for and information can be saved in the data part.

The above organization of a subroutine enables the subroutine to perform the same function for each calling program when it is entered concurrently or serially by several programs in a multiprogramming environment. Such program organization is known as *reentrant* program organization and the procedure part of the program is called *pure* procedure.

For large programs, the pure procedures of the programs can save considerable storage. For example, if a FORTRAN compiler is programmed reentrantly, then all the user FORTRAN programs can share the same compiler. In other words, the user FORTRAN programs become the (input) data parts of the compiler and the compiled programs become the (output) data parts of the same compiler. Because the compiler consists of pure procedures, its compilation of the present program will not be effected inadvertently by the other programs. However, the saving of storage does not imply the saving of the main memory. If the main memory is small, then for large programs, such as a FORTRAN compiler, only one execution phase of the compiler is brought into main memory at a time. It is unlikely that the same execution phase is needed by all the user FORTRAN programs at the same time since different programs may be in different stages (therefore, phases) of the compilation. Thus, multiple copies of the compiler in terms of execution phases are still used. For systems with large main memory, such as IBM 360/370 MVT, an entire reentrant program can be kept in the main memory for sharing. In this case, the system must provide a means by which the reentrant program is known to the system in the main memory and through which different user programs may call the procedures of the reentrant program as subroutines. In IBM 360/370 MVT, such means is called LINK PACK. In either case, the use of pure procedure can save considerable secondary storage. Because the logic of a program cannot be changed in the course of its execution, there is no need to save multiple copies of the same program onto secondary storage even if the execution of the program is partially completed. The need to transfer the entire program and its input and output data onto secondary storage (called swapping) because of temporary suspension from execution—for example, due to running out of the time slice—may now be restricted to the swapping of its associated input and output data, thus, not only reducing the swapping time, but also saving secondary storage.

4.6.1 A LINKAGE CONVENTION FOR REENTRANT PROGRAMS

By *linking* we mean the exchange of control between a calling program P_i and a called subroutine P_j. The linkage is initiated in the calling program by the execution of a set of instructions referred to as a *calling sequence*; and the linkage is further maintained and completed in the called subroutine by the execution of two sequences of instructions known, respectively, as the *entry initialization* and *exit return*. In this

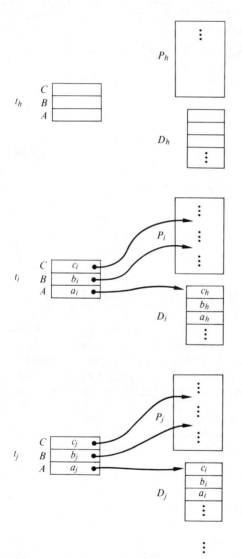

Explanation
Assume that these are snapshots taken at different times—
first at t_h, next at t_i,
and then at t_j.

Consider only P_i and P_j and their associated data parts D_i and D_j. We note that D_j contains among other things the content of the registers A, B, and C when P_j was called. In this case, it is evident that P_i was the calling program since information saved in D_j consists of a_i, b_i, and c_i.

Fig. 4.7 A linkage convention.

convention the calling program P_i must provide

1. the address a_i of its data part D_i in register A, in case P_i is to be called by other programs; and
2. a calling sequence which includes the parameter list address in register B, the return address in register C and the transfer to the subroutine P_j.

When it is entered, the subroutine P_j must issue the entry initialization sequence to

3. save in its data part D_j the contents of all the registers; and
4. provide the address a_j of D_j in register A.

When it exists, the subroutine P_j must provide exist return sequence to

5. restore all register contents saved in D_j;
6. restore a_i in register A in particular; and
7. transfer to the calling program P_i via register C.

We note that in this convention the register A always contains the address of the data part of a program currently in control, the register B maintains the parameter list address of the calling program, and the register C is used for return address. In addition, each called subroutine saves all the register contents in its data part when it is entered and restores the same contents just before it returns. To dynamically allocate area for the data part, the called subroutine P_j can issue a REQUEST–MEMORY macroinstruction. The return of the instruction is the beginning address a_j of the allocated area. The relations of P_i and P_j and the contents of registers A, B, and C are depicted in Fig. 4.7.

4.6.2 AN EXAMPLE OF THE LINKAGE CONVENTION FOR A REENTRANT SUBROUTINE

In IBM 360 and 370 assembly languages, the basic calling sequence of the calling program P_i and the entry initialization and exit return sequences of the called subroutine P_j are listed below. In addition, the data part D_j of the called subroutine is included for illustration. Not included in the illustration are the pseudoinstructions which declare the subroutine entry and parameter list addresses in the calling program.

Calling Sequence (in P_i)

L	15,ADCON	Subroutine entry address in register 15.
LA	1,PLIST	Parameter list address in register 1.
BALR	14,15	Return address in register 14.

Entry Initialization (in P_j)

STM	14,12,12(13)	Save contents of registers 14,15,0–12, in D_j.
LA	12,DJ	Address a_j of data area in register 12.
ST	12,8(13)	Place a_j in the data area at a_i.
ST	13,4(12)	Address a_i in the data area at a_j.
LR	13,12	a_j in register 13.

Exit Return

LM	14,12,12(13)	Restore registers 0–12,14,15.
L	13,4(∅,13)	Replace its data part address with that provided by the calling program. This instruction is needed because the calling program may have been called by another routine.
BR	14	Return via address in register 14.

Word	Displacement	Contents
1	0	Unused
2	4	Address a_i of the data part of the calling program (backward link).
3	8	Address a_j (stored by the called program P_k if P_j calls P_k) of its data part (forward link).
4	12	Return address (register 14 content).
5	16	Entry point address (register 15 content).
6	20	Register 0
7	24	Register 1
8	28	Register 2
9	32	Register 3
10	36	Register 4
11	40	Register 5
12	44	Register 6
13	48	Register 7
14	52	Register 8
15	56	Register 9
16	60	Register 10
17	64	Register 11
18	68	Register 12
(the remaining part of D_j)		

Figure 4.8

4.7 POSTSCRIPT

The discussion of file integrity and I/O deadlock problems in IBM 360 TOS/DOS system can be found in [2]. Although considerable information on IBM MFT and MVT systems are available—[12], [13], [14], [15], [16], [17]—the study of their system deadlock problems is sketchy. We have derived most of our information from [10]. Synchronization and interlock mechanisms have been proposed and introduced in [7] and [16], but the first theoretical treatment on the synchronization and interlock mechanisms was presented in [8]. In the presentation, the terminology of semaphore p- and v-operations was proposed. For this reason, computer manufacturers are also inclined to use this terminology. However, the mechanisms proposed in Section 4.1 are somewhat more elaborate than the ones suggested in [8]. The stories of the sleeping doctor and smart banker are originated in [8].

The first recognition of system deadlock is given in references [8] and [10]. For our convenience, we have relied on the characterization, prevention, detection, and recovery of system deadlock as presented in [3].

The study of sufficient conditions for system deadlock is not included here. The reader may refer to [9] and [11].

REFERENCES

1. B. W. Arden, B. A. Galler, T. C. O'Brien, and F. H. Westervelt. "Program and Addressing Structure in a Time-Sharing Environment." *J. of ACM* **13**, 1 (January 1966): 1–16.

2. G. Bender, D. N. Freeman, and J. D. Smith. "Function and Design of DOS/360 and TOS/360." *IBM Systems Journal* **6**, 1 (1967).

3. E. G. Coffman, M. J. Elphick, and A. Shoshani. "System Deadlocks." *Computing Surveys* **3**, 2 (June 1971): 67–78.

4. C. J. Conti, D. H. Gibson, and S. H. Pitkowsky. "Structural Aspects of the System/360 Model 85—I General Organization." *IBM Systems Journal* **7**, 1 (1968): 2–14.

5. P. A. Crisman (Editor). *The Compatible Time-Sharing System—A Programmer's Guide,* Second Edition. Cambridge, Mass.: The MIT Press, 1965.

6. A. J. Critchlow. "Generalized Multiprocessing and Multiprogramming Systems—Status Report." *Proc. of FJCC,* 1963, pp. 107–126.

7. J. B. Dennis and E. C. Van Horn. "Programming Semantics for Multiprogrammed Computations." *Comm. of ACM* **9**, 3 (March 1966): 143–155.

8. E. W. Dijkstra. "Co-operating Sequential Processors." *Programming Languages—NATO Advanced Study Institute,* Edited by F. Genuys. New York: Academic Press, 1968, pp. 43–112.

9. A. N. Habermann. "Prevention of System Deadlocks." *Comm. of ACM* **12**, 7 (July 1969): 373–377, and 385.

10. J. W. Havender. "Avoiding Deadlock in Multitasking Systems." *IBM Systems Journal* **7**, 2 (1968): 74–84.

11. R. C. Holt. "Some Deadlock Properties of Computer Systems." *Computing Surveys* **4**, 3 (September 1972): 179–196.

12. "IBM System/360 Operating System—Introduction to Control Program Logic," Program Logic Manual, Form &28-6605.

13. "IBM System/360 Operating System—Control Program with Option 2," Program Logic Manual, Form Y27-7128.

14. "IBM System/360 Operating System—Fixed Task Supervisor," Program Logic Manual, Form &28-6612.

15. "IBM System/360 Operating System—MVT Control Program Logic Summary," File No. S360-36, Form Y28-6658-1, Second Edition, January 1968.

16. "IBM System/360 Operating System—MVT Supervisor," File No. S360-36, Form No. Y28-6659-3, Fourth Edition, November 1968.

17. "IBM System/360 Operating System—Supervisor and Data Management Macro-Instructions," File No. S360-36, Form No. C28-6647-0, First Edition, February 1967.

18. "IBM System/370 Principles of Operation," GA22-7000-3, Fourth Edition, January 1973.

19. W. C. McGee. "On Dynamic Program Relocation." *IBM Systems Journal* **4**, 3 (1965): 184–199.

20. T. H. Simpson, R. P. Crabtree, and R. O. Ray. "HASP-II/Houston Automatic Spooling Priority System with Remote Job Entry." IBM Program Information Department, Hawthorne, N.Y., Order No. 360D-05.1.04, September 1968.

EXERCISES

1. (E. W. Dijkstra) Consider the following conditions and sample procedures. Find out which procedures have what conditions and explain your findings.

   Explanation

   a) A procedure section is *critical* if control of the CPU during its execution should not be switched to another procedure.

   b) The use of *mbegin* and *mend* enables the tasks between a pair of mbegin and mend to be multiprogrammed with other pairs.

   c) The procedures are written in ALGOL and the computer system has only one CPU.

   Conditions

   a) If one of the tasks is running well outside of its critical section, it should not lead to any potential blocking of other tasks. Otherwise, the condition is unnecessarily restrictive.

   b) A condition may occur which causes the execution of a critical section before the execution of the present critical section is completed.

   c) A condition may exist which causes mutual blocking of each other among running tasks.

   ```
   "begin integer c1,c2;
         c1: = 1; c2: = 1;
         mbegin
         task 1: begin A1 : c1: = 0;
                     L1 : if c2 = 0 then goto L1;
                          critical section 1;
                          c1: = 1;
                          remainder of cycle 1;
                          goto A1
               end;
   ```

```
        task 2: begin A2 : c2: = 0;
                      L2 : if c1 = 0 then goto L2;
                           critical section 2;
                           c2: = 1;
                           remainder of cycle 2;
                           goto A2
                 end
            mend
end".
```

```
"begin integer c1,c2;
        c1: = 1; c2: = 1;
        mbegin
        task 1: begin L1 : if c2 = 0 then goto L1;
                             c1: = 0;
                             critical section 1;
                             c1: = 1;
                             remainder of cycle 1;
                             goto L1
                  end;
        task 2: begin L2 : if c1 = 0 then goto L2;
                             c2: = 0;
                             critical section 2;
                             c2: = 1;
                             remainder of cycle 2;
                             goto L2
                  end
            mend
end".
```

```
"begin integer turn; turn: = 1;
        mbegin
        task 1: begin L1 : if turn = 2 then
                      goto   L1;
                             critical section 1;
                             turn: = 2;
                             remainder of cycle 1;
                             goto L1
                  end;
        task 2: begin L2 : if turn = 1 then
                      goto   L2;
                             critical section 2;
                             turn: = 1;
                             remainder of cycle 2;
                             goto L2
                  end
            mend
end".
```

2. Emulate the semaphore and synchronization primitives as proposed in Section 4.4.1 in either an assembly language or high-level programming language. If they are emulated in an assembly language, then represent these primitives as macros. If they are done in some high-level language, then compose them as procedures or subprograms. By issuing macro calls or procedural calls, test the semaphore and synchronization primitives with examples given in the chapter.

3. State the sequence of events after first *p*-operation is executed. List all assumptions. Assume that semaphore (SYSSEM) is 1 when first *p*-operation is executed.

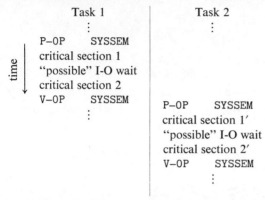

4. The following definitions will be needed in answering the questions. A *directed graph* is a pair (N, E), where N is a nonempty set of *nodes* and E is a set of *edges*. Each edge in E is an ordered pair (a, b), where a and b are nodes in N. (For given nodes a and b, we will allow E to contain more than one edge of the form (a, b).) An edge (a, b) is said to be *directed from* node a and *directed to* node b. The graph is said to be *bipartite* if the set of nodes N can be partitioned into disjoint subjets Π and RHO such that each edge has one node in Π and the other node in RHO.

A *sink* is a node with no edges directed from it, and an *isolated node* is a node with no edges directed to or from it. A path is a *sequence* $(a, b, c, \ldots, r, s)$ containing at least two nodes, where $(a, b), (b, c), \ldots,$ and (r, s) are edges. A *cycle* is a path whose first and last nodes are the same.

The *reachable set* of node a is the set of all nodes b such that a path is directed from a to b. A *knot* is a nonempty set K of nodes such that the reachable set of each node in K is *exactly* set K.

a) In a bipartite graph having no more than one edge directed from given node a to given node b, what is the maximal number of edges in E?
b) Illustrate a bipartite graph which consists of a sink, a cycle, and a knot.
c) Prove that a graph does not contain a knot if and only if each node is a sink or has a path directed from it to a sink.

5. (R. Holt) We define a *system* as a pair (Σ, Π) where Σ is a set of *states*

$\{S, T, U, V, W, \ldots \}$,

and Π is a set of *tasks*

$\{T1, T2, T3, \ldots \}$.

Each task is defined as a mapping from the system states into the subsets of system states. In the figure, we illustrate a system whose states are $\{S, T, U, V\}$ and whose tasks are

$\{T1, T2\}$. In this system, task $T1$ maps state S into $\{T, U\}$. We may interpret this to mean that when the system is in state S, task $T1$ may change the state to either T or U.

If task T_i maps state U into a subset of Σ containing state V, then we write

$$U \xrightarrow{i} V.$$

(Read "task T_i takes U to V.") Thus in the figure we have the following: $S \xrightarrow{1} T$, $S \xrightarrow{1} U$, $T \xrightarrow{1} S$, $T \xrightarrow{2} S$, $T \xrightarrow{2} V$. If the system allows the following sequence of zero or more changes of state: $S \xrightarrow{i} T$, $T \xrightarrow{j} U, \dots, V \xrightarrow{x} W$, then we write

$$S \xrightarrow{*} W.$$

For example, in the figure, $S \xrightarrow{1} T$ and $T \xrightarrow{2} V$; thus $S \xrightarrow{*} V$.

When T_i can no longer take one state to another, we say T_i is *blocked*; if T_i will never again be able to change states, we say T_i is *deadlocked*. Formally:

Task T_i is *blocked* in state U if there exists no state V such that $U \xrightarrow{i} V$. Task T_i is *deadlocked* in state U if for all V such that $U \xrightarrow{*} V$, T_i is blocked in V.

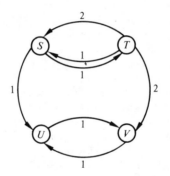

a) Identify in the figure the task which is blocked but not deadlocked and the state in which the blockage occurs.

b) Identify in the figure the task which is deadlocked and the states in which the deadlock takes place.

c) Does the following statement follow from the definitions?

"A task T_i is not deadlocked in state U if and only if there exists a state V such that $U \xrightarrow{*} V$ and the task T_i is not blocked in V."

d) If one or more tasks are deadlocked in state U, then we may say U is a *deadlock* state. If all tasks are deadlocked in U, we say U is a *total deadlock* state. In the figure, identify the deadlock and total deadlock states, if any.

e) We shall say that a state is safe if it cannot be changed by any task into a deadlock state. That is:

"State U is *safe* if for all V such that $U \xrightarrow{*} V$, V is not a deadlock state."

We shall say a system is *safe* if it contains one or more safe states.

Suppose $U \xrightarrow{*} V$. Prove that if U is a deadlock state, then V is a deadlock state. Also prove that if U is a safe state, then V is a safe state.

5

Virtual Memory Operating Systems

REMARKS

In this chapter, our aim is to answer the following questions:

1. Why do we need virtual space?
2. What are the types of virtual space and their capabilities?
3. How are multiprogramming systems utilizing virtual space structured?

In answering question (1), we will point out that virtual space is designed primarily to resolve the problems concerning dynamic memory allocation, repetitive program relocation, program overlay, and run-time growth of programs and data. Because different developers of virtual memory computers have aimed to resolve one or more of the above problems, there are various types of virtual spaces. To this end we will try to classify the types of virtual spaces and illustrate them with examples. The examples will include CDC 3500, IBM 360/67, UNIVAC Spectra 70/46, IBM 370 and Honeywell 645. Thus we can answer the question posed in (2).

In answering question (3), we try to outline a "generalized" multiprogramming operating system which includes some of the important common characteristics of four operating systems, namely, TSOS on UNIVAC Spectra 70/46, TSS on IBM 360/67, OS/VS2 on IBM 370, and MULTICS on the Honeywell 645. The presentation is in the form of a design study. Thus, the basic system organization and detailed program logic are provided. It is hoped that by studying the generalized multiprogramming system the reader can get an overview of the system and can become familiar with the interfaces of various components of the system.

5.1 THE CONCEPT OF VIRTUAL SPACE AND ADDRESS TRANSLATION

5.1.1 DYNAMIC MEMORY ALLOCATION

5.1.1.1 Memory Utilization Requirements

In a multiprogramming environment with several programs concurrently residing in main memory, the demand for more efficient utilization of this memory is apparent. To achieve a more efficient main memory utilization, the system must provide a *memory allocation mechanism*

1. to make available main memory for accommodating other programs and data once the residing program and its data are no longer needed;

2. to place the new programs and data in some available main memory locations; and

3. to handle memory allocation dynamically, since the arrival of the new programs in a multiprogramming environment is unpredictable.

In order to accomplish (1), the system must keep track of the available memory. Although memory fragmentation may result in several disjoint available memory blocks, the amount of work in keeping track of these blocks is not unmanageable. The difficulty lies in fitting the new program and data into the available blocks dynamically.

5.1.1.2 Program Fragmentation and Compacting Operation

Consider the example below where the main memory is occupied at time t_0 by programs A, B, C, and D. At a later time t_1, programs B and D are not needed. Thus the memory occupied by these programs should become available.

Figure 5.1   At time t_0 At time t_1

We note in Fig. 5.1 that the available memory (shaded areas) constitutes two separate blocks. Now let us place a program E in the memory. If the program size is greater than either one of the blocks and less than the total available memory, then the system must either fragment program E into two parts or consolidate the available blocks into one before placing the program in the main memory.

The former requires that the operating system keep track of various fragments of a program. Since memory fragmentation tends to get worse as time goes on, the task of keeping track of program fragments will become intolerable.

The latter requires the system to perform the *compacting operation,* i.e., the consolidation of the available blocks by moving programs and their data in the memory. The result of the compacting operation on the memory shown in Fig. 5.1 is shown in Fig. 5.2.

Figure 5.2   At time t_2

The problems associated with the compacting operation are as follows:

1. Since the compacting operation is a main-memory-to-main-memory operation, it requires the interruption of the running program during its entire operation.* In other words, the execution of the current program has to be suspended because some other program has requested additional main memory.

2. The program and data being moved (e.g., program C in Fig. 5.2) may contain address-dependent information (say, the absolute address of an entry point in the same program). Since addresses as well as constants are stored in the memory as numbers, it is not possible for the compacting operation to distinguish addresses from constants. The information which can be used to distinguish addresses from constants is called relocative information, which is produced by the language translator—say, the assembler in the internal relocation symbol dictionary—and used by the linking loader for calculating absolute addresses. However, the linking loader as presented in Chapter 1 does not save this information, without which the readjustment of the absolute addresses for repetitive relocation of a program which has been relocated is not possible. Such a linking loader is usually termed a *static linking loader,* and the relocation performed by static linking loading is referred to as the *static relocation.* Hence, the compacting operation is incapable of updating the absolute addresses with respect to their new program locations because relocative information about these addresses is no longer available.

We note that the compacting operation is really an attempt to relocate a program after the program has been relocated once in the main memory by the linking loader.

---

*   For example, in IBM 370/165 with a high-speed (cache) memory of 80 nanoseconds and main memory of 2 microseconds, the Move instruction, which moves N characters from one main memory location to another, requires approximately $t \ (= 0.56 + 0.24N)$ microseconds for large N. In other words, if the compacting operation is realized in hardware as the Move instruction, then during a compacting operation of a program the program of N bytes will have to wait t microseconds before its execution can be resumed.

The failure of the compacting operation in relocating a program is due to the fact that, in general, once the program is statically relocated, it cannot be relocated again. For these reasons, the compacting operation is seldom used. Thus, to provide a more efficient dynamic memory allocation mechanism, we must provide a solution to the relocation of a program after the program has been relocated once.

5.1.1.3 Dynamic Memory Allocation and Repetitive Program Relocation

One solution to the aforementioned problem lies, perhaps, in the ability of the computer system to provide a function which can "remember" the original program addresses and their corresponding new locations. By not associating two different original addresses with the same new location, and by not corresponding an original address with two different new locations, the function can remember unique correspondence between original addresses and new locations. Mathematically, such a function is said to be 1-1 and single-valued.

More formally, we let f be a single-valued and 1-1 function whose domain of definition is the set V of all addresses of a program, and whose range is the set M of all memory addresses. In symbols we have

$$f(a_i) = b_i$$

where

$$a_i \in V \quad \text{and} \quad b_i \in M.$$

If f is an identity function I, then we have

$$I(a_i) = b_i$$

i.e.,

$$a_i = b_i \quad \text{for all } i.$$

In other words, the addresses used in the program (more specifically, in its load modules) are exactly the memory locations. In this case, the relocation of a program requires the relocation of the program addresses again. As we've learned from previous sections, this is difficult, if not impossible.

If f is not the identity function, then the addresses used in the program need not be the same addresses at which the program resides. The exact correspondence between the program addresses and the memory addresses is provided by the function f.

Referring to Fig. 5.3, we observe the following:

1. Since f_D maintains the correspondence, the program addresses are still the same regardless of their memory locations. Thus there is no need for relocating the program.

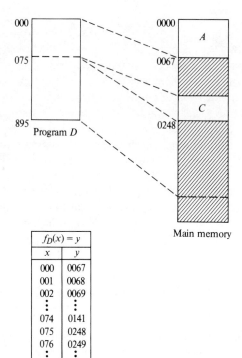

Main memory

$f_D(x) = y$	
x	y
000	0067
001	0068
002	0069
⋮	⋮
074	0141
075	0248
076	0249
⋮	⋮
895	1068

Figure 5.3

2. Since f_D keeps track of corresponding memory locations, it does not matter to the program whether the locations are scattered or contiguous. A memory-compacting operation is therefore not necessary.

3. Dynamic memory allocation for the program amounts to an inspection of available memory and the construction of the function f_D.

With the availability of f_D, both the relocation of program C and the compacting operation become unnecessary. However, the system must have the capability of constructing and using the above function.

We note that a running program D can be dynamically and repetitively relocated in any available space as long as it is provided with an updated function f_D^t after each relocation time t. Thus, the realization of f_D^t in computer systems will help us to eliminate the compacting operation and will facilitate dynamic allocation and repetitive relocation.

5.1.1.4 Virtual Address, Virtual Space, and Address Translation

In executing an instruction of program D, the instruction may refer to a specific location. The address field of the instruction of course contains the address of the specific location (subject to the usual base and index registers modification). However, this address is not the memory address but the program address. The program address is used by the system for computing the memory address based on the function f_D. Once the memory address is computed, it is used for actual reference. The process of computing memory addresses is called *memory translation*, and the function f_D is usually called the *translation function* or *translation table* (if the function is in a tabulated form) associated with program D. To distinguish program addresses from memory addresses, the former are called *virtual addresses* and their addressing space *virtual space*, while the latter are called *physical addresses* and their addressing space *physical memory*. In this new terminology, we say that the user is given a virtual space and his programs are compiled and assembled in virtual addresses. After the program is loaded in the physical memory, and before its execution, a translation function is made for the program. For each reference to virtual space during execution, the virtual address is translated into a physical address via the translation function. The physical address is then used by the system for physical memory reference. It should be clear by now that the memory in which the information physically resides is not the same memory in which the information is referenced by the user. A computer system employing virtual space is called a *virtual memory system*.

5.1.1.5 Practical Considerations in Constructing Translation Functions

The above discussion indicates that for each program in the system there is associated a translation function f^t at relocation time t. Since these programs may be dynamically and repetitively relocated, it is difficult to develop closed formulas for the translation functions f^t. Instead, translation tables are used and the change of the translation tables from f^{t_1} to f^{t_2} amounts to updating the entries in the translation table f^{t_1}. This difficulty is the main reason that prompts the current virtual memory computer systems to employ translation tables. To conserve the storage for these tables and to reduce the processing time in translation, it is desirable to have small tables.

Referring to Fig. 5.3, we note that if program D were as large as virtual space, then the translation table would have as many entries as the size of virtual space, since there is an entry for each address used in the program. This is clearly impractical. Assuming that the size of virtual space is equal to the size of the physical memory, the entire physical memory would have to be used for storing the table, and there would be no room for entering the program. A practical solution is therefore needed.

Consider the following organization of physical memory and virtual space:

1. Divide the physical memory into equal units of words, or bytes, and call these units *blocks*.

2. Divide the virtual space into equal units, called *pages*, whose size is the same as the block size.

3. Construct for each program a translation table whose entries associate the pages of the program and the blocks in which the pages reside.

From the above, we note that the maximum number of entries in the translation table is equal to the number of pages available in the virtual memory.

More precisely, we let

2^m be the size of the virtual space,

2^n be the size of the physical memory, and

2^k be the size of the block or page, all in numbers of words or bytes.*

Thus the virtual address is m bits long and the high order $(m - k)$ bits can be used to number pages. For this reason, these $(m - k)$ bits are called *page numbers*. Similarly, the high order $(n - k)$ bits of the n-bit physical addresses are called *block numbers*. From (3) we learn that, in general, the entries in the translation table associate the page numbers with block numbers.

From Fig. 5.4, we note that the page number can be used to locate the proper entry in the translation table. The entry contains among other information (such as access control and memory protection bits) the block number for that page. The $(n - k)$ bit block number is then used to form the n-bit physical address. During

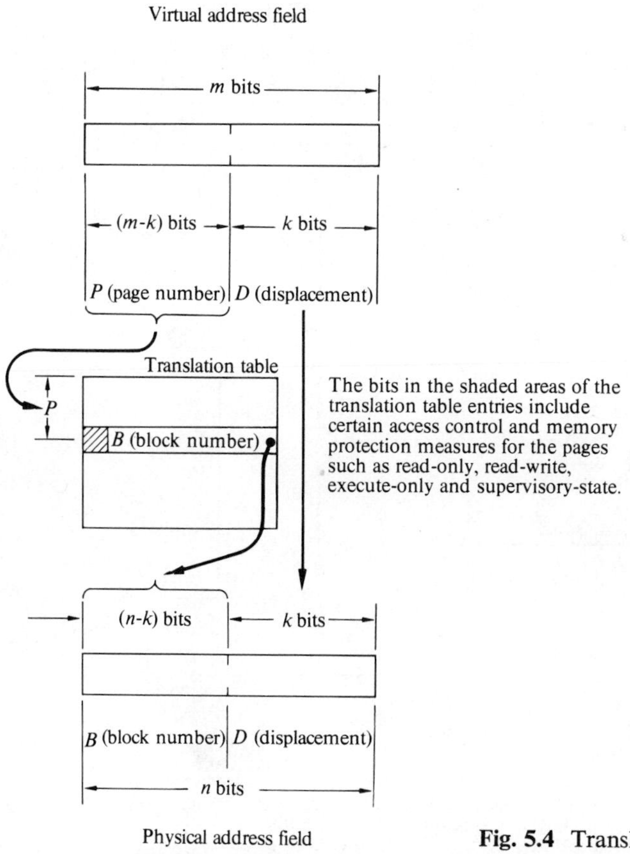

Virtual address field

The bits in the shaded areas of the translation table entries include certain access control and memory protection measures for the pages such as read-only, read-write, execute-only and supervisory-state.

Physical address field

Fig. 5.4 Translation of an address.

---

* The use of binary addressing scheme is expedient. Logically, any number system can be employed for addressing as long as the computer hardware is of the same number system.

the translation process, the k-bit displacement is used as it is. The displacement is the offset in a given block or page.

The simplest virtual memory computers are those whose virtual space and physical memory have the same size, i.e., $m = n$. This is incorporated in the standard model of the CDC 3500 (see Fig. 5.5) computer and is also available on the CDC 3300 as an option. The maximum CDC 3500 virtual space consists of 262,144 24-bit words. The size of the page is 2,048 words. Thus, there are 128 pages. Since the sizes of virtual space and physical memory are the same, there are exactly 128 blocks in the physical memory. The translation table (called *page index file*) consists of 128 entries each of which is 12 bits long. The 12-bit entry (called *page index*) consists of a 7-bit block number and some 5-bit control information. This control information is used for (1) access control, e.g., read-only, read/write, and unaddressable, and (2) handling partial page, e.g., quarter, half, and three-quarter page. If partial page is specified, then page length and address must be provided.

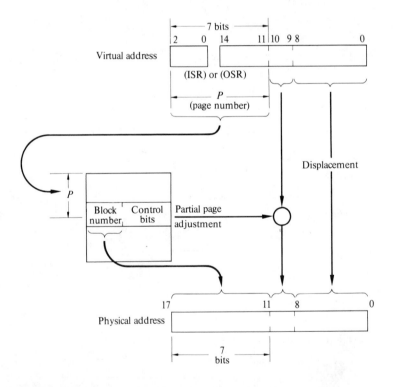

The effective page number in the CDC 3500 is formed by the three bit contents of the Instruction State Register (ISR) or Operand State Register (OSR), and the four higher order bits of the address field. The contents of these registers are maintained and changed by the operating system.

Fig. 5.5 The CDC 3500 virtual address and memory translation.

Because there is only one translation table, all programs must be in the same virtual space. Furthermore, there is no need of a *physical-memory-utilization map* showing whether a block is being used to accommodate a page, since all the occupied blocks have their block numbers in the translation table. The ones being unused do not have their block numbers in the translation table.

The (program and data) pages are of course produced by the language translators and subsystems. The operating system with the aid of the linking loader assigns the available blocks to incoming pages via the translation table. When the blocks are filled, the execution of the programs (i.e., their pages) begins.

5.1.2 TOWARD A VIRTUAL SPACE WITHOUT PROGRAM OVERLAY

The CDC 3500 virtual memory systems resolves the problem concerning dynamic memory allocation and repetitive relocation of programs. However, it does not provide a solution to other problems regarding (virtual) space and (physical) memory utilization. One such problem is concerned with program overlay—a topic which has been discussed in Chapter 1 in conjunction with physical memory utilization. Let us review it again. If a program is larger than the space available, then special operating system features must be provided so that certain addresses can be used by different sections of the program at different times. (See Fig. 5.6).

In this example, program A is the main program which calls on subprograms B at time t_0 and C at time t_1. Both subprograms B and C share the same space. Because the program logic of B and C are independent of each other, they can be executed at different times.

The program overlay technique requires that

1. sections of the program to be overlayed must be logically independent of each other;

2. careful program linkages and calls must be employed to avoid addressing conflict; and

3. the operating system must be informed about the overlay structure so that the linking loader can relocate sections of the program properly.

This obviously places a great deal of burden on the part of the user and operating system.

Having reviewed the overlay problem, we note that the need of overlay feature in a computer is not unique to CDC 3500 but is universal in virtual memory systems with small virtual spaces and in real memory systems with small real memories.

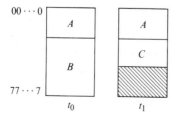

Figure 5.6

5.1.2.1 Linear Virtual Memory Systems

Attempts have been made to utilize the basic notion of the virtual space for resolving the overlay problem. By making the virtual space sufficiently large, on the one hand, it is hoped that the need of program overlay will not be necessary. By keeping the physical memory sufficiently small, on the other hand, it is hoped that the additional cost of the computer memory will not be considerable. The price to pay is the cost and performance for the memory translation and backing storage, which will be discussed later. Meanwhile, we will give an example of a virtual memory computer whose virtual space is greater than the physical memory.

The UNIVAC Spectra 70/46 computer system is a virtual memory computer. Its virtual space consists of 512 4K-byte pages and its physical memory 64 4K-byte blocks. In other words, the virtual space is 8 times bigger than the physical memory. Since there are 512 pages, there are, at most, 512 entries in the translation table (called the *translation memory*). Each entry is composed of a 6-bit block number and 10-bit status and control information. The latter indicates whether the page is

1. modified or not;
2. present or absent;
3. privileged only to the operating system or not;
4. read-only or read/write;
5. half or full page; and
6. a half-page address, in case the page is a half page.

Since the virtual space is 8 times larger than the physical memory, it is not possible to have all the virtual pages reside in the blocks. For this reason a backing storage is provided. The backing storage is usually one or more direct access devices such as drums and disks.

During memory translation, the status information (2) may indicate that the page being referenced is absent from the physical memory. In this case, the page is not in any block, and a page-fault results. The *page-fault* is a hardware interrupt which causes the operating system to initiate a *paging process* to bring the desired page into the physical memory, from the backing storage, and to place it in an available block. While the page is being brought in, the operating system may pass control to another program by replacing the current translation table with the translation table of the other program. The paging routine of the operating system is responsible for managing the backing storage (say, the drum) and storing and retrieving pages. Contrary to the compacting operation mentioned earlier, the paging is not a main-memory-to-main-memory operation. It is primarily an I/O operation. By giving control of the CPU to another program, it is hoped that overlap of I/O and computation operations can be obtained. Furthermore, the program being interrupted due to paging is the same program requesting additional space rather than some other program in execution.

The 2 million bytes of UNIVAC virtual space is an attempt to resolve not only the dynamic memory allocation and repetitive program relocation problem but also the problem of program overlay. Potentially, each user can be given 512 pages—a virtual space of 2 million bytes. The pages of each user's program compete for the 64 blocks of the physical memory. In reality, this is not so because of

1. the small backing storage, i.e., the drum, which has only space for 800 pages; and
2. the restriction placed by the operating system on reserving the last 256 entries of each translation table for itself.

Comparing Figs. 5.5 and 5.7, we note that both address translation processes are similar. The main difference is that in Fig. 5.7 the page number has more bits than the block number, whereas in Fig. 5.5 these two numbers have the same number of bits. Because both CDC 3500 and UNIVAC Spectra 70/46 virtual memory are addressed in a linear fashion, i.e., from $(00 \cdots 0)$ to $(77 \cdots 7)$, they are called *linear virtual memory systems*. Their memory translation is characterized by a one-dimensional (or one-step) search of the translation tables. For this reason, they are often referred to as *one-dimensional virtual memory systems*. When the virtual space is larger than the physical memory, the additional requirements are as follows:

1. The need of a backing storage such as drums or disks.
2. The capability of the operating system to retrieve pages from, and to store (new or updated) pages in, the backing storage. The retrieval process is called the *paging-in operation* and the storing process the *paging-out operation*. Collectively, they are referred to as *paging*.
3. The management of a *backing-storage-utilization map* and a *physical-memory-utilization map*. The former is used to keep track of the utilization of storage units (e.g., sectors or tracks) on the backing storage for pages; the latter, on the blocks in the main memory for paging. Because of these usages, they are also called, for brevity, *virtual space map* and *physical memory map*, respectively.

The use of a physical-memory-utilization map enables the virtual memory system to support several translation tables (therefore, several virtual spaces). Since the pages of different virtual spaces may be in the blocks, the map can show for a given block the space from which the page belongs. When available blocks are scarce, certain pages may have to be "purged" from the physical memory. In this case, the virtual spaces of the purged pages must be identified. Once identified, their corresponding translation tables can be found and table entries for those pages can then be updated.

A more thorough discussion on paging operations, map and table managements, and multiple virtual spaces will be presented in later sections. Here we point out simply the potential power of a linear virtual memory system, in which the virtual space is larger than the real memory, and the elaborate system operating overhead which may significantly increase the cost and degrade the performance of the system. The rationale for a larger virtual space is the belief, of course, that the backing storage is cheaper than physical main memory, the paging operations for one program are mostly overlapped with the execution of another program, and the management of maps and tables is not excessive. Furthermore, these systems provide repetitive program relocation, dynamic memory allocation, and overlay structure elimination.

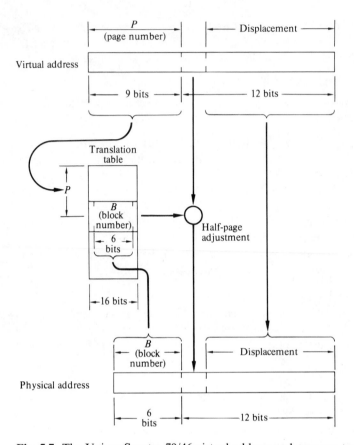

Fig. 5.7 The Univac Spectra 70/46 virtual address and memory translation.

5.1.2.2 Linear Segmented Virtual Memory Systems

The IBM 360/67 virtual memory computer system has a maximum virtual space of 2^{32} (over 4 billion) bytes. Since the page size is 4K bytes, there are over one million $(2^{32} \div 2^{12} = 2^{20})$ pages. As was mentioned earlier, there is an entry for each page used in the translation table which relates the page number with the block number. The maximum size of the translation table is therefore 2^{20}. A one-dimensional search of 2^{20} entries in the translation table would require a 20-bit index register. Furthermore a linear table is prohibitively long.

A two-dimensional search (2-step table search) is therefore developed to eliminate the need of a large index register and a long linear table. Referring to Fig. 5.8, the pages of the virtual space are grouped into *segments*. There are 2^{12} segments, each of which consists of 2^8 pages. A table, called the *segment table*, contains for each entry the origin of another translation table, called the *page table*. The maximum number of entries in the segment table is 2^{12}. In other words, there are at most 2^{12} page tables. Each page table contains 2^8 entries, and this relates the page numbers

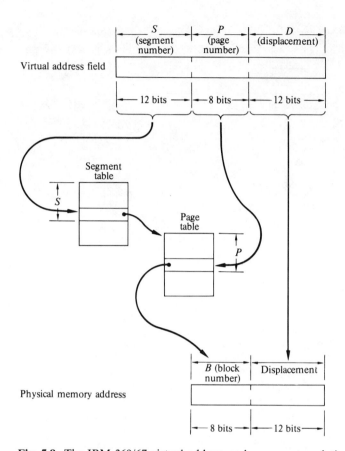

Fig. 5.8 The IBM 360/67 virtual address and memory translation.

with their corresponding block numbers. Thus, instead of 2^{20} page table entries, there are now 4352 $(2^{12} + 2^8)$ entries.

Address translation is accomplished by decoding the first 12 high-order bits of the virtual address, the *segment number*, via the segment table. From the entry in the segment table, the origin of a page table can be found. The next 8 bits of the virtual address are used as a page number. By locating the proper entry in the page table, a block number may be found. The block number and the displacement form the physical memory address.

As we have seen, the address translation is a two-dimensional search. For this reason, the IBM 360/67 type of virtual space is called a *two-dimensional virtual memory system*. The segmentation and paging of the virtual space also earns for the system the name *linear segmented virtual memory system*.

The IBM 370 represents a refinement of the linear segmented virtual memory system. In the IBM 370, there are several virtual space configurations to choose from, depending on the desired sizes of the segments and pages. Since there are two different segment sizes (64K and 1M bytes) and two different pages sizes (2K and 4K bytes), four configurations are possible. Furthermore, the displacement within a page is effected by the page size. The formats of the four virtual addresses and two physical addresses are depicted in Fig. 5.9.

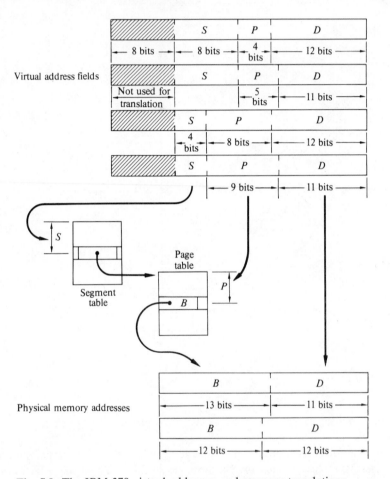

Fig. 5.9 The IBM 370 virtual addresses and memory translations.

Regardless of which one of the four configurations is chosen for an installation, the first 8 bits of the virtual address is (presently) not used for address translation. Thus only the remaining 24 bits are used as the virtual address. We also note that the physical address is 24 bits. Since both the virtual and physical addresses have the same number of bits, the sizes of the virtual space and the physical memory are the same as those in the case of the CDC 3500.* The difference between CDC 3500 and IBM 370 virtual memory system lies in the fact that in the IBM 370 there can be more

---

* Although not all IBM 370's have the full 2^{24} byte physical memory capacity installed.

than one virtual space, whereas in the CDC 3500 there is only one allowed. The number of virtual spaces that the IBM 370 can support is determined by the size of the backing storage, as in the case of UNIVAC Spectra 70/46, and is not constrained by the address translation facility. More specifically, the IBM 370 virtual memory system can be configured to provide either a single virtual space with 2^{24} bytes or a multiple number of virtual spaces each of which is 2^{24} bytes in size. The physical memory has, nevertheless, a maximal size of 2^{24} bytes.

It is interesting to note that there are two ways to achieve a large virtual space. One way is to allow more bits in the virtual address than in the physical address. Because the virtual address field is longer than the physical address field, the virtual space is larger than the physical memory. The other way is to allow a multiple number of virtual spaces. In this case, even if the virtual address has the same number of bits as the physical address, the multiplicity of the spaces effectively multiplies the memory size. The latter, of course, is the IBM 370's direction. Furthermore, if the virtual address is longer than the physical address and the multiplicity of virtual spaces is greater than one, then the effective memory is expanded in both directions, such as in cases of UNIVAC Spectra 70/46 and IBM 360/67. Consider Fig. 5.9 again; we note that the unused portion (8 bits) of the IBM 370 virtual address can be employed for future expansion of each individual virtual space.*

In summary, the large linear segmented virtual memory systems—such as the IBM 360/67, UNIVAC 70/46, and IBM 370—can resolve the problems dealing with (1) dynamic memory allocation, (2) repetitive program relocation, and (3) program overlay.

5.1.3 SPARSELY USED LINEAR SEGMENTED VIRTUAL SPACE
5.1.3.1 The Concepts of Segmentation and One-level Storage

Consider the following example. Let A, B, and C be three running programs. If we anticipate that program B will grow during its run, we can reserve additional space (shaded area) for B so that its growth will be confined in the reserved area. Otherwise, program B must dynamically request space from the operating system.

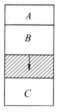

---

* Another way to expand the size of IBM 370 virtual space is to form new virtual space units. The unused 8-bit address field can be employed to designate the numbers of the new units. To find a segment table, the new-unit table is consulted. The new-unit number is used as an offset to locate the entry which is the origin of the segment table. The remaining translation process is similar to the one in Fig. 5.9.

As we know, memory management will greatly increase the complexity of the operating system. The necessity for the programmer to reserve space for program gowth is largely due to the fact that the virtual space is used as a linear address space. In a linear address space, the growth of one program may affect its neighboring programs. Even with the foresight of reserving additional space, the program may still outgrow its allotted space. This is especially true where the growth of the program is unpredictable. An example is the dynamic array feature in ALGOL and PL/1 in which arrays are not "dimensioned" with fixed numbers. Thus their growth is usually open ended. Another example is in the handling of files. Because files can be considered as collections of data (in fact, they are termed *data sets* by IBM), they also have the growth problem.

One solution to the problem of program and data growth is to use the linear segmented virtual space *sparsely*. For example, if we always assign a segment to a program or data set, then the growth of the program or data set within the segment requires only the addition of an entry in the page table for that segment. As long as there are enough segments which can accommodate a sufficient number of programs and data sets and each segment contains enough pages so that program or data set growth will unlikely exceed the segment size, then the problem concerning growth is resolved.

There are other benefits. In the case of a reentrant program, for example, we may assign the pure procedure of the program to one segment and its data to another segment. Consequently, the invariant program logic is separated from the variant data. Furthermore, the linkages among the pure procedures and the bookkeepings of their associated data can be more clearly (not necessarily more efficiently) handled as intersegment communications. In the case of file handling, we may discipline ourselves to use segments as files. References to a file become references to a segment. Thus, data processing of files is apparently viewed by the user as data transfers in a virtual space. The traditional view of data processing as I/O operations involving secondary storage such as tapes and disks may suddenly fade away. As far as the user is concerned, his files, programs, data, and common subroutines are all stored in the virtual space. The various levels of backing storage, such as drums, disks, tapes, and others, are "invisible" to him. This concept of utilizing the virtual space is referred to as the *one-level storage concept*. We note that the emphasis of segments has changed considerably from the usual notion of segmentation. Here, the segmentation is not just another dimension of a virtual space, but is also a discipline in treating programs and data sets in the virtual space.

Although the use of segments for handling program growth and the use of the concept of one-level storage have separate origins elsewhere, as noted in the postscript at the end of this chapter, the integration and generalization of the well-disciplined segmentation and one-level storage concepts for a virtual memory system has been demonstrated at MIT. MIT's MULTICS is implemented on a Honeywell 645 virtual memory system which contains up to 2^{14} (16K) segments and each segment is composed of 256 10K-word pages. In other words, one can conceivably write or create 2^{14} programs and files and each program or file can grow up to 2,560K words. The address translation in Honeywell 645 is similar to the one in IBM 360/67, i.e., a two-dimensional search. We will not dwell on it again.

5.1.3.2 Sparsely Used Linear Segmented Virtual Memory Systems

The MULTICS-Honeywell 645 virtual memory computer is called a *sparsely used linear segmented virtual memory system*. It is perhaps the most ambitious system that directs itself to resolve the five most outstanding problems encountered in systems programming, namely,

1. dynamic memory allocation,

2. repetitive program relocation,

3. program overlay,

4. run-time program and data growth, and

5. one-level storage handling.

One may inquire at this point whether future virtual memory systems should all strive for solutions to problems (4) and (5) in addition to problems (1) through (3). As long as the data sets are small and temporary (e.g., parameter lists for program calls, but not permanent files), problem (4) can be alleviated by present linear segmented virtual memory systems, such as the IBM 370, without difficulty. There are considerable differences of opinion, however, as to the solution to problem (5). In order to facilitate the one-level storage concept in a segmented virtual memory system, the following conventions, facilities, and technologies must be available.

1. All segments must be able to have symbolic names. (We note that files have file names.)

2. The "traditional" file system must be replaced by a segment management system. The catalogued file names will have to be replaced by catalogued segment names. (See discussion on catalog and file system in later sections.)

3. The size of a segment must be large enough to accommodate large files. (At present, the 2,560K-word segment in the Honeywell 645 is not adequate.)

4. Effective paging algorithms and efficient intersegment communication mechanisms must be found to enhance data processing of files. Unlike interactive programming such as program preparation and debugging, where only a small number of programs and data sets is involved, and where program and data set references are localized and infrequent, the number of files involved in a data processing environment is great. Furthermore, the quantity of data is huge, the frequence of data references is high, and references are also scattered. Without a more effective algorithm, the paging traffic will be excessive. Furthermore, frequent intersegment communications (say, branch and link across segment boundary by symbolic names) can be time-consuming.

5. The memory technology must be well advanced so that the problems of organization of memory hierarchy, using various auxiliary storage devices, and of automatic percolation of data within the hierarchy based on cost and duration of usage can be resolved.

At present, we do not understand item (4) well. Furthermore, the memory hierarchy technology still has a long way to go. The incompatability between a file generated and managed by a segment management system and a file generated and managed by a traditional file system has further compounded the movement toward one-level storage. Simply stated, What do we do with all the existing files if we are to introduce a sparsely used linear segmented virtual memory system? The IBM 370 linear segmented memory system takes a cautious approach. The traditional file system is retained and the one-level storage concept is not incorporated. Instead, an interface known as the virtual storage access method (VSAM) is provided which allows a data set stored on secondary storage to be mapped into a virtual space at the time of request for the data set. (See our discussion of a virtual access method in Section 5.2.2.4.) Once it is mapped into the virtual space, the data set can be directly referenced. Because different developers of virtual memory computers have aimed to resolve one or more of the above problems, there are various types of virtual space organizations and implementations. To this end we have illustrated the types with examples including CDC 3500, UNIVAC Spectra 70/46, IBM 360/67, IBM 370, and MULTICS-Honeywell 645.

5.2 A GENERALIZED MULTIPROGRAMMING OPERATING SYSTEM

The purpose of presenting a generalized multiprogramming operating system using virtual space is twofold:

1. to summarize the common characteristics of some of the multiprogramming operating systems so that the reader can get an overview of these systems; and

2. to outline the architecture of a generalized multiprogramming operating system from which discussions of important concepts can be elaborated and specialized.

The system has been abstracted from four current virtual memory systems: TSOS on UNIVAC Spectra 70/46, TSS on IBM 360/67, MULTICS on Honeywell 645, and OS/VS2 on IBM 370. The parts of the system that most heavily influence physical resource allocation are detailed in this design. Thus, the following features are shown explicitly: multiprogramming, demand paging, multitasking, multiple-paths to I/O devices, dynamic loading, a hierarchical file catalog, and a virtual access method. Algorithms which vary widely from system to system, such as the task initiator or dispatcher, and the paging algorithm, are not shown in any detail; however, their place and function within the system are made explicit.

5.2.1 THE HARDWARE REQUIREMENTS

The multiprogramming system under discussion is a system with a single processor. The results that are obtained from the discussion may be extended to a multiprocessor system. The principal method of dynamic memory allocation is demand paging. The four hardware sections include

1. the processor (also called the central processor unit or CPU),

2. the physical memory (also called main memory or core memory),

3. the backing storage (also called backup or swapping memory), and

4. the I/O channels and secondary storage devices (also called external devices).

Each will be discussed individually in the following sections.

5.2.1.1 The Processor

In order for a task to gain control of the processor, the following operations must take place:

1. The general-purpose registers, that are controlled by the programs of the task, must be set to the proper values for the task.

2. Other registers of the CPU, such as those that contain information determining the task's privilege and status, must be set.

3. The hardware mechanism which translates the virtual address to physical address must be activated. The activation involves the restoring of the pointer to the task's translation table in an all-important register, for example, the Descriptor Base Register in MULTICS-Honeywell 645 or the Control Register 1 in IBM 370. Obviously, this is the register which separates one virtual space from another. Furthermore, it is also the register which leads other related tasks of the current task to the same virtual space. In addition, any concurrent translation device utilizing associative memory registers or high-speed buffer registers, if available, must also be activated. These registers are few and contain only block numbers most recently assigned to the pages which are still in those blocks. By utilizing these registers, the translation process can be shortened if the virtual address is indeed referring to a page whose block number is in the registers. Otherwise, a typical one-(two-) dimensional search via (segment table and) page table must be performed.

4. The program counter, containing the virtual address of the next instruction to be executed, must be set to the next address to be executed within the task. This action is actually a transfer to the task.

When a task gives up the processor, all of the above information must be saved. Switching tasks on the processor thus involves some overhead.

The amount of processor time that is needed for a computation will be proportional to the amount of data traffic to and from the memory unit that the processor is using. The external devices will, in general, be rotating and will have tight tolerances on the time in which each byte must be transferred. Therefore, they will take memory cycles as they need them. The processor will then be delayed by the amount of memory cycles that are taken by the channel.

5.2.1.2 The Physical Memory

The blocks of the physical memory will at all times contain the following:

1. Programs and data areas which are either being used by the processor, or are awaiting execution by the processor.

2. I/O buffer areas, which are either awaiting an I/O unit, or channel, or are transmitting their contents to, or receiving them from, a channel.

3. Programs for which there is currently no user, but which are being kept available in case they are requested, possibly because they are needed with rapid response, or because the expectancy of their use is high.

4. Programs and data areas of tasks which are awaiting completion of an I/O operation or other operation which prevents processing.

5. Nothing useful. These blocks are therefore available for allocation.

Although physical memory may be organized into banks or modules which can be separately accessed, enabling channel operations to take place in one bank without interfering with processing in another, such a memory system will not be considered directly, even though it adds another dimension to the problem of resource utilization. The discussion in the following sections can be extended to be applicable to a memory system containing n memory banks. For example, if a paging operation must take place, it must be determined whether *any* of the n memory banks in the generalized system would require the paging actions, and if so, to which bank the action should be directed. The rules by which the banks interact with each other and the rest of the system are not readily generalizable.

5.2.1.3 The Backing Storage

The backing storage may be either a drum, a fixed-head disk, or bulk core. Recent reports of systems employing bulk-core storage as a backup to primary memory seem to indicate a significant improvement in overall performance, especially in demand paging systems. Most multiprogramming systems still utilize the more inexpensive drum or disks.

We will assume that the large bulk core storage is truly a random access device, i.e., any location can be accessed with the same access time, which is very small in comparison with the drum or disk unit. The drum (disk) will have pages distributed on n different sectors (tracks) from which an operation can begin periodically once every revolution. Only one page can be read from a sector (track) at any one time. Thus, if two page requests for one sector (track) occur simultaneously, one will be satisfied after a latency period, averaging one-half a revolution period; the other must wait one entire revolution longer.

The physical memory will be served by one paging channel. This can be extended to many paging channels, with some effort, as in the case of multiple memory banks.

The paging channel itself will at any time be performing one of the following activities:

1. Demand page-in, the highest priority activity. This is bringing a page into physical memory in order to allow a task in physical memory to continue processing.

2. Pre-paging. This is bringing pages of a task into physical memory before the task is given to the processor.

3. Page-out. This is removing a page from physical memory to the backing storage.

5.2.1.4 The I/O Channels and Devices

The I/O section of the system contains multiple data channels, serving direct access devices of varying sizes and speeds. The assignment of devices to channels is not unique; in general, it is possible to access one I/O device through different channels.

The I/O devices include the communications unit, which provides the interface with the user terminals. Because the terminals are very slow compared with the channels, all the terminals will be multiplexed on one communications unit, which may itself be multiplexed with other slow speed units on one channel. Communications with the user terminals create a relatively constant load on the communications unit, because of the slowness of the terminals. The underutilization of the communications channel or device, due to slowness and idleness of the terminals, must be tolerated, because the underutilization cannot be overcome solely by internal modifications to the system. Therefore, the scheduling of this channel will not be a significant part of the overall resource allocation problem.

The random access I/O devices are not as fast as the paging device, although their transfer times are of the same order of magnitude. They are dedicated to files, catalogs of files, and other off-line and on-line storage.

5.2.2 THE SOFTWARE SYSTEM ARCHITECTURE

As a virtual memory system, the virtual spaces of the system are organized with the following restrictions:

1. Several segments of each virtual space with the same segment numbers (usually either the low end or the high end, or both ends) are permanently assigned to the system. In other words, the user tasks will not be able to use these segments directly. When the use of these segments is deemed necessary, the user request for these segments will result in an interrupt such as the supervisor call (SVC).

2. Some of these segments are permanently kept in the physical memory.

The permanent assignment of parts of a virtual space for system use is accomplished by controlling the entries of the segment table. Since the operating system creates the segment tables for the user tasks, it can reserve several segment table entries in a segment table for its own use. For example, in the UNIVAC Spectra 70/46 the last 256 entries of each translation table are reserved for the TSOS operating system. In the IBM 370, the OS/VS2-2 also reserves several segments for its own use as depicted in Fig. 5.10. Furthermore, certain pages of these segments are kept in the physical memory blocks at all times. Such pages constitute, for example, the nucleus of the operating system as depicted in Fig. 5.10.

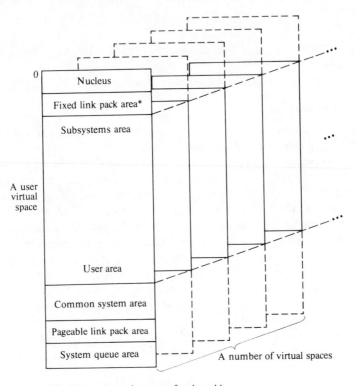

*The link pack area is an area for shareable
reentrant programs (see also Chapter 4).

Fig. 5.10 The IBM 370 OS/VS2-2 virtual spaces layout.

The operating system allocates the various system hardware resources to the tasks operating within the system. Another view is that the operating system schedules the tasks for the hardware resources. For each task the operating system maintains a *task control block (TCB)* for all the information relating to the task. Each task will also be characterized by a mapping from virtual addresses of the virtual space allocated for the task to the physical addresses of the main memory blocks. This mapping will be given by the task's segment and page tables.

5.2.2.1 Resident Parts of the Operating System

When an interrupt or SVC takes place, the interrupt-handling hardware of the CPU causes information pertaining to the interrupt—such as the location at which the interrupt occurred—and a number identifying the type of interrupt to be placed in program-accessible registers. The hardware then transfers control to a particular location, within the supervisor, which is the beginning of a routine called the *interrupt analyzer*.

The interrupt analyzer identifies the type of interrupt, and transfers to the appropriate *interrupt-response routine* which processes the interrupt. This may be done, for example, by consulting a *branch table*. The table contains the virtual addresses of the interrupt response routines, with the identifying number of the interrupt response routines, with the identifying number of the interrupt as an index. (See Fig. 5.11.)

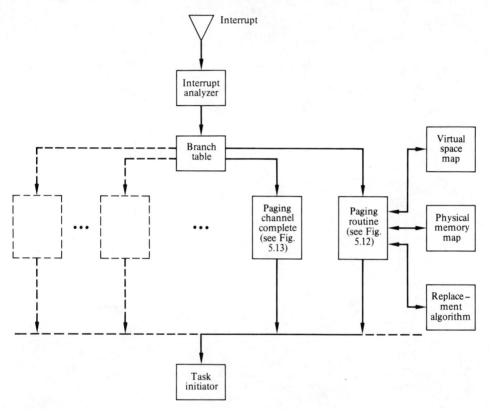

Fig. 5.11 The resident parts of the operating system.

Branching to an address of an interrupt response routine could be done by the hardware interrupt mechanism directly, by merely setting the location counter to the proper location within the branch table.

When a program references a virtual address for which no block has been allocated, the *page-fault* interrupt occurs. The response to the page fault is the *page-fault-interrupt-response routine*, or the *paging routine*. The paging routine must find in the backing storage the secondary address of the required page. To do this, it must have the *virtual space map* table which gives a mapping from the virtual address to the secondary storage address for every page of the task using the processor.

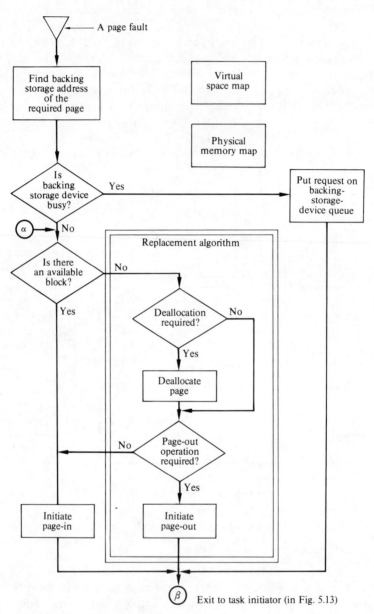

A page fault

Find backing storage address of the required page

Virtual space map

Physical memory map

Is backing storage device busy? — Yes → Put request on backing-storage-device queue

α — No

Is there an available block? — No

Replacement algorithm

Deallocation required? — No

Yes

Deallocate page

Page-out operation required? — No

Yes

Initiate page-in

Initiate page-out

Yes

β Exit to task initiator (in Fig. 5.13)

Fig. 5.12 The paging routine.

The paging routine (Fig. 5.12) must also find an available block in the physical memory in which to place the required page. Thus, it must have a record of the usage of all the blocks in the *physical memory map*. If there is no block available in the physical memory, or if the availability of blocks is too scarce, the paging routine must initiate the *replacement algorithm*. The algorithm will deallocate a block which contains a page of some task. The deallocation of a block is therefore the logical operation of breaking the correspondence of a page of a task and the block in which the page resides. If the task has not altered the contents of the page while it is in the block, the operation involves merely the removal of the block number in an entry for the page in the page table associated with the task. If the task has altered the contents, the contents must be saved in the backing storage before the block can be reallocated. Thus, the physical operation of paging-out must be performed as well.

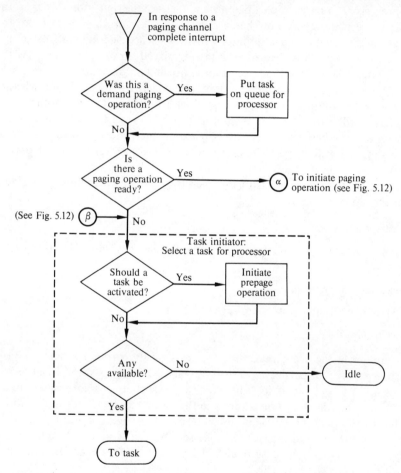

Fig. 5.13 The paging-channel-complete-interrupt-response routine.

The *paging-channel-complete-interrupt-response routine* (Fig. 5.13) initiates the paging operations which have been placed in the backing storage queue during the time the storage device was busy. A channel completion marks the end of a demand paging operation and also indicates that a task is ready for the processor. Because it must sense the channel completion signals, the paging-channel-complete-interrupt-response routine is made resident. The ready task will not always be immediately returned to the processor for execution because this action may not be the most efficient task schedule. Instead, the routine places the task on queue and transfers to a subroutine called the *task initiator*. It is the task initiator's function to select the next task for the processor. For this reason, the task initiator is also known as the dispatcher or scheduler.

The task initiator is called in two different circumstances. First, a task may demand the processor. For example, paging channel completion indicates that the task which had been in paging now has a demand for the processor. Second, the operating system may call the task initiator at various scheduled intervals by setting an *interval timer* to some time slice when a task is placed on the processor. At the specified time later, the interval timer will expire, causing an interrupt. The response to this interrupt will be a call on the task initiator, which will again decide whether to allow the task to continue on the processor, or to replace it with another task. The task initiator will also determine the amount of processing time allocated to the task. Its decisions are based on each task's place on the processor queue, external priority, run time, allocation, etc. This set of decisions comprises the major part of the scheduling algorithm for the system.

Thus, the following are the parts of the operating system which must be resident by virtue of their function:

a) the interrupt analyzer,

b) the paging routine with its maps (the physical memory map and the virtual space map),

c) the replacement algorithm,

d) the paging-channel-interrupt-response routine, and

e) the task initiator.

The remainder of the operating system can exist in the virtual space and be run under demand paging. In particular, interrupt response routines can exist in virtual space. When an interrupt occurs for which the response routine is not resident in the physical memory, the transfer to the address in the branch table will result in another interrupt due to the page fault. This interrupt and the paging operation must be completed before the original interrupt can be serviced. The system would operate inefficiently in this manner, because paging delays would often occur for functions that should be executed immediately.

In this operating system, all the interrupts due to paging channel completion signals, page faults, and interval timer expirations will be serviced immediately by resident routines. On the other hand, program-forced interrupts, or SVC's, may or may not be handled by the resident routines, depending upon the frequency with which they are called.

5.2.2.2 Physical I/O Operations and the PIOCS

A. Management of Channel Queues

I/O devices are operated by orders issued through the channels. In general, an I/O device or a set of I/O devices, through their device controller, may communicate with the CPU and physical memory via one of several channels. This flexibility allows greatly increased efficiency of I/O device operation, since congestion at one channel can be alleviated by directing operations to a less utilized channel. An order to an I/O device will be delayed only if every one of the channels that could receive the order is busy. The principal I/O device orders are:

Seek. A seek is a positioning of the access mechanism of the I/O device so that the physical record, e.g., cylinder, may be read or searched. During the positioning, the channel may be idle or may perform I/O operations on some other device.

Search. A search looks for a particular physical record (e.g., track) after the seek has been completed. A search involves sampling some data (the key field) on the physical track to determine the position of the particular record. The channel is busy during the search.

Read or *Write.* After the proper location has been found, the data is read from the (track) area or written onto the (track) area.

A particular advantage of a multiple-path arrangement is in the execution of seek orders during periods of heavy I/O use. Seek operations do not require constant utilization of the channel; they merely require the availability of a channel for an instant in order to send the order to the device controller. Thus, if a requested I/O device is not busy, the seek operation for that device need be delayed only until any one of the channels that can communicate with the I/O device completes an operation. This delay is generally much less than the delay in which only one channel is connected to that device.

An I/O operation is queued for one of the two following reasons. First, the I/O device may be busy performing a seek or search operation. In this case, the operation will be placed on a queue for the device. Second, all available paths to the device may be busy. The I/O operation will then join a queue for the path set to that device. A *path set* of an I/O device is defined as the set of all channels which can communicate with the I/O device. Conversely, for a given path set of channels, the devices which are connected to the channels are said to be attached to the path set. Consequently, a channel belongs to the path set of each device that can be connected to the channel and becomes a member of several path sets. A path set is not available if each of the channels in the path set is busy. It is available if at least one channel in it is not busy. An example of path sets is depicted in Fig. 5.14.

There are two queues for each path set. One is a queue of seek operations to available devices attached to the path set. As long as no two different seek operations, directed to the same device attached to the path set, are on queue for the path set,

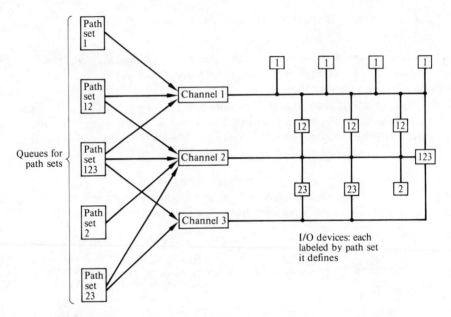

Queues for path sets

Fig. 5.14 Examples of path sets.

this queue will be empty when a channel of the path set becomes available. In this case, all the seek orders can then be sent to the devices via this channel. The other is a queue of search operations. When a channel of the path set becomes available, one of the search operations on queue is selected. The selection criteria could be dependent upon task priority, path set priority, and I/O device and operational requirements, such as the position of access mechanism, the latency period, and expected length of the I/O operation. In general, the algorithm should favor a path set of fewer channels over larger path sets, since there will be fewer opportunities to service the smaller path sets. This selection priority will ultimately depend upon the number of devices belonging to each path set and the frequency of reference to these devices.

Channel operations are initiated when calls are made on the PI/O macro. (See the following section on the PI/O macro.) If either the device or the path set of the device is busy when the I/O operation is requested, the operation is placed on the corresponding queue. These operations must be initiated when a device or a channel becomes free as the result of the completion of an operation.

B. The Operation of I/O Devices

In a multiprogramming environment, secondary storage devices for files are shared. To safeguard the integrity of the files and to facilitate more efficient sharing, the physical I/O instructions are made privileged and are issued from the operation system. When a user task has a need for an I/O operation, it employs an SVC called the *physical-I/O SVC*. This results in an interrupt, to which the response is the *physical-I/O-response routine*, briefly called the *PI/O macro*. If the device is available

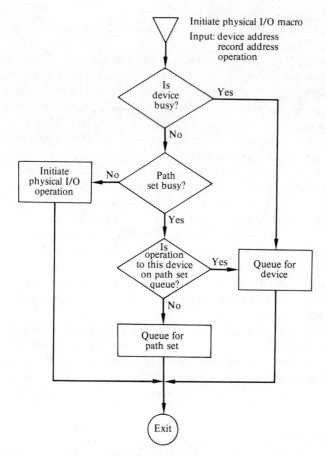

Fig. 5.15 The physical I/O initiation.

the PI/O macro (Fig. 5.15) issues the channel commands and device orders that initiate the operation on the device. If the device is not available, the macro puts the operation on the queue for the device for later execution, when the device becomes available.

The input to the PI/O macro is contained in the device control blocks which were elaborated upon in Chapter 2. We shall not repeat that discussion here. However, we shall discuss the operation of the PI/O macro from the point of view of *resource allocation*.

Although the three types of orders—namely, seek, search, and read or write—are needed for a typical I/O operation, the processor need not send each order via the channel to the device explicitly and singly. The orders, along with channel commands, can be organized into a *channel program* from which the channel will issue a new order when the current I/O order is completed. The physical I/O macro is responsible for setting up such a channel program, and for issuing an execute-channel-program instruction.

In this operating system, the I/O operations for direct-access devices such as disks are divided into two steps, for which two instructions (two channel programs) are issued. First, a channel program consisting of the seek order is issued. Upon completion of the positioning operation, the channel causes a channel-complete interrupt signifying the completion of that channel program. The interrupt response program then issues an instruction for the search, and read or write, operations. Thus, two channel-complete interrupts take place for each physical I/O operation, and the channel-complete interrupt response routine takes different actions, depending upon which channel program has been completed.

There are two reasons why the I/O operations for direct-access devices are carried out in two steps. First, in order to obtain a complete record of the utilization of the devices and channels, it would be useful to record when the seek (for which the channel is not utilized) ends, and the search begins. Second, it allows greater flexibility in I/O scheduling. For example, if a high priority I/O operation must be initiated on a channel that is executing the channel program for a seek, then the channel program for a subsequent search can be deferred until completion of both seek and search of the high-priority I/O operation.

The cost of executing the I/O operations in this fashion is an extra interrupt for each operation. In most cases, there will be no high priority interrupt; therefore, when a seek program completes, the channel-complete-interrupt-response routine will only check for the presence of a higher priority I/O operation, then issue the instruction for the already prepared second step. Thus, the extra interrupt takes little processor time.

C. The Channel-Complete-Interrupt Response

The channel-complete-interrupt occurs at the completion of either a seek or a search and read or write, operation. An interrupt caused by the completion of a seek means that the channel was available to transmit the interrupt to the CPU. It also means that no search operations are on queue for the channel since an available channel requires no deferment of any seek operation. Therefore, the search and read or write operation can be initiated immediately upon the interrupt marking the completion of a seek operation.

If the interrupt is for the completion of a read or write operation, there may be other operations placed on queue for the channel during its busy period. First, other seek operations may have completed. The (inhibited) interrupts for these operations are held by the devices or device controllers until the channel becomes free. The channel-complete-interrupt-response routine (Fig. 5.16) will note these inhibited interrupts and service the interrupts by placing their corresponding search operations on the path set queues which include the free channel as a member.

Second, there may be another operation on queue for the device just terminating. In general, it will be a new seek, but if it is directed to the same cylinder as the operation just completed, only the search part is necessary. If it is a seek, it is initiated

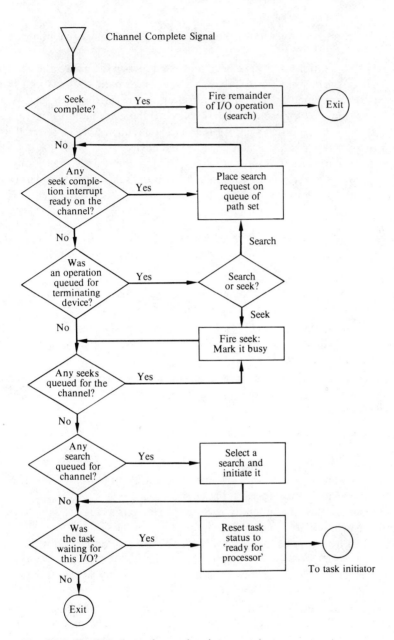

Fig. 5.16 The I/O-channel-complete-interrupt response.

immediately. If a search, it is queued for the path set along with other potential search operations.

Third, new I/O operations may have been requested during the period the channel was busy. Each of the new requests, for which the entire path set had been busy until this point, is represented by a seek operation on queue for the path set. These seek operations are initiated for each available device. If there are multiple operations directed toward one device on the path set queue, one operation is selected for initiation and the others are put on the queue for the device.

Last, one search operation is selected from among the search operations on queue for this channel. The selection is dependent upon I/O scheduling considerations previously mentioned.

D. The Task Initiator

The task initiator is the system program which decides which task will take control of the processor. It selects the task from a pool of available tasks. A task may not be available for the processor for one of several reasons.

1. The task is on queue for paging because a required page is not in the physical memory. Its return to available status is imminent.
2. The task is awaiting data requested in an I/O operation. During this period the blocks associated with the task may, of course, be taken by another task, according to the replacement algorithm.
3. The task is waiting for a response from a terminal. Since this wait is expected to take a long time, no system resources will be allocated to the task. The task is called a *dormant task*.

In case (1), the page-fault interrupt signals the system to block the processing of the task. The page-fault-interrupt-response routine of the system then removes the task from the status of being available for the processor.

In case (2), when an active task must wait for the completion of an I/O operation, it does not enter an "idle" loop. Instead, the task issues an I/O WAIT SVC. This tells the system that this task should be removed from the status of being available for the processor and the task initiator may place another task on the CPU.

Likewise, when a task must await a response from the terminal, as in case (3), it issues a TERMINAL WAIT SVC. In response to the TERMINAL WAIT SVC, the operating system places the task in a dormant state (possibly allows the task's pages to be paged out) and transfers to the task initiator to find another task for the processor.

Tasks whose processing has been halted for paging and I/O waits are returned to the active status by the paging channel or (I/O) channel-complete-interrupt-response routines. A dormant task is returned to active status by the routine which responds to the interrupt marking the completion of an input message from a terminal. This routine, called the *terminal-I/O-complete-interrupt-response* routine, is outlined in Fig. 5.17.

In summary, we note that physical I/O operations are tedious to prepare and subtle to manage. Nevertheless, such preparation and management are functions of the

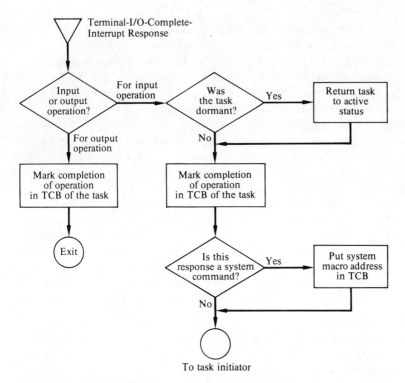

Fig. 5.17 The terminal-I/O-complete-interrupt response.

operating system. The collection of interrupt response routines, channel and device management routines, the device control blocks, and path set queues constitutes the basic elements of the *physical I/O control subsystem* (PIOCS) for the operating system.

5.2.2.3 Logical I/O Operations, LIOCS, and the File System*

In a multiprogramming system the user programs do not have direct control over the hardware of the system. Hence they do not specify I/O operations by physical addresses of secondary storage devices and the addresses of data areas on the devices. Instead, the operating system assigns to user data their locations on the storage

---

*   Logical I/O operations are needed in batch processing systems as well as in multi-programming systems. The file system is also a necessary part of online batch processing systems and multiprogramming systems as noted in Chapter 3. The reasons that the dis-cussions of the file system and logical operations are "belatedly" included in this chapter are as follows:

1. The logical I/O operations in batch processing systems and multiprogramming systems with or without virtual spaces are traditionally alike. By presenting the logical I/O operations in a more general environment (i.e., in virtual memory systems environment),

devices and issues for the user the hardware commands which require these hardware addresses. Furthermore, the operating system establishes and maintains the correspondence between the user names for data and the physical locations of the data. The correspondence between the user names and the physical locations of data is made in a set of system macros called *logical I/O* (or LI/O) *operations*. (See the exercise on logical I/O in Chapter 2.) More specifically, the user data are handled as logical records. Each logical record is assigned by the user program an alphanumeric *keyword*. In order to store records onto secondary storage, the user must first create a *file* for the records and assign a *file name* for the file. The creation of a file will cause the operating system to allocate secondary storage for the incoming records; the assignment of a file name will allow the user to refer to the collection of records as a logical entity. Consequently, the user program can employ logical I/O (LI/O) operations to store and retrieve records by referencing the records with their file names and keywords without the need to know their secondary storage addresses. The correspondences among the file names, record keywords, records, and addresses are maintained in the file system which will be discussed in the following section. The logical I/O operations which perform storage and retrieval of records and constitute the major part of the *logical I/O control subsystem LIOCS* will be elaborated upon.

A. A Simple File Structure

A file in secondary storage has three parts: a definition, a directory, and records. The *definition* contains the information concerning the file creation, access control requirements, and the secondary address of the file directory. The file *directory* is the set of (keyword, physical address) pairs that defines a mapping from the keyword of

---

the use of logical I/O operations in batch processing and multiprogramming systems can be specialized and derived. Thus, there is no need to repeat here some of the material that was presented in earlier chapters.

2. Logical I/O operations in virtual memory systems involve the understanding of virtual spaces. Any attempt to present the logical I/O operations in an earlier chapter would necessarily be incomplete because the notions and terminology of virtual space were not yet introduced.

3. Although traditional logical I/O operations are still supported by virtual memory systems, this support is available largely due to the requirements for program compatability. In other words, they have been implemented for virtual memory systems because old (user) programs using logical I/O developed on earlier systems without virtual spaces must be run on newer systems with virtual spaces. For example, the IBM 370 OS/VS2-1 supports logical I/O operations established by IBM 360 MFT. Likewise, IBM 370 OS/VS2-2 supports logical I/O operations of IBM 360 MVT. In these cases, user programs on IBM 360 can be moved to IBM 370 without causing any incompatibility of logical I/O operations. However, there are more efficient operations. One of them is called the *virtual access method* (VAM) which is available only on virtual memory systems. Therefore, the discussion of logical I/O alongside of the discussion of VAM may serve as a contrast for more efficient I/O. It is hoped that the user of the new systems will use VAM for his new program activity and gradually replace the logical I/O with VAM in his old programs.

The rationale to include the discussion of the file system in this chapter is similar to the one made for logical I/O.

each record in a file to the physical address of the record in secondary storage. It will be structured in multiple levels if it is too large to be contained in a single track. (To aid clarity, we will not use the term physical record or block. The former may be confused with logical record; the latter with the main memory block for paging.) If the keywords of the records in the file are arranged in alphanumeric order, and the set of (keyword, physical address) pairs extends over more than one track, a two-level directory is necessary as depicted in Fig. 5.18. The first level is the set of (high-keyword, second-level track address) pairs, where high-keyword is the largest (and last) keyword on the corresponding second-level track. The second level will be the pairs that define the mapping, extending over as many tracks as are necessary.

Letting K_i denote keyword i, we have:

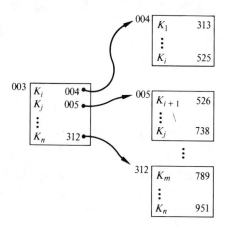

Figure 5.18 A two-level directory implementation of a simple file.

The records of the file are stored on tracks. If more than one record is stored on a single track, the records on the track are ordered lexicographically by their keywords. The file structure is recursively extendable in the following way: the records of one file may become the file definition of another. Referring to Fig. 5.19, we note that the file definition of B is a record of File A. Thus, we say that file A is the *predecessor* of file B and B is the *successor* of A. In symbol, we have $A = P(B)$. A user program may refer to file B by the *qualified file name A.B*.

B. Address Transformation of User Files

A list of all the files, known as the *system catalog* (Syscat), is maintained in the system. It takes the form of a nonhomogeneous tree, i.e., starting from the root of the Syscat (the file whose definition is not a record of another file), the number of files that must be searched in order to reach an endpoint (which is a user file) is not the same for each endpoint. Figure 5.20 is a representation of the Syscat as a tree.

A particular file may be specified by a fully qualified file name—that is, the name may be composed of the concatenation of several file names—each of which specifies

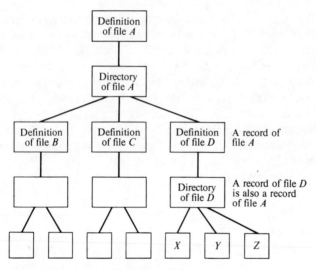

Fig. 5.19 The structure of file A.

the branch that is taken in the Syscat tree in the search for that file. For example, in Fig. 5.20, the file name *A.B.E.F.H.* is a fully qualified name; it specifies one user file. The name *A.C.* is partially qualified; it specifies a file of user files.

The name of the user that owns a particular file appears as some part of the fully qualified file name. A file named after an owner of any file therefore appears at some level of the Syscat. This file is the root of a subtree of the Syscat tree, which defines a file whose elements are all the files owned by that user. This root will be called the user's *file of files* (FOF).

The first level of Syscat is a file with a multilevel directory; the first level of the directory is resident in virtual space, and the remaining directory levels are resident on a secondary storage device. The records of the Syscat are the file definitions of user private and shared files.

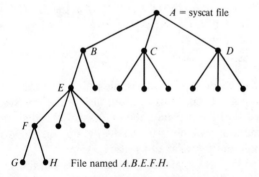

Fig. 5.20 Abstract structure of naming convention.

Figure 5.21 is a representation of a typical system catalog. It has two levels for each of the files that are owned by a user, and one level for the public files. The records of the first level of the Syscat are therefore either the definitions of the FOF's for the various users or the definitions of public files.

This is the Syscat structure that will be used to demonstrate the operation of the logical I/O operations. It has the features of a multilevel structure; however, for our discussion, the two levels of file structures are sufficient. The generalization to an arbitrary multilevel structure is straightforward.

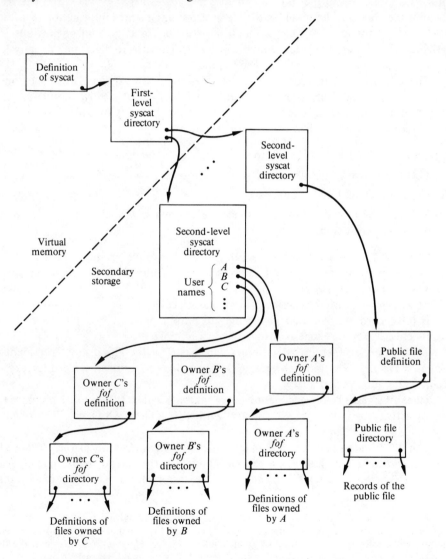

Fig. 5.21 Structure of Syscat.

C. Logical I/O Operations

In general, a user task requests logical I/O operations by issuing an SVC for the
GET and PUT macros. These macros bring, or store, a record from or to the file,
respectively.

The input to each macro consists of (1) the virtual address to or from which the
record is to be moved, (2) the file name, and (3) the keyword of the record.

During the time that a file is active for I/O operations, the system maintains
information relevant to the status of the file in a *file control block* (FCB). The FCB
contains the file name, a pointer to the file directory, and status information regarding
those parts of the file that can be found in virtual space as a result of previous I/O
activities. The latter is referenced by the logical I/O macros to determine the physical
I/O operations which must be executed for the macros.

The GET and PUT macros assume that files to be operated on have previously
been opened. Otherwise, an error condition will result. Basically, the file-opening
operation has the effect of placing the address of the directory of a file F in the FCB.
The macro GET F, X will then perform the following steps:

a) Bring the directory of file F into virtual space.

b) Locate the track containing the record whose keyword is X in the directory.

c) Bring this track into virtual space.*

d) Relocate the record X in virtual space. (For brevity, record X means the record
whose keyword is X).

The next time the GET macro is called—GET F, Y, for example—it will not be
necessary to perform step (a) because the directory of F already resides in virtual space.
Likewise, it is not necessary to perform step (b) if record Y is on the same track as
record X, since this track is resident in virtual space.

If the record is not found in the file, an output parameter of the macro is set
to this effect. The GET macro is outlined in Fig. 5.22.

The GET macro therefore determines which part of the file, if any, is resident in
virtual space before issuing physical I/O instructions to bring the file directory or
record track into virtual space.

Since a file must be opened before its GET macro is called, the user task prepares the
file for activity by issuing an OPEN macro with SVC. The OPEN macro is outlined in
Fig. 5.23.

The OPEN macro calls the GET macro to obtain the definition of the file F. The
input parameters to this call are the file name and the record index in the form:
GET P(F),F. (Recall that $P(F)$ means the predecessor of F.) The open macro then

---

* It is not imperative that the entire track be brought into virtual space, since the hardware
may search for the required record and bring just that into virtual space. However, this
method will conform to the method of greatest efficiency for sequential processing of the file.
In sequential processing, it is assumed that if record X is obtained, records Y and Z, which
are on the same track, will be required imminently, therefore, they might as well be obtained
with record X by reading the entire track.

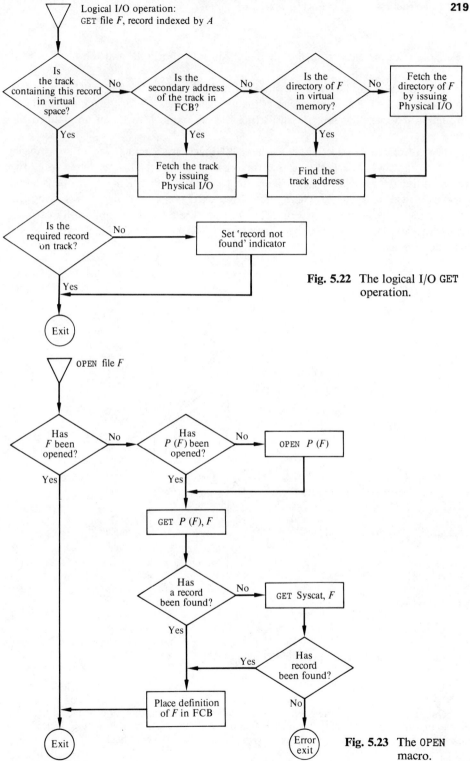

Fig. 5.22 The logical I/O GET operation.

Fig. 5.23 The OPEN macro.

places the relevant data from the file definition into the FCB, and the file F is thus opened.

If a FOF was the input to the call on the OPEN macro, the file P(FOF) is in fact the Syscat. If the file F is not found in the file $P(F)$, a search for the file F is initiated throughout Syscat (first level), considering the file name F to be an unqualified file name.

The entire operation of the OPEN and GET macros is summarized in an example shown in Fig. 5.24. It is assumed that the user, for whom the task is defined, and the owner of the files needed by the task are the same.* The first time a user opens a file, the user's FOF is opened. The Syscat is searched, via a GET macro specifying the user's name. Operation (1) in Fig. 5.24(a) brings the second level of the Syscat into virtual space. Operation (2) then brings in the Syscat record, which is the user's FOF definition.

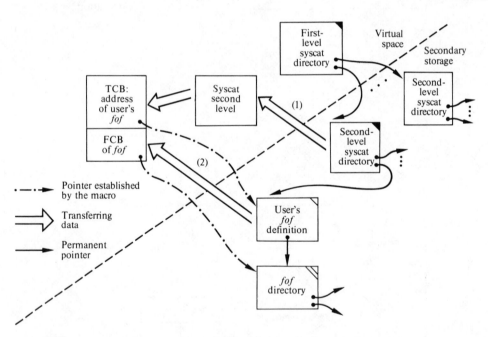

(a) 'GET Syscat, user name' is called by 'OPEN fof' which is, in turn, called by the 'GET P(A), A'

Fig. 5.24(a) Physical operations in file OPEN and GET.

---

*   This is not necessarily the case. The two individuals' names may, however, be equated in the LOGON process, and the owner's name will then be available in the TCB. The operation is subject to security and privacy procedures not covered here.

By means of a GET P(A),A macro, operation (3) brings in the directory of the FOF, the listing of the names and locations of all the user files (see Fig. 5.24(b)). This listing will remain resident in virtual space and serve as the *user catalog* (Usercat). From then on, all user-specified file operations will first consult the Usercat before searching for file names in Syscat.

Having found the secondary address of file A in the Usercat, the file definition of file A is brought into virtual space by operation (4). File A is then opened. Next, the Usercat is modified to replace the secondary address of the file definition with the virtual address of file A in FCB.

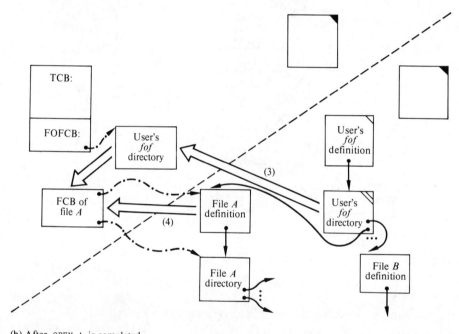

(b) After OPEN A is completed

Figure 5.24(b)

Lastly, the macro GET A,X involves two operations shown in Fig. 5.24(c). Operation (5) will now find the secondary address of the directory of file A in Usercat and bring the directory into virtual space. Operation (6) will bring the track containing the record indexed by X into virtual space. Later, when the GET macro is called again for a record in file A, not all of the physical I/O operations associated with the GET macro will be necessary.

The PUT macro restores a record to a file. Its operation is quite similar to that of the GET macro. We will not discuss it here.

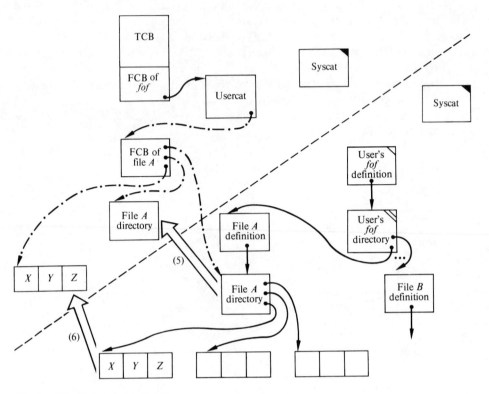

(c) After GET   A,X is accomplished

Figure 5.24(c)

In summary, we note that the logical I/O operations are operations on files whose records are usually smaller than the physical record (e.g., track) size. By retrieving the larger physical record and utilizing deblocking, the logical records can be dispatched to the user task in a GET operation. On the other hand, the smaller logical records are blocked into a physical record for a PUT operation. The use of a large blocking factor (thus large physical record size) is primarily designed to take advantage of the high transfer rate of the I/O channels and devices on the one hand, and to offset the long access time of the secondary devices on the other hand. However, none of these design considerations have taken seriously the effects of logical I/O operations in virtual memory systems. This problem is particularly acute since the block sizes for I/O (e.g., track or cylinder sizes) are usually very large, and the block size for paging (i.e., the page size) is small. By requiring large block size for logical I/O operations and by performing deblocking and blocking in virtual space for large physical records, a great number of pages (thus physical memory blocks) are required.

Therefore, attempts have been made to improve the traditional logical I/O operations for virtual memory systems. We will discuss these attempts at greater length in the following section.

The logical I/O macros, such as GET, PUT, OPEN and others, constitute the basic elements of the logical I/O control subsystem (LIOCS). The function of the LIOCS to perform blocking, deblocking, buffer switching, and management (say, keeping all the buffer pages in physical memory blocks) is usually referred to as the I/O buffering subsystem (IOBS). Because secondary storage devices must be identified before use, it is necessary for the LIOCS to verify these devices (say, removable disk packs) by their labels. The part of the LIOCS which retrieves, writes, and verifies labels is commonly called the I/O verification subsystem (IOVS). (For a discussion on IOBS and IOVS, the reader may refer to Chapter 2).

On-line batch processing systems, multiprogramming systems, and virtual memory systems made the use of on-line storage devices and central information repository a necessity. Information is organized into files and records. References to files and records are made by their names and keywords. Directories are created to keep track of the whereabouts of files and records. In particular, the system catalog which serves as a master directory to all other directories, files, and records is made a part of the operating system. The catalog, the directories, the files and records, and the facilities which maintain them are collectively called the *file system*.

5.2.2.4 The Virtual Access Method (VAM)

The virtual access method to be discussed in the sequel is a set of logical I/O operations which take advantage of the organization of the virtual space and the address translation mechanism of the system. Thus it is unique to virtual memory operating systems. Obviously, the influence of the virtual space organization and the translation mechanism on the method is significant. Both the file structure and the record organization must be reformatted. For convenience, we shall refer these files, directories, and records as VAM files, VAM directories, and VAM records. Nevertheless, the catalog scheme discussed in the previous sections is still applicable here.

A VAM record of a VAM file may extend over several pages of the virtual space. The records are therefore variable length. One page of a VAM record contains the *table of contents* (*TOC*) which refers to the specific items in the remainder of the record. In calling for a VAM record, the user does not specify the virtual address at which he would like the retrieved record to reside; instead, the access method (macro) obtains all the virtual space that is needed and provides the user task with the virtual address of the record. The access method also provides the task with the address of the TOC for the record. The TOC will contain addresses which are relative to the beginning of the record. The user task can therefore locate the specific items of interest in the virtual space allocated for the VAM record.

Thus, retrieving a VAM record of a file for a user is equivalent to allocating virtual space for the entire file and its directory. However, not all of the allocated space is placed in physical memory. The user may then access selected portions of the VAM records within the VAM file, causing only the needed portions of the VAM record to be transferred into physical memory.

The efficiency of the virtual access method is obvious because, in addition to the table of contents, only the parts of a record that are needed are brought into physical memory.

The operation of this access method parallels the paging operation. When a page of a virtual space has not been placed in the physical memory, the page table entry for that page is marked "not-in-physical-memory." The address in this page table entry is then the address of the page on the backing storage. This address is used by the paging routine to initiate a physical I/O operation to the backing storage. The same technique is now extended to include pages residing on secondary devices for files. When the virtual space is allocated to the pages of VAM records, page table entries are assigned to the pages, but these entries are marked "not-in-virtual-space" and the address associated with the entries are their addresses on the secondary storage device. When a page marked "not-in-physical-memory" is referenced, a page-fault interrupt occurs, resulting in an I/O operation from the backing storage (i.e., paging device). When a page marked "not-in-virtual-space" is referenced, a page-fault interrupt will also occur. In this case the paging operation that results will be a read operation from the secondary storage device instead of the paging device. Thus the similarity between the paging operation and virtual access method is apparent.

The operation of the virtual access method will now be discussed in some detail. Although the VAM records of a VAM file are of variable length, no indication of record lengths are contained in the file directory. In particular, a VAM record's TOC may also be of variable length. On the other hand, the physical records are of fixed length because both the page size and track size are of fixed length. Thus, variable length VAM records must be fitted into a standard fixed length format. The choice of fixed length format varies from one virtual memory system to another. Unlike the physical record size in a nonvirtual memory system which can be more flexible, the physical record size chosen for a virtual memory system must be related to the page size in addition to the track size. Usually this format size is a fixed multiple of the page size (or half-page size if the facility to reference half-pages is available). For this discussion, we will refer to physical records as *tracks*.

A way of fitting those records into fixed length format is to define a TOC for the TOC—essentially constructing a TOC in the form of a multilevel directory. Henceforth, TOC for a VAM record will refer to only the first, fixed length portion of the TOC. Starting from the TOC, then, the accessing of any particular item within the record may occur in a multistep operation.

The remainder of the VAM record will be on the physical tracks following the TOC track, in the address space of the secondary device. Then, with the physical (secondary) address of the beginning of the VAM record known, and the logical address (with respect to the beginning of the record) of a data element known, the address of the track containing the data element will be known.

An outline of the steps of the VAM GET macro is depicted in Fig. 5.25. First, the VAM GET macro calls on a system routine to allocate enough virtual space to contain the TOC for a record of this file. Then, the TOC which contains the record length

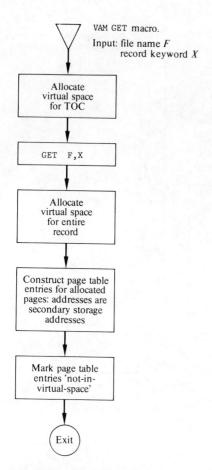

Fig. 5.25 VAM GET macro.

will be brought into virtual space. The accessing of the VAM TOC may be performed by the regular GET routine previously described. With the virtual space allocated for the TOC of record *A*, the GET F,A operation will be assumed to bring the TOC of record *A* into virtual space. This is operation (1) in Fig. 5.26.

Next, enough virtual space is allocated to contain the entire record, and the page table entries for this virtual space are constructed. These are (2) and (3) of Fig. 5.26. The page table entries will contain a "not-in-virtual-space" flag. The secondary addresses of the pages are calculated from the initial secondary address of the record, and placed in the page table. This is operation (4) of Fig. 5.26.

It is interesting to note that not only can the files and records on the secondary storage be "logically" moved into virtual space by updating the translation tables and utilizing I/O operations similar to paging, but one can go several steps further by considering all the storage (other than the physical memory), whether it is backing storage for pages or secondary storage for files and records, as parts of a hierarchy

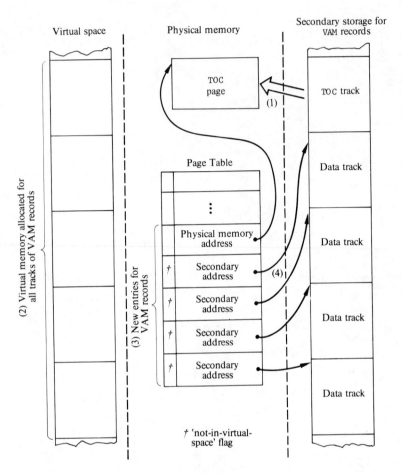

Fig. 5.26 The operation of VAM GET.

of storage. The physical (main) memory is the memory in which programs are executed. The hierarchy is for on-line storage and retrieval of information. In order to provide "unified" I/O operations to store and retrieve information in the hierarchy, these I/O operations must be "intelligent" enough so that more readily needed information such as program pages will be stored in high-performance storage for rapid retrieval and storage and less frequently used information such as journal tapes will be stored in low-performance storage for less frequent access. Such a hierarchy is, perhaps, the first step toward the one-level storage concept as outlined earlier.

5.2.2.5 Economization of Virtual Space

The use of virtual spaces in a virtual memory system can also be viewed as an attempt to economize the physical memory of the system. When an active task operates in physical memory, the expensive physical memory is conserved by allocating to the task only the physical memory (usually a block or two) that is absolutely necessary to its operation at any instant. For the remainder of the task (i.e., the less active part), low-cost backing storage is substituted for the higher-cost physical memory.

At some point, even the backing storage, which now contains the entire virtual space of each task, will become excessively large relative to its cost. The same technique used to conserve physical memory can be applied again to conserve virtual space. That is, only the parts of the task that are actively in the virtual space are allocated with backing storage. Of course, the operating definition of "active" here must be considerably less stringent than the definition which allows a part of the task to reside in physical memory. The remainder of the virtual space is kept resident on some even less expensive mass memory device. The logical extension of this is, of course, a hierarchy of memory devices, each device in the hierarchy being bigger, slower, and less expensive (per unit of information) than a device at the level above. Programs and data will move up and down in the hierarchy, based on their utilizations over periods ranging from fractions of microseconds at the top, to years at the bottom. This extension is again the concept of one-level storage. Here the hierarchy represents the organization of memory devices. However, as far as the user or user task is concerned, the entire hierarchy is his virtual space. In other words, the hierarchy is transparent to him, making the storage supported by the devices look like a single level.

A. The Use of Reentrant Programs for Storage Economization

The technique of writing user programs to be reentrant has been discussed in previous chapters. This technique represents a saving of physical memory only if one user requires a page of program (more specifically, an execution phase of the program) at the same instant that another user is using that page (i.e., another user has allocated physical memory for it). Because this usage is difficult to achieve, the saving of physical memory due to reentrant programming technique is hard to achieve. However, this technique results in a greater optimization of backing storage, because only one copy of the program need be resident in the backing storage for all users of the program.

B. The Use of Dynamic Call for Storage Economization

Another economy of backing storage is the *dynamic call*. Assume a user task is executing one program *A*, which requires the services of another program *B*. Both of these programs must be loaded into the same virtual space, so that they can communicate with each other. Traditionally, these programs have been loaded into the same virtual space and linked together before the task is run, i.e., before the execution of program *A* has begun. (This loading and linking process is characterized by static relocation as reviewed in the earlier part of this chapter.) Thus, the virtual space of the task must be large enough to include both programs throughout the operation of the task.

A saving of virtual space for the task is apparent if the program *B* is not loaded into the virtual space of the task until the actual call on *B* takes place. The system

CALL macro will perform the function of loading and linking program *B*, and transferring to it. The CALL macro therefore utilizes a loader known as the *dynamic linking loader*. In the following section, we will discuss the dynamic loader, the use of the CALL macro, and the new loading and linking process.

5.2.2.6 Dynamic Linking

A. The Functions of the Dynamic Linking Loader

The loader performs the following functions:

1. Allocates the virtual space required for a program.
2. Moves the program into virtual space.
3. Resolves all internal relocation and external symbols in the program.

In performing the first function, the loader must first (a) determine the size of the program to be loaded, (b) reference the system tables to allocate backing storage tracks for the program, and (c) create entries for this program in the page table of the task which requested the program.

The second function entails physical I/O operations which move the program into virtual space.

For the third function, there is an implicit I/O operation which must be performed to bring the data required for the resolution of addresses into virtual space, to be used by the loader. Resolving the internal relocation symbols of a program can then be performed in virtual space. The resolution of external symbols, however, may involve several physical I/O operations, and, in fact, may result in another call on the loader.

B. Resolution of Address References

Let us review the process of address resolution. This process was, of course, discussed in Chapter 1. Nevertheless, we will repeat it for virtual memory systems, relating the following discussion to the material presented in Chapter 1.

Each instruction in a program potentially contains a virtual address which is the specification of the operand of the instruction. At the time a program is assembled or compiled, the program is not contained in any virtual space. Therefore, addresses contained within the program are not completely specified. The addresses are written as displacements relative to the beginning of the program, and are called relative addresses (see Section 1.4.4). When the program is loaded into virtual space, the specification of the addresses contained within the program must be completed. The loader does this, in general, by adding the absolute virtual address of the beginning of the program to each relative address contained within the program. Such a process is called *address resolution*.

There are several methods of reducing the number of addresses that must be resolved by the loader. One is the technique of base register addressing. At the beginning of the execution of a program, a few instructions place both the starting address of the program and the beginning address of the data area into base registers.

Throughout the remainder of the program, instructions which use the addresses in the base registers replace those which would have contained the addresses explicitly. By referring to addresses implicitly via base registers and eliminating the use of explicit addresses throughout the main part of a program, the program may be considered to reside in more than one virtual space. Such a program can be used as a *shared program* by several virtual spaces.

Using the above technique, the problem of resolving the addresses of internal relocation symbols of a program when it is relocated in virtual space can be alleviated.

The more difficult task in the address resolution occurs when addresses that are used in one program A are defined within another program B. If A and B were compiled or assembled separately, the language processor of program A has no knowledge of the values of the symbols that are defined within B. Aside from the fact that these symbols are not defined within any virtual space, their value even relative to program B is unknown. Therefore, the language processor of A leaves those external symbols in the form of alphanumeric names. The values of these symbols must be determined at the time the program is loaded into virtual space. In other words, the output of a language processor (i.e., an object module), consists of program proper (i.e., the instructions and constants that comprise the program itself) and two dictionaries of address-specifying information: the internal relocation symbol dictionary and the external symbol dictionary. Obviously, the information used by the loader for calculating the values of the symbols is contained in the aforementioned dictionaries.

The first dictionary contains a specification of locations within the program which contain addresses. The loader needs this dictionary in order to modify those locations when the program is loaded into virtual space.

The second dictionary contains two types of information (see also Section 1.3.3.2). The first type is the set of external symbolic names called *externally defined symbols* (REFS). These are names used within program A which are defined within some other program. These alphanumeric names are placed in a *REF table* by the language processor. In general, there may be many points within A which contain a reference to one externally defined symbol. Therefore, the program proper of the object module will contain a pointer to an entry in the REF table at each point where an external reference is made. Although the REF table entry may include pointers to each location within the program at which the address is required, this technique is usually not used. In either case, the loader must be capable of placing the proper definition of the external reference into the program. The link between the program word (or byte) that requires the address and the name itself must be present.

The second type of address information is the set of entry points called *symbol definitions* (DEFS). These are the symbolic locations within program A that may be referenced by some other program. The language processor creates a table of correspondence between the DEF's, which are represented by alphanumeric names, and their values, which are their addresses relative to program A. This table is called the *DEF table*.

Two object modules containing explicit representations of the links in the REF and DEF tables are shown in Fig. 5.27.

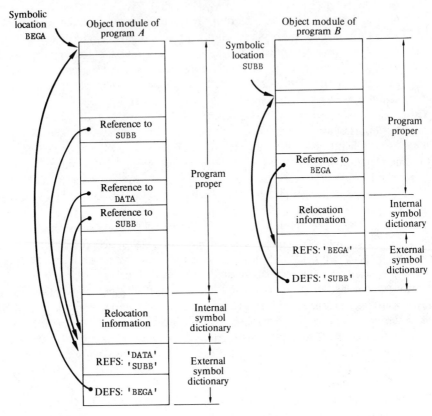

Fig. 5.27 Address specifying information contained within object modules.

After the program has been loaded into a virtual space, the relocation information (for internal addresses) may be discarded, since all of the internal references have been specified. Then, the REFS must be resolved. The loader cannot complete the loading of program *A* until the DEFS of program *B*, which are REFS of program *A*, are assigned virtual addresses. The loader allocates space for program *B* and loads it into virtual space before returning to complete the loading of program *A*. The REFS in program *A* are given their virtual addresses, and then the table of REFS is discarded. Because programs that are loaded later may contain a REF to a location within program *A*, the DEF table of program *A* must be saved. Furthermore, the DEF table need not now contain relative addresses. Since each symbol in the DEF table now has a value which is a virtual address, the table is updated to contain the correspondence between DEF symbols and their virtual addresses.

Potentially, there are as many DEF tables as there are loaded programs for a task. To consolidate the tables and facilitate the resolution, these tables are moved into a separate area called the *task dictionary* (TDY) of the task. Each time a new program is loaded for a task, the TDY of the task will be searched for each new REF. If every REF of the new program is found in the TDY, no recursive call on the dynamic linking loader will be necessary to load new programs in order to resolve REFS.

C. Loading and Linking Operation

In order to load a program for a task into virtual space, the loader must perform the following five steps, although some of the steps do not necessarily have to be completed before other steps are performed.

1. Allocate virtual space for the program.
2. Move the text of the program (i.e., the program proper) to the virtual space.
3. Update each relative address in the text of the program. The relocation information in the internal relocation symbol and external symbol dictionaries must be be available during this step.
4. Update the DEF table by completing the address of each symbol in this table. The DEF table is now consolidated into the TDY of the task which may be referenced by the loader during the loading of another program containing a REF to this program.
5. Define each entry in the REF table. This process involves
   a) a search of the TDY for each REF symbol,
   b) a search of the user file catalog for the symbol if it is not found in the TDY, and
   c) a search for the symbol in the Syscat if it is not found in the user file definition area.

In cases (b) and (c), the REF is to be found in a program that is not yet loaded. Thus, the REF cannot be defined until the corresponding program is loaded. Consequently, the program containing the symbol must be found and a recursive call on the loader must be made before this step can be completed. When the symbol is defined, each reference to it in the program is completed. Finally, when this is done, the REF table may be discarded.

In Fig. 5.28, we show by way of an example how each of the REF's in program A given in Fig. 5.27 is resolved as A is loaded. Before A is loaded, on the program ORIG resides in the virtual space of the task as depicted in Fig. 5.28(a). During loading of the program A, the REF SUBB is not found in the TDY, which contains all the external symbols defined in previously loaded programs as depicted in Fig. 5.28(b). A search through the file catalog shows that SUBB is defined in program B. Therefore, the program B is loaded, and the updated DEF table of the program B is added to the TDY. The address within A can now be completely specified as depicted in Fig. 5.28(c).

D. Loading and Linking With the Virtual Access Method

As presented in the preceding section, the loader is a heavy user of the I/O operations. To achieve whatever economies of machine utilization are possible during these I/O operations, the loader will use the virtual access method (VAM). When the virtual

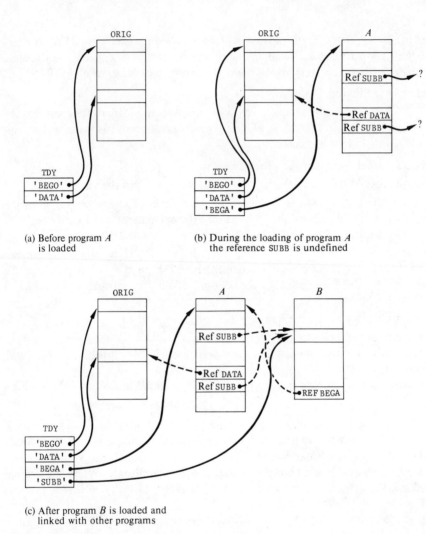

(a) Before program *A*
is loaded

(b) During the loading of program *A*
the reference SUBB is undefined

(c) After program *B* is loaded and
linked with other programs

Fig. 5.28 Resolution of external symbols.

access method is employed, the data is physically moved only as the data is used, one
page at a time. In this case, a page of a program will be brought into virtual space
only when it is accessed in the course of executing the program. In other words, the
program is "forced" into execution before it is completely loaded and linked. The
loader, however, must resolve the program's addresses after the program proper is
brought in from the secondary device. This implies that the loader operation must
be distributed so that, as the pages are brought in from secondary storage, the loader
will operate on one page of a program at a time.

If the loader is called to load one page at a time, it must maintain all the address-specifying information in virtual space until each page of the program is loaded. The address-specifying information for each page must be available in physical memory as the page is loaded.

Two separate operations are therefore needed. One is the preparation for the loading of a program; this operation, called the *program-load* operation, is called once for each program to be loaded. The program proper is not moved during this operation.

The second load operation, the *page-load* operation, will be performed as each page of the program to be loaded is accessed for the first time. The obvious way to call the page-load operation is in response to a page fault.

The program-load operation which uses the VAM can be implemented as a macro as follows. Using the name of the program as an argument, the operation calls the VAM GET. The VAM GET will return the virtual address allocated to the program, the length of the program, and the virtual address of the table of contents (TOC). In the case of an object module (VAM) record, the TOC contains the addresses of the relocation-specifying information (including DEF table and REF table) of the object module. The operation then moves the DEF and REF tables to the TDY, so that they may be referenced later during the page-load operation. As soon as this information is accessed, a page fault occurs and an implicit call on the VAM paging routine occurs. This brings the page containing the program relocation-specifying information into physical memory.

Since the VAM call provided the virtual address at which the program is to be loaded, the loader can make the correspondence between each relative address within the program and its virtual address. In particular, the loader can complete the DEF table for the program. The REF table may be completed when the REFS are needed, at the time of the call for page-load operation.

Lastly, the (VAM) page-load operation must be informed whether the page contains data or program. This information is left in the page table. Along with the not-in-physical-memory and the not-in-virtual-space bits, there will be an unprocessed-by-loader bit for each page that contains program sections.*

A summary of the load operation is depicted in Fig. 5.29.

E. The Page Loader

When a page fault occurs during the execution of a program, the page-fault-interrupt-response routine checks the not-in-virtual-space bit of the page table. If it is set, the paging routine initiates a physical I/O operation for the page. When the physical read operation is completed, the routine checks the unprocessed-by-loader bit for the page.

---

*   Not every page in the program proper of a program will require loading operations, because programs can be written at least in part without containing any address constants. For example, a reentrant program contains no addresses of modifiable data.

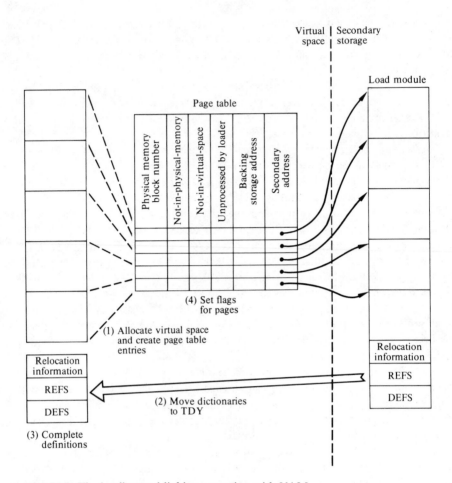

Fig. 5.29 The loading and linking operation with VAM.

If it is set, a loading process must begin. The system program which handles the load-ing of program pages is called the *page loader*.

The page loader finds the relocation information corresponding to this page in the TDY. The address computation for each specified word in the relocation inform ation table is performed. If any address requires the definition of a REF, the TDY is searched for the REF. If this search is not successful, first the user catalog, and then the system catalog are searched for the symbol definition. If it is found, the program containing the symbol must be loaded in order that the REF may be resolved.

The operation of the page loader is outlined in Fig. 5.30.

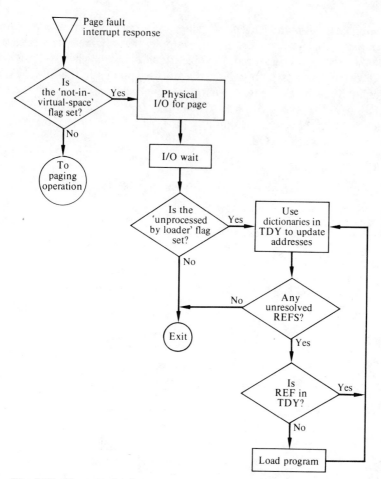

Fig. 5.30 The page loader.

5.2.2.7 Multitasking

The concept of multitasking has been motivated in the previous chapter. The need for synchronization and interlock mechanisms for the purpose of coordinating running tasks has also been presented there in the context of system deadlock over shared resources. We will not repeat those discussions here. In this section, we will discuss the process of creating and destroying tasks without which the notion of multitasking will not take place.

The desire to create new tasks is often prompted when one task is required to perform several logical functions. By creating another (sub-) task to perform one or more of these logical functions, it is hoped that there will be a reduction in the total time required, since some functions will then be performed in parallel. The task and the subtask may run in parallel even on a single-processor system, by competing for system resources. One consequence is, for example, that one task may take the processor while the other is waiting for an I/O operation. In creating a TCB for a new subtask, only a virtual address representing the starting point for the new task is required. Other data—such as the page table for the new task, file security, and access control information—may be copied directly from the TCB of the originating task. In fact, the subtask may have only a dummy TCB, containing little more than a pointer to the originating task's TCB.

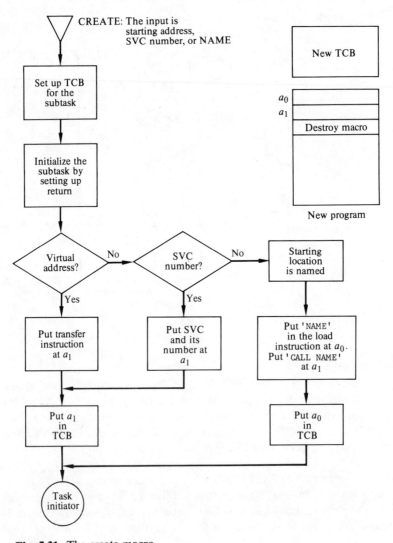

Fig. 5.31 The create macro.

The CREATE macro, used to create subtasks, may operate in one of several ways, depending upon how the subtask's starting location is specified. This may be specified by one of the following three ways: (1) as a literal name of a program, (2) as the SVC number of a system program, and (3) as the virtual address of a program. In the first case, the CREATE macro searches the Syscat for the name of the program, locates it, and transfers to it. In each case the CREATE macro performs the transfer by constructing a small program to receive the return of the routine, then inserting either the SVC or the transfer instruction in that program, and then transferring to the created program.

In Fig. 5.31 the operation of the CREATE macro is outlined. The three general methods of specification of the starting point for the subtask are deciphered by this macro, and the program representing the beginning of the subtask is shown. The operations of the subtask occur in a subroutine in this representation, and the program for the subtask consists of a transfer instruction to the subroutine and a return point.

After it is run, the subtask can be removed from the system by issuing a DESTROY macro. The DESTROY macro works in an analogous way to the CREATE macro and will not be detailed here.

5.2.3 SUMMARY

The presentation of the generalized virtual memory system follows the same approach as the presentation of the batch processing systems. The approach is to examine first the resident parts of the operating system, then the PIOCS and LIOCS, and finally the file system. There are considerable similarities among the batch processing system, the multiprogramming system, and the virtual memory system in terms of their basic capabilities in handling physical operations and resources such as channels, devices, and I/O operations. For on-line systems, whether they are batch processing, multiprogramming, or virtual memory systems, the need for a set of logical I/O operations and a centralized file system is universal. Thus it is not surprising that the better endowed virtual memory system can also support batch processing—on-line or off-line. What makes the virtual memory system unique is its ability to provide *interactive processing*. In an interactive processing system, the overwhelming emphasis is on fast response time. As we recall, by response time we mean the elapsed time between the demand of output and the arrival of output. To facilitate fast response, the time slice and turn-taking procedure are used to schedule the user jobs. By taking turns and receiving a time slice from the system, a competing job can proceed with some processing, and generate some output, resulting in some responses. When it is the turn of the job to proceed, the virtual memory system must relocate it in the memory, allocate space for its data and routines, retrieve filed data and routines for its use, and load and link its routines dynamically. These requirements can be met because the virtual memory system has the capability to relocate programs repetitively, allocate space dynamically, access data and routines on secondary storage efficiently (via VAM), and load and link routines on the fly. There are additional means to improve the response time. For example, the omnibus job can be organized into more refined tasks. The concept of multitasking is therefore introduced. The multitasking concept also improves system utilization, since more refined tasks are always easier to manage for system throughput than are omnibus jobs. With good response time and system throughput, an interactive virtual memory system can serve many users where an individual user may think that he has all the system resources at his disposal, although most of the resources are shared with other users. Such a system is often referred to as a *time-sharing system*.

5.3 POSTSCRIPT

The discussion of virtual space is based on the views outlined in [10] and [18], Specific examples of virtual space implementations are derived from [14], [15], [24], [27], [30], and [31]. The one-level storage concept is originated in [16] and the concept of segmentation is due to the Burrough's B5500; these concepts are generalized in [6]. The generalized virtual memory system is designed with some of the prevailing notions and common approaches found in [5], [19], [23], [28], and [32]. The first draft of the sections on the generalized virtual memory system was written for the 1970 Summer Program on *Multiprogramming Systems Design Principles* (as noted in the preface) and was subsequently included in [21].

The recent introduction of IBM 370 operating systems such as OS/VS2 Release 1 and Release 2 has added the impetus toward virtual memory systems. The OS/VS2 Release 1 and Release 2 are intended to replace the OS/360 MFT and MVT, both of which have been discussed in Chapter 4. The major difference between Release 1 and Release 2 lies in the support of virtual spaces. In Release 1 there can only be a single virtual space; in Release 2 there can be one virtual space for each user. The multiplicity of virtual spaces is discussed in the earlier part of this chapter. The virtual memory system included in this chapter can serve as an introduction to these large systems. For example, the file catalog scheme is a simplification of the ones used in Release 1 and 2. The virtual access method (VAM) is an introduction to VSAM and VIO of these two releases. For references on OS/VS2 Release 1 and Release 2, the reader may begin with [28].

Due to limited space, this chapter cannot discuss some of the topics such as paging algorithms, the influence of paging on programs, demand paging and other paging strategies, and storage fragmentation in paged memory. However, the reader may find some interesting references on paging algorithms in [2], the influence of paging on programs in [4], demand paging in [7], [17], and [29], paging strategies in [9] and [26], storage fragmentation in paged memory in [25], and backing storage for paging in [8].

No exercise is included in this chapter. However, the generalized virtual memory system outlined in the chapter can be used as the basis for design and implementation studies on various system components. A more ambitious undertaking may include the development of a complete system on a virtual memory computer using the system components resulting from the studies.

REFERENCES

1. M. A. Auslander, and J. F. Jaffe. "Functional Structure of IBM Virtual Storage Operating Systems—Part I: Influences of Dynamic Address Translation on Operating System Technology." *IBM Systems Journal* **12**, 4 (1973): 368–381.

2. L. A. Belady. "A Study of Replacement Algorithms for a Virtual Storage Computer." *IBM Systems Journal* **5**, 2 (1966): 78–101.

3. J. P. Birch. "Functional Structures of IBM Virtual Storage Operating Systems—Part III: Architecture and Design of DOS/VS." *IBM Systems Journal* **12**, 4 (1973): 401–411.

4. B. S. Braun and F. G. Gustavson. "Program Behavior in a Paging Environment." *Proc. AFIPS 1968 FJCC* **33**, 2 (1968): 1019–1032.

5. F. J. Corbató and V. A. Vyssotsky. "Introduction and Overview of the MULTICS System." *Proc. AFIPS 1965 FJCC* **27**, 1 (1965): 185–196.

6. R. C. Daley and J. B. Dennis. "Virtual Memory, Processes and Sharing in MULTICS." *Comm. ACM* **11**, 5 (May 1968): 306–322.

7. W. M. Demeis and N. Weizer. "Measurement and Analysis of a Demand Paging Time Sharing System." *Proc. of 24th National Conference of ACM*, 1969, pp. 201–216.

8. P. J. Denning. *Queuing Models for File Memory Operation*, MAC-TR-21 (M.S. Thesis), Project MAC, MIT, October 1965.

9. P. J. Denning. "The Working Set Model for Program Behavior." *Comm. ACM* **11**, 5 (May 1968): 323–333.

10. J. B. Dennis. "Segmentation and Design of Multiprogrammed Computer Systems." *Journal of the ACM* **12**, 4 (October 1965): 589–602.

11. H. Hellerman. "Some Principles of Time-Sharing Scheduler Strategies." *IBM Systems Journal* **8**, 2 (1969): 94–117.

12. D. Howarth. "The ATLAS Supervisor Program, Introduction to System Programming." *System Programming.* Edited by P. Wegner, New York: Academic Press, 1964, pp. 227–238.

13. D. K. Hsiao et al. *A Manual for RCA SPECTRA 70/46 TSOS Subsystem Writers.* Technical Report, Moore School of E.E., University of Pennsylvania, June 1969.

14. "IBM System/360 Model 67 Functional Characteristics," File No. S360-01, Form A27-2719-0, 1967.

15. "IBM System/370 Principles of Operation," GA22-7000-3, Fourth Edition, January 1973.

16. T. Kilburn, D. B. G. Edwards, and F. H. Sumner. "One-Level Storage System." *IRE Transaction on Electronic Computers*, April 1962.

17. C. J. Kuehner and B. Randell. "Demand Paging in Perspective." *Proc. AFIPS 1968 FJCC* **33**, 2 (1968): 1011–1017.

18. W. C. McGee. "On Dynamic Program Relocation." *IBM Systems Journal* **4**, 3 (1965): 184–196.

19. G. H. Mealy, B. I. Witt, and W. A. Clark. "The Functional Structure of OS/360—Part I: Introductory Survey; Part II: Job and Task Management; Part III: Data Management." *IBM Systems Journal* **5**, 1 (1966): 2–51.

20. D. Morris, F. H. Sumner, and M. T. Wyld. "An Appraisal of the ALTAS Supervisor." *Proc. of 22nd National Conference of ACM*, 1967, pp. 67–75.

21. A. Noetzel. "The Design of a Meta-System for Measurement and Simulation of Time-sharing Computers." *Ph.D Dissertation*, University of Pennsylvania, 1970.

22. R. W. O'Neill. "Experience Using a Time-Shared Multiprogramming System with Dynamic Address Relocation Hardware." *Proc. AFIPS 1967 SJCC* **30**, (1967): 611–621.

23. G. Oppenheimer and N. Weizer. "Resource Management for a Medium Scale Time-Sharing Operating System." *Comm. ACM* **11**, 5 (May 1968): 313–322.

24. E. I. Organick. *The Multics System: An Examination of Its Structure.* Cambridge, Mass.: The MIT Press, 1972.

25. B. Randell. "A Note on Storage Fragmentation and Program Segmentation," *Comm. ACM* **12**, 7 (July 1969).

26. B. Randell and C. J. Kuehner. "Dynamic Storage Allocation Systems." *Comm. ACM* **11**, 5 (May 1968): 297–306.

27. "RCA SPECTRA 70/46 Reference Manual." 70-46-601, March 1968.

28. A. L. Scherr. "Functional Structure of IBM Virtual Storage Operating Systems—Part II: OS/VS2-2 Concepts and Philosophies." *IBM Systems Journal* **12**, 4 (1973): 382–400.

29. J. L. Smith. "Multiprogramming under a Page on Demand Strategy," *Comm. ACM* **10**, 10 (October 1967).

30. "3300 Computer System Reference Manual." Control Data Corporation, Pub. No. 60157000, 1966.

31. "3300/3500 Computer Systems—Master—Reference Manual." Control Data Corporation, Pub. No. 60213600, April 1969.

32. V. A. Vyssotsky, F. J. Corbató, and R. M. Graham. "Structure of MULTICS Supervisor." *Proc. AFIPS 1965 FJCC* **27**, 1 (1965): 203–212.

6
Data
Base
Management
Systems

REMARKS

It is not the aim of this chapter to survey data base management systems. Instead, we have concentrated our study on two of the most important aspects of the systems:

1. Data structure, access and update.

2. Data security.

To facilitate the study, we have introduced an abstract model. Although the abstraction may be somewhat formal, it is carefully derived from working data base management systems.

We first model data structure—access and update—and then data security. It is hoped that by studying the model we can gain a better understanding of the basic concepts and prevailing notions in data base management systems without ever resorting to detailed expositions of the system elements involved.

Because the model is rather complete, no prior knowledge of specific data management systems is needed here. Nevertheless, the reader does need to know what a sequential file and an indexed sequential file are and should have a good understanding of the organization and use of random access storage devices, such as disks.

6.1 INTRODUCTION

Data base management systems are important because there are indications that future operating systems will be oriented primarily toward data base management. The indications result from the increasing on-line use of computer systems, and from the proliferation and mass introduction of multilevel secondary storage devices which can offer on-line storage ranging from very inexpensive, high capacity, slow speed archival memory to very expensive, low volume, high speed fixed head rotating devices. Thus, the traditional view of an operating system as a manager of physical resources is too limited. Furthermore, the problems of managing physical resources in terms of main memory and virtual space, input/output operations, data channels, and buffers are better understood. On the other hand, the sheer size of on-line data bases in future computer systems requires the operating system to become, in addition, a logical resource manager. The management of logical resources is concerned with the organization, security, access, and storage of data and programs in the data base. To this end, we have proposed an abstract model of a generalized data base management system which represents a unified approach to structure, protection, and use of data bases.

There are many reasons which have prompted the unified approach.

1. The seemingly diverse structures in data base management systems have common characteristics. It is therefore possible to propose a unified treatment of the structures by means of a generalized data structure which includes a large number of well-known structures as special cases. By data structures we mean the logical record organization and file structures for the on-line storage, access, and update of data on secondary storage. The need for a large number of data structures in a data base system is motivated by the fact that different data structures can facilitate different data base management tasks. For example, an indexed sequential file structure can facilitate the management of program files where the line numbers of the program statements are used as indices (keywords), statements of the program are handled as records, and the program is treated as a file. Other data structures can facilitate query, browsing, and transaction-oriented operations. However, commercial data base management systems can only handle a few data structures. Thus, by studying the generalized data structure, one can not only review many seemingly diverse structures as special cases of the generalized one, but one can also strive for the design and implementation of a data base management system which hosts these structures.

2. The various access and update methods in data base management systems also bear some intrinsic resemblance to each other. We note that the mere availability of a large number of data structures in a data base system will not necessarily lead to a more efficient system. Since these data structures are for secondary storage, efficient methods to access and update the structured data are also needed. It is therefore not surprising that whenever a data structure is introduced, an access and update method is also included. A good example is the ISAM (indexed sequential access method of IBM) associated with the indexed sequential structure. Multiple data structures in a data base management system require multiple access and update methods. The requirement that a data base management system supports a large number of data structures and their update methods complicates not only the design and implementation of the data base management system but also the discussion of these methods. Due to the intrinsic resemblance of the methods, it is therefore feasible to devise a unified access and update method specifically for the generalized data structure. Because the method works for the generalized structure, it works for every special structure. Further, we can show that the access and update method is at least as efficient as the tailor-made methods for the individual special structures.

3. Access control and privacy protection mechanisms in data base management systems are needed regardless of which data structure and access and update method are used. It is therefore more appropriate to discuss the mechanisms for access control and privacy protection in a generalized system environment. The need for control and protection in data base management systems is prompted by the emphasis on intelligent growth of integrated data bases. To grow intelligently, the system must encourage the users to share their data, since it is through the sharing of data that users may benefit from their fellow users' experiences—past mistakes, present endeavors, and future undertakings. However, the basis of data sharing must be voluntary. In other words, if a data base owner wants to make certain portions of his data available to the public, a few users, or no users at all, he should be able to do so. An involuntary information sharing system is one in which every piece of information once stored in the system is available to every user of the system. Such a system has its merit in a more restricted environment, for instance, when the users of the system are from the same project. However, in a general environment with users from various disciplines and data of different degrees of sensitivity, it is not desirable to make data sharing compulsory. Such a compulsory act may even discourage the use of the system.

In sharing data there arises the problem of privacy and of safeguarding of the proprietary information. In order to make data-sharing voluntary, the system must provide means to protect the privacy of, and to control the access to, a user's data. Once a user learns that he will be free from an invasion of privacy, he may gain confidence in using the system. He could then generate a private data base, accumulate data in it, improve it, and, under the access control of the system, gradually make part or all of his data available to a select few, or to the public, at his discretion.

6.2 DATA STRUCTURES

6.2.1 AN ANALOGY

Recent proliferation of data base management systems resembles the early development of programming languages. In language development, attempts are usually made first to identify the type of applications that the language is designed for. This process involves the characterization and classification of the type of data and the kind of operations to be used in the application. Whether the application is symbol manipulation, mathematical computation, or business data processing, one of the most important tasks in language development is to select for the type of data a data structure which can facilitate convenient and efficient operations. Without a suitable data structure, data for applications cannot be easily represented in the language. Without proper data representation, efficient procedures are difficult to develop. We are, of course, familiar with the use of arrays for mathematical computations, strings for symbol manipulations, and hierarchies for data processing. Once a data structure is chosen, operations which manipulate the structure and procedure elements which sequence these operations are then developed. Although different languages may have significant differences in syntax, vocabulary, and convention, these differences are largely for the human factor and aesthetic considerations. Even the differences in basic arithmetic, logical and I/O operations are relatively slight. What really distinguishes one language from another is the data structures and the efficient operations provided to manipulate these data structures.

With such distinctions in mind, a programmer would utilize, for example, the array and its mathematical functions in FORTRAN for mathematical applications, string and its operators in SNOBOL for symbol manipulations, and hierarchy and its reserved words in COBOL for data processing. However, difficulties arise when an application involves all these data structures and diverse processing and computation requirements. This calls for a programming language with a rich collection of data structures and a large set of efficient operators and functions for these structures. PL/1 is an attempt to provide these facilities. The need for a large variety of data structures, operators, and functions seems natural as the complexity of the applications increases. Yet, such variety is not economical unless the computing resource can handle it. Thus, PL/1 did not arrive on the scene until recently when large capacity computers came within the reach of many organizations.

An analogous development occurs in the data base management field. The need for data base management systems is motivated by the desire to handle large data bases on secondary storage devices. For each data base management system, a data structure which represents the organization of data in secondary storage is usually chosen and developed with a view toward efficient storage, access, or update. Because different data structures are good for different data base management requirements and few data structures alone can meet all these requirements, there is a proliferation of data structures and their data base management systems. For example, the SDC's TDMS specializes in the inverted file structure, the IBM's GIS allows only indexed sequential files, and Xerox's DATRIX utilizes exclusively the multilist file structure. However, with the recent phenomenal growth of data bases and increasing demand to support diverse applications, the usefulness of a data base management system may lie not only in its ability to specialize on individual data structures, but also in its capability to provide a rich collection of existing and new data structures, on the one hand, and a large set of efficient data base management functions for these structures, on the other hand. The discussion of the variable structure and rapid access data base management system model in this chapter is an attempt to provide these capabilities.

6.2.2 VARIABLE STRUCTURE

Data structures are considered in two distinct ways: record organization and file structure. The consideration of the characteristics of data items and the formation of these data items as units for storage and access is the study of the record organization. Although a record may consist of one or more data items, it is the smallest unit of data which can be stored and accessed at one time. With this notion of records, it is possible for the model to optimize the storage and access process and to provide efficient data base management functions.

Just as the record organization determines how the individual data items in the record are interrelated, so the file structure determines how the individual records in the file are interrelated. Here, we utilize a generalized file structure which includes several of the widely used file structures as special cases. The key to an understanding of the generalized file structure is the notion of the keyword and list on which the notions of directory and file structure are based.

6.2.2.1 Record Organization

Consider two undefined terms: a set A of "attributes" and a set V of "values." A *record R* is a subset of the Cartesian product $A \times V$ in which each attribute has one and only one value. Thus R is a set of ordered pairs of the form: (an attribute, its value).

An *index* for a record R is a set of its attribute-value pairs which collectively characterize R. In practice, it is useful to choose attribute-value pairs which are relatively short and simple to express. These ordered pairs in the index are called the *keywords*. The symbol K or K_i will be used to denote a keyword.

Every record is assigned a unique positive number, called its *address*, which indicates the whereabouts of the record in a given storage space. In a computer system, the storage space may include many types of storage devices, but a record must still be assigned a unique address in accordance with its storage device.

Sometimes a record R has associated with one of its keywords K the address of another record with the same keyword. Such an address is called the *pointer* of R with respect to K, or, more briefly, the K pointer of R. When R does not have an address associated with K, it is customary to say that R has a *null pointer* with respect to K. In a *data base record*, every keyword of the record is associated with a pointer. Henceforth, by a record we mean a data base record.

A *list L* of records with respect to a keyword K, or, more briefly, a *K list*, is a set of records containing K such that

a) the K pointers are distinct;

b) each nonnull K pointer in L gives the record address of a record within L and L only;

c) there is a unique record in L not pointed to by any other record containing K— it is called the *beginning* of the list;

d) there is a unique record in L containing the null K pointer—it is the *end* of the list; and

e) there exists, for every record R at its record address a_n ($n > 1$) in L, a sequence of K pointers

$$(a_1, a_2, \ldots, a_n)$$

where

  i) a_1 is the address of the beginning of L, and

  ii) the record at its address a_j contains a K pointer a_{j+1} for $j = 1, 2, \ldots, n - 1$.

Consequently, if there are two K lists for the same keyword K, then they do not have a record in common.

For example, in Fig. 6.1, the record R contains six keywords, one of which, K_1, is assigned the null pointer. We know in this case that the null pointer does not direct R to any other record containing K_1. On the other hand, the K_6 pointer of R first directs R to R' and in turn the K_6 pointer of R' directs R' to R''. This directed path determined by keyword K_6 is then terminated because the K_6 pointer of R'' is null.

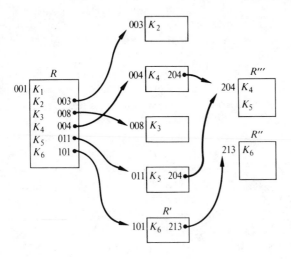

Figure 6.1

We note that in the example there are exactly six lists:

The K_1 list contains the single record R, which can be regarded as a directed path with just one point.

The K_2 list contains records at addresses 001 and 003, and thus determines the (directed) path 001, 003.

The K_3 list has as its path 001, 008.

The K_4 list has path 001, 004, 204.

The K_5 list has path 001, 011, 204.

The K_6 list has path 001, 101, 213.

A set F of records is called a *file* if every K list containing one or more of these records is contained in F. To distinguish among several files, every file is given a unique name, called its *file name*.

The characteristics of an attribute-value pair and its relation with other attribute-value pairs can be specified to reveal the information type and the organization of the data items in a file. We say that the attribute-value specifications of a file determine the *record organization* of the file. Intuitively, a file may consist of one or more records, and a record may be composed of one or more attribute-value pairs. The attribute-value pairs designated as keywords have pointers. The relation between files, records, attribute-value pairs and keyword pointers is depicted in Fig. 6.2. The entire data base is represented by a circular node which consists of many files designated with square nodes. File names are enclosed in the nodes. Each file consists of many records represented by hexagons. Each record is depicted as a hierarchy of attribute-value pairs. The attribute is separated from its value by a comma. A keyword is the attribute-value pair underlined with an arrow. Some of the pointers are shown by way of dotted lines which characterize the record addresses of the identical keywords.

Because all records in a file have the same information type and record organization, attribute-value pairs of one record always have the same information type and are related to each other in the same way as attribute-value pairs of another record. What differs from one record to another record are the values of the attributes and the absence and presence of certain optional attribute-value pairs in the record organization. For an example, in Fig. 6.2 we note that all part number records in part number file have the same types (attributes) of information and the same organization (four pairs related in the same order and with the same indentation), but that they differ in the values associated with the attributes (e.g., part number in one record is TX4240 and in another is TX0035). In the purchase order file some orders contain part description, others do not.

The record organization discussed here is characterized by the following attribute-value specification features which properly include all of the specification features in COBOL. We term the record organization a *generalized record organization.*

A. Level of an Attribute-Value Pair

Each pair is assigned a level number. These *level numbers* for all of the pairs establish a hierarchical record organization. Thus, a record may be viewed as a tree structure where each node of the tree is an attribute-value pair and the depth of the node in the tree represents a level number. The root of the tree and its pair are assigned the level number zero. Nodes of depth N will have their attribute-value pairs assigned the level number N.

For a given nonterminal node of the tree, there is always a subtree whose root is that node. We call the attribute-value pair associated with that node a *superior pair* and the attribute-value pairs associated with the subtree *subordinate pairs* of the (superior) pair. Obviously, the level number of an attribute-value pair is less than the level number of each subordinate pair. In particular, we call those subordinate pairs whose level numbers are one greater than the level number of the superior pair the *immediate subordinate pairs* of the (superior) pair. Conversely, we call the superior pair the *immediate superior pair* of the immediate subordinate pairs.

In Fig. 6.2, we adopt the convention that the attribute-value pairs at the same level lead from the same vertical lines. More specifically, we note that the pairs containing vendor number and vendor sources are at the same level. Although the pairs containing vendor name, vendor address, purchase order, and date of purchase are at one level, this level is "below" the level of the pair containing vendor source. Thus, these pairs are immediate subordinates to the pair containing vendor source.

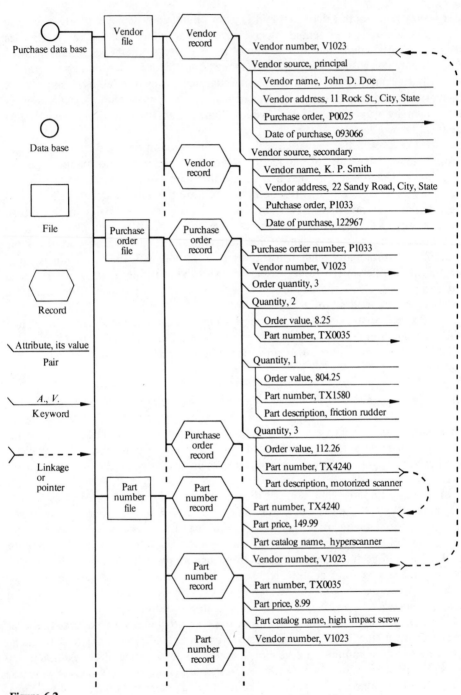

Figure 6.2

The number is assigned to a pair either explicitly by the programmer or by default. In case of assignment by default, the level number assigned to the pair is the same level number assigned to the previous pair. The level number 01 is always assigned to the first pair of a record in case of default. The organization of pairs in terms of level or hierarchy in a record can be used to identify related pairs as subgroups, groups, and divisions for the ease of reading and modifying the pairs. An example of levels of attribute value pairs in a record is depicted in Fig. 6.3.

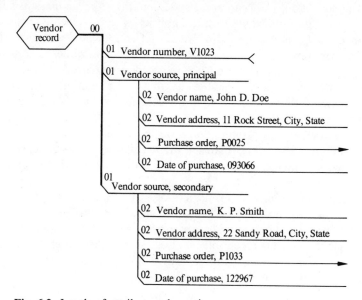

Fig. 6.3 Levels of attribute-value pairs.

B. Occurrence of an Attribute

In referring to the purchase order in Fig. 6.2, we note that the attribute "Part description" appears first under "Quantity 1" and then under "Quantity 3." However, there is no part description under "Quantity 2." This is a case where an attribute does not occur uniformly in the record. Furthermore, an attribute may not occur uniformly in every record of a file. Such an occurrence of an attribute is termed an *optional occurrence* of the attribute. On the other hand, the attribute "Purchase order number" appears in every purchase order record. Such an appearance of an attribute is termed a *uniform (or mandatory) occurrence* of the attribute.

In addition, if the occurrence of an attribute of an attribute-value pair is optional, then the occurrence of each attribute of its immediate subordinate pairs will be determined by the following:

a) The attribute must occur if it is uniform and the optional attribute of its immediate superior pair appears.

b) The attribute cannot occur, even though it is uniform, if the optional attribute of its superior pair does not occur.

Thus, the optionality and uniformity of the occurrence of the attribute of an attribute-value pair are relative to the optionality and uniformity of the occurrence of the attribute of its immediate superior pair.

C. Repetition of an Attribute

In a record, some attributes may appear once, and some may appear many times. For example, in Fig. 6.2, the following attributes appear twice in a record: vendor source, vendor name, vendor address, vendor order, and date of purchase. This is quite common in business reports or records. However, it becomes rather tedious to specify these attributes each time they have to be repeated in a record. To ease the programmer's effort in specifying a repetitive attribute, a repetition number is assigned to the attribute. When an attribute does occur in a record, the *repetition number* of the attribute indicates the number of repetitions of the attribute in the record. In addition, the repeated attributes will have the same level as the original one and every attribute of a level lower than the original one will also be repeated. The absence of a repetition number indicates, by default, that the repetition number is zero. Thus, for example, in specifying the attribute "Vendor source," one needs only to assign it a repetition number 1. Furthermore, in specifying the attributes vendor name, vendor address, purchase order, and date of purchase, one does not need to assign any repetition number. The absence of a repetition number will indicate implicitly that there is no repetition involved. Since these four attributes are at a level lower than the repetitive attribute, they will be repeated each time the attribute "Vendor source" is repeated (as they are in Fig. 6.2).

D. Type of Value

The *value* of an attribute may be alphanumeric, integer, real, packed, unpacked, binary, etc. Such specifications can be useful to a processing program in handling the value.

E. Size of Value

The *size* of a value is the number of characters that compose the value. This number may be fixed or variable. In the case where the number is fixed, the value of the attribute will have the same size in every record where the attribute appears; otherwise, the size of a value may vary from record to record.

F. Keyword Designation

An attribute-value pair may or may not be used as a keyword for accessing purposes. For example, a short pair, such as one whose attribute is "Vendor name," might be used in a retrieval statement, whereas, for practical reasons, a long one such as "Vendor address" might not. Attribute-value pairs designated by the user as keywords for subsequent retrieval and inquiry purposes can be used by the data base management system for constructing a keyword directory for the file. (Discussions of directory and file are in later sections.)

G. Linkage and Pointers

The records belonging to different files may "relate" to each other because they have the same attributes and values. For example, the purchase of a part from a vendor could result in three records: a purchase order record showing the cost of the purchase and the vendor from whom the purchase is procured, a vendor record describing the vendor source and date of purchase, and a part record documenting the sale price, name, and supplier of the parts. These three records belong to three different files, namely, the purchase order record in a purchase order file, the vendor record in a vendor file, and the part number record in a part number file. However, they are all related to this purchase. As illustrated in Fig. 6.2 by the dotted lines, the pair "Part number TX4240" under "Quantity 3" in the purchase order record refers to the part number record whose part number is TX4240. In the same part number record, the pair "Vendor number V1023" refers to the vendor record whose vendor number is V1023. We note that these three records are in three different files, and yet they are "related" because the part TX4240 which cost \$112.26 to stock and which is selling at a price of \$149.99 was purchased from the vendor K. P. Smith. In order to establish an effective cross-reference among these records so that a user's application program can "trace" through the dotted lines for related information, linkages must be provided for these fields. For example, qualified file names, Boolean expressions of keywords, and attributes can be used as logical pointers to reference attribute-value pairs of records in other files. On the other hand, to relate one attribute-value pair (i.e., the keyword) of a record to the same attribute-value pair of another record in the same file, there is no need to use qualified file names. As defined earlier, the use of the record address as a pointer is sufficient. However, the choice of a convention for linkages or pointers is not a subject to be discussed here. What we propose here is to allow the user to specify such an option.

From the preceding discussion, we summarize that an attribute-value pair is characterized by the following eight parameters:

1. an attribute A;

2. its value V;

3. its level number L;

4. an indication O of uniform ($O = 1$) or optional ($O = 0$ or blank) occurrence of A;

5. the type T of V where $T = I$ (Integer), $T = A$ (Alphanumeric), $T = D$ (Decimal), $T = $ (no value), etc;

6. the size S of V;

7. a designation k of keyword ($k = 1$) or nonkeyword ($k = 0$); and

8. an indication P of the need ($P = 1$) or not ($P = 0$ or blank) for a pointer or linkage.

Thus, by leaving out its value V, we can explicitly specify for every attribute-value pair in a record organization its information type and its relation with others as follows:

(A, L, O, T, S, k, P).

In case a repetition number R is associated with the attribute A, then A is to be repeated R times. Each repetition will result in a new pair. In addition, all the pairs which have a level number greater than L, and are subordinate to the attribute-value pair, will be repeated. Such repetition will also result in a set of new pairs. We note that the new pairs may or may not contain the same value V. To characterize the information type and the relation with other pairs of a set of attribute-value pairs whose attribute is A and whose repetition number is R, we modify the above tuple as follows:

(A, L, R, O, T, S, k, P).

6.2.2.1.1 THE RECORD TEMPLATE CONCEPT

Records are collected together to form a file because they contain the same type (attributes) of information. Referring to Fig. 6.2, for example, all records in a vendor file are likely to contain the attribute "Vendor source." Thus, it is reasonable to expect that there will be only a limited number of different attributes in each new record of a file, even though the total number of attributes may be large. Because of this characteristic of records in the same file, it is possible to save considerable file storage space by removing the attributes from the records themselves and storing the unique attributes in some central place associated with the file. This central place is called the *record template*, for short, *template*. It is important to note that records collected in a file usually have not only the same type (attribute) of information, but also the same general organization. Consequently, the template contains not only the unique attributes but also information regarding the relations among the attribute-value pairs. Since these relations determine the general record organization of a file, this information is referred to as the *global record structural specification* of the file.

What remains to be stored in the individual records is, in addition to various nonstructural information such as values of the attributes, the information about the presence and absence of certain global structural features for a given record organization. This information which is local to a record is referred to as the *record control information* of the record.

With this in mind, we store the eight-tuples for all the unique attributes in the template; and for each user record, we create a *record control block* for storing its record control information. Thus, in storage, a record consists of all the values of its attributes and a record control block. To distinguish the record as perceived by the user from the record as it appears in storage, we call the user record the *logical record*, and its organization the *logical record organization*; we call the stored record consisting of values and the record control block the *physical or system record*, and its organization the *physical record organization*. In other words, logical records are what the user and his programs see, and the system records are what the system handles.

More precisely, we learn that the physical record organization is based on the concept of the record template.

Each entry of the record block corresponds to an attribute-value pair and is of the form:

(a control number, size of the value)

where the control number is a positive integer. The assignment of unique positive integers as control numbers to attribute-value pairs is done by the record input program according to a prescribed algorithm and does not concern the user.*

Before entering records, the user specifies the record organization. The result of the specification is a set of eight-tuples in a template. When user records are being entered, the record input program will check each incoming record against the template. If a record conforms to the global structural specification in the template, the record is then processed by the record input program for calculating its control numbers, constructing its record control block, and generating its storage image. As far as he is concerned, he is not aware that storage images of his records do not contain any attributes and that the unique attributes of all his records are placed in the template. He still views his records as sets of related pairs, each of which is composed of an attribute and its value.

6.2.2.1.2 RECORD ORGANIZATION TYPES

To make the preceding discussion more apparent to the reader, we will use the illustration in Fig. 6.2 for case study.

Case 1: UF Type

The record structural specification for the records in the vendor file may be as follows:

(	A	,	$L,$	$R,$	$O,$	$T,$	$S,$	$k,$	$P)$
(Vendor record,		00,	,	1,	,	,	,	)
(Vendor number,		01,	,	1,	$A,$	5,	1,	1)
(Vendor source,		01,	1,	1,	$A,$	9,	1,	)
(Vendor name,		02,	,	1,	$A,$	20,	1,	)
(Vendor address,		02,	,	1,	$A,$	50,	,	)
(Purchase order,		02,	,	1,	$A,$	5,	1,	1)
(Date of purchase,		02,	,	1,	$I,$	6,	1,	).

This specification indicates that every vendor record has the same number of attributes. In addition, every value is of a fixed size. Thus the records generated by

---

* In this discussion, the algorithm treats each pair of a record as a node of a tree (with the possibility of having a null node for the root). Each node is assigned a positive number starting at the root of the tree, traversing the right subtree, then traversing the left subtree. For a treatment on tree traversal algorithms, the reader may wish to refer to [16].

this specification will all have the same length. Since the occurrence of the attributes is *u*niform and the sizes of their values are *f*ixed, the record organization is said to be of *uniform-fixed type* (*UF type*). UF-type records do not require any record control information to be built into individual records. Thus, the storage images of these records do not have record control blocks. The control numbers to be generated by the record input program are listed on the left-hand side of each attribute-value pair specification as follows:

	(A ,	$L,$	$R,$	$O,$	$T,$	$S,$	$k,$	P)
0	(Vendor record,	00,	,	1,	,	,	,	)
1	(Vendor number,	01,	,	1,	$A,$	5,	1,	1)
2,7	(Vendor source,	01,	1,	1,	$A,$	9,	1,	)
3,8	(Vendor name,	02,	,	1,	$A,$	20,	1,	)
4,9	(Vendor address,	02,	,	1,	$A,$	50,	,	)
5,10	(Purchase order,	02,	,	1,	$A,$	5,	1,	1)
6,11	(Date of purchase,	02,	,	1,	$I,$	6,	1,	).

We note that the third specification is assigned with two control numbers since it contains a repetition number 1. The other pairs assigned with two control numbers are the subordinate pairs whose level numbers are greater. From the control numbers, we learn that every vendor record has exactly 11 attribute-value pairs. Furthermore, we note that pairs whose attributes are vendor number, source, name, purchase order, and date of purchase are designated as keywords and that the records are linked to records in other files having the same vendor number and purchase order.

Case 2: OF-Type and OV-Type

The record specification for the records in the purchase order file may be as follows:

	(A ,	$L,$	$R,$	$O,$	$T,$	$S,$	$k,$	P)
0	(Purchase order record,	00,	,	1,	,	,	,	)
1	(Purchase order number,	01,	,	1,	$A,$	5,	1,	1)
2	(Vendor number,	01,	,	1,	$A,$	5,	1,	1)
3	(Order quantity,	01,	,	1,	$I,$	1,	,	)
4,8,12	(Quantity,	01,	2,	1,	$I,$	1,	,	)
5,9,13	(Order value,	02,	,	1,	$D,$	6,	,	)
6,10,14	(Part number,	02,	,	1,	$A,$	6,	1,	1)
7,11,15	(Part description,	02,	,	0,	$A,$	,	,	).

The occurrence indicator in the last specification is set to zero which means that the attribute "part description" does not occur uniformly in a record. In accordance with this, we provide local record control information to be included into individual records. For the first purchase order record in Fig. 6.2, the record input program constructs the following entries of the record control block where each entry is of the form:

(a control number, size of the value).

(0,)
(1,)
⋮
(6,)
(8,)
⋮
(10,)
(11,16)
(12,)
(13,)
(14,)
(15,18)

The absence of (7), indicates that the attribute for this optional pair is not to be generated for this record. The absence of the second components in (0,), (1,) and others indicates that the sizes of values of pairs with control numbers 0, 1, and others are fixed by the global record specification in the template. If all of the record control entries do not have the second components, then the record specification is termed of *optional-fixed type* (*OF type*). It allows the *o*ptional occurrence of attributes in the individual records; however, the sizes of the values are *f*ixed. The case that we are studying now is not an OF type because we have record control information such as (11,16) and (15,18) where the individual record can control the size of the values of their attributes. In this case, the attribute "Part description" with control number 11 has a value of 16 characters. And the same attribute with control number 15 has a value of 18 characters. If at least one record control entry has a second component, then the record specification is called *optional-variable type* (*OV type*). The above example is a record specification of OV type.

Case 3: UV Type

Finally, we proceed to specify a record organization for the records in the part number file. We note that each part number record has a *u*niform occurrence of four attributes. One of the attributes takes a *v*ariable value size and the other attributes take fixed values. The following is a typical case of *uniform-variable type* (*UV type*) record specification.

```
0  (Part number record,  00,  , 1,  ,  ,  ,  )
1  (Part number,         01,  , 1,  A,  6,  1,  1)
2  (Part price,          01,  , 1,  D,  6,  ,  )
3  (Part catalog name,   01,  , 0,  A,  ,  ,  )
4  (Vendor number,       01,  , 1,  A,  5,  1,  1).
```

The record control block in each record must provide information to control the size of the variable values. For the first record, we provide

(0,)
(1,)
(2,)
(3,13)
(4,).

For the second record, we provide

(0,)
(1,)
(2,)
(3,18)
(4,).

In conclusion, we emphasize that, in a real situation, record organization may involve various types, levels, and repetitive patterns. With the aid of this study, we have developed a comprehensive scheme to accommodate these variations.

6.2.2.1.3 REORGANIZATION AND MULTIPLE ORGANIZATION

By *reorganization* we mean the change of record information type and global structure from an existing organization to a new one. Because the information type and global structural information of records of a file is concentrated in a single template, reorganization of records of the file amounts to a change of the template. More specifically, it requires the modification of the 8-tuples in the template. For large files, there is considerable saving in terms of record processing time. Since individual logical records can be reorganized without requiring their storage images (i.e., values and record control blocks) to be processed, the processing is restricted to the template. For example, the existing vendor records in Fig. 6.3 may be reorganized to reflect a new application and user requirement as in Fig. 6.4. Such reorganization would result in a simple change from the template described in Case 1 above to the one below:

(	A	,	$L,$	$R,$	$O,$	$T,$	$S,$	$k,$	P
(Seller record,			00,		1,		,	,	)
(Seller identification,			01,		1,	$A,$	5,	1,	1)
(Seller file,			01,	1,	1,	$A,$	9,	1,	)
(Name,			02,		1,	$A,$	20,	1,	)
(Business address,			03,		1,	$A,$	50,	,	)
(Purchase order,			02,		1,	$A,$	5,	1,	1)
(Date of purchase,			03,		1,	$I,$	6,	1,	).

We note that in this reorganization, some of the original attributes and the level numbers of attribute-value pairs containing business address and date of purchase have been affected.

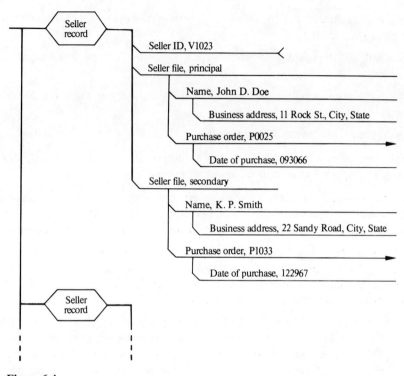

Name, John D. Doe
Business address, 11 Rock St., City, State
Purchase order, P0025
Date of purchase, 093066

Figure 6.4

From the discussion, we note that there are two templates associated with the records—one for the original record organization as illustrated in Fig. 6.2 and another for the new organization as sketched in Fig. 6.4. In other words, there are two record organizations for the same set of records. With this in mind, we can develop a data base management system which keeps track of multiple templates for the same file. Since each template determines a record organization of the file, a file with multiple templates can enjoy multiple record organizations.

In summary, we have deliberately used elementary examples to illustrate simple reorganizations. For elaborate reorganization of records with complex hierarchy, careful consideration must be given to the design of the template, the choice of an algorithm for assigning control numbers, and the construction of the record control block.

6.2.2.1.4 CONCLUSIONS

Although additional access and processing are needed to implement the record template concept, its advantages significantly outweigh the overhead. More precisely, the use of the record template can

1. save storage space by removing attributes from every individual logical record and placing the distinct attributes in the template;

2. allow the reorganization of the entire file by modifying the template alone without processing individual records;

3. permit additional record organizations for the same file by introducing new templates;

4. permit application programs to be written independently of the physical layout of the records; and

5. facilitate the enforcement of access control to individual data items and records.

The attempt to concentrate all the data definition and structural description of records into a template has several far-reaching effects.

1. To manipulate records, the user (or user program) no longer has to include the data and format descriptions of the records in his program. In the case of COBOL, this amounts to the elimination of most parts of the data division of the program.

2. By having a centralized template of data definition and structural description information, different user (or user programs) will have the same understanding and interpretation of the data format and record organization of the records, thus eliminating misinterpretation of information.

3. The owner of the records may assign to another user of his records a new record template derived from the original template. The new record template may only have enough data definition and structural description information for a part of the record organization. Consequently, the user will not be able to use the other part of the records since that part of record organization is not specified for the user in his template. Such a template is called a *derived template*. The use of derived templates may enhance data integrity and protection. By *data integrity*, we mean that the data will not be altered or contaminated due to accessing errors. By *data protection*, we mean that the data will remain anonymous as a result of having no access to the data. Because the derived template does not have any information about the parts of records which are safeguarded for integrity and protection purposes, there is no way for the user (or user program) to access that part of the records.

6.2.2.2 File Structures

In referring to the definition of list and keyword in previous sections, we note that no two lists for the same keyword have in common a record containing that keyword. Furthermore, if a record is characterized by two different keywords, the record will belong to two different lists. Intuitively, the former implies that for a given keyword, if the system can establish access to a record via one list, there is no need to access the record via a different list; the latter implies that for multiple keywords the system must determine the records which are characterized with these keywords by way of their respective lists. For example, the record R depicted in Fig. 6.5 cannot exist in a data base management system. Since the keyword K_3 appears more than once in R, R is not a record by definition of the K_3 list. In practice, there is no reason for information (i.e., the keyword) to be stored in a record redundantly.

Fig. 6.5 Record not allowed.

We also note that the notion of the keyword enables the user to relate one record to another and the notion of the list allows the system to establish an access path to the related records. To utilize the lists of records, the notion of directory and storage cells for a file is introduced.

6.2.2.2.1 THE CELL, DIRECTORY, AND GENERALIZED FILE STRUCTURE

Let F be a file whose records contain just m different keywords. For each keyword K let n be the number of records containing K and let h be the number of K lists in F. Further, we denote by a_j the beginning record address of the jth K list. Let p_j be the number of records in the K list with beginning address a_j. By definition, the number n of records containing keywords K_i is given by

$$n = \sum_{j=1}^{h} p_j. \tag{1}$$

We denote by $|F|$ the number of different possible addresses in the "file space." Thus, for each record address a we see that

$$0 \le a_{ij} \le |F| - 1.$$

Consider the set of beginning addresses, and let E be a relation defined for a fixed positive integer s, $0 < s \le |F|$, as follows.

Two beginning addresses a and a' are related, i.e., aEa', if and only if

$$a = es + r$$

and

$$a' = es + r'$$

where

$$0 \le r < s \quad \text{and} \quad 0 \le r' < s.$$

Since the a's are positive integers, the values of r, r', and e are nonnegative integers. Furthermore, E is an equivalence relation. Thus, the set of a's can be partitioned by E into equivalence classes, called *secondary storage cells*, or more briefly, *cells*. The number of cells is one greater than the maximum value of e. The integer s is called the *cell size*, and is the number of different addresses possible in the cell. At any time, we may compute the cell corresponding to a given address, a, by the ratio:

$$C = \left[\frac{a}{s}\right], \qquad \text{where the brackets indicate the integral part of the ratio.}$$

Each cell is assigned a unique positive number, called its *cell address*, which is computed according to the formula:

$$c = s \cdot C, \qquad \text{where } c \text{ is the cell address corresponding to the cell } C.$$

The notion of cell is introduced for the purpose of studying efficient record storage and access strategies. The use of an abstract and neutral term such as cell is deliberate. The real-world interpretation of the cell will depend upon the particular installation (e.g., the number of disk modules installed for on-line storage), the refinement of access strategy (e.g., accessing disk module, therefore cylinders, in parallel or disk tracks in parallel only), and the chosen file structure. Thus a cell may be regarded as a disk module in one installation and as a disk cylinder in another installation. Consequently, the interpretations of cell address and record address will also be determined accordingly.

For convenience, we introduce for each beginning address a of keyword K the triple

$$(c,(a,p))$$

where c is the address of the cell within which a belongs and in which p records of the K list lie. *We require that, for a given K list, all records of the K list lie within the same cell.* However, it is possible that there may be several K lists in a cell for the same keyword.

With this notation available, we define the *directory* of F as the set of sequences

$$\{K,n,h; (c_1,(a_1,p_1)), (c_2,(a_2,p_2)), \ldots, (c_h,(a_h,p_h))\} \tag{2}$$

where there is one sequence for each of the m distinct keywords.

We note that with (1) the above expression can be simplified as

$$\{K,h; (c_1,(a_1,p_1)), (c_2,(a_2,p_2)), \ldots, (c_h,(a_h,p_h))\}. \tag{3}$$

We will henceforth refer to the set of entries $(c_j,(a_j,p_j))$ for a given K as $D(K)$. Thus, the above expression becomes $\{K,h; D(K)\}$.

Using subscript i to identify district keywords, the expression (3) can also be stated as follows:

$$\{K_i,h_i; (c_{i1},(a_{i1},p_{i1})), (c_{i2},(a_{i2},p_{i2})), \ldots, (c_{ih_i},(a_{ih_i},p_{ih_i}))\}$$

and

$$D(K_i) = \{(c_{i1},(a_{i1},p_{i1})), (c_{i2},(a_{i2},p_{i2})), \ldots, (c_{ih_i},(a_{ih_i},p_{ih_i}))\} \tag{4}$$

for $i = 1, 2, \ldots, m$.

In short, we have $\{K_i,h_i; D(K_i)\}$.

A *generalized file structure* is a file with its directory. We shall now proceed to show in the following sections that many specialized file structures can be derived from the generalized file structure.

6.2.2.2.2 INDEXED SEQUENTIAL AND RANDOM FILE STRUCTURES

An *indexed sequential file* is a generalized file structure in which for every keyword K, we have $n = h = s = 1$. Furthermore, for any keywords K_i and K_j, if K_i is lexicographically followed by K_j, then $a_{i1} < a_{j1}$. Thus such a file has only one keyword per record, and the records in the file are stored sequentially on the basis of the lexicographical order of the keywords (see Fig. 6.6).

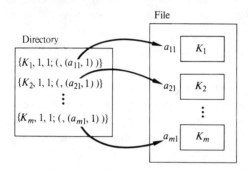

Fig. 6.6 An indexed sequential file.

If the a_{i1}'s are not ordered, then the file is an *indexed random file*.

A. The Use of Indexed Sequential and Random File Structures

Because the lexicographical order of the keywords of an indexed sequential file reflects the sequence of the records, the indexed sequential file structure is widely used to maintain (source) program files for program preparation and debugging. For example, a FORTRAN program file can be structured indexed-sequentially by designating the line numbers of the FORTRAN program statements as keywords, the program statements as records, and the program name as the file name. In this application, the line numbers not only can be used to access individual program statements so numbered, but also can be employed to maintain the sequence of program statements. By asking the data base management system to retrieve from his file all the program statements between one line number and another (higher) line number, the user can have a list of his program statements sequenced by their line numbers.

In the course of inserting new statements, the user must assign a new line number to each new statement. The new line number, say K_j, is therefore between two existing line numbers K_i and K_k, indicating that the user desires to insert the new program statement between the statements numbered K_i and K_k, respectively. Again, if the user requests a new listing of his program statements, the statements will be listed in a sequence as reflected by the alphanumeric order of the keywords. In other words, the statement numbered K_i will be listed before the statement numbered K_j, which in turn will be listed before the statement numbered K_k. Although the program statement sequence is preserved by line numbers (i.e., keywords), the record addresses (i.e., a_{i1}) no longer satisfy the condition where $a_{11} < a_{21} < \cdots < a_{m1}$. This is due to the fact that some of the newly inserted statements (records) are stored at the "end" of the file, since there was no room between existing statements (records). In other words, the original indexed sequential file gradually becomes an indexed random file. Nevertheless, the user is not aware of the fact that the records of his indexed sequential file may be rather randomly stored after considerable update. Sequential listing of records of an indexed random file is still possible. However, in an effort to support the apparent sequence, additional repositioning of the storage device's access mechanism may be needed.

B. The Implementation of Indexed Sequential File Structure

An implementation of the directory of an indexed sequential file is described in Section 6.2.2.2.2 and illustrated in Fig. 5.18 of the previous chapter. We shall not repeat it here. In fact, we shall not discuss the implementation of the structures in the following sections. All these structures have been implemented in real-world systems. Due to limited space, we shall concentrate on the discussion of their logical properties instead of their physical implementations.

6.2.2.2.3 THE INVERTED FILE STRUCTURE

An *inverted file* is a generalized file structure in which every list contains only one record, and for every keyword K_i, the cell addresses $c_{i1}, c_{i2}, \ldots, c_{ih_i}$ are distinct, i.e., $n_i = h_i$ and $s = 1$. This means that every record is contained in its own cell whether or not the record utilizes all the space in the cell. For brevity, we have not shown the cell addresses of the inverted file depicted in Fig. 6.7.

A. The Notion of Inverting a File

In the early days of file processing, a file F was taken to be merely a collection of records each of which was assigned a unique address. The unique addresses were collected into a set, called the directory. In order to locate a set E of records having some common keywords, which is in general much smaller than F, all the addresses in the directory were used for bringing in the corresponding records for examination. The general steps involved in this kind of file processing are to get a record address, then to examine the keywords of the record so addressed. These steps are shown as follows with an arrow indicating the sequence of the steps.

$$\text{Get the address of every record } R_i \text{ in } F$$
$$\downarrow \tag{1}$$
$$\text{Search } R_i \text{ for the given keywords.}$$

Let r be the ratio of the amount of effort and time in processing F to obtain E versus the amount of effort and time in processing every record in F. Step (1) yields $r = 1$, which constitutes a rather uneconomical file processing.

Directory

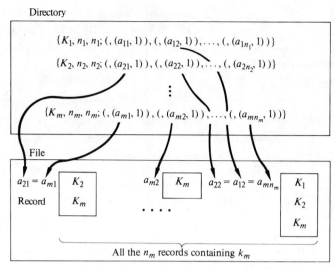

Fig. 6.7 An inverted file.

An inverted file differs from the above file by keeping copies of its keywords in the directory and by assigning each keyword with the addresses of all those records which contain that keyword. To find a set E of records containing a common keyword K, one needs only to locate the addresses associated with K in the directory. The steps are

$$\text{Given a keyword } K$$
$$\downarrow$$
$$\text{Get the addresses of the records}$$
$$R_i \text{ which contain } K.$$

(2)

Comparing (1) and (2), one gets the impression that (2) is "inverted" from (1), since (1) goes from records to keywords and (2) goes from keywords to records.

In this case, the ratio r is small. However, the directory of an inverted file is usually large, because for every keyword there is associated a sequence of record addresses. And a record address may appear many times in different sequences (e.g., the address a_{22} appeared three times in the directory shown in Fig. 6.7, namely at K_1, K_2, and K_m entries). Thus a great deal of effort is expended in processing the directory.

B. The Use of the Inverted File Structure

There are several useful features of the inverted file structure.

1. It allows a record to be associated with more than one keyword—a feature which is not available to the indexed sequential and random file structure. For example, if a record is a payroll record, then it may be necessary to have the name, the salary, and the job title of the payee as keywords.

2. It enables the user to collect statistical information about the records in the file without having the records retrieved for the collection. By referring to the directory alone, the data base management system can answer, for example, the following question imposed by the user.

   "How many payees are there whose salary is \$15,000 and whose job title is foreman-first-class?"

This question can be answered by processing the directory without accessing the file. Since (salary, \$15,000) and (job title, foreman-first-class) are keywords, they appear in the directory as two different entries. Associated with each of the entries is a sequence of record addresses. By identifying and counting those addresses which occur in *both* sequences, the number of payees is therefore obtained.

The use of multiple keywords for a record allows more refined characterization of the record. The inclusion of all the addresses of the records for each keyword which characterizes the records enables the user to inquire about the file. These features obviously require considerably more (directory) storage and processing cost and effort than the indexed sequential and random files.

6.2.2.2.4 THE MULTILIST FILE STRUCTURE

A *multilist file* is a generalized file structure in which there is just one list per keyword and the cell size is equal to the size of the file space, i.e., $h_i = 1$, and $s = |F|$. The requirement that $s = |F|$ means that there is only one cell in the file, and all records in the file are in the same cell.

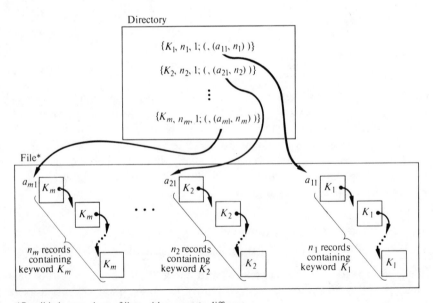

*Possible intersections of lists with respect to different keywords are not shown in the figure.

Fig. 6.8 A multilist file.

A. The Notion of Multilist

In a multilist file the sequences in the directory correspond to lists. Only the beginning address of each list occurs in the directory. The successive records are obtained by means of the pointers. It is important to keep in mind that the lists shown in the file of this example can intersect by having one or more records in common.

Directory

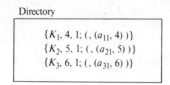

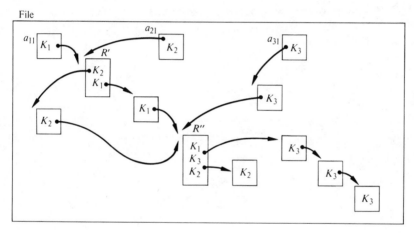

Figure 6.9

The terminology "multilist" stems from the fact that a record R is a member of multiple K_i lists whenever R contains these K_i. Referring to the above illustration, we note that record R' is a member of two lists, namely K_1 and K_2 lists, and that record R'' is a member of three lists, the K_1, K_2, and K_3 lists.

B. The Use of Multilist Files

Unlike the directory of the inverted file, a multilist directory does not always give exact statistical information about the records in the file. For example, in referring to the example illustrated above, the number of records containing K_1 is 4. In other words, $n_1 = 4$. We also have $n_2 = 5$ and $n_3 = 6$. Nevertheless, the total number of records in the file is *less* than the sum of n_1, n_2, and n_3. More specifically, there are exactly 12 records in the file, and yet the sum of the n_i is 15. In order to get the exact record count for any inquiry involving the keywords, the file must be searched. This, of course, is a rather expensive operation.

On the other hand, there are files whose primary function is to supply texts in the records. In this case, the search of records in the file is mandatory. For example, a bibliographical file of scientific abstracts of technical papers can be facilitated by a multilist file structure. Here, the author names, keywords and phrases, and category numbers can be used as keywords. Because records of the same keywords are in the same lists, it is possible to have a list of all the abstracts written by an author, characterized by certain key phrases, or numbered under some category.

6.2.2.2.5 THE CELLULAR MULTILIST FILE STRUCTURE

A cellular multilist file is a generalized file structure in which, for every keyword K_i, the cell addresses $c_{i1}, c_{i2}, \ldots, c_{ih_i}$ are distinct and $0 < s < |F|$.

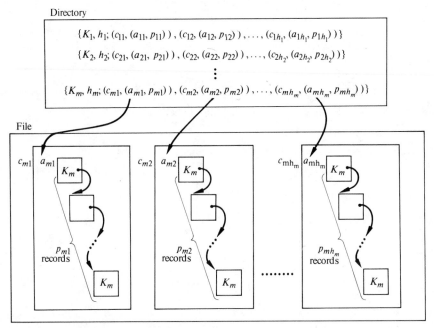

Directory

$$\{K_1, h_1; (c_{11}, (a_{11}, p_{11})), (c_{12}, (a_{12}, p_{12})), \ldots, (c_{1h_1}, (a_{1h_1}, p_{1h_1}))\}$$

$$\{K_2, h_2; (c_{21}, (a_{21}, p_{21})), (c_{22}, (a_{22}, p_{22})), \ldots, (c_{2h_2}, (a_{2h_2}, p_{2h_2}))\}$$

$$\vdots$$

$$\{K_m, h_m; (c_{m1}, (a_{m1}, p_{m1})), (c_{m2}, (a_{m2}, p_{m2})), \ldots, (c_{mh_m}, (a_{mh_m}, p_{mh_m}))\}$$

Note: The possibility of an intersection of K_i-list and K_j-list for $i \neq j$ and the equality $c_{ij} = c_{uv}$ for $i \neq u$ *does* exist and is not illustrated here.

Fig. 6.10 A cellular multilist file.

The cellular multilist file structure is intended to utilize the notion of cell. By controlling the number of records in a list and the number of lists in a cell, the cellular multilist enables the data base management system to make use of almost all the possible storage in the cell. In other words, the system can now fit the lists of records into the cells for better storage utilization. On the other hand, by keeping track of the cell addresses and the addresses of beginnings of the lists, the cellular multilist file structure allows the data base management system to take advantage of storage devices for more efficient access. The latter will be discussed in considerable detail in the section on access algorithms. We will therefore forgo any elaboration here.

In cellular multilist file structure, no two lists in a given cell are for the same keyword. However, there can be one or more lists (each is for a different keyword) in the cell. Furthermore, if a record is characterized by several keywords, then the record lies in the lists for the keywords.

6.2.2.2.6 NEW FILE STRUCTURES FOR DIVERSE APPLICATIONS

By varying the number of cells, the number of lists in a cell, and the number of records in a list, one can generate a large variety of file structures. In particular, we can generate a file in which records associated with one keyword are structured as index random, with another keyword as multilist, and with remaining keywords as inverted.

An example is included here to illustrate the choice of file structure for an application. It will be shown that the proper choice of file structure can result in considerable saving in storage and processing for the application.

Using a collection of publication abstracts, we compare a file organized by the generalized file structure with a file organized by a pure inverted file structure. Estimates are made in terms of storage and access requirements. This example is deliberately made simple so that some of the concepts can be demonstrated without resorting to a detailed exposition.

The example. A collection of 30,000 publication abstracts (about 1000 characters per abstract) which are characterized by their:

classification numbers (assume these are universal decimal classification numbers; there is one prime and an average of four secondary UDC numbers per abstract);

languages (assume 50 languages, and one or more per abstract; average 1.5 per abstract);

publishers (assume 300 publishers, and equal distribution of abstracts over publishers);

accession numbers (one unique number per publication);

abstracts (consist of variable length text—average 100 words); and

authors (one or more per abstract; average of two abstracts per author and about 15,000 names).

User's processing requirements for the example:

1. Individual abstracts should be readily retrievable by their unique accession numbers.
2. There should be a tally of the number of abstracts in a given language and published by a specific publisher.
3. A rapid retrieval of the abstracts tallied in (2).
4. Text processing of *all* the abstracts by universal decimal numbers.

A. Suggested Generalized File Structure

For the accession numbers, we select indexed random file structure since there is a one-to-one correspondence between the accession numbers and the abstracts.

For the attribute languages and publishers, we choose inverted file structure.

This choice enables the user to get an exact tally and fast retrieval response from a large collection of abstracts of books since only a small number of books in the collection are written in the same language and published by the same publisher.

For the classification numbers, we recommend a multilist file structure, in which the abstracts are ordered by the prime UDC number and are threaded by lists of secondary UDC numbers. By tracing through the lists of UDC numbers, abstracts can be retrieved in the classes one at a time for text processing.

The processing requirements for the attribute author are not specified. However, we recommend a structure in which each keyword author has, at most, two lists, since there are approximately two abstracts per author.

B. An Arbitrarily Chosen File Structure

Without regard to the user's processing requirements as stated before, we arbitrarily choose the inverted file structure for the application to permit a comparison with the generalized file structure.

The directory storage requirements for attributes ACCESSION NO., AUTHOR, LANGUAGE, PUBLISHER, and their values are the same. However, for the attributes PRIME CLASS. NO. and SEC. CLASS. NO., additional storage is needed.

C. Comparison of Two File Structures in Terms of Directory Storage and Access Requirements

Gross computations for the generalized file structure as proposed in (A) and the pure inverted file structure as arbitrarily chosen in (B) are listed below:

1. The assumptions made for the attributes of the keywords are as follows.

   Prime classification numbers: One number per abstract and five abstracts per value. Thus, there are 6000 different values.

   Secondary classification numbers: An average of four numbers per abstract and 20 abstracts per value. Again, there are 6000 different values.

   Languages: About 50 different languages and an average of 1.5 languages per abstract.

   Publishers: Equal distribution of the abstracts over the publishers. Therefore, 100 abstracts per publisher.

   Accession numbers: One number per abstract and one abstract per value.

   Authors: 15,000 different names, and about 2 abstracts per author.

2. Directory storage for the generalized file structure.

   For the attribute ACCESSION NO., the indexed random file structure requires

   10 characters for the attribute (all attributes are truncated to ten characters),
    2 characters for its control information,
   10 characters for a value,
    4 characters for its control information, and
    6 characters for an address of the (record which is the) beginning of the list.

Thus,

$$(10 + 2) + (10 + 4 + 6) \times 30{,}000 = 600{,}012 \text{ characters} = \frac{600{,}012}{2K}$$

= 300 physical records (with the assumption that the size of a physical record is 2K characters).

Similarly, for the attribute LANGUAGE, the inverted file structure requires

$$(10 + 2) + 50(10 + 4) + 1.5 \times 6 \times 30{,}000 = 270.712 \text{ characters}$$
$$= 136 \text{ physical records.}$$

For the attribute PUBLISHER and 300 publishers, it requires

$$(10 + 2) + 300 \times (10 + 4) + 6 \times 30{,}000 = 184{,}212 \text{ characters}$$
$$= 93 \text{ physical records.}$$

For the attribute AUTHOR and 15,000 different names, it requires

$$(10 + 2) + 15{,}000 \times (10 + 4) + 6 \times 30{,}000 = 390{,}000 \text{ characters}$$
$$\cong 195 \text{ physical records.}$$

For the attribute PRIME CLASS. NO., the multilist file structure requires

$$(10 + 2) + (10 + 4) + 6 = 32 \text{ characters}$$
$$< 1 \text{ physical record}$$

For the attribute SEC. CLASS. NO., the multilist file structure requires

$$(10 + 2) + (10 + 4) + 6 \times 6{,}000 = 36{,}026 \text{ characters}$$
$$\cong 36 \text{ physical records.}$$

Thus the total directory storage requirement is

$$300 + 136 + 93 + 195 + 1 + 36 = 761 \text{ physical records.}$$

3. Additional storage requirement for a pure inverted file structure.

For PRIME CLASS. NO., it requires

$$(10 + 2) + 6{,}000 \times (10 + 4) + 6 \times 30{,}000 = 264{,}012 \text{ characters}$$
$$= 132 \text{ physical records.}$$

For SEC. CLASS NO., it requires

$$(10 + 2) + 6{,}000 \times (10 + 4) + 6 \times 4 \times 30{,}000 = 804{,}012 \text{ characters}$$
$$\cong 402 \text{ physical records.}$$

Therefore, there is an additional storage requirement of $132 + 402 = 534$ physical records. Total directory storage requirement for an all-inverted file is

$$817 + 534 = 1{,}351 \text{ physical records.}$$

4. Gross computations for access requirements.

ACCESSION NUMBER	(30,000 values each with an ABL*)

LANGUAGE	English with 12,500 ABL's
	French with 5,000 ABL's
	German with 5,000 ABL's
	Italian
	Spanish with 625 ABL's
	Portuguese with 625 ABL's
	Dutch with 625 ABL's

PUBLISHER	(300 values each with 100 ABL's)

PRIME CLASSIFICATION NUMBER	0000000000 with one ABL

SECONDARY CLASSIFICATION NUMBER	One value each with one ABL

AUTHOR	15,000 values each with one ABL

*ABL stands for the *a*ddress of the (record which is the) *b*eginning of the *l*ist.

Fig. 6.11 The layout of the directory of the generalized file structure.

In these computations, we are concerned with the number of accesses to the physical records which constitute the directory. Naturally, these numbers are sensitive to a particular implementation of the directory. However, this is not the place to compare various implementations of a directory in terms of the directory access. What we try to illustrate is the number of accesses in a given implementation with respect to various query types. Although these numbers may change from one implementation to another, we believe that they would stay approximately the same relative to each other.

For queries of the type LANGUAGE = ENGLISH & PUBLISHER = A.B. DOE (user's processing requirements 2 and 3), there are approximately 38 physical records ($6 \times 12,500 = 75,000$ characters = 38 physical records) containing English language abstracts, and one record (300 publishers distributed over 93 records) containing the said publisher. The maximum number of records access is therefore $38 + 1 = 39$. This estimate holds for both the generalized and pure inverted files.

For text processing of all the abstracts containing a prime classification number (user's processing requirement 4), we note that file searches of these abstracts in both structures are the same. What differentiates the two structures is the number of physical records involved in the directory to determine the addresses of the abstracts. In the case of pure inverted file structure, there are 132 physical records in the directory containing addresses of the abstracts. Thus these records must be used to determine the addresses of the abstracts. On the other hand, in the generalized file structure, there are only 37 physical records containing the addresses of the abstracts with "least" secondary universal decimal number. Thus, directory access in this case is minimal.

For queries of the type: ACCESSION NO. = *nnnnnnnnnnnn*, we note that there is only one record in both the generalized file and the pure inverted file directories. Since the directory will allow direct retrieval of this record without sequential search of the directory, access requirement is one physical record for each file structure.

In summary, we have the following estimate (Fig. 6.12).

		Generalized file structure (one indexed random, two multilist, three inverted)	Inverted file structure only
	Directory storage requirement (number of physical records)	761	1,351
Maximal number of physical records required for directory decoding	For query of the type: LANGUAGE = ENGLISH and PUBLISHER = A. B. COX (User's processing requirements 2 and 3)	39	39
	For text processing of all the abstracts containing a prime classification number. (User's processing requirement 4)	37	132
	For Query of the Type: ACCESSION NO. = 0123456789 (User's processing requirement 1)	1	1

Figure 6.12

6.3 QUERY

A keyword K is *true* for a record R if $K \in R$. A *query* (with respect to a file F) is a proposition given by a Boolean (and arithmetic) expression of keywords (which characterizes the records in F). A query is said to be *true* for a record R if this proposition holds for R; in this case, R is said to *satisfy* the query. For our discussion, every query is assumed to be in its disjunctive normal form (DNF):

$$(K_{11} \wedge K_{12} \wedge \cdots \wedge K_{1r_1}) \vee (K_{21} \wedge K_{22} \wedge \cdots \wedge K_{2r_2}) \vee \cdots$$
$$\vee (K_{t1} \wedge K_{t2} \wedge \cdots \wedge K_{tr_t}),$$

where $\wedge$ represents AND, and $\vee$ denotes OR.

For example, the following queries are well-formed DNF's.

(Line Number, 1102.1),
(Employee, John Doe) $\wedge$ (Salary, 15,000),
((Year, 1964) $\wedge$ (Month, April))
$\qquad \vee$ ((Year, 1964) $\wedge$ (Month, May) $\wedge$ (Time, 11:00 AM)).

The first query is a disjunctive normal form with only one keyword. The second query is a disjunctive normal form with one conjunct. In this conjunct there are two keywords. The last query consists of two conjuncts, one has two keywords and the other has three keywords.

Consider the following user request for records:

(Subject, Computer) $\wedge$ ((Area, Organization) $\vee$ (Concentration, Architecture))

This request is of course not in disjunctive normal form. However, it is known that any Boolean (and arithmetic) expression of keywords can be transformed into a disjunctive normal form. We thus have a DNF for the above request.

((Subject, Computer) $\wedge$ (Area, Organization))
$\qquad \vee$ ((Subject, Computer) $\wedge$ (Concentration, Architecture)).

At the beginning a user request for records is always transformed into a Boolean (and arithmetic) expression of keywords in disjunctive normal form. With the DNF as input, the directory decoding procedure will process the directory entries and produce the desired information for subsequent use by the file searching function.

The Boolean (and arithmetic) expression of keywords not only can be used as a query for directory decoding and file search, but also can be used as the specification of a set of records for many other purposes. For this reason, occasionally we call the DNF, for short, the *expression* or *description*.

6.4 DIRECTORY DECODING AND FILE SEARCH

Consider in the directory of a file any sequence

$$\{K, h; D(K)\} \qquad \text{where } D(K) = \{(c_1,(a_1, p_1)), (c_2,(a_2, p_2)), \ldots, (c_h,(a_h, p_h))\}.$$

We now introduce several operators which allow information to be extracted from the directory.

The *cell entry operator d* gives the number of records in the storage cell c for a given keyword K. Note that for a given keyword K there may be more than one entry $(c_j(a_j, p_j))$ in $D(K)$ associated with the storage cell c. Thus the operator sums up all those p_j whose c_j is identical to c. In symbols we write

$$d(K, c) = \sum_j p_j \quad \text{for those } (c_j,(a_j, p_j)) \in D(K) \quad \text{where } c_j = c.$$

Henceforth, we will refer to the sum corresponding to keyword K and the cell at c as P_j. Thus, the application of d for a given cell and keyword produces the sum of record counts as contained in various entries for the same cell and keyword.

The *cell identifier operator b* determines the storage cells associated with a given keyword. In symbols, we write

$$b(K) = \{c|(c,(a, p)) \in D(K)\}.$$

The *directory search operator f* determines the beginning addresses a_{ij} associated with a given keyword and storage cell. In symbols, we write

$$f(K, c) = \{a|(c,(a, p)) \in D(K)\}.$$

A keyword is *decoded* if all its beginning addresses a_{ij}, its associated cell addresses, and the number of records in each cell have been determined by the application of f, b, and d. To apply the above operators for decoding a given keyword, the cell identifier operator must first be applied to the keyword in order to obtain the set of all cell addresses associated with the keyword. Then the other two operators may be applied with each cell address in this set to obtain the number of records in the cell for the keyword, and the beginning addresses for the keyword lists. The use of these operators will be described further when the access algorithm is discussed.

In addition to the operators for directory decoding discussed above, it is also useful to have a function g, called the *file search function* for a given file F. The domain of g is the cartesian product $K \times A$ of the set K of all keywords in F with the set A of all addresses in F, while the range of g is A. In effect, g tells how to trace through each list from the beginning address to each consecutive pointer. In symbols, we write

$$y = g(K, x)$$

where y is the K pointer of the record whose address is x. For completeness, we set $y = 0$ if y is a null K pointer. In accordance with our intuition, a record R is said to be *retrieved* or *accessed* if a K pointer of R has been produced by g. We note that the mere presence of the address of a record does not imply the retrieval of the record. The record is retrieved only if its address has been used by g for the production of a pointer.

Let us again use, for example, the records illustrated in Fig. 6.1. First, apply g to R and one of its keywords. Since the address of R is 001, we have $g(K_6, 001) = 101$, the address of R'. Then by applying g to R' and the same keyword K_6, we obtain $g(K_6, 101) = 213$, the address of R''. Finally, we have $g(K_6, 213) = 0$, which indicates the absence of any more records in the K_6 list. In this case, with the given R we have retrieved R' and R''.

We can also retrieve the remainder of the records by applying g to other keywords of R as follows:

$$g(K_1, 001) = 0$$

$$g(K_2, g(K_2, 001)) = g(K_2, 003) = 0$$
$$g(K_3, g(K_3, 001)) = g(K_3, 008) = 0$$

$$g(K_4, g(K_4, g(K_4, 001))) = g(K_4, g(K_4, 004))$$
$$= g(K_4, 204) = 0$$

$$g(K_5, g(K_5, g(K_5, 001))) = g(K_5, g(K_5, 011))$$
$$= g(K_5, 204) = 0$$

$$g(K_6, g(K_6, g(K_6, 001))) = g(K_6, g(K_6, 101))$$
$$= g(K_6, 213) = 0$$

The records retrieved by the function g in the above example are those with addresses 001, 003, 004, 008, 011, 101, 204, and 213. Since record R''' at address 204 contains two keywords, it has been retrieved twice.

To a large degree efficient data base management functions are dependent upon the performance of the directory decoding procedure and file accessing strategy provided by the system. Unless these algorithms can facilitate rapid access to the desired records as they are requested by the user, the data base management functions of the system can hardly be made efficient. For this reason the system must employ an intelligent directory decoding procedure and an efficient file accessing strategy to support the data management functions.

To contrast more efficient procedures and strategy with less efficient ones, we formulate two algorithms for accessing all records in a generalized file structure.

6.5 TWO ACCESS ALGORITHMS

We now describe an algorithm for accessing all the records in a file F which contain a single keyword K_i. We then describe an algorithm for the access of all the records in F satisfying a given description in terms of keywords. Finally, we will study the difference between these two algorithms.

6.5.1 THE SERIAL ACCESS ALGORITHM

All the records containing K in F can be accessed by the following procedure:

1. Apply the cell identifier, cell entry and directory search operators (b, d, and f) until K is decoded. This results in a sequence ψ of h beginning addresses of K lists.

2. Apply the file search function g first to a beginning address a in ψ. Assume that the cell contains p records in the K list. Then apply the file search function g

iteratively to each of the pointers found in (2) until all p records containing K are retrieved.

3. Remove a from ψ; continue the algorithm at (2) until ψ becomes empty.

This algorithm is called *serial processing of lists*. An intuitive explanation follows. For a given keyword, first find out all the beginning addresses of its lists. Choose one such list and then trace through it from the beginning record to each consecutive record until there are no more records in the list. In this case, another list is chosen and is to be traced through in the same manner as above. This will be repeated until no more lists are available. While a list is being traced, one cannot begin the tracing of another list. Thus lists must be processed in turn, i.e., serially.

Consider the simple file as depicted in Fig. 6.13. We shall demonstrate the use of serial access algorithm by retrieving every record in the file. Since there are only three keywords in the directory, this demonstration amounts to record retrieval on the basis of a user query as follows:

$$K_1 \lor K_2 \lor K_3.$$

A. Now apply the serial access algorithm to K_1.

Step 1. Apply the cell identifier operator b, and obtain for this keyword the storage cell address, 00. Apply the cell entry operator d, and learn the number of records in the cell for the keyword K_1. More specifically,

$$n_1 = p_{11} = 5.$$

Apply the directory search operator f, and determine all the beginning addresses for K_1, i.e.,

$$a_{11} = 04.$$

This results in a sequence ψ of one beginning address only.

$$\psi = (04).$$

Step 2. Apply the file search function g to ψ.

$$g(K_1, 04) = 05,$$
$$g(K_1, 05) = 06,$$
$$g(K_1, 06) = 07,$$
$$g(K_1, 07) = 09,$$
$$g(K_1, 09) = 0.$$

Step 3. Remove 04 from ψ. Now ψ is empty. Therefore, every record containing K_1 has been retrieved. In fact, there are five such records whose addresses have been revealed in Step 2.

B. Similarly, we repeat the serial search algorithm (i.e., the three steps) on keyword K_2. The result is a set of three retrieved records containing K_2.

Directory

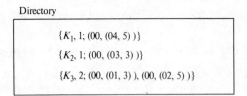

File

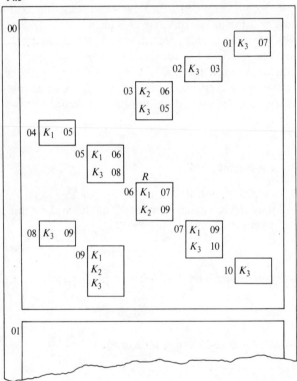

Figure 6.13

C. Finally, we apply the serial search algorithm on keyword K_3. Because there are two K_3 lists, the sequence ψ contains two beginning addresses:

$\psi = (01, 02).$

In applying the file search function g to the first address in ψ, we have

$g(K_3, 01) = 07,$
$g(K_3, 07) = 10,$
$g(K_3, 10) = 0.$

Now the second address in ψ is used.

$g(K_3, 02) = 03,$
$g(K_3, 03) = 05,$
$g(K_3, 05) = 08,$
$g(K_3, 08) = 09,$
$g(K_3, 09) = 0.$

In other words, eight records are retrieved.

In summary, we note that this example not only demonstrates the simplicity of the algorithm but also points out the limitation of the serial access.

In order to retrieve from the file those ten records which satisfy the query, the algorithm has made sixteen $(5 + 3 + 8 = 16)$ record accesses. Letting *precision* be defined as the ratio of the number of records which satisfy a query to the number of records accessed during the file search, we have

$$\text{precision} = \frac{10}{16} = \frac{5}{8},$$

indicating that the serial search algorithm is imprecise. Obviously, absolute precision can occur only when the value of the precision is 1.

Some improvements of the algorithm can be achieved by always applying the file search function g to a beginning address a which belongs to the cell with lowest cell address. In other words, all the K lists in a cell will be serially processed before any K list in another cell is searched. Furthermore, cells will be accessed in a sequential manner from the lowest cell address to the highest one. However, for a major improvement we introduce the following algorithm.

6.5.2 THE PARALLEL ACCESS ALGORITHM

We now formulate an algorithm for accessing all the records in a generalized file F satisfying a given query which we recall is expressed in the disjunctive normal form of keywords. Let the query be as follows:

$$(K_{11} \wedge K_{12} \wedge \cdots \wedge K_{1r_1}) \vee (K_{21} \wedge K_{22} \wedge \cdots \wedge K_{2r_2}) \vee \cdots$$
$$\vee (K_{t1} \wedge K_{t2} \wedge \cdots \wedge K_{tr_t})$$

where there are t terms of the given query and r_i keywords in the ith term.

1. *Determine cell addresses.* For each of the t terms, apply the cell identifier operator b repeatedly until all the r_i keywords of the term have been processed. This results in a collection of sets θ_{ij} of cell addresses $j = 1, \ldots, r_i$. Form the intersection of these sets

$$\theta_i = \bigcap_{j=1}^{r_i} \theta_{ij}.$$

We note that records which are not contained in cells whose addresses are in the set θ_i do not satisfy the ith term of the query (because these records do not contain one of the keywords of the ith term). Therefore, only records in the cells of θ_i for $i = 1, \ldots, t$ will be considered for further processing.

2. *Choose prime keywords.* Consider the ith term of the query

$(K_{i1} \wedge K_{i2} \wedge \cdots \wedge K_{ir_i})$ and its set θ_i of cell addresses.

For ease of discussion, we drop the subscript i and refer to the term and its set of cell addresses respectively as follows:

$(K_1 \wedge K_2 \wedge \cdots \wedge K_r)$ and θ.

With this simplification, the expression in step (1) becomes

$$\theta = \bigcap_{j=1}^{r} \theta_j.$$

This implies that, for every $c_v \in \theta$,

$(c_v,(a_{uv}, p_{uv})) \in D(K_u)$ for every u.

In other words, c_v are the cell addresses of cells containing records characterized not only by K_u but also by every other keyword of the term.

Apply the cell entry operator d repeatedly for each cell address c_v in θ and each keyword K_u of the term. The result is a set of sums $(d(K_u, c_v) =)P_{uv}$, one such sum for each distinct pair of keyword K_u and cell address c_v. Recall that the sum $d(K, c)$ is the number of records containing keyword K which lie in the cell at c.

Choose the smallest P_{uv} for each cell C_v. The corresponding keyword is designated as the *prime keyword* K_v' for the cell. We note that the prime keyword for one cell may be different from the prime keyword for another cell. Nevertheless, these prime keywords are keywords of the ith term of the query, and therefore characterize any record which satisfies the ith term.

Since the prime keyword of a cell is the keyword whose lists are the smallest relative to the lists of other keywords in the same conjunct (i.e., the ith term of the query), this keyword will be used in lieu of all the keywords of the conjunct for subsequent file search in the cell. This obviously improves the precision, by accessing the smallest lists of records which can possibly satisfy the conjunct instead of large lists which may also satisfy the conjunct. However, there are many cells containing records satisfying the conjunct. We must therefore have a prime keyword for each cell.

From this information, we form a set γ' of pairs of the form

(K_v', c_v) where K_v' is the prime keyword for the cell addressed by c_v, and there is one such pair for every cell address in θ.

Having obtained γ' for the term, we repeat the process for each term in the query, thus obtaining a γ_i' for each of the t terms in the query. The union of these γ_i', γ, is used for directory decoding.

3. *Decode the directory.* For each (K', c) pair in γ, apply the directory search operator f to obtain the beginning addresses of record lists to be searched during retrieval. Initialize the sequence ψ to be the sequence of addresses corresponding to the complete application of f to the set ψ. Note that ψ initially contains beginning addresses of K lists. In step (6) of the algorithm, K pointers will be added to ψ, and in step (4) addresses they will be removed from ψ. Let E be an initially empty set to be used in the retrieval process.

4. *Search the file.* Let σ be the monotone subsequence of ψ obtained by discarding from ψ every occurrence of an address after its first occurrence.

If all the addresses in σ have been used by the file search function g, then the search has been completed, and the algorithm continues at step (7). Otherwise, in σ pick the first address which has not yet been used by g, and call it a. Also delete this address from ψ. (If σ is monotone increasing, then the address is the smallest address in σ. If σ is monotone decreasing, then the address is the largest).

We note that a is either a beginning address of a K list or a K pointer. In either case, a is the address of a record R. Apply g to a and K repeatedly for every keyword $K \in R$ which is a prime keyword for the cell containing record R, to obtain a sequence σ_1 of K pointers. That is, before $K \in R$ may be used in g, the pair (K, c_a) must be in γ, where c_a is the cell address of the cell containing record R.

We note that the record at a is retrieved. Remove all the null pointers from σ_1.

5. *Examine the record.* Keeping in mind that the purpose of this algorithm is to retrieve all records in F satisfying the given query, examine the record just retrieved to determine whether the record satisfies the query. If so, include it in the set E. Otherwise, do not include it in E.

6. *Prepare to retrieve the next record.* Move all the addresses from σ_1 to ψ. Now the algorithm is repeated at step (4).

7. *Complete the retrieval.* In E we have all the records which satisfy the given query.

This algorithm is called the *parallel processing of lists.* It differs from the serial one in that while one list is being traced, it is possible to trace other lists. In other words, several lists may be traced without any one of them being completed. In essence, these lists are being processed in parallel. More specifically, the algorithm can search on more than one prime keyword per term in the query. In fact, it searches, in parallel, on one prime keyword *per storage cell* per term.

Significant points. Several significant points of this algorithm deserve to be emphasized.

A. We note that step (1) of the algorithm is designed to skip unnecessary storage cells whose records may satisfy certain individual keywords of a conjunct but nevertheless fail to satisfy the conjunction of the keywords.

B. Within the set of keywords occurring in a conjunct, the number of records chosen for retrieval is as small as possible.

Consider a term (conjunct) of a given description

$$(K_1 \wedge K_2 \wedge \cdots \wedge K_r).$$

Let L_{ij} denote the K_i list whose beginning address is a_{ij}, and whose cell address is c_{ij} and L_i the union of the K_i lists in the same cell. We have

$$L_i = \bigcup_{j=1}^{w} L_{ij}, \qquad i = 1, 2, \ldots, r; \qquad w \le h_i.$$

We note that each L_i contains exactly $\sum_j p_{ij}$ records. The set S of records satisfying the above conjunct is, in fact, the intersection of the L_i's. That is,

$$S = \bigcap_{i=1}^{r} L_i = \bigcap_{i=1}^{r} \bigcup_{j=1}^{w} L_{ij}.$$

Furthermore, we note the S is a subset of L_i for every i. However, these L_i may vary in size. It is obvious that it will take more effort to obtain S from a large L_i than from a small L_i. To minimize the effort in obtaining S, one should trace through the K_i lists of the smallest L_i. The selection of the prime keywords enables us to determine a smallest set of records for every conjunct of the query for record access.

We reiterate that in determining these lists, consideration is given to the cells in which these lists lie. The criterion is to select the smallest list on a per cell basis. Thus, for a given conjunct, there are lists for only one keyword to be traversed in a given cell and those lists contain the smallest number of records. The keywords of these keyword lists are known as prime keywords, which may vary from one cell to another. Nevertheless, they are keywords of the conjunct. Step (2) is designed to determine the shortest lists of satisfying records for retrieval.

C. As we have observed in Fig. 6.13, the record R (at 06) was retrieved twice because it contains two keywords. In general, a record may have many keywords. Thus by tracing through the lists of every keyword the record will be retrieved many times, although only one retrieval is needed. This is especially apparent in the use of the serial access algorithm. The parallel access algorithm assures that a record once accessed will not be accessed again because, in file searching, the algorithm uses the address sequence σ instead of ψ and chooses an address a in σ which has never been used for the file search function. This results in considerable saving in retrieval effort.

D. The ordering of the addresses and the discarding of the redundant addresses in step (4) enables the movable access mechanism of a storage device to make a sweep from one end of the storage device to the other, with minimal repositioning. Depending on the monotonicity of the address sequence σ in step (4), the mechanism will sweep one way or another. If the sequence is monotone decreasing, then the mechanism will sweep from "high end" to "low end." If the sequence is monotone increasing, then the sweep will be from low to high. On the other hand, the serial access algorithm may cause the repositioning each time it begins the access to a list.

E. In step (5), we note that the set F of retrieved records may properly contain the set E of records satisfying the query (i.e., there may be records in F which are not in E). However, in the case of inverted file structures, these two sets F and E are identical due to the intersection performed in step (1). In this case, the retrieval precision is therefore absolute.

F. Although it handles only one query, i.e., one disjunctive normal form of keywords at a time, the algorithm can be easily extended to batch queries. The extension requires the addition of a query queue, the formation of multiple queries into a (combined) disjunctive normal form, and the dispatch of satisfying records to a user based on the part of the combined disjunctive normal form which corresponds to the user's query. The queue is used to stack up the queries. Each of the queued queries will be transformed into a disjunctive normal form. At the end of a waiting period, a combined DNF of the following format is then formed:

$$(DNF)_1 \ \lor \ (DNF)_2 \ \lor \cdots \lor \ (DNF)_n.$$

In this case, there are n users and $(DNF)_i$ denotes the disjunctive normal form of the user i. Obviously, the disjunction of disjunctive normal forms is again a disjunctive normal form. It is this combined DNF that will be used by the parallel access algorithm as input. When a satisfying record is retrieved, the record must satisfy the DNF. More specifically, the algorithm knows that the record satisfies $(DNF)_i$ for some i. A dispatch of the record to the user i may take place immediately. Such extension is especially useful in on-line and time-sharing environments where multiple queries from various users about the centralized data base are involved.

G. The parallel algorithm can be extended to handle queries for network and hierarchy file structures. Let us first discuss the extension of the generalized file structure to these structures. Basically, there is a directory at each level of the hierarchy. At the "root" of the hierarchy, there is the (master) directory. An entry of the directory is composed of the keyword K_i^1, the number h_i^1 of the lists, and the 3-tuples of cell address c_j^1, beginning of the list a_{ij}^1, and the record count p_{ij}^1 of the list. Of course, a_{ij}^1 is the address of the first record of the list. This record may or may not be a directory. If the record is a directory, then we have an additional level of file structure. In other words, at address a_{ij}^1, we can locate a directory of a file at the level 2. By the same token, an n-level file structure is realized if there is a directory at $(n - 1)$ level of the file structure as is depicted in Fig. 6.14.

To locate a collection of records at level n, the system performs the directory decoding and file search at level one. The file search is said to be successful if a record is found such that the record is the directory of a file at the next level. Again, the directory decoding and file search procedures are conducted using the directory at the new level. Eventually, the directory for $(n - 1)$ level is found from which the set of records at level n can then be located.

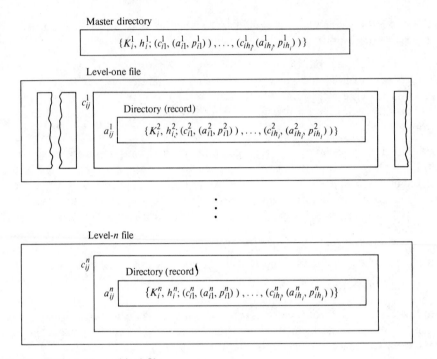

Fig. 6.14 A hierarchical file.

For the network and hierarchy file structures, the query is in the form of multilevel Boolean expressions of keywords. At each level, the Boolean expressions of keywords for that level is used. Unless there is at least one record which satisfies the Boolean expression at that level, there is no need to proceed the directory decoding and file search at the next level. In other words, if there is no record satisfying the expression $(K_{11}^m \wedge K_{12}^m \wedge \cdots K_{r1}^m) \vee \cdots \vee (K_{t1}^m \wedge K_{t2}^m \wedge K_{tr_t}^m)$, there is no need to proceed the directory decoding and file search for the expression $(K_{11}^{m+1} \wedge K_{12}^{m+1} \wedge \cdots \wedge K_{1s_1}^{m+1}) \vee \cdots \vee (K_{u1}^{m+1} \wedge K_{u2}^{m+1} \wedge \cdots \wedge K_{us_u}^{m+1})$.

The above searching strategy is very useful in conducting problem solving in terms of goals and subgoals. The problem solving goal can be expressed as query of the "highest" level, i.e., $m = 1$. When the goal is reached, the subgoals can then be pursued. For the subgoals, we have queries at the second level, i.e., $m = 2$. If one of the subgoals is realized, then the subsubgoal can be directed. In this way, the problem is solved when the final goal is reached.

In summary, the parallel access algorithm is characterized by the following:

1. It accepts disjunctive normal form of keywords as input.

2. It retrieves all records satisfying a query from one storage cell before it retrieves records from other storage cells for the same query.

3. It selects, for each storage cell, the smallest set of records which could possibly satisfy a given query for retrieval.

4. It determines, for inverted files, exactly those records which satisfy a given query prior to record retrieval.

5. It eliminates any duplicate retrieval of records.

6. It can be extended to handle the disjunction of queued disjunctive normal forms of keywords and multilevel access to hierarchical files.

These characteristics of the algorithm tend to minimize the movement of the access mechanism for moveable-head storage devices, reduce the number of accesses to secondary storage, eliminate imprecise record retrieval in the case of inverted files, and enhance on-line and time-sharing access to a data base.

The only file structures which do not take the advantage of the parallel access algorithm are the indexed sequential and random files. Because a record in these files can only be characterized by a single keyword, there can be no query in the form of conjunction of keywords. Without conjuncts, prime keyword selection is unnecessary. For the same reason, considerations for the elimination of redundant retrieval of a record when the record is an intersection of two or more lists is also unnecessary. In the case of these files, the serial access algorithm will suffice.

6.5.3 THREE EXAMPLES

The operation of the parallel access algorithm may best be illustrated with the following examples.

An Example On Parallelism

Consider a simple generalized file structure with only one cell as depicted in Fig. 6.15. This file is identical to the file as depicted in Fig. 6.13. However, we shall illustrate the file differently with nodes and directed graphs. Let us denote the records by nodes and lists of records by solid lines. It is understood that a node, which is the intersection of lists, contains the keywords of those intersecting lists. For example, the record at 09 is the intersection of K_1 list, K_2 list and K_3 list, and contains keywords K_1, K_2, and K_3. In this file, there are ten records and one K_1 list, one K_2 list, and two K_3 lists. The directory of the file is

$\{K_1, 1; (00, (04, 5))\}$

$\{K_2, 1; (00, (03, 3))\}$

$\{K_3, 2; (00, (01, 3)), (00, (02, 5))\}.$

For a query of the form

$K_1 \lor K_2 \lor K_3,$

the effective file search is depicted in Fig. 6.15 by a dotted line which shows that the algorithm will search these three lists in parallel and access every one of these records once and only once. Furthermore, it makes a sweep of records from the lowest address to the highest one.

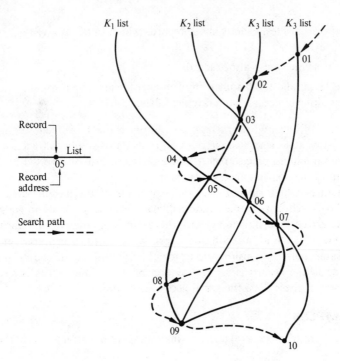

Fig. 6.15 Parallel access.

The prime keywords for this description are K_1, K_2, and K_3. Directory decoding will result in a sequence σ of beginning addresses:

$$\sigma = (01, 02, 03, 04).$$

The file search is tabulated in Table 6.1. Since the serial access algorithm has also been applied to the same file for the same query, it is easy to compare the relative efficiency between the serial and parallel access algorithms. We note that in this example the parallel access algorithm made ten (10) record accesses to retrieve just those ten records satisfying the query. On the other hand, the serial access algorithm produced the same ten records by accessing sixteen records.

An Example on Minimal Access

Consider the cellular multilist file of Fig. 6.16, in which there are four cells, with cell size = 10, and the query $K_1 \wedge K_2$ for record retrieval.

Step 1. Since there is only one term $K_1 \wedge K_2$, we apply the cell identifier operator first to K_1 and determine the set of cell addresses {00, 10, 20, 30}, and then to K_2 and determine the set of cell addresses {00, 10, 20}. Intersecting these two sets, we have the set θ of cell addresses {0, 10, 20}.

The interpretation of this step follows. Since any record satisfying the term must contain both keywords K_1 and K_2, only storage cells for which lists for both K_1 and

a	$Y = g(K, a)$	σ_1	σ
			(01, 02, 03, 04)
01	$07 = g(K_3, 01)$	(07)	
02	$03 = g(K_3, 02)$	(03)	($\underline{01}$, 02, 03, 04, 07)
03	$05 = g(K_3, 03)$ $06 = g(K_2, 03)$	(05, 06)	($\underline{01}$, $\underline{02}$, 03, 04, 07)
04	$05 = g(K_1, 04)$	(05)	($\underline{01}$, $\underline{02}$, $\underline{03}$, 04, 05, 06, 07)
05	$06 = g(K_1, 05)$ $08 = g(K_3, 05)$	(06, 08)	($\underline{01}$, $\underline{02}$, $\underline{03}$, $\underline{04}$, 05, 06 ,07)
06	$07 = g(K_1, 06)$ $09 = g(K_2, 06)$	(07, 09)	($\underline{01}$, $\underline{02}$, $\underline{03}$, $\underline{04}$, $\underline{05}$, 06, 07, 08)
07	$09 = g(K_1, 07)$ $10 = g(K_3, 07)$	(09, 10)	($\underline{01}$, $\underline{02}$, $\underline{03}$, $\underline{04}$, $\underline{05}$, $\underline{06}$, 07, 08, 09)
08	$09 = g(K_3, 08)$	(09)	($\underline{01}$, $\underline{02}$, $\underline{03}$, $\underline{04}$, $\underline{05}$, $\underline{06}$, $\underline{07}$, 08, 09, 10)
09	$0 = g(K_1, 09)$ $0 = g(K_2, 09)$ $0 = g(K_3, 09)$	(0)	($\underline{01}$, $\underline{02}$, $\underline{03}$, $\underline{04}$, $\underline{05}$, $\underline{06}$, $\underline{07}$, $\underline{08}$, 09, 10)
10	$0 = g(K_1, 10)$	(0)	($\underline{01}$, $\underline{02}$, $\underline{03}$, $\underline{04}$, $\underline{05}$, $\underline{06}$, $\underline{07}$, $\underline{08}$, $\underline{09}$, 10)

Table 6.1

K_2 are present must be searched. Therefore, the cell at 30, which contains no K_2 list, may be eliminated from the search.

Step 2. The application of the cell entry operator for K_1 and K_2 with respect to θ results in the set $\{(K_1, 3), (K_2, 2)\}$ for the cell at 00, the set $\{K_1, 2), (K_2, 3)\}$ for the cell at 10, and the set $\{(K_1, 1), (K_2, 1)\}$ for the cell at 20. For cell 0, the record count for K_1 is 3 and the record count for K_2 is 2, so we choose K_2 as the prime keyword for cell 0, since its record count is smaller. In a similar way, K_1 is chosen as the prime keyword for the cell at 10. For the cell at 20, K_1 is arbitrarily chosen as the prime keyword because all record counts are the same for that cell. Thus

$$\gamma = \gamma' = \{(K_2', 00), (K_1', 10), (K_1', 20)\}.$$

The interpretation of this step is as follows. Since the K list for one cell is entirely separate from the K list for any other cell, the "prime keyword" for a term must be determined separately for each cell. Within a given cell, the prime keyword is determined by choosing the keyword with the fewest associated records. This assures

Directory

$$\{K_1, 4; (00, (06,3)), (10, (12,2)), (20, (23,1)), (30, (35,1))\}$$
$$\{K_2, 3; (00, (03,2)), (10, (14,3)), (20, (20,1))\}$$
$$\{K_3, 3; (00, (09,1)), (10, (14,2)), (20, (21,1))\}$$
$$\{K_4, 3; (10, (16,2)), (20, (22,3)), (30, (37,1))\}$$

File

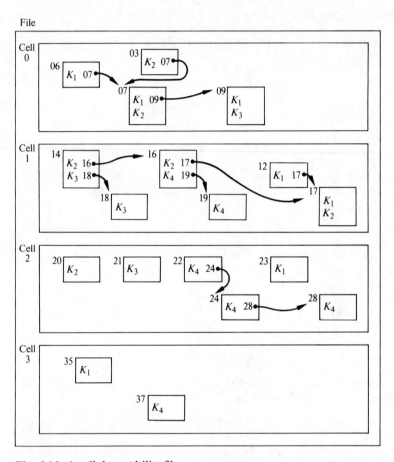

Fig. 6.16 A cellular multilist file.

fewer records retrieved during the file search than would be the case in a search on arbitrarily selected keywords. Note that, although the prime keyword turned out to be the same for two of the three storage cells involved, this is not necessarily the case in general.

Step 3. Referring to the directory in Fig. 6.16, the application of the directory search operator to $(K'_2, 00)$ yields the address 03, to $(K'_1, 10)$ yields address 12, and to $(K'_1, 20)$ yields address 23. Thus $\psi = (03, 12, 23)$. The keywords have now been decoded in the directory, and the beginning addresses of record lists are available to the file search process.

Steps 4, 5, 6, and 7. These remaining steps involve the retrieval of the records as shown in Table 6.2. We have $\sigma = (03, 12, 23)$. Applying the file search function to K_2 and the smallest address in σ which has not been used for retrieval yields $g(K_2, 03) = 07$, a pointer to another record. In other words, the record at 03 is retrieved. Since it contains only K_2, the record does not satisfy the query $K_1 \wedge K_2$. The newly obtained address forms an address sequence σ_1, which is then merged with σ. For noting an address in σ which has been used as a parameter for g, we underline the address. Thus we have

$$\sigma_1 = (07), \qquad \sigma = (\underline{03}, 07, 12, 23).$$

To retrieve the next record, g is applied to K_2 and the address 07, since it is the smallest address in σ which has not been used for g. We obtain $g(K_2, 07) = 0$, and the record satisfies the query.

The remaining steps are similar to the above and are tabulated in Table 6.2. They are not discussed in detail here. Note that different prime keywords are used for storage cells as determined in step (2) above.

In this example, we have shown that the generalized file structure accurately models the cellular multilist file structure. Another advantage of the file structure and algorithm is that they accurately model the directory decoding process for inverted files. This will be shown in the example below.

a	$Y = g(K', a)$	σ_1	σ	E
			(03, 12, 23)	
03	$07 = g(K_2, 03)$	(07)		
07	$0 = g(K_2, 07)$	(0)	($\underline{03}$, 07, 12, 23)	
12	$17 = g(K_1, 12)$	(17)	($\underline{03}$, $\underline{07}$, 12, 23)	07
17	$0 = g(K_1, 17)$	(0)	($\underline{03}$, $\underline{07}$, $\underline{12}$, 17, 23)	
23	$0 = g(K_1, 23)$	(0)	($\underline{03}$, $\underline{07}$, $\underline{12}$, $\underline{17}$, 23)	07, 17
			($\underline{03}$, $\underline{07}$, $\underline{12}$, $\underline{17}$, 23)	

Table 6.2

An Example on Absolute Precision

Consider the inverted file of Fig. 6.17, and the query $K_1 \wedge K_2 \wedge K_3$.

For the inverted file structure, the directory decoding process will intersect the three sets of beginning addresses associated with the three keywords. Having thus selected a set of distinct record addresses, the file search process can retrieve exactly

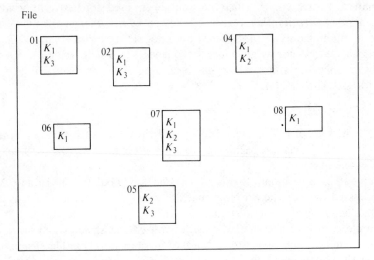

Directory

$\{K_1, 6; (\ , (01,1))\ , (\ , (02,1))\ , (\ , (04,1))\ , (\ , (06,1))\ , (\ , (07,1))\ , (\ , (08,1))\}$
$\{K_2, 3; (\ , (04,1))\ , (\ , (05,1))\ , (\ , (07,1))\}$
$\{K_3, 4; (\ , (01,1))\ , (\ , (02,1))\ , (\ , (05,1))\ , (\ , (07,1))\}$

File

Fig. 6.17 An inverted file.

those records satisfying the three keywords. Thus, the algorithm would proceed as follows.

Step 1. Apply the cell identifier operator to K_1, K_2, and K_3 which yields the sets {01, 02, 04, 06, 07, 08}, {04, 05, 07}, and {01, 02, 05, 07}, respectively. By intersecting these three sets, we have the set {07}. Therefore, only records in cell 07 can possibly satisfy the query, $K_1 \wedge K_2 \wedge K_3$.

Step 2. The application of the cell entry operator for K_1, K_2, and K_3 in the cell at 07 yields the set $\{(K_1, 1), (K_2, 1), (K_3, 1)\}$. Since the record counts are the same for all three keywords, we arbitrarily choose K_1 as the prime keyword. Thus

$$\gamma = \gamma' = (K_1, 07).$$

Step 3. The application of the directory search operator to $(K_1, 07)$ yields the address 07. Thus, $\psi = (07)$.

Steps 4, 5, 6, and 7. The record at 07 is retrieved. Since pointers in all records are null, the retrieval process is complete.

Note that the intersection of sets of beginning addresses in the directory for inverted files is accurately modeled by the generalized algorithm. This is because the set-intersection process is an integral part of the algorithm.

6.6 UPDATE

6.6.1 THREE UPDATE ALGORITHMS

A file must be updated when keywords are added, deleted, or replaced.

The addition of an existing keyword K_i to a record R' may be handled in several different ways. Since K_i does exist, there is an entry for K_i in the directory of the file. Thus, we may select a $(c_{ij}, (a_{ij}, p_{ij}))$ for consideration. The selection criterion is defined as follows:

Let a'_{ij} be the record address of R' and s be the uniform cell size. We

1. compute

$$c'_{ij} = s \left[\frac{a'_{ij}}{s} \right]$$

where the brackets indicate the integral part of the ratio,

2. select, if possible, an entry $(c_{ij}, (a_{ij}, p_{ij}))$ where $c'_{ij} = c_{ij}$,

3. create, otherwise, a new entry $(c_{ij}, (a_{ij}, p_{ij}))$ where $c'_{ij} = c_{ij}$, $a_{ij} = 0$, and $p_{ij} = 0$.

Update Algorithm I. This algorithm performs the front end insertion. It

1. retrieves the record R' from the address a'_{ij};
2. inserts the keyword K_i into R';
3. inserts a_{ij} of $(c_{ij}, (a_{ij}, p_{ij}))$ into R' as the K_i pointer;
4. stores R' at a'_{ij}; and
5. replaces $(c_{ij}, (a_{ij}, p_{ij}))$ in the directory with $(c_{ij}, (a'_{ij}, p'_{ij}))$ where $p'_{ij} = p_{ij} + 1$.

In this algorithm, the updated record R' becomes a member of the K_i list whose beginning address is a'_{ij}. In other words, R' is the beginning of the K_i list. The only restriction to the algorithm is that the cell whose address is c_{ij} must be sufficiently large to accommodate the expansion of the record R' as depicted in steps (2) and (3).

Update Algorithm II. This algorithm performs the replacement. It

1. retrieves the record R' from the address a'_{ij};
2. saves a copy of R';
3. places a *deletion tag* in R';
4. stores R' at a'_{ij};
5. removes the K_i pointers, if any, from the copy of R';
6. inserts the new keyword K_i into the copy of R'; and
7. enters the copy of R' as a new record into the file.

A record with the deletion tag is a record whose content is no longer of any interest to the user and whose K_i pointers are still useful to the access algorithm of the system to establish the K_i lists. Thus, for the purpose of accessing other records in the K_i lists, the record is not physically deleted from the file even though it is transparent to the user.

The process of placing a new record R' in the file involves the assignment of a_{ij} of $(c_{ij},(a_{ij},p_{ij}))$ as K_i pointers to K_i in R'. Furthermore, these $(c_{ij},(a_{ij},p_{ij}))$ will be replaced by $(c_{ij},(a'_{ij},p'_{ij}))$. Finally, after each K_i in R' has been assigned a K_i pointer and every corresponding triple $(c_{ij},(a_{ij},p_{ij}))$ in the directory has been processed, the record R' is then stored at a'_{ij}. This process is similar to the steps (3), (4), and (5) in Algorithm I, except that these three steps must be performed for each and every K_i appearing in R'.

The Algorithm II is not handicapped by the requirement that a newly updated record must be small enough to be fitted into an existing cell, as was required in Algorithm I. Since the updated record is entered as a new record, allocation of a fresh cell for accommodating the record is an easier task. However, there is the necessary task of removing tagged records at a later time.

Update Algorithm III. This algorithm combines both front-end insertion and replacement. It takes advantage of the aforementioned two update algorithms. Whenever a newly modified record can be fitted into the same cell from which it was retrieved, Update Algorithm I is used. Otherwise, Algorithm II is employed. This algorithm tends to minimize the number of tagged records and to avoid overflowing existing storage cells.

To add a new keyword to a record, the same algorithms may be used. The only difference between adding an existing keyword and a new keyword is in the selection of $(c_{ij},(a_{ij},p_{ij}))$. Since there is no entry in the directory corresponding to the new keyword K_i, the following entry is created:

$$\{K_i,1;(c_{i1},(0,0))\}.$$

We shall not discuss the deletion and replacement of keywords which will be studied as part of the exercise.

6.6.2 THE PHENOMENON OF STRUCTURAL MIGRATION

From the preceding discussion, we note that the addition of either new or existing keywords to records in a file tends to generate directory entries whose triples are of the form

$$(c_{ij},(a_{ij},1)).$$

In other words, new K_i lists containing only one record may result from frequent update. Thus, the update process can cause a given file structure to become a new file structure whose lists are short. Such a phenomenon is termed *structural migration.*

Accessing lists containing only one record per list does not require extensive file search. Thus, the new file structure is especially suitable for restructuring because the overhead of file search is low. Restructuring an existing file is particularly meaningful if the file has been updated often. Via restructuring, the file can then be tailored to a new processing requirement as demonstrated in the example in Section 6.2.2.2.6.

6.6.3 THE GARBAGE COLLECTOR

6.6.3.1 The Role of the Garbage Collector

Recovering storage space occupied by tagged records and regenerating every list of a file so that no record in the list is a tagged one is the task of a *garbage collector*.

A cell is said to be *dead* if every record in the cell has been tagged for deletion. A list is said to be *inactive* if every record in the list has been tagged. Thus, in a dead cell every list of the cell is inactive. If no record has been deleted since the file was generated, then every list is active and, furthermore, every cell is live. When records are tagged for deletion, two possibilities occur:

1. *A list may become inactive.* In this case, the part of the cell occupied by the inactive K_i list is wasted. Furthermore, the directory entry associated with K_i serves no useful purpose for the access of records because it points to an inactive list. The situation may become more acute if the cell is dead. Hence there is the need for purging every directory entry which points to an inactive list, and recovering the storage area.

2. *An active list may have many tagged records.* In order to access all the records in the list, it is necessary to pass through the tagged records. Thus, besides wasting the cell storage occupied by the tagged records, time is wasted during any access to the list. This seems to warrant the attempt to "shorten" an active list by removing all tagged records in that list.

6.6.3.2 The Garbage Collection Algorithm

The algorithm employed here for the garbage collector involves two phases. Phase I is performed *only once* for the file and phase II is executed *repeatedly* when necessary. The phases are described below.

Phase I. In phase I the collector reads as many records of a cell as possible from the cell storage into main memory. It discards tagged records, and processes only the nontagged ones. For every nontagged record, it

a) extracts the keywords in the record;

b) places them in a buffer, called the *keyword-buffer*, if they are *different* from the keywords already in the keyword-buffer;

c) computes a new record address for the record;*

d) saves the address along with the keywords now in the keyword-buffer;

e) writes the record onto an auxiliary storage unit;* and

---

* This is a new record address in $|F|$, i.e., the file space. It has nothing to do with the address in the auxiliary storage unit which serves only as a temporary storage. Thus, whenever we refer to the address a_{ij} of the record, we mean the new record address in the intended file space even though the file has *not* been copied onto the permanent file space yet. Nevertheless, the system knows the temporary address at which the record resides on the auxiliary unit.

f) if a keyword of the record is *identical* to a keyword in the keyword-buffer, it is not placed in the keyword-buffer. Instead, the address, saved along with the keyword in the keyword-buffer, is inserted into the record along with the keyword. And steps are resumed at (c).

This algorithm assures that at any given point every keyword of last record in a cell contains the address of the previous record containing the same keyword. Since there may be many keywords in a record, the last record processed is also the first record of the lists. We note that keywords in the keyword-buffer are distinct, and furthermore, each keyword is associated with a pointer to the first record in a list. This algorithm is applied to every cell in the file. The size of the keyword-buffer is restricted by the main storage available to the collector. If it is not big enough to accommodate all the distinct keywords of the file, file processing will be continued in phase II. Otherwise, it will be terminated in phase I and there is no need to initiate phase II.

In either case, at the end of phase I, the collector generates a directory from the keywords in the keyword-buffer and replaces the old directory of the file. If it is not necessary to proceed into phase II, the processed records that are stored on the auxiliary unit are then written back onto the cell storage. (See Fig. 6.18.)

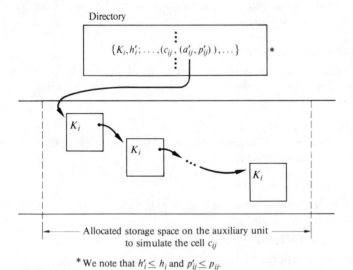

Directory

$$\{K_i, h'_i; \ldots, (c_{ij}, (a'_{ij}, p'_{ij})), \ldots\} \quad *$$

K_i

K_i

$\cdots$

K_i

Allocated storage space on the auxiliary unit to simulate the cell c_{ij}

*We note that $h'_i \leq h_i$ and $p'_{ij} \leq p_{ij}$.

Fig. 6.18 At the end of phase I.

Phase II. The algorithm used here is the same as the one in phase I, except that in processing a keyword, the collector saves not only the address a_{ij} of the last processed record (thus first of the list) containing the keyword, but also the address a^t_{ij} of the first processed record *in this phase* containing the keyword. (See Fig. 6.19.) Unlike

a_{ij} and a'_{ij}, the addresses of permanent file space, the a^t_{ij} is an auxiliary storage address. At the end of phase II, each keyword in the keyword-buffer (in main memory) that is generated by phase II must be either identical to a keyword in the directory (generated by phase I) or different from all the keywords in the directory.

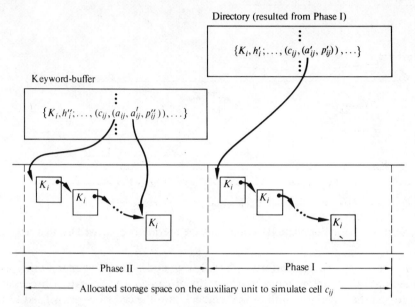

Fig. 6.19 Each keyword in phase II has two pointers.

Case 1. If the keyword is different, then the collector inserts it into the directory.

Case 2. If the keyword, K_i, is identical to a keyword in the directory, the collector fixes up the linkages by

a) retrieving from a^t_{ij} the first record processed in phase II containing this keyword and bringing it into main memory;

b) finding from the directory the pointer, a'_{ij}, of the last processed record containing this keyword;

c) inserting the above pointer into the retrieved record and placing the record back where it belongs (now the first processed record of this phase is linked to the last processed record in the previous phase); and

d) replacing the pointer, a'_{ij}, associated with the directory with the one, a_{ij}, associated with the same keyword in the main memory keyword-buffer. Now the keyword in the directory is pointing to the last record in this phase.

In short, case 2 involves the establishment of the dotted lines shown in Fig. 6.20. It is performed with the intent to preserve the list if the processing of the list was interrupted at the end of phase I.

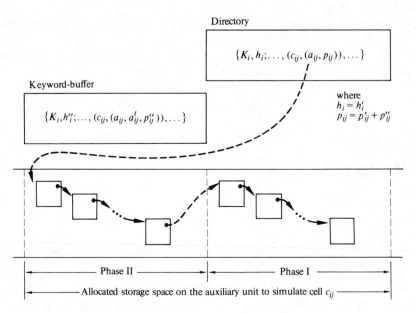

Directory

$$\{K_i, h_i; \ldots, (c_{ij}, (a_{ij}, p_{ij})), \ldots\}$$

Keyword-buffer

$$\{K_i, h''_i; \ldots, (c_{ij}, (a_{ij}, a'_{ij}, p''_{ij})), \ldots\}$$

where
$h_i = h'_i$
$p_{ij} = p'_{ij} + p''_{ij}$

Phase II $\longleftrightarrow$ Phase I

Allocated storage space on the auxiliary unit to simulate cell c_{ij}

Fig. 6.20 At the end of phase II—continuing the previously processed list in a cell.

In general, the collector performs phase I once and phase II as many times as it is required until there are no more records to be processed. At the end of processing, the records on the auxiliary unit are written back into the cell storage assigned to the file.

6.6.4 ADDRESS MONOTONICITY

The primary consideration in developing the garbage collection algorithms is centered on the preservation of the monotonicity of the record address sequence in any list. This consideration is based on the observation that if all record addresses of any list in the file are monotonically increasing (decreasing), then the parallel access algorithm will cause the movable read/write head of a direct access storage device to make a *single sweep* from the low (high) end of the storage device to the high (low) end of the same device. Otherwise, nonmonotonic address sequence of a list will cause the repositioning of the read/write head which is time-consuming. Thus, to really make effective use of the access algorithm, we must preserve the monotonicity of the record addresses for every list.

Record addresses of a given list are always in monotonic order when the file is newly created. If the order is preserved during update, then the effectiveness of the access algorithm will be assured. For this reason, we should strive to develop update algorithms which can preserve for every list the monotonicity of the record addresses in the list.

Consider the example where the original file is depicted in Fig. 6.21. We assume that the record R in Fig. 6.21 containing K_j and K_n is to be characterized by an additional keyword K_i. In other words, the record R must be put on a K_i list. The updated file as depicted in Fig. 6.22 is not acceptable since the address sequence of the K_i list is not in monotonic decreasing (increasing) order. Should this happen, the access algorithm would cause the movable read/write head mechanism of the device to reposition the mechanism for the record R after the record R' has been retrieved. On the other hand, there is no repositioning of access mechanism necessary for the updated file as depicted in Fig. 6.23. In this case, we merely create a new K_i list.

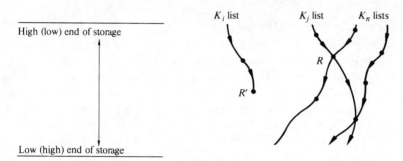

High (low) end of storage

Low (high) end of storage

Figure 6.21

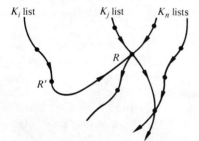

Figure 6.22

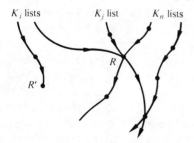

Figure 6.23

6.7 DATA SECURITY—A STUDY OF LOGICAL ACCESS CONTROL

Data security means different things to different people. The reason perhaps lies in the data security problem itself. It is a large problem which involves security considerations in procedures, computer hardware, system software, and data base. Thus research and development in data security have been aimed at resolving one or more of these problem areas. A completely secure system of course requires successful resolution of security problems in all four areas. To aid our understanding of data security in general and the security roles of hardware, software, and data base in particular, we introduce the jeweler's story.

6.7.1 THE JEWELER'S PROBLEM

A jeweler not only sells gems but also handles for his customers the jewels which he sold to the customers. In addition to repair and service, the jeweler must sometimes keep his customers' jewels in the safe, especially if these are regular and important customers. He knows that the safety of the jewels is only as good as the security of the safe. To this end he must have well-made safes with elaborate protection mechanisms and combinations. Quite often he has to transport the jewels from one place to another. In this situation, he must devise a secure procedure for transportation. Although safes may be included in the transportation, there is still the need for special vehicles (e.g., armored cars) to carry the safes. Furthermore, he must take great precautions when the jewels are being moved from one vehicle to another (say, from a car to a boat). Until he can secure very good safes and devise very reliable means and procedures for the transportation, the jeweler will not be able to safeguard his customers' jewels adequately.

The security problem is compounded when one day the jeweler realizes that in an effort to safeguard the jewels, he has kept the jewels hidden, and has thus interfered with one of the most important uses of the jewels, i.e., display. He then asks himself whether it is possible to provide maximal display of jewels on their rightful owners or their designated users, and at the same time provide maximal security. Being a jeweler, he naturally investigates the possibility of developing security devices within the bracelets, necklaces, and ornaments. Such devices, if effective, can protect the jewels while they are displayed by their rightful users. In this case, both the intended use of and the security of the jewels are realized.

There is a close correlation between jewels in the jeweler's story and data in data base systems. Just as jewels are intended for display, data in data base systems are destined to be shared. It is through sharing of data that the users of the systems can benefit each other intellectually. However, the basis of data sharing must be voluntary. In other words, the system must be able to safeguard the anonymity of the user's private data and to control access to shareable data. Safeguard measures in computer systems can be viewed in different levels. As in the case of using safes to protect jewels, the use of real memory and virtual space units to protect data is an approach. Such approach is termed *memory protection*. Like jewels which must be transported from one place to another, data must also be moved in computer systems. The active agents for such data movement are referred to as *procedures*. These entities are composed mainly of programs. Thus, another approach is aimed to develop *procedure protection*. Both memory and procedure protection mechanisms, which deal with physical hardware and software elements, are collectively called *physical protection and access control mechanisms*. Finally, in an attempt to incorporate protection mechanisms along with the data, there is the need of more subtle protection mechanisms which we refer to as the *logical protection and access control mechanisms*.

6.7.2 THREE LEVELS OF ACCESS CONTROL AND PROTECTION

The study of access control and protection mechanisms in computer systems is therefore concerned with effective means to protect the anonymity of private information, on the one hand, and to regulate the access to shareable information on the other hand. Effective means for access control may now be considered in three levels: memory level, procedure level, and logical level.

At the memory level, access control mechanisms are those which regulate access to memory in terms of units of memory. The main point is that protection applies to the containers, i.e., the memory units, not the contents. As a consequence, everything inside the container is subject to the same access control as the enclosure itself. Furthermore, the contents are safe only as long as they are kept in protected containers.

Typically, physical memory protection schemes employ memory bounds registers or storage protection "keys" which control access to bounded memory areas. Other, more sophisticated, schemes are possible. The idea of having an $m \times m$ matrix of control bits to keep track of access rights to m memory areas has been advanced. For example, an entry A_{ij} would determine the access rights to ith area from the jth area. The A_{ij} may correspond to various access rights such as read-only, read/write, execute-only and privileged mode.

In general, one user's access rights to an area may differ considerably from another user's access rights to the same area. In a multiprogramming and shared data base environment, the system must therefore provide dynamically different access matrices for different users. The use of virtual space may, therefore, enhance the implementation of the matrix scheme. Here, page and segment tables are consulted by the hardware at instruction decoding time. Each user is assigned his own tables and therefore cannot get into a segment of space which does not have an entry in those tables. As a result, elaborate schemes, such as the access matrix, are more easily implemented with virtual space. Yet, even in virtual space, we note that the protected areas are again units of space.

The second level of access control is concerned with procedure access control and protection. A procedure is simply a set of programs and associated data. Thus, unlike memory protection, the notion of procedure protection and control is concerned with access to and protection of programs. To this end, we must develop mechanisms which can determine when and under what conditions programs can pass control from one to another. In other words, the mechanisms must be able to monitor the execution of programs in terms of their calls, returns, and transfer of parameters.

An elaborate procedure access control and protection mechanism was proposed and known as the "ring mechanism." This concentric ring mechanism allows one program to give control to another without violating any of the access control rights of either program, thereby safeguarding each program's working tables, data, intermediate results, etc. Conceptually, the concentric ring mechanism requires the user to arrange his procedures hierarchically, that is, procedures at the lower part of the hierarchy (i.e., outer rings) have less privileged access rights. It is a generalization of a simple hierarchy of two rings. In the simple hierarchy of two rings, procedures are run either in the inner ring (i.e., supervisory state) or the outer ring (i.e., the user-program state). To communicate with procedures in the supervisory state, a procedure in the user-program state must go through a gate or a set of gates. The implementation of gates varies from one computer system to another computer system. It may be implemented as supervisory calls (SVC) or as software system macros. On the other hand, to access procedures in the user-program state, no procedure in the supervisory state is required to go through gates. With the generalization the ring mechanism allows many program-running states where each state is realized in a concentric ring. It is therefore possible to have, for example, the system-supervisory state (in the innermost ring), the user-supervisory state (in next ring), the user-subsystem-monitor state, the user-subsystem state, and the user-subsystem-program components (in the outermost ring). This mechanism can be implemented in a computer whether or not it has virtual space. Therefore, one should not indulge in the misconception that virtual space protection and procedures protection are one and the same.

The highest level of access control is logical. It is natural that, in a large data base environment, the user will first organize his data into some logical structure. He will then refer to his structured data in terms of logical entities such as fields, arrays, records, subfiles, and files. The important point is that these entities are logical units of information which may have little resemblance to their physical or virtual storage images. By allowing the user to associate access control requirements and protection measures with the logical units, the access control mechanism can facilitate direct control and protection of the information, regardless of the whereabouts of that information. Furthermore, the mechanism does not require the user to be familiar with the physical or virtual storage structure of the computer system.

Logical access control mechanisms must therefore have the facility for the user to describe his shareable and private data in terms of logical entities of the data base, to assign access rights and protection requirements to these entities, to determine the collections of these entities and the types of access that other users may have, and to incorporate additional authentication and checking measures.

6.7.3 A LOGICAL ACCESS CONTROL MODEL

We will not discuss here in great detail the complex logical access control mechanisms in some of the working data base management systems. Instead, we present a simple model on which some of the important concepts and salient features of these mechanisms may be achieved.

Basically, the logical access control model consists of three parts:

1. A shared data base to which access must be controlled.

2. A group of users whose access to the data base must be regulated.

3. A set of mechanisms which govern the accessing of the data base by the users.

In order to develop the model, solutions to the following problems must be provided. These solutions are discussed in separate sections.

1. A method to identify the logical elements of the data base.

2. A representation of the types of access the user can have to the data base.

3. A concept on which a user can assign and change access types of other users to his data base.

4. A basis on which the system can determine who could perform what data management functions on accessible data.

5. A methodology for effective implementation of various access control requirements as specified in the access types.

6.7.3.1   Identification of the Logical Elements of the Data Base

Logical elements in the data base must be uniquely identified so that the system can resolve their different identities and control access to individual elements. However, the burden of assigning unique identifiers to individual elements of data base should not be placed on the user. One requirement is, therefore, that the system, not the user, have the responsibility to assign a unique identification number to each and every datum in the data base. What the user must have is a means to describe his logical elements for access control purpose and to specify his access control requirements for these elements. In order to describe his logical data elements for access control purpose, the user must be able to declare their structures; and in order to provide a priori and posteriori controls over access to these data elements, the user must be able to specify their authentication and checking procedures. We note that the user already has a data description language for declaring data structure in data base creation and a data manipulation language for specifying data base management requirements. It follows that the same data description language may be used to declare the structure of the logical elements for access control purposes. The use of the same description language for both data base creation and control not only is expeditious but also eliminates the possibility of false identification due to ambiguity in language translation. Similarly, the same data manipulation language may be employed to specify the authentication and the checking procedure for access control to data base elements. Thus, a second requirement is that the means employed to describe elements of the data base for access control purposes and to specify their access control requirements should be the same as the ones used to declare data structure and to specify data manipulation requirements for data base creation and processing.

These are indeed the requirements that the model attempts to meet. In this model elements of the data base are identified as fields (i.e., attribute-value pairs), groups of fields, keywords, records, subfiles, and files. References to fields are made by field names (attributes), to groups by group names and relations of the fields, to records by selection criteria in terms of Boolean and arithmetic expressions of fields and field names, to subfiles by Boolean and arithmetic expressions of keywords, and to files by file names. All these names and expressions can be used in the procedures for data definition, manipulation, and access control purposes. We shall illustrate their use in later sections. In this model, procedures can be written in either data description and manipulation command languages or data management assembly language macros, on the one hand; or in higher-level languages such as FORTRAN and COBOL which have been extended to include data definition, manipulation, and access control facilities, on the other hand.

6.7.3.2 Representation of Access Types

We represent the types of access a user has to the data base as an *authority item*.

Conceptually, there is one-to-one correspondence between the users and the authority items.

An authority item consists of the following:

1. User identification.

2. Names of all the user's accessible files.

3. Options (i.e., access privileges) regarding the use of the files. Some of the options are listed below:

ND	Directory reading is not allowed
RR	Read records only
RE	Read either directory or records
EP	Execute program records
ER	Enter new records
RW	Read or write records
TB	Temporarily block the access of other users while the file is being modified
OWN	Own the file

4. Program entries for file-level procedural authentications.

5. Record access control descriptions (i.e., Boolean and arithmetic expression of keywords, filed names, and fields) for opening portions of files, for being temporarily blocked from access to portions of files, for allowing or denying one's use of certain portions of files.

6. Program entries for record-level procedural checking.

7. Field access control descriptions (i.e., Boolean and arithmetic expression of field and field names).

8. Program entries for field-level procedural checking.

The entire collection of the authority items may be viewed as an *access control matrix* with the user identified with the rows and logical units of data base with the columns. The entry A_{uv} contains a series of access rights and restrictions held by user u to logical unit v.

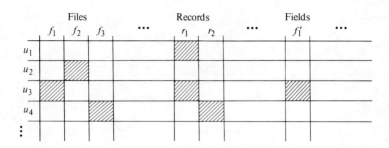

For implementation the matrix is too sparse to be stored as it is. For ease of change and update of access privileges and restrictions, the matrix should be organized like any other records of a (system) file. Because access privileges and restrictions to the same data units differ from one user to another, and because there are more data types than users, the implementation of authority items as records is user-oriented instead of data-type oriented. In other words, there is one authority item for a user.

6.7.3.3 The Concept of Ownership

We introduce the concept of ownership to facilitate for the user the granting and denying of access privileges.

A user can grant and deny other users access to a file if he is the *owner* of the file.

To become an owner of a file the user must satisfy and comply with a set of rules and regulations which may vary from one installation to another. In particular, the system administrator is a de facto owner. Since he owns the file of authority items, he effectively owns every file in the system. There are therefore special requirements imposed on the system administrator whose access to authority item file may be inherent and whose use of the file may, nevertheless, be stringent. When a user becomes an owner of a file, the system assigns an OWN option for the file in the user's authority item. In this model, the creator of a file will automatically become the owner of the file. As an owner of the file, the user can grant and deny any other users access to that file. In other words, a user with OWN option on a file can assign any option to other users for the file.

In summary, the concept of ownership establishes for the system a hierarchy of users as depicted in Fig. 6.24.

6.7.3.4 The Basis for the Use of Data Management Commands and Macros

The use of data management commands and macros by a user is dictated by the user's assigned options in his authority items. The authority item of a user is used by the data base management system at all times to determine whether the user can perform a specific data base management function as indicated by his use of certain command or macro. For example, only the owner of a file can give others access to

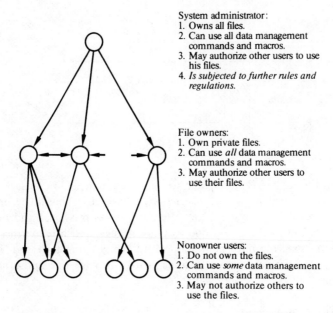

System administrator:
1. Owns all files.
2. Can use all data management
   commands and macros.
3. May authorize other users to use
   his files.
4. *Is subjected to further rules and
   regulations.*

File owners:
1. Own private files.
2. Can use *all* data management
   commands and macros.
3. May authorize other users to
   use their files.

Nonowner users:
1. Do not own the files.
2. Can use *some* data management
   commands and macros.
3. May not authorize others to
   use the files.

Fig. 6.24 A hierarchy of users.

the file. Thus, to exercise the following command, the user of the command must be an owner, i.e., there must be an OWN option in the user's authority item.

> XFILES ACCESS/(user's name)/(user's project name)/(file name)/(option)/(protection description)

The XFILES ACCESS command enables a file owner to delegate access rights to other users for use of his file. It takes basically five parameters, namely the following:

1. User's name: This may be a name or a disjunction of names.

2. User's project name: a single project name.

3. File name: This may be a file name or a disjunction of file names.

4. Option: (See option list in previous section.)

5. Protection description: a Boolean and arithmetic expression of keywords which characterizes a subfile for permanent protection from access.

```
XFILES ACCESS/BROWN/OSU/
            FILE1/RR/(INFORMATION TYPE, PRIVATE)/
            FILE2/RR/(CLASSIFICATION, CONFIDENTIAL)V
                (PRIORITY, IMPORTANT)
```

The above example indicates that Brown may have access to both FILE1 and FILE2. He can read all records except those satisfying the protection description (INFORMATION TYPE, PRIVATE) in FILE1 and (CLASSIFICATION, CONFIDENTIAL)V PRIORITY, IMPORTANT) in FILE2.

On the other hand, there are commands which may be exercised by the user on a file without being the file owner.

```
XFILES OPEN
XFILES OPEN/A₁/B₁/A₂/B₂/ · · · /Aₙ/Bₙ
XFILES OPEN/A₁/B₁/A₂/B₂ · · · /Aₙ
```

The first open file executive command will open all files that are accessible to the user. The other two forms will open the portion (i.e., the subfile) of A_i, which satisfies the Boolean and arithmetic expression B_i as long as it is accessible to the user. In case B_i is null or absent for some i, the file A_i is opened entirely.

But A_i may be either a single file name or a disjunction of file names. For instance, if a user wants to open a subfile for processing consisting of all the employee records in which the job title is foreman-first-class, he may exercise the following:

```
XFILES OPEN/EMPLOYEE–FILE/(JOB–TITLE, FOREMAN–FIRST–CLASS)
```

where EMPLOYEE–FILE is a file name and (JOB–TITLE, FOREMAN–FIRST–CLASS) is a keyword.

In Fig. 6.25 we list some of the commands on files and subfiles and their associated options for exercising the commands.

Options (access rights) to be provided to the system by the user's authority item to permit use of the command	Some of the commands (and their explanations)
None	New file (to create a new file)
OWN	Delete file (to delete an existing file)
RR,RE,RW,OWN,EP or ER	Open subfile or file (to open a subfile or file for accessing)
None	Close file (to close a file)
OWN	Access subfile or file (to give others access rights to his subfile or file)
OWN	No-access subfile or file (to remove given access rights to his subfile or file)
TB or OWN	Temporarily block subfile or file (to claim exclusive access to a subfile or file)
None	Unblock file
RW or OWN	Reorganize file (to collect garbage)
None	Log-in for a file (to enter necessary parameters at opening time for the file-level procedure)
OWN	Enter a log-in program (to incorporate a file-level authentication procedure for the file)

Fig. 6.25 Data management commands.

System macros are subject to the same option controls as the commands. These macros are used in the user's assembly programs as data management functions. Through the compiler, the user can also employ these macros as data management subprograms and subroutine calls.

All macro calls have the following schematic form:

GSR $P, (S_1, S_2, \ldots, S_n)$

where GSR is the data management system macro name, S_i are service names, and P may be null, the symbolic address of a Boolean and arithmetic expression of keywords, or a number.

For example, if the user program wants to enter a new record into an open file, then he can issue the macro call with the following data management service.

Service name	Meaning
IT,FQ	Enter a new record into a specific file.

Macro Call

GSR   ,(IT,FQ)

with address of the record, IT in register i and file name, FQ in register j.

Returns from the call

1. If service is completed successfully, then register i contains zero.

2. Otherwise, register j contains all ones and p-bit is set.

In this example the parameter P is null. In the following examples, we demonstrate the use of parameter P as a pointer to a Boolean and arithmetic expression and as a number.

Service name combination	Meaning
DL, IM, FQ	Delete records by description from a specific file.

Macro call

GSR   ADDR,(DL,IM,FQ)

with address of the description at ADDR and file name in register FQ.

The following macro enables a program to fetch parameters as operands of an executing command.

Service name	Meaning
DES	Get the address of the specified operand of the current command.

Macro call

GSR   N,(DES)

where N indicates the Nth operand.

The mere availability of the above service macros for data management does not provide every user of the system the right to receive such data management services. In fact, without the ER option in his authority item, the user cannot exercise the first macro (i.e., the one with IT, FQ service names). Unless he is the owner of a file, the user cannot delete records of the file by issuing the second macro (i.e., the one with DL, IM, and FQ). The use of DES in a macro requires no option. The rationale is that one's program can always know the parameters of one's command. In fact, this is an effective way for an executing program to communicate with an ongoing command. As a summary, we list a set of data management macros and their required options in Fig. 6.26.

6.7.3.5 The Security Procedure

Regardless of the type of access the user may desire, there is a *security procedure* through which all access to the data base must be validated and monitored.

1. Identify the command or macro call.

2. Check to see whether the user has access to the files involved, i.e., consult his authority item.

3. If the user has access to a file, then check to see whether the file is currently open for his use.

4. If the file is open, then check to see if the user has the proper file-option with respect to the call (e.g., read-only option for retrieval, write option for input, etc.).

5. If a user has the correct option for using the file, set up certain necessary information for the system programs involved.

6. Perform a priori analysis of the expression. Remove keywords and attribute-value pairs from the expression if these keywords and pairs are prohibited.

7. Call the proper system program or programs to perform the requested service.

8. Keep track of the status of the service. Since a data management service may not be completed without repeated calls, it is necessary to save some information for the continuation of the service at a later time.

9. Update and save the information that was originally set up for the system programs.

10. Continue the service on the next open file, if step 3 involves more than one open file.

11. Make sure that each output record belongs to the open portion of a file, not temporarily blocked from use by others, and not permanently protected from access.

12. Satisfy the procedural checking at record level.

13. Make certain that fields protected from access are removed from the outputting record, i.e., posterior control.

14. Satisfy the procedural checking at field level.

Some of the Data Management Macros   GSR $P, (S_1, S_2, \ldots, S_n)$

Options required to permit the use of macros	Macro Call	Meaning
RE	GSR , (KY)	Fetch keywords from the directories of all open files.
	GSR , (KY,FQ)	Fetch keywords from the directory of a specific file whose name is in mq register.
	GSR A, (DL,IM,D)	Delete data records only by Boolean expression of keywords at A.
	GSR A, (DL,IM,MP,ND,NMU,NSYS)	Delete program records only by expression at A.
OWN	GSR A, (DL,IM,MU,ND,NMP,NSYS)	Delete command procedure records only by expression.
	GSR A, (DL,IM,SYS,ND,NMP,NMU)	Delete system records only by expression.
	GSR A, (DL,IM,D,MP,NMU,NSYS)	Delete data and program records by expression.
(None)	GSR N, (DES)	Get the address into accumulator of the Nth parameter of executing command.
RR	GSR A, (NDL,IM)	Retrieve records by Boolean expression at A.
	GSR A, (NDL,IM,FQ)	Retrieve records by expression from a specific file.
ER	GSR , (IT)	Enter a new record into an open file where the record address is in accumulator.
	GSR , (IT,FQ)	Enter a new record into a specific file.

Fig. 6.26 Some data management macros.

Let us discuss some of the steps in the security procedure.

Steps 1 and 4 require the system to identify the types of options which are necessary for the issuance of the particular command or macro call. As was indicated in previous sections, the data management commands and macros that a user can exercise are determined by the type of options assigned to him. For example, without the OWN option the user is not permitted to delete a file through the issuance of the data management command DELETE FILE or the macro call IM–DL–FQ (with a Boolean expression characterizing all records in the file). To this end, the system consults the user's authority item. Since options regarding a file are always associated with the name of the file as a part of the third entry in the authority item, the system can determine whether the user has proper options for the use of that command or macro call.

For step 2, the system consults the second entry of the authority item. We note that in this entry the names of all the accessible files to the user are listed; but files which are not accessible to him do not have their names in his authority item. In other words, inaccessible files are completely transparent to the user.

The inclusion of step 3 in the security procedure provides for a file owner the first opportunity to employ authentication programs to screen all users of the file. Typically an authentication program for a file consists of a set of owner-written routines which are loaded into the system by the file owner through the use of the command ENTER–A–LOG–IN–PROGRAM at the file creation. When a user attempts to open the file, he involuntarily invokes the authentication program for the file. Although the program may demand various input from the user [via GSR n, (DES) macro], it always produces either one of two standard outputs indicating either a positive or negative authentication. Since programs written for authentication purposes can employ data management macros, they can store and retrieve information regarding the number of file opening attempts and combinations of user passwords. Without positive authentication, the file will not be opened for access.

We note that the program entry points for file-level checking are placed in the fourth entry of the authority item. Thus, thoughtful use of the authentication programs (also known as log-in procedure) at file level can provide very good protection of the file as a whole.

Step 5 and steps 7 through 10 are self-explanatory. We shall not elaborate here. In step 6, we remove keywords which are prohibited from use by this user. The description of the prohibited keywords is incorporated in the fifth entry of the user's authority item. By removing the keywords from the user's query, macro descriptions, and command descriptions, no access based on these keywords will ever take place. Thus, the user will not be able to infer the existence or nonexistence of the keywords and their associated records by referring to their successful or unsuccessful retrieval. In step 11, the security procedure carries the access control from the file level as in step 3 to the subfile level. By using Boolean and arithmetic expressions of keywords, fields, and field names as a means to partitioning a file into subfiles, the system can control access to the subfiles. However, in this case the partitions are virtual and no subfiles are actually being generated. The reasons for not physically making duplicate subfiles are to safeguard the integrity of the data base on the one hand and to facilitate update on the other hand. Virtual subfiles can be readily created by introducing new Boolean and arithmetic expressions. In fact, there can be a multiplicity of subfiles for various access purposes, as illustrated in Fig. 6.27.

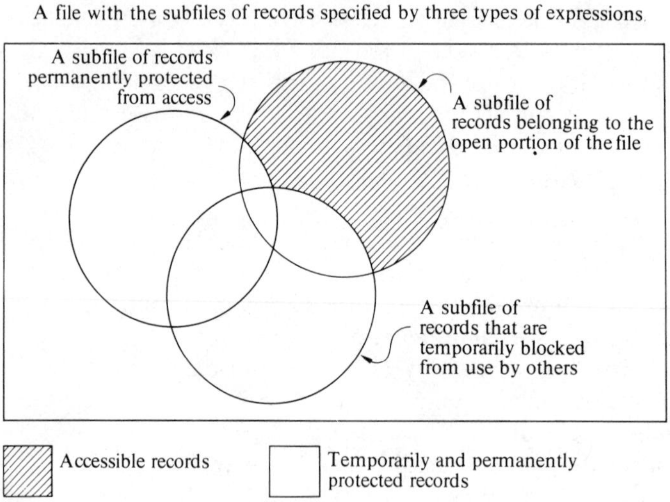

A file with the subfiles of records specified by three types of expressions.

Fig. 6.27 Subfile protection.

On a need-to-know basis, many subfiles may be defined for the same file as depicted in Table 6.3. The multiplicity of subfiles for various access control requirements may grow large. However, the mechanism needed by the system to verify whether a record belongs to a subfile is straightforward. (See Fig. 6.28.)

Expression intended for subfile level access control	Does the record satisfy the expression?	Record accessibility
Permanent protection from use	Yes	Deny
	No	Permit
Temporarily open for use	Yes	Permit
	No	Deny
Temporarily blocked by others from use	Yes	Deny
	No	Permit
⋮	⋮	⋮

Table 6.3 The use of Boolean and arithmetic expressions to define subfiles for various access control purposes.

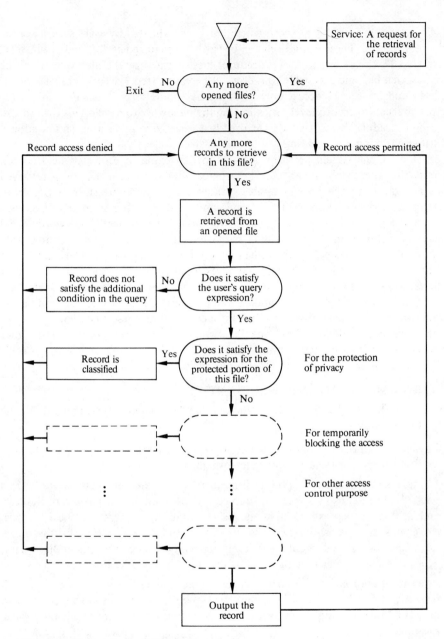

Fig. 6.28 Expression validations in record access.

An accessible record is a record which has been validated by every security check at the subfile level. These validations can be easily mechanized as depicted in Fig. 6.28.

In step 12, the system allows procedures incorporated by the file owner to check records which become accessible to a user. Whereas in step 3 access control is at the file level and in step 11 access control is at the subfile level, this step enables the control of access at record level. By allowing the file owner to develop his own record checking procedure, records which are already accessible to other users can be subject to further checking and auditing.

In step 14, the system performs a posteriori checking of protected field names. We note that the checking can only take place after the record has been retrieved from secondary storage into system's working area. In contrast to a posteriori checking, a priori checking of field names and fields (in step 6) at query or user program running time involves the removal of all the protected keywords, field names, and fields from the user's data management and macro calls. In this way, no access will be initiated by any "invalid" keywords. Step 14 is the last step in the security procedure. It is in this step that access control is finally brought to the user at the field level. Because many access control requirements are dependent upon some combination of field names and/or values, matching of names and computing of values must take place dynamically. By incorporating these matching and computing procedures at the field level, the file owner can have direct control of the other user's access to his individual datum.

The security procedure is an integral part of the data base management system.

6.7.4 SUMMARY ON DATA SECURITY

We have discussed a simple logical access control model. The highlights of the model are as follows:

1. Logical references for both data base access and access control—No reference to physical memory and virtual space organizations is made.

2. Flexible compartmentalization technique to aggregate information for access control—The aggregates are files, subfiles, records, and fields. The use of Boolean and arithmetic expressions as a means to compartmentalize the files, records, and fields eliminates the need of creating subfiles physically. Furthermore, expressions are stored in authority items and away from compartmentalized data. This allows flexible change of compartments by simply updating the expressions.

3. Procedural approaches for further checking and authentication—At each logical level (i.e., file, subfile, record, or field level) the file owner can introduce his own programs for auditing, monitoring, and screening other users of his data base.

4. Modular security procedure—The use of procedural checking and compartmentalization means by the user can vary. On the one hand, for public files there can be no compartmentalization of data within the files and no procedural checking at any level. On the other hand, multilevel checking on well-compartmentalized files can be demanded by the file owners. The security procedure

is modular so that it can systematically invoke the right degree of security checking to support the user's security requirements.

5. Interlocking mechanism for blocking and unblocking multiple access to the same data aggregates—This mechanism is needed in on-line environment where, for example, one user may update some data aggregates and another user may want to access the same data aggregates before the completion of the update.

6. A priori and a posteriori control of field level access—A priori control is performed at assembly time on query statements and at execution time on commands and macros. A posteriori control is enforced at the time that an aggregate of data is about to be outputted to the user. The former is intended to prevent any access from taking place as a result of an invalid query and malicious command and request; the latter is designed to remove small datum of highly classified nature from system output.

7. Ease of use—The introduction of the concept of ownership enables the users of the system to have an orderly way of obtaining and denying access privileges and restrictions. Because access control information is stored in the authority items, as records of a system file, it can be updated very easily by the system administrator. Furthermore, the separation of access control information from the raw data enables the change of a user's access requirements without having to process the raw data base.

6.8 POSTSCRIPTS

The generalized record organization is derived from the work in [8]. An implementation of the record template can be found in [5]. The generalized file structure and its parallel access algorithm are based on the work in [11], and [13]. The garbage collector is derived from [7]. For a survey of some of the commercial data base management systems, the reader may refer to [1]. Some of the well-known file structures such as the indexed sequential [15], inverted file [22], multilist [21], and cellular multilist [18] have been used in real-world applications. Attempts to improve the parallel access algorithm can be found in [20]. For the generalization of keywords to represent minterms of attribute-value pairs and the use of minterms to determine pointers in lists or record addresses in the directory, the reader may look up the work in [23].

The access control mechanism for data security systems is modeled after the work in [6] and [9]. One of the first working systems, as noted in [4], can be found in [7]. The extension of the access control from the subfile level to datum level was advanced by [2]. The use of data secure systems in medical application for safeguarding sensitive information was demonstrated in [2] and [14]. References on memory protection using a matrix scheme can be found in [17], on process protection employing the ring concept can be motivated by [3], and on logical protection using security deadlock mechanism, context protection and consistent control are outlined in [10].

REFERENCES

1. CODASYL Systems Committee. *A Survey of Generalized Data Base Management Systems*, ACM, New York, May 1969.

2. M. Gelblat. "Computers for Medical Problem Solving—A New Medical Environment." Ph.D. Dissertation, The Moore School of Electrical Engineering, University of Pennsylvania, December 1971.

3. R. M. Graham. "Protection in an Information Processing Utility." *Comm. ACM* **11**, 5 (May 1968): 365–369.

4. L. J. Hoffman. "The Formulary Model for Access Control and Privacy in Computer Systems." Ph.D. Dissertation, Stanford University, May 1970.

5. M. Horton. "Reading, Writing, Creating and Updating Records and Files in a Generalized File Structure." Master's Thesis, University of Pennsylvania, 1971.

6. D. K. Hsiao. "Access Control in an On-Line File System." *File Organization-Selected Papers from File 68*, IFIP ADP Group, Amsterdam: Swets and Zeitlinger, 1969.

7. D. K. Hsiao. "A File System for a Problem Solving Facility." Ph.D. Dissertation, University of Pennsylvania, May 1968, NTIS AD 671 826.

8. D. K. Hsiao. "A Generalized Record Organization." *IEEE Transactions on Computers* **C20**, 12 (December 1971): 1490–1495.

9. D. K. Hsiao. "Logical Access Control Mechanisms In Computer Systems." *Proceedings of ADP Secure Data Sharing Conference*, Washington, D.C., September 1972. Also available as a technical report (OSU-CISRC-TR-73-4), The Ohio State University, Columbus, Ohio.

10. D. K. Hsiao et al. "Research on Data Secure Systems." *Proceedings of the AFIPS 1974 NCC* 43, AFIPS Press, Montvale, New Jersey, May 1974.

11. D. K. Hsiao and F. Harary. "A Formal System for Information Retrieval from Files." *Comm. ACM* **13**, 2 (February 1970): 67–73; Corrigenda. *Comm. ACM* **13**, 4 (April 1970): 266.

12. D. K. Hsiao and F. Manola. "A Uniformed Approach to Structure, Access and Update in Data Base Systems." *Proceedings of European Computer Congress 74*, London, England, May 1974.

13. D. K. Hsiao and F. Manola. "Data Management with Variable Structure and Rapid Access." *Proc. of First USA-Japan Computer Conference*, Tokyo, Japan, October 1972.

14. D. K. Hsiao and K. Nakanishi. "A Cardiac Catheterization Information System—An Application of an Advanced Data Management Facility." *Proc. of ISLANDS OF APPLICATIONS—Tokyo Conference*, IEEE Computer Society, Tokyo, Japan, June 1972.

15. "IBM System/360 Operating System: Data Management," Form C28-6537-2, IBM Thomas J. Watson Research Center, Yorktown Heights, N.Y. (November 1966).

16. D. E. Knuth. *The Art of Computer Programming, Vol. 1, Fundamental Algorithms*. Reading, Mass.: Addison-Wesley, 1968, pp. 316–329.

17. B. W. Lampson. "Scheduling and Protection in an Interactive Multi-Processor System." Ph.D. Dissertation, University of California at Berkeley, March 1967.

18. D. Lefkovitz and R. V. Powers. "A List-Structured Chemical Information Retrieval System." *Proceedings 3rd National Colloquium on Information Retrieval*, Philadelphia, Pennsylvania, May 12–13, 1966.

19. F. A. Manola. "An Extended Data Management Facility for a General-Purpose Time-sharing System," Master's Thesis, May 1971, NTIS AD-724 801.

20. J. Pomeranz. "Fewer Retrievals in the Hsiao-Harary File Structure." *ICR Quarterly Report No. 27*, The Institute for Computer-Research, University of Chicago, November 1, 1970, II D-1 to II D-4.

21. N. S. Prywes. "Man-Computer Problem Solving with Multilist." *Proc. IEEE* **54**, 12 (December 1966): 1788–1801.

22. A. H. Vorhaus and R. D. Wills. "The Time-Shared Data Management System: A New Approach to Data Management." System Development Corp., Santa Monica, California (February 1967) (SP-2747).

23. E. Wong and T. C. Chiang. "Canonical Structure in Attribute Based File Organization." *Comm. ACM* **14**, 9 (September 1971): 593–597.

EXERCISES

1. Design a simple data definition language for record specifications. Write a *record input program* which accepts the data definition language as its input and produces a record template for the specified organization as its output. Furthermore, the record input program must accept new logical records as its input, verify the records on the basis of the information in the template, generate the proper record control block for each individual record if valid, and produce as its output the record control blocks and their associated storage images of the records.

2. On the basis of the record control blocks and storage images of the records generated in the first exercise, define an additional record template which reflects a new record organization. Write a *record output program* which accepts the new template and the existing record images and control blocks as its input and produces logical records as its output.

3. (W. Kuhn) By viewing the record organization as a rooted, ordered, and labeled tree, we can determine the number of permissible configurations for a given record organization. More specifically, develop for a given record organization with n attributes a set of recursion formulae which computes the number of permissible configurations where (1) k or less attributes are involved, and (2) exactly k attributes are involved.

4. Except in the case of cellular multilist file structure, the concept of storage cell is not well taken in the definitions of other known file structures. In other words, we let the size of cell be arbitrarily fixed in one case. (e.g., $s = 1$ in indexed sequential, indexed random file structures) and exceedingly flexible in another case (e.g., $s = |F|$ in the inverted file structure). Propose improved definitions for these file structures so that the cell size can be more reasonably specified. Show the impact of the new definitions and cell size specifications on the serial and parallel access algorithms.

5. Develop a set of programs which constructs the directory and the file of a generalized file structure.

6. Write a set of directory decoding programs for the cell entry, cell identifier, and directory search operators.

7. Write programs for the serial access algorithm. The input to the programs is a disjunction of keywords and a generalized file structure. The output from the programs is a sequence of snapshots showing the manner in which each keyword list is traced.

8. Implement the parallel access algorithm. The input to the algorithm is the disjunctive normal form (DNF) of keywords. Assume that there are at most two conjuncts in the DNF and three keywords in every conjunct. Test the algorithm with the examples illustrated in Section 6.5.3. To show the working of the algorithm, a sequence of snapshots in terms of record access as depicted in Tables 6.1 and 6.2 in the same section should be included. Finally, generate some results with new sample files.

9. (F. A. Pomeranz) In the parallel access algorithm, the selection of prime keywords for file search is determined on the basis of the record counts in the directory. Although different keywords of a conjunct may become prime keywords for different cells, a keyword once selected for the cell as the prime keyword of the conjunct (because it has the smallest record count) stays as the prime keyword for that cell. By keeping track of the record counts of the keywords of the conjunct, and by reducing the respective record counts of the keywords that each time a retrieved record contains those keywords, we may discover in the course of a file search that the prime keyword has a greater record count than the record counts of some other keywords. If this should happen, we immediately switch prime keywords. In other words, we dynamically designate a keyword as the new prime keyword whenever the record count of the keyword becomes the smallest.

Show how the *dynamic choice of prime keywords* is worked out. Also show the improvement in retrieval precision and the overhead of tallying the record counts. Is the improvement in retrieval precision at the expense of repositioning of read/write mechanisms of movable head devices? Will this improvement work in a file whose record addresses are not monotonic?

10. (E. Wong and T. C. Chiang) One of the difficulties in obtaining absolute precision in multilist and cellular multilist files is that lists in these files have records in common. In other words, these lists do intersect. A more subtle application of the generalized file structure and a clever interpretation of the notion of keyword list may result in a multilist or cellular multilist file structure in which no two lists have a record in common.

Consider a generalized file structure with m keywords. It is well known in Boolean algebra that there are 2^m possible minterms; each of the m variables appears in each minterm. By treating the keywords as variables, we have 2^m possible minterms of keywords. It also follows in Boolean algebra that for a given record containing some keywords, the record satisfies one and only one minterm. Furthermore, not all minterms may have satisfying records in the file. Nevertheless, we term those minterms that have satisfying records in the file the *atoms*. It is obvious that for each atom there is at least one record in the file which satisfies that atom. Furthermore, the atoms partition the file into mutually exclusive lists of records. By keeping the atoms in directory instead of the keywords, we then have a generalized file structure whose lists do not intersect. In the new generalized file structure, the notion of keyword list is expanded to mean the atom list.

Illustrate the approach with examples. Study the problems of directory entry deletion and addition due to decreasing and increasing the number of keywords.

11. Write programs for the three update algorithms as outlined in Section 6.6.1. Prepare several test examples in order to illustrate the working of the algorithms. In each test, the directory of the file should be displayed before and after the update.

12. Design and write programs for the garbage collection algorithm as outlined in Section 6.6.3.2. Input to the programs is a file of records some of which have deletion tags. Output from the programs is a new file of records without deletion tags. The directory of the file should also reflect its new entries. Particular efforts should be made to show that the garbage collection algorithm may involve, in one case, phase I only; and, in another case, both phases I and II.

13. Show that the necessary programs which examine a retrieved record against a given query in step 5 of the parallel access algorithm can be used as the verification mechanism for access control purpose as outlined in Fig. 6.28.

Epilogue

Future operating systems will primarily be oriented toward data base management. In other words, these systems not only must manage physical resources in terms of main memory and virtual space, input/output operations, data channels and buffers, and devices and terminals, but also must be concerned with the structure, protection, and use of logical and physical resources. With this view of operating systems, we may conclude that the system will be comprehensive and sophisticated enough to incorporate many system features discussed in the preceding chapters. To this end, we outline a data base system architecture in Fig. E.1. By referring to the roles of its system components, we can thereby relate in the system the material included in the chapters.

The job supervisor (1) accepts jobs for the system and dispatches output to the user. For off-line job I/O (Section 3.2.4.1, Chapter 3) and remote job entry (Section 3.3.2.2, Chapter 3), the job supervisor may have to interface with one or more satellite computers. When on-line programming is being supported, the job supervisor must manage for each user a pair of (job) input and output buffers in which the user's program statements, data, and commands can be accumulated and edited (Section 3.3.1.1, Chapter 3). Because user jobs are "stacked" in the buffers, preprocess of job input, postprocess of job output, and interpretation of on-line commands can be facilitated (Section 3.3.1.3.2, Chapter 3). Some of this processing and interpretation may be performed at the entry of the job, say a satellite computer system (Section 3.3.1.2, Chapter 3), or at a centralized place where a more powerful computer system is available (Sections 3.2.4.2 and 3.3.2.1, Chapter 3). For handling jobs in high volume, via multiple entries, and through slow unit-record devices, the job supervisor may need a job spooling system (Section 3.3.2.3.1, Chapter 3). Once the job input/output is completed, the jobs are sequenced for processing.

For more effective utilization and control of system resources, the omnibus jobs are organized into tasks. For each task, the system creates a task control block and an authority item (3). The task control blocks are used by the task monitor (2)

316

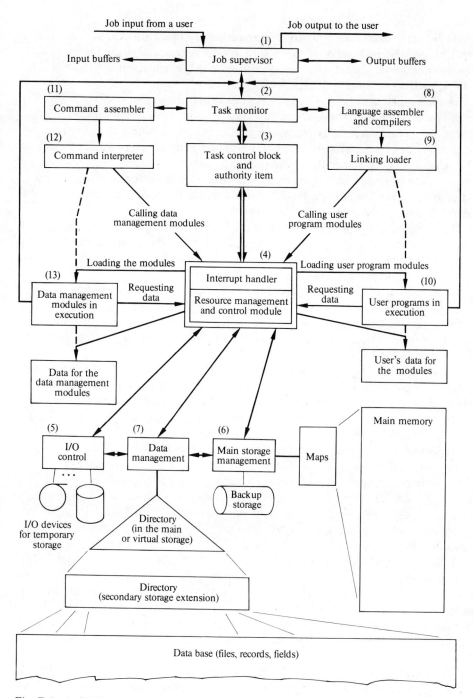

Fig. E.1 A data base system architecture.

to schedule task execution. A turn-taking procedure based on certain time slice is employed by the task monitor to ensure better turnaround time (in particular, response time) and to create balanced utilization of system resources (Sections 4.2 and 4.3, Chapter 4; Section 3.2.7, Chapter 3).

The authority item is used by the resource management and control module (4) for the purpose of controlling access to logical and physical resources (Section 6.7, Chapter 6). Because tasks may request access to resources dynamically, these requests are received as (machine) instructions via SVC's by the interrupt handler (Section 5.2.2, Chapter 5). Whether the requests are for physical devices, memory units, or data sets, the resource management and control module determines the granting and denying of the requests on the basis of the requester's access attributes and the system's available resources.

If the request is for physical devices and I/O operations, the input/output control system (5) will be activated. In this system, devices are verified, buffers are allocated and being switched, and channels are utilized for concurrent processing (Section 2.4, Chapter 2; Sections 5.2.2.2 and 5.2.2.3, Chapter 5).

If the request is for virtual space and main memory, the main storage management system (6) will be activated. In this system, the backup-storage-utilization and physical-memory-utilization maps are consulted so that the paging operation involving program relocation and memory allocation can be performed (Sections 5.2.2 and 5.2.2.1, Chapter 5).

If the request is for data sets, the data management system will be activated (7). Directory decoding is followed by file search. Update and garbage collection of the data base are carried out routinely (Sections 6.6.1 and 6.6.3, Chapter 6).

The data management system also utilizes IOCS for physical as well as logical I/O operations. However, in utilizing IOCS the data management system may employ more effective strategy to access the secondary storage so that high precision, minimal redundancy, and low access time may be achieved (Section 6.5.2, Chapter 6).

Security procedure must be followed when requested resources become available (Section 6.7.3.5, Chapter 6). To dispatch the resources such as data and programs to the requester's virtual space, the main storage management system is interfaced. In this case, the (address) mapping of resources into the virtual space may involve special handling such as virtual access method (Section 5.2.2.4, Chapter 5).

Program preparation and execution are important functions of the system. The relation of assembler (8), linking loader (9) and program execution phases (10) is very similar to the relation of (interactive or on-line) command language assembler (11), interpreter (12), and command module execution phases (13). The similarity lies in the manner with which they make requests for resources and with which they interact with the task monitor, interrupt handler, and resource management and control module.

The assembly system (Chapter 1) and the command processor (Section 3.3.1.3.2, Chapter 3; Section 6.7.3.4, Chapter 6) may utilize either static or dynamic linking loader for subroutine linking and loading (Section 1.5, Chapter 1; Section 5.2.2.6,

Chapter 5). Furthermore, during program execution, the program requests and calls in the form of system macros may take place (Section 5.2.2.3, Chapter 5; Section 6.7.3.4, Chapter 6).

Although the preceding chapters are organized around unique systems concepts and features, these concepts and features can and will appear collectively and integrally in large and advanced systems.

Index